The Last Voyage of the Andrea Doria

Also by Greg King and Penny Wilson

Twilight of Empire: The Tragedy at Mayerling and the End of the Habsburgs

Lusitania: Triumph, Tragedy, and the End of the Edwardian Age

The Resurrection of the Romanovs:
Anastasia, Anna Anderson, and the World's Greatest Royal Mystery

The Fate of the Romanovs

Also by Greg King

The Assassination of the Archduke:
Sarajevo 1914 and the Romance that Changed the World
(with Sue Woolmans)

Wallis: The Uncommon Life of the Duchess of Windsor

Twilight of Splendor:
The Court of Queen Victoria During Her Diamond Jubilee Year

The Court of the Last Tsar:
Pomp, Power, and Pageantry in the Reign of Nicholas II

The Mad King: A Biography of Ludwig II of Bavaria

The Murder of Rasputin:
The Truth About Prince Felix Youssoupov and the Mad Monk
Who Helped Bring Down the Romanovs

The Last Empress: Life and Times of Alexandra Feodorovna, Tsarina of Russia

The Last Voyage

of the

Andrea Doria

*The Sinking of
the World's Most Glamorous Ship*

GREG KING AND PENNY WILSON

ST. MARTIN'S PRESS

NEW YORK

To Pierette Simpson, whose devotion to the Andrea Doria's
memory and generosity helped make this book possible

First published in the United States by St. Martin's Press,
an imprint of St. Martin's Publishing Group

www.stmartins.com

The Library of Congress Cataloging-in-Publication Data is available upon request.

ISBN 978-1-250-19453-4 (hardcover)
ISBN 978-1-250-19455-8 (ebook)

Our books may be purchased in bulk for promotional, educational, or business use.
Please contact your local bookseller or the Macmillan Corporate and Premium Sales
Department at 1-800-221-7945, extension 5442, or by email at
MacmillanSpecialMarkets@macmillan.com.

First Edition: April 2020

10 9 8 7 6 5 4 3 2 1

The Last Voyage of the Andrea Doria

Prologue

———◆◆———

In the summer of 1956, readers were captivated by Walter Lord's *A Night to Remember*, which chronicled the sinking of the magnificent *Titanic* on her maiden voyage to New York in April 1912. As the story of the impossibly splendid, doomed *Titanic* took the world by storm, another liner prepared to set sail from its berth in the bustling port of Genoa. *Andrea Doria* was so famous for her beauty and luxurious onboard life that many people diverted travel plans from other vessels and even airplanes to book passage on this wonderful and happy ship.

The proud flagship of the Italian Line, *Andrea Doria* represented not only the nation's postwar recovery but also its glamorous, creative, and artistic march toward modernity. "A living testament to the importance of beauty in the everyday world" was how the Italian Line described the *Doria* on her maiden voyage in 1953. Her seven-hundred-foot-long sleek hull, shimmering black and topped by a cascade of white decks, was somehow traditional while still looking to the future. Previous liners had sported elaborately paneled rooms crowned with stained glass domes and crowded with opulent, overstuffed furniture modeled on British country house interiors. The *Doria* was starkly different: her modern rooms—all concealed lighting, wooden veneers, aluminum strips, and boldly colored, angular furniture—caused a sensation. The cutting-edge décor and oceangoing Italian hospitality drew a diverse contingent of passengers to this voyage, representing a true microcosm of the twentieth century: aristocrats and heiresses; actors and ballet stars; celebrity politicians and media moguls; a burgeoning rock-and-roll musician and American tourists hoping to indulge in la dolce vita; and immigrants reluctantly leaving their villages to seek new lives in the United States.

It was ironic that so many of the passengers on this trip, the *Doria*'s 101st Atlantic crossing, carried copies of *A Night to Remember* to their cabins, setting them on bedside tables or tucking them beneath pillows in anticipation of cracking open the spine and enjoying the story of *Titanic*. Not one seems to have worried that reading about a maritime disaster while at sea might result in an inadvertent but ominous sense of déjà vu. That first night, and all the days and nights that followed, the *Doria*'s passengers, snug in their berths or reposing on sun-drenched deck chairs, knew that they were quite safe from *Titanic*'s fate. It was summer; the *Doria* traveled an iceberg-free southern route; and radar and modern technologies seemingly ensured safety at sea.

And then, on the morning of July 26, people turned on their television sets to stunning news. The previous night, the Swedish liner *Stockholm* had rammed the *Doria* just off Nantucket. The images were shocking, stark, unbelievable: the great liner on her side in the Atlantic, abandoned as the ocean slowly but surely took possession. It was the first time that a maritime tragedy had played out before millions of eyes. Over the next few days, viewers saw heartrending scenes of survivors arriving in New York as they pushed past cameras and microphones for emotional reunions with desperate relatives. There were tales of heroism and allegations of cowardice, of joy and of loss, and, above all, a sense of disbelief that a tragedy like that which had befallen *Titanic* could occur in the modern age. But icebergs, as *Doria*'s passengers had discovered, could take many shapes.

In 1956 there would be no *Titanic*-like casualty figures. Thanks to the valiant efforts of the *Andrea Doria*'s captain and crew, as well as heroic actions by a handful of ships like the French liner *Ile de France* that had raced to the scene of the collision, only fifty-one lives were lost. Ten were children aboard *Andrea Doria*, their lives tragically cut short; speaking to their surviving siblings today, the pain remains sharp, the loss incalculable, their memories undimmed by the passage of time.

Arrogance played a part in the *Titanic* disaster, but *Andrea Doria* had done nothing to tempt fate. From the gracious and paternal captain to his competent officers to the smiling and helpful employees of the ship's "hotel," the passengers had discovered a world of peace and quiet, recreation and reflection, art, entertainment, and new friends—a place to spend an enjoyable week away from the pressures of everyday life until, contented and recharged, they were delivered safely to their destination port. The fact that this expected happy ending to the voyage was torn away from those on the *Doria* less than twelve hours before they were due to dock in New York made the tragedy all the more poignant.

After a century of books, films, and musicals, *Titanic* remains maritime history's best-known disaster. Yet *Andrea Doria*'s story is more immediate. Many vividly recall watching footage of the sinking and the emotional reunions as survivors arrived in New York. The *Doria* is closer in time to us than *Titanic*, and many of her survivors are still alive today. From girls in sundresses sliding down rough ropes into lifeboats, to a young boy venturing into the lower decks of the ship to retrieve his sleeping little sister from their cabin, survivors of the *Andrea Doria* confronted danger with great bravery and fortitude. Their stories are inspiring, dramatic, and occasionally tragic and deserve to be better known.

The *Andrea Doria* disaster did not deliver a death blow to the liner industry: it was the increase in commercial air flights that did that. But looking back, it is impossible not to read her tragic death as the foreshadowing of a future already being written in vapor trails against the sky even as her hull disappeared beneath the waves.

Chapter One

A t nine o'clock on the evening of Monday, April 16, 1956, millions
of Americans tuned in to CBS to watch the latest episode of the
hit comedy *I Love Lucy*. Since January, viewers had followed the mad-
cap adventures of the Ricardos and their friends the Mertzes on a trip
to Europe. After episodes set in London, Scotland, and Paris, Lucille
Ball and company moved on to Italy. That Monday night's episode,
"Lucy's Italian Movie," had the comedienne preparing for a role in a
fictional film called *Bitter Grapes* by stomping her way through a vat of
fruit at a local vineyard and ending in a riotous brawl that became one
of the most celebrated moments in the series.

"Lucy's Italian Movie" cemented the shift in American attitudes toward the former World War II enemy. After liberating Naples and
Rome, soldiers had returned to the United States with memories of
sun-drenched piazzas and endless feasts of pasta washed down by flowing wine; a fair number also returned with brides who were surprised
to find an America enraptured with pizza and entertainers like Frank
Sinatra, Tony Bennett, and Dean Martin. They flocked to movies by
Roberto Rossellini and Vittorio De Sica and witnessed the rise of Italian stars like Anna Magnani, Gina Lollabrigida, and the sultry Sophia
Loren, who flaunted her affair with married director Carlo Ponti.

Everything Italian seemed to be in vogue. Fashions, sleekly stylish
yet somehow traditional, boasted exquisite materials and impeccable
tailoring, suggesting an elegant yet casual approach to life.[1] Even some-

thing as mundane as transportation was swept up in this new renaissance. Gentlemen, imagining themselves stylish playboys or indulgent tycoons, suddenly wanted to drive an Alfa Romeo, a Ducati, a Maserati, a Fiat, or a Ferrari. After Gregory Peck and Audrey Hepburn famously appeared in the 1953 film *Roman Holiday* riding a Vespa through the capital's narrow streets, everyone wanted one of the little scooters.

Lured by low production costs, Hollywood began churning out Italian-made films at Cinecittà (cinema city), an enormous movie studio and lot on the southeastern edge of Rome. So many major motion pictures started shooting at Cinecittà that *Time* magazine soon dubbed the studio "Hollywood on the Tiber."[2] Films like *The Barefoot Contessa* and *Three Coins in the Fountain* only added to Italy's allure with their own evocative moments, seemingly summoning moviegoers to this enchanted nation.

Hollywood came to the Tiber to work but it stayed in Italy to play. Katharine Hepburn, Greta Garbo, and Ava Gardner were soon joined by Henry Fonda, Humphrey Bogart, Clark Gable, Lauren Bacall, Rita Hayworth, Orson Welles, Rex Harrison, and Cary Grant. Elizabeth Taylor might be spotted shopping in a quiet boutique; Ingrid Bergman might be pushing past ranks of the new paparazzi who were eager to report on her scandalous affair with Roberto Rossellini. Aristocrats came and went along the beautiful Amalfi Coast: the Duke and Duchess of Windsor, the former king Farouk of Egypt, and a host of dukes, barons, and princes who could be seen sipping martinis in elegant outdoor cafés.[3]

The films, the fashion, the resorts, the food, the style, the effortless way of life—all chronicled in pictures and magazines—enticed the world to Italy. The country was not only returning to life, it had grabbed life by the throat and was proudly marching forward. The tourists came in ever greater waves, all eager to soak up their own slice of this exotic, enchanted land. And, in true Italian style, getting them there was itself quickly raised to an art form.

The end of World War II marked the end of the golden age of the ocean liner. Nations devastated by the conflict struggled as depressed economies and tightened budgets restricted travel. Cunard's *Queen Mary* and *Queen Elizabeth* returned to transatlantic service, offering speed and luxury aligned to British probity and mannered elegance, even if their once-chic, 1930s art deco interiors now seemed slightly dated. Compagnie Générale Transatlantique—the French Line—ran the former German liner *Europa* as SS *Liberté* alongside their grand old *Ile de France* of 1927. The latter had lost her third funnel; between the remaining two a series of ten-foot-high letters composed of electric lights spelled out the ship's name at night like some Times Square billboard.

In 1950 America challenged this stagnant, motley collection of prewar transatlantic refugees. American Export Lines built two liners, the SS *Independence* and the SS *Constitution*. Stretching nearly seven hundred feet and modern in appearance, the sisters entered service on the increasingly popular Manhattan-to-Genoa run. To challenge on the Atlantic, the United States Lines commissioned a new vessel designed by naval architect William Francis Gibbs. She was the first liner to make extensive use of aluminum for her superstructure, funnels, and fittings. On her maiden voyage in July 1952, the new SS *United States* shattered all previous speed records: her top speed of just over 38 knots was so fast that the crashing waves chipped paint away from her sharply raked bow. At 990 feet and 53,330 tons, she was the largest liner ever constructed in America: her white superstructure and immense twin red funnels ringed in white and topped with flying blue sampan-style wings looked revolutionary and cleanly crisp.[4] But critics struggled with words like "sterile" and "cold" when describing the vessel and her fittings, suggesting that she had little of the warmth of previous liners.[5]

A new phenomenon now challenged transatlantic liners: regularly scheduled airline flights across the ocean. Pan Am had begun transatlantic flights in 1939, utilizing Boeing Clippers, but those demanded refueling stops, and a flight was a long ordeal. Howard Hughes used his Hollywood connections to push TWA Airlines and promote "civilized" air travel, though this meant sixteen hours aboard a Boeing Stratocruiser to reach London from New York. Flying was an innovation, and an expensive one, with tickets averaging as much as the modern equivalent of $10,000 for a round-trip flight across the Atlantic. A modicum of glamour prevailed: since airlines generally carried only a small number of well-to-do passengers, they all dressed for the occasion and spent their hours smoking and drinking aboard Constellations, Comets, and DC-4s. Flying, though, was still often an unnerving experience: lacking pistons, planes vibrated terrifyingly in turbulence, and accidents were not infrequent. Growth was inevitable. In 1948, some 273,000 travelers flew across the Atlantic; by 1951 the number had risen to 342,000, and by 1955 airlines could lay claim to almost half the transatlantic passengers.[6]

The ocean-liner industry struggled against these unwelcome aerial interlopers. Unable to beat the speed of airplanes, they sold the journey as its own end, offering a more pampered and relaxed experience— "Getting there is half the fun!" ran one Cunard ad.[7] Aboard a ship there was time to drink, dance, read, and sleep; lavish meals full of exotic foods contrasted with the frequently unpalatable portions meted out from Radaranges in the sky. But increasingly, as Captain Harry Grattidge of the *Queen Mary* recalled, "there was a subtle change in the mood" aboard transatlantic liners.[8] "First class," wrote one maritime historian, "began to reflect the incursion into what was left of society by those who belonged more strictly to café society, along with pashas of the expense account and tycoons of the credit card. Instead of carrying fastidious women to the Paris openings," liners were "more apt to carry . . . the entrepreneurs of Seventh Avenue. Instead of individuals bound, guidebooks in hand, for Mont-Saint-Michel and the chateaux of the Loire," there were "business people with an eye out for something French or 'French-y' on which to slap their company labels. The dining habits of these new passengers were so fixed and unadventuresome that the expert chefs and sommeliers serving them suffered erosions of spirit. Prepared to serve up exquisitely subtle dishes in commemoration of Auguste Escoffier, wines preserved in rows as hushed as the vaults of Cartier, they found themselves responding to endless requests for planked steaks, mashed potatoes and double J & B's on the rocks."[9]

This was the dichotomy Italy now faced as it struggled to reclaim its traditionally rich nautical heritage. The Italian Line, officially called

Società di navigazione Italia, had come into existence in 1932 as part of Mussolini's consolidation of industry in his fascist state. The line had built two immense and glamorously luxurious liners in the 1930s, *Rex* (which was then the fastest ship afloat and briefly captured the famed Blue Riband) and *Conte di Savoia*. Neither survived the war or its aftermath. What remained were four smaller liners, all at least a decade old: *Conte Biancamano, Conte Grande, Saturnia,* and *Vulcania*. Increased emigration after the war promised immense revenues, as did the gradual return of tourist travel. The problem was funding. Italy was still suffering through the years of postwar depression, and Prime Minister Alcide De Gasperi successfully turned to America, asking for and receiving loans through the Marshall Plan so that his devastated country could rebuild its merchant fleet.[10]

Two new liners were commissioned in 1950. Not only were they to reclaim Italy's seafaring traditions, but they would also carry larger, more symbolic messages: that Italy had recovered from the devastation of World War II; that it offered tourists exciting and beautiful adventures; and that they, too, could enjoy its art, culture, and traditions, on land and also on the sea. The ships were to be floating Italian ambassadors, containing the work of her most prestigious artists and designers and equipped with the latest technology. As one of the ships' interior designers, Gio Ponti, once explained, the new liners were not only a means of transport but also, more importantly, "a manifestation of the arts of the country that the ship represents . . . There is no reason why passengers who come to Italy attracted by Italian art should not find its expression (naturally its most noble expression) on ships which are themselves Italian."[11]

The liners were born in Genoa. The great Italian port city had produced two memorable maritime figures: Christopher Columbus and Admiral Andrea Doria. The first made his name and reputation traveling the oceans, mapping trade routes, and searching for new lands; the second helped establish Genoa as a sea power, repelling the French, the Turks, the Spanish, and an onslaught of pirates in the fifteenth century, frequently changing his allegiances to take advantage of the fortunes of war. He ended his days ensconced in a palace in Genoa, celebrated for his heroic deeds and ruthless determination.

Founded in 1853, Giovanni Ansaldo & Company sprawled at Sestri on the outskirts of Genoa. It had long been one of the country's oldest engineering companies and had a proud tradition of naval architecture. On February 9, 1950, the keel for the first of the new liners was laid on the company's massive Slipway No. 1, the same slip where *Rex* had been built.[12] Designated only as No. 918, the new liner took sixteen months to frame, plate, and deck.[13] Gradually a massive hull began rising from the slipway, encased in a web of orange gantries, cranes, and scaffolding swarming with workers. The intimidating bow towered above the yard; plating began to shape her graceful stern. By the spring of 1951, framing neared completion. The still unfinished hull, reported *The New York Times*, was "visible for miles," its red bottom adding "color to this otherwise drab and dreary part of Genoa."[14]

Inauspiciously the launch had to be postponed by six days while work continued at a rapid pace. Finally, on the morning of June 16, 1951, an immense crowd gathered beneath a beautiful, sunny sky at Ansaldo to watch the festivities. Scaffolding and tools had been cleared to provide a pristine dais for the new ship. Cardinal Giuseppe Siri, archbishop of Genoa, blessed the vessel before Giuseppina Saragat, wife of the former minister of the Italian Merchant Marine, stepped forward, and, with a small silver hatchet, sent a bottle of sparkling wine smashing into the bow of the newly christened *Andrea Doria*. Amid cheers the great hull slowly freed itself from its ways and drifted down its slip into the water with an immense splash, the rumble of her drag chains temporarily drowning out the applause and the band playing the national anthem.[15]

Another eighteen months were spent finishing and fitting out the new liner at Ansaldo, even as her sister ship, to be christened the *Cristoforo Colombo*, rose on a nearby slipway. Not until December 1952 was *Andrea Doria* completed. She was 697 feet long—nearly two hundred feet shorter than *Rex*—ninety feet wide, and at 29,100 tons almost half the size of her illustrious predecessor. Everything about her suggested the streamlined aesthetic of the modern 1950s era. From her sharp bow with its bulbous nose, her black hull stretched back, topped with a white superstructure largely built from aluminum alloys to save weight. Aft, three decks cascaded gracefully down to the gently curved stern, each pierced with its own swimming pool, a reminder that the vessel sailed the usually sunny southern Atlantic route. Topping the liner was the Belvedere Deck, left clear for games but dominated by a single, thirty-eight-foot-high funnel, raked back slightly, its main body of white topped with a slender ribbon of green and a larger band of red, the colors of the Italian flag.[16]

Andrea Doria boasted a number of technological innovations and improvements on past Italian liners. She was completely air-conditioned (even the garage on B Deck was climate-controlled), and all cabins had a telephone connected to the ship switchboard.[17] Great efforts had gone into ensuring that she was fireproofed: special flame-resistant insulation was used in nearly all interior spaces, and automatic doors could quickly seal off entire sections of the ship in the event of a fire. In addition to the automatic sprinkler system, the *Doria* boasted a special carbon dioxide–suppression system and even had its own small but dedicated fire brigade.[18]

Safety concerns extended to the bridge. The liner was equipped with the latest navigational systems, with two radar screens; a radio direction finder; and the relatively new loran system, to assist in long-range navigational bearings.[19] And, should unforeseen disaster ever strike, there would be no repeat of the *Titanic* disaster. The liner carried sixteen aluminum lifeboats, eight on each side, operated by electric winches: two emergency boats, each capable of holding fifty-eight passengers; two motorized boats, each holding seventy; and twelve regular Fleming lever boats, each capable of carrying 168 persons.[20] Together, these lifeboats could hold 2,008 people, some two hundred more than the *Doria* was designed to carry.[21]

Twin sixteen-foot-diameter bronze screws, driven by steam turbines capable of attaining 35,000 horsepower, propelled the *Doria* through the water. Three diesel and two steam turbine generators powered the ship and gave her a top speed of 25.3 knots. For added safety, the main electrical generators were in a separate watertight compartment from the main engine room; there was also an emergency diesel generator, situated in its own compartment on a higher deck, designed to run emergency amber lights and power the bilge and ballast pumps in the event of a crisis. Fuel oil tanks in the ship's bottom and along her port and starboard sides allowed the *Doria* to carry just more than four thousand tons of diesel.[22]

Fuel oil and fresh water also served as ballast in the side tanks and in the tanks spaced along the ship's double bottom. These offered additional protection in the event of any collision or if the ship struck something along the bottom of its hull. Steel bulkheads divided the liner into eleven watertight compartments; these rose as high as A Deck. Designers followed the requirements outlined in the 1948 Convention for the Safety of Life at Sea (called SOLAS): the *Doria* could float if any two adjoining watertight compartments were breached. These same standards theoretically assured that the liner would never be subject to more than a list of 7 degrees to either port or starboard; even so, the *Doria* exceeded these requirements, being capable of surviving a list of up to 15 degrees. No one could envision a scenario in which any ship would acquire a list beyond 20 degrees and still remain afloat: such a list would render the watertight bulkheads extending to A Deck largely useless, enabling water to flood into the ship unchecked.[23]

Getting the ship safely from port to port was of course the greatest concern, but nearly as much thought and attention went into ensuring that *Andrea Doria*'s passengers reached their destinations in style. Some eighteen months were devoted to the liner's final fitting out and decoration.[24] In addition to the cabins, there were more than two dozen public rooms. The breakdown in these accommodations, spread over ten decks, signaled a new reality for ocean liners. They still clung rigorously to class divisions, although the new names bestowed on the tiered accommodations were meant to emphasize progress and mobility. Thus Second Class became Cabin Class, with its implication of privacy, while Tourist Class, replacing the outdated terms "Steerage" and "Third Class," as maritime historian John Maxtone-Graham wrote, suggested "respectability" and "frugality."[25]

The Italian Line had never been quick to follow modern trends. *Rex*'s interiors had walked an uneasy—and ultimately discordant—line between historicism and modernity, but *Conte di Savoia* was more adventuresome, reflecting a kind of art deco merged with insistent modernity as exemplified in the First Class Lounge, where a coved and painted ceiling resting on neobaroque marble columns sheltered above overstuffed club chairs covered in startling zebra patterns.[26]

But the era of maritime period revival was dead. *Andrea Doria* was the first Italian liner to break from this somewhat contradictory heritage. She would be futuristic, dramatic, and starkly different, following the prevalent *alta moda* trend of the 1950s: her modern rooms caused a sensation, as did her murals, marquetry panels, and sculptures.[27] Even the furniture, influenced by the 1950s mid-century modern aesthetic of Charles Eames and Eero Saarinen, was contemporary, with sparse wooden or metal legs and bold color schemes. "In many respects," writes maritime historian Peter Kohler, "she was the most decoratively daring postwar North Atlantic liner."[28] Ironically she would be one of the last ships to sport such innovative maritime décor: the liners that followed soon lapsed into a kind of shared hotel glamour, all sleekness, sharp corners, and generic interiors that were virtually indistinguishable from one another.

From the first, *Andrea Doria* was envisioned as the embodiment of Italian culture and heritage. No matter how modern her interiors, she was to represent the paintings, sculptures, and artistry that had made Italy famous in the Renaissance. This linkage of past to present also underlined the overarching message that a country so recently devastated by war had been reborn and could boast of a proud tradition that no conflict could erase. The Italian Line did something unique with the *Doria:* rather than assign decoration to a single firm, it held competitions to outfit the various interiors and selected the best contemporary designers and artists to adorn her rooms. Gio Ponti was in general charge of organizing the design, and with Giovanni Zoncada, he received commissions for many of the First Class rooms on the Promenade Deck. Born in 1891, Ponti was one of Italy's most successful architects, but he was also celebrated for his ceramics, furnishings, and even cutlery, all designed in bold, modernist shapes and colorful tones. Both Ponti and Zoncada had a long history of maritime decoration, having refitted the *Conte Biancamano* and the *Conte Grande* when America returned those older liners to Italy after their seizure during World War II. On the *Doria*, Ponti gave free rein to modernity: he treated the ship like a stage set, creating theatrical interiors adorned with decorative veneered panels; glass doors and partitions; sculpted ceilings set with indirect fluorescent lighting; anodized aluminum in shades of gold, silver, or bronze; vibrant bursts of purple, orange, and yellow in fabrics; and abstract murals and stylized ceramics to provide visual interest.[29]

The First and Cabin Class dining rooms of *Andrea Doria*, along with the foyers and staircases, were given to Milanese architect Antonio Ramelli. Other First Class spaces, including the Belvedere Lounge, the Card Room, and the Reading and Writing Room, were designed by architect and designer Gustavo Pulitzer Finali, who had previously worked on the *Conte di Savoia* as well as the Grosvenor House Hotel in London and the Palace of the League of Nations in Geneva. Spaces for Cabin Class passengers were designed by Matteo Longoni, Ugo Ratti, and by the Genoa firm Arredamenti Navali Unione Artisti, which also fitted out most of the rooms in Tourist Class.[30]

The Italian Line took advantage of the latest technologies to publicize and promote its new liner and the adventures promised by a voyage aboard her. "The British gave the Atlantic Ferry its reliability," wrote Peter Kohler, "the Germans its speed, and the French its style, but the Italians transformed it from passage to pleasure. The indolent, sun drenched Lido life was a preferable alternative to the fogbound damp of the northern routes."[31] The goal was no longer attracting the once-lucrative emigrant trade; that would continue, of course, but now the emphasis shifted to pleasure, to the idea of a voyage as a holiday unto itself. Promotional posters, brochures, and advertisements featured colorful sketches and photographs of happy passengers: elegantly dressed, white-gloved ladies descending the *Doria*'s modern First Class Staircase; women in fashionable ensembles exchanging gossip over martinis in their lounge; delighted diners in crisp dinner jackets standing before tables laden with gastronomic delicacies while white-jacketed stewards served up lobster; and children romping on deck as their parents looked on from the edge of the ceramic-lined swimming pools.

The new *Andrea Doria*, the Italian Line promised, was something absolutely unique: "First of all, a ship that is worthy of the name must be a ship. She must be able to function as a huge machine . . . to provide light and heat and numerous essential hotel services to her passengers. She must be able to cleave the ocean waves efficiently and safely, no matter what the weather conditions. She must get her passengers where they want to go with reasonable dispatch, adhering to a schedule announced in advance. But today a ship must be more than that. For the period of her voyage she must be a whole way of life for her passengers. She must provide them with an experience that will somehow be different and better than a comparable experience they could have anywhere else. This experience must be one they will enjoy while they have it . . . and one they will never forget as long as they live. The *Andrea Doria* is, we think, unique. She was designed to be a huge, completely efficient machine, a real ship. She was also designed as a living testament to the importance of beauty in the everyday world."[32]

In another advertisement, the Italian Line pondered, "What gives a ship that thing called personality? From where come those qualities of warmth and friendliness? How do you take the coldness out of steel? How do you breathe life into glass and tile? You won't find the answer in blueprints. You can't do it with money or calloused hands. You build such a ship with your heart. Into every detail of this lovely vessel have gone the skill and pride of the greatest artisans of Italy. Every mural, every tapestry, every rug and chair . . . each exquisite bit of glassware and every glowing tile is the work of craftsmen. Yes, a ship is built of many hearts. This is the tradition of Italy. This is the *Andrea Doria*."[33]

But the Italian Line was not merely selling a voyage on the *Doria*: sketches captured alluring vistas of azure Mediterranean bays where flowers bloomed in profusion, people lingered languorously in enchanting sidewalk cafés, and sun-washed Italians waited with open arms to welcome the world. It was all, one advertisement promised, "a chapter in your life you'll never forget. All too few are the occasions in life so gloriously, immeasurably perfect in every way that one cherishes their memory for a lifetime. Yet the moment you step aboard your luxurious Italian Line flagship you'll know in your heart that this trip was one of them. You sail away from worry and care into another world of leisurely living, gracious service, superb cuisine, and exciting visits in fascinating lands. You return rested, refreshed . . . rich in experiences you will treasure always as you relive them in memory again and again."

By November 1952 work on the *Doria* was complete, and Ansaldo Shipyards formally turned her over to the Italian Line. During her acceptance trials at sea the first week of December, the *Doria* managed an average speed of just over 26 knots. Mechanical issues kept her from making her maiden voyage on December 14; instead, she would finally set sail for New York on January 14, 1953.[34]

On that morning, all of Genoa it seemed had turned out to bid the liner farewell. Flags flew, streamers fluttered, bands played, and an immense crowd lining the waterfront cheered with pride as the new *Andrea Doria* slowly steamed out of the harbor. Everything went well until the liner neared the end of its voyage: off Nantucket, she encountered a terrible storm, with strong winds and crashing waves that sent her rolling in the rough seas. After one particularly large wave, the *Doria* listed some 28 degrees; tables and chairs tumbled—"we were swimming around in filet mignon, spaghetti, and antipasto mixed with a little champagne," recalled one passenger. Twenty people suffered minor injuries.[35] The ship soon recovered, but this wasn't supposed to happen: *Andrea Doria* was designed to take a 15-degree list; anything over that risked unchecked flooding and severe loss of buoyancy.

Finally, having passed off Long Island, Sandy Hook, and the Ambrose Light, the *Doria* turned north, steaming through the Narrows off Staten Island into New York City's North River (also known as the Hudson). A contingent of whistling tugs, fireboats spouting sprays of water, and thousands of spectators greeted the liner as she slipped past a skyline of silver skyscrapers and slowly eased into her berth at Pier 84. Mayor Vincent R. Impellitteri, himself an Italian immigrant, was on hand to welcome this floating symbol of Italian pride. Reporters scoured the ship, stumbling over themselves to capture her magical effect. "Her name," wrote columnist Robert C. Ruark, "is *Andrea Doria*, and she is as beautiful a new piece of marine construction as I ever saw . . . A ship is a wonderfully solid thing, making sense in a shaky world. A ship doesn't hurry too much. It's nearly impossible to sink one or set it painfully afire. It works faithfully for its master, and takes on a portion of his personality. The man, in turn, is influenced by his vessel and comes to be like her."[36]

New, modern, glamorous, and full of beauty, *Andrea Doria* soon attracted a roster of celebrity passengers, cementing the Italian Line's resurgence in the transatlantic trade. In 1955 the Italian Line carried more than 100,000 passengers, second only to the Cunard Line.[37] In April 1953 Clare Boothe Luce, the new American ambassador to Italy, traveled aboard the liner with her husband, publisher Henry Luce: not surprisingly, his *Life* magazine commemorated the sailing in its pages. Also aboard was director John Ford, who unfortunately had to keep to his cabin for most of the voyage as he was suffering from sensitive eyes. A year later, writer Tennessee Williams accompanied Italian actress Anna Magnani when she traveled to America aboard the *Doria* to shoot *The Rose Tattoo*, a film that gained her the Academy Award for Best Actress. A galaxy of celebrities soon followed: *Andrea Doria* saw Kim Novak, John Steinbeck, Ramon Novarro, Cary Grant, Tyrone Power, Orson Welles, Spencer Tracy, and Richard Widmark all enjoying passage to and from Italy in the liner's first years. There was even a brief appearance in the 1954 film *On the Waterfront*, with the *Doria* steaming in the background during a rooftop scene between Marlon Brando and Eva Marie Saint.

Andrea Doria was rarely without a celebrity on board. The experiences of actress Joan Crawford and her family give a glimpse of this side of the liner's life. In January 1956 Joan, along with her husband, Pepsi magnate Alfred Steele, and her four children Christina, Christopher, and twins Cynthia and Cathy, were returning to America aboard the liner, having spent the Christmas holidays in Switzerland. "Joan would never fly," says her grandson Casey Lelonde, and she "would never allow her kids to fly," so they always went to Europe by liner, on either the *Ile de France*, a Cunard ship, or on the *Andrea Doria*.[38] Christina, then sixteen, recalls the dichotomy of the trip: before they boarded the luxurious liner, they visited Naples, where she was shocked to see thin, barefoot children on the cold streets begging for bread or families huddled together around fires in the ruins of bombed-out buildings. "People accosted Joan in Naples," Christina recalls, "trying to grab her jewelry. I felt really embarrassed as Joan and I dressed in fur coats. I gave the children what little money I had. The stark contrast between our 'photo-op' first class publicity tour and life for Europeans after the War was upsetting. It was an introduction to the real world that no one else in our group seemed to see or talk about, but I never forgot."[39]

The family boarded *Andrea Doria* in Cannes on January 8, graciously welcomed aboard by Captain Piero Calamai. The captain held a private cocktail party for Joan, her husband, and Christina, and two days into the voyage, he entertained them at his table in the First Class Dining Room. On January 12 he put in an appearance at Joan and Al's private cocktail party in their suite, and the next morning he had the entire family up to the bridge for a tour. Throughout, Christina found him "quite charming but formal, and he treated my brother and me with kindness, and spoke to us as people, not children."[40]

Having just come from a holiday filled with tours of classical museums, Christina found "the art and décor on the *Andrea Doria* in stark contrast. It was bright, modern, sleek and very stylish. The furniture was very comfortable and, of course, everything was almost brand new." The liner encountered rough seas, and many passengers were seasick, giving it an almost abandoned feeling. Christina took advantage of this freedom. She played Ping-Pong with her brother and "walked on deck a lot, even in the wind and rain." Every afternoon recent movies were shown—she remembers seeing *Vera Cruz, Kismet, The Tender Trap*, and *She Couldn't Say No*. The food "was delicious" and "the service was great. The men in charge of our table had lots of funny conversations with us, partly in English. At that time, I spoke French and understood some Italian." And after dinner, she was allowed to go dancing, though she deemed it a "pretty boring crowd," but "it was fun and everyone was nice to me. Usually, since I was alone, I sat with a Jesuit representative from the Vatican who was the most interesting, well educated person."[41]

While Christina enjoyed her time on the ship, a nanny named Mrs.

Howell looked after young twins Cathy and Cindy.[42] Their ninth birthdays fell during the voyage. "Captain Calamai," Joan recalled, "asked me if it would be all right if the girls planned the menu for the whole of the First Class passengers." They did so, Joan insisted, without any advice from her, choosing vodka and caviar for the adults, followed by soup, New York–cut steaks, mixed vegetables, salad and cheese, and an immense birthday cake accompanied by champagne.[43] It was a memorable voyage. But Cathy and Cindy would soon have a less pleasant experience with the *Andrea Doria*.

Chapter Two

L ate into the night of July 16, 1956, the Genoa pier buzzed with activity. As the rest of the city slept, *Andrea Doria* was awash with preparations for departure the following day. Cabins were cleaned, linens changed, bathrooms scrubbed, corridors vacuumed, public rooms polished, decks and windows washed, and every surface shone. Trucks and vans disgorged tons of provisions: food, wine, and fresh flowers to adorn tables. Dining room tables were laid with linen, china, silver, and crystal in anticipation of luncheon, the first meal to be served to passengers the following afternoon.

Tuesday, July 17, 1956, dawned warm and clear in Genoa. Stretching along her pier, *Andrea Doria* glistened beneath the sun. Pacing the bridge was Piero Calamai, *Andrea Doria*'s fifty-eight-year-old captain, six feet tall, sturdily built, and with the slightly weathered face of a career mariner. Born on Christmas Day in 1897, Calamai came from a seafaring family. His father, Oreste, had founded the journal *The Merchant Navy*, while his younger brother commanded the Italian Naval Academy at Leghorn. Calamai graduated from the San Giorgio Nautical Institute in Genoa in August 1916 and went to sea during World War I, serving as an ensign with the Italian Navy. At the age of eighteen he won the Italian War Cross for valor in action. In 1919 he entered the Italian Merchant Marines as a second lieutenant and finally attained the rank of first officer. In this capacity, Calamai served on a number of liners, including the *Conte Biancamano*, the *Conte de Savoia*, and the

Conte Grande. While on the last, Calamai leaped overboard and saved the life of a passenger who had fallen into the sea, winning a medal for his bravery. Calamai returned to military service as a reserve lieutenant commander during World War II, once again winning a military cross for saving Italian torpedo cruiser *Caio Duilio* and its men after it had been torpedoed by British forces. In 1947 he finally resumed his career with the Italian Line, attaining the rank of superior commander.[1]

In 1953 the Italian Line had given Calamai command of the new *Andrea Doria* for its maiden voyage; it was his twenty-eighth ship. The company respected his efficiency and knowledge, and paid Calamai $625 a month.[2] Like most captains, Calamai had a deep emotional attachment to his ship: as an Italian he was proud of this living embodiment of Italy's resurgence, and as a Genoa native, he shared the sense of pride in this magnificent liner that had been born in its shipyard. Now, as he walked the *Doria*'s sleek bridge it was with a tinge of regret: this would be his last westward voyage on the liner. When he brought her back to Italy, he was scheduled to take his summer holiday before assuming the helm of her sister ship *Cristoforo Colombo,* whose captain was retiring.[3]

In his private life Calamai was shy and retiring. He lived quietly in Genoa with his wife, Anna, and two teenage daughters, Marina and Silvia. He disliked alcohol, loved music, and remained unpretentious. He carried these attitudes onto the *Doria.* Calamai was a gentlemanly, almost courtly captain, courteous and so sensitive to the feelings of others that he had never given way to displays of temper and had never been known—as had many captains—to dress down the officers beneath him in front of other witnesses: if a situation arose, Calamai would pull the offender aside for a private chat. This won him great respect from his crew, who recognized and reflected his dedication to duty.[4]

Captain Calamai, recalled Guido Badano, his second officer on *Andrea Doria,* was "a brilliant and ambitious man, shy in personal relationships, a modern gentleman, simple and humane with everyone." He was "precise, prudent, and had a gentle touch with the passengers." Eugenio Giannini, the *Doria*'s third officer, concurred, calling Calamai "a gentleman, loved and respected by his crew, and a decent, indeed, an exceptional, person."[5] Giannini added: "I never saw him lose his temper during the months I served under him. I always saw him judge things calmly and with good sense."[6]

All of these were admirable traits in a man, and perhaps even in a shipmaster, but in many ways they conflicted with the social role expected of a liner captain. "The captain's duty," wrote John Malcolm Brinnin, "to cater to the self-regard of his clientele made it essential that he be a social arbiter. Once his ship's safety was assured he was expected to act as host and do all in his power to induce his guests to travel again in the same ship or in another of the line." A captain had to entertain and appease those passengers in his care, assuring and guiding them and doing his best to meet their social needs. The wealthiest and most prominent passengers often demanded special attention: tours of the ship, the captain's presence at private cocktail parties, and the social recognition of their importance by being allowed at his table for gala dinners. Most captains "had to train themselves to act with a social grace for which few of them had the background, disposition or aptitude."[7]

This was anathema to Calamai. He was retiring under the best of circumstances; with his dislike of alcohol he found cocktail parties an ordeal. Somehow he managed a detente of sorts. He'd greet passengers, show celebrities the bridge, and smile for photographs, but his social presence on the *Doria* was limited: he would make a concession to dine publicly twice during a voyage, but only rarely could he be pushed beyond these compromises. Instead, he took most of his meals with his senior officers in a private dining room.[8] On the *Doria*, the majority of the social responsibilities fell to Osvaldo Magagnini, *comandante in seconda*, or second in command, whose position as staff captain was meant to appease passengers hoping to bask in favor from the ship's officer.

By eight, when the first gangway doors opened, taxis, buses, and cars crowded into a long line snaking toward the pier. Clad in bibs emblazoned with ITALIA, longshoremen unloaded luggage onto carts. Signs directed arrivals to one of three lines: First, Cabin, or Tourist Class. Within the immense hall, officials behind desks checked tickets, passports, and visas; passengers identified trunks, suitcases, and valises, which were then tagged with a colored slip indicating its destination, red for the holds or yellow for the cabins, before being loaded onto conveyor belts that carried them into the ship's hull. Passengers moved toward the vast open doorways and onto the narrow gangways leading into the ship, where stewards waited to direct them to their cabins. Temporary confusion reigned: up or down staircases and along corridors, passengers pushed past cabin boys holding farewell baskets, boxes of candy, telegrams, and floral bouquets amid shouted directions and a din of eager voices excited to embark on what they hoped would be a memorable voyage.[9]

First Class accommodations spanned seven decks: the Belvedere and Sun Decks were given over to open spaces for promenades and games, while the public rooms occupied the Lido, Boat, Promenade, Upper, and Foyer Decks, with cabins disposed on the Boat, Upper, and Foyer Decks. The last third of the Boat Deck was devoted to Cabin Class, with a gymnasium on the port side and the Children's Playroom, with a jungle-themed mural on the walls, on the starboard side. The Cabin Class Foyer and the Cabin Class Dining Room were both situated on the Foyer Deck, separated by pantries and kitchens from the First Class Dining Room in front and the Tourist Class Dining Room toward the stern. Tourist Class passengers had an open area on the ship's Promenade Deck bow area below the bridge, while the deck near the stern was given over to their Lido, Veranda, and Swimming Pool. The last quarter of the Upper Deck offered them four public rooms: the Tourist Class Card Room on the starboard side, with the Tourist Class Reading and Writing Room on the port side, and beyond them, the Tourist Class Lounge and finally the somewhat smaller Tourist Class Social Hall with a bar, both surrounded by an enclosed Tourist Class Promenade Deck. Differences in decoration were subtle: the decoration of the Tourist Class Dining Room was notably simpler than in First Class, and the wooden chairs had no arms.

Segregation by class was most obvious in the passenger cabins. Accommodations for the 218 First Class passengers took pride of place, situated from the front of the superstructure to midship. The 320 passengers traveling in Cabin Class had cabins at the rear of the superstructure and on A and B Decks, while the 703 people who booked Tourist Class passage were relegated to the areas near the stern and in the lowest decks.[10] These differences were reflected in ticket prices. During high season, which ran from July to October, a standard First Class cabin cost between $335–$360; a Cabin Class room could be had for between $260–$300; and prices for accommodations in Tourist Class ranged between $205–$250.[11]

Most of the liner's privileged passengers entered *Andrea Doria* through the First Class Foyer, situated amidships on the Foyer Deck and, with its elevators and Grand Staircase, a principal point of access to other parts of the ship. An elongated oval, the First Class Foyer featured walls of alternating wooden veneer stripes and an elliptically shaped ceiling fringed with concealed lighting. The First Class Forward Staircase marked a significant departure in design. Most liners before World War II had devoted considerable space and luxurious decoration to grand staircases: frequently topped with impressive domes, they provided the ultimate in theatrical entrances for ladies in sweeping gowns. But the modern, less formal *Doria* broke from this tradition. The staircase was still there, cascading down in divided flights between polished wooden railings and ornate wrought iron scrolls, but it offered no grand approach into any of the liner's principal public rooms. Aside from the light blue linoleum on the risers and treads, the staircase's only decorative element was a ceramic mosaic by Alfonso Bortolotti, which hung on the main landing.[12]

Having found their accommodations, passengers explored the ship before taking to the open decks: masses of white, green, and red streamers draped from the railings to the pier, and the strains of jovial music and the hum of excited exchanges filled the air.[13] At eleven, the ship's loudspeakers crackled to life, announcing, *"La nave è in partenza!"* ("The ship is departing!") Whistles blew in alert as visitors reluctantly returned to the pier and waved handkerchiefs and upraised hands as gangways pulled away.

Calamai paced along his neat bridge and chart room, past the wheel, radar screens, chronometers, barometers, and all the other technical developments that the Italian Line had installed to ensure the *Doria*'s safety. An internal telephone brought news that the engine room crew was ready. Hatches were sealed, moorings were loosened, and lines were coiled before Calamai ordered his ship slow astern. Standing on the teak decks, passengers could feel the low rumble of vibrations beneath their feet as the engines came to life. Slowly, *Andrea Doria* backed out of her berth as tugs eased her round so that she could make her exit. With a final three blasts from her whistle, she slipped through the harbor, smoke trailing from her funnel, gulls dancing overhead against the clear blue sky, and her two bronze propellers churning a white ribbon of foam in her wake as she steamed away from Genoa's embracing hills, setting sail for New York on her 101st transatlantic crossing.

Eighteen-year-old Andrew Stevens boarded the liner with his parents Archie and Herminia, bound for America and a return to their home in Mamaroneck, New York. Born in 1888, Archie had received a degree in mechanical and electrical engineering from Stanford University and his career took him all around the world. He'd met schoolteacher Herminia Burke, fourteen years his junior, during a posting to Buenos Aires, and the couple married in 1933; five years later, Herminia gave birth to their son, Andrew.

In 1952 Archie took a position in Paris working as a liaison between International Telephone and Telegraph, where his fluent French stood him in good stead; Herminia and Andrew followed in 1954, and the family lived in an apartment on Avenue Hoche in Paris, with Andrew attending the American School of Paris. "It was difficult when I first moved to Paris," he recalls. "I did not speak any French." Still, he joined his friends from school and explored the countryside, spending three days walking on a pilgrimage from Paris to Chartres. He found it easier to get around when he bought an expensive Pequot motorcycle, and traveled to watch the races at Le Mans and for holidays in Switzerland, enjoying the freedom of his youth. Once he narrowly avoided disaster when a car came too close as he and a friend were riding back to Paris. The car missed Andrew but sent his friend crashing through the window of a bakery; he was relieved to find him unhurt, sitting in a jumble of ruined pastries and "licking his fingers with delight."[14]

When Andrew graduated from school in Paris, his father gave him an expensive Oneida watch as a present, which was now strapped to his wrist as he explored the *Doria*. Herminia was bringing back more than a hint of France for their American home: crates in the hold contained clothing, jewelry, and a full set of specially commissioned Limoges china, while their new car had been loaded into the fully air-conditioned garage on B Deck. Young Andrew was enchanted: "We had a lot of fun," he recalls. "It was a beautiful ship."[15] On board the *Doria*, Andrew quickly settled into his own First Class cabin on the starboard side of the Sun Deck.

On the Upper Deck, Istvan Rabovsky and his wife, Nora Kovach, inspected their cabin, No. 56. It was typical of *Andrea Doria*'s First Class accommodations: two twin beds, separated by a built-in chest of drawers, nestled against the light wood veneer paneling. A bureau and two low armchairs upholstered in beige fabric faced the beds, while two portholes, draped in beige-and-maroon-plaid curtains, pierced the outer wall. A long corridor led to the private bathroom, closets draped in more beige-and-maroon-plaid curtains, and to the door opening to the corridor.[16] Istvan quickly decided that they didn't need both a bathtub *and* a shower—luxuries that he found just a bit too expensive. They could save $60 if they switched to a smaller inside cabin, with only a single porthole down a narrow, dead-end corridor and a bathroom with only a shower. After some hasty conversation, a steward duly moved them to Upper Deck Cabin No. 77 on the port side.[17]

Twenty-six-year-old Istvan and twenty-five-year-old Nora were Hungarian ballet stars. Born to an unwed mother, Istvan had suffered a peripatetic childhood, pawned off on various foster families and relatives until he was finally reunited with his mother. After seeing Fred Astaire, Istvan decided he wanted to dance and was enrolled in the Hungarian State Opera ballet school in Budapest. He was a rising star when he met a fellow ballet student, the fiery Nora Kovach, who had trained at the Kirov Ballet in Leningrad. Her socially prominent parents opposed the romance, but the couple eventually married in 1952, taking up an uncomfortable residence with her mother and father until they could afford their own apartment.[18]

Istvan and Nora toured Eastern Europe and the Soviet Union for a year. As Nora later said, they "were members of the privileged class and had money, an automobile and a nice home but never what we wanted most: freedom."[19] The fame and privilege under the Communist regime failed to overcome this most basic desire. In May 1953 they joined the Hungarian National Ballet's engagement in Soviet-occupied East Berlin, eight years before the Berlin Wall went up. By accident, they learned that there was a subway stop beneath their hotel; as their comrades were preparing for an evening performance, Istvan and Nora slipped into the station and rode to West Berlin, where they sought asylum.[20] They were the first Soviet bloc ballet stars to defect to the West. "Because they disappeared during a performance," recalled Paul Szilard, Hungarian tour manager, "it was regarded as a huge scandal."[21]

The defection was nerve-racking: the couple had no passports and several times they had to evade the police. Once accomplished, Nora suffered from guilt: "I was thinking of mother [sic], home, family," she said. "It's a very big problem. But freedom is better."[22] American impresario Sol Hurok immediately signed Istvan and Nora, knowing he—and they—could capitalize on the international publicity their daring feat had garnered. He took them to London, where they first appeared with the Festival Ballet at the Royal Festival Hall in an August production of Don Quixote.[23] Western audiences had not yet experienced Soviet ballet: not until 1956 did the Bolshoi finally make a London appearance. Istvan and Nora, all athleticism and power, were a stunning revelation. The couple, enthused The Spectator, "danced with magnificently effortless style and technical completeness. Nora Kovach is lovely, steady, coordinated, and a born lyrical dancer, while Istvan Rabovsky out-spins and out-jumps every other male dancer seen here during twenty-five years; after some requisite polishing he will go on astounding us for a long time."[24]

In November Hurok took the couple to America, where they made a debut on Ed Sullivan's television show The Toast of the Town to great interest and even greater acclaim. Tours of the United States, Europe, and Latin America followed: in July 1956 the couple had just completed an appearance in Genoa before they boarded *Andrea Doria* for the return trip to America.[25]

Barbara Boggs boarded the *Doria* in Genoa, along with her second husband, Dr. Robert Boggs, and two of her children—Barbara Bliss, sixteen and a daughter of her first marriage; and twelve-year-old Robert F. Boggs (called Bobby)—and settled into their cabin on the Boat Deck. Barbara Boggs was probably the wealthiest and most privileged of all the *Doria* passengers, but that wealth and privilege had been accompanied by a fair dose of pain.

She was born January 16, 1918, the first daughter of Chicago department store heir Marshall Field III, who inherited a fortune estimated at $120 to $160 million (about $4.5 to $5 billion today), and his first wife, Evelyn.[26] Barbara was brought up in an enchanted world: there was a massive New York City mansion; European cruises on her father's yacht *Corisande;* and languid days at Caumsett, the 108-room house Field built on Long Island's Gold Coast.[27] On the surface Barbara wanted for nothing. At Caumsett a staff of eighty—English butler, Scottish housekeeper, French chef, footmen, valets, maids, laundresses, governesses, nurses, chauffeurs, gardeners, grooms, and florists—ensured that every whim was indulged; one man even ironed the morning newspaper before it was presented to Marshall Field.[28] But, as Barbara recalled, "I had been a rather lonely child for several reasons. I was brought up in enormous and isolated places, and in what seemed to me dark, cold and somewhat frightening houses. I was taken care of by a string of nurses, governesses, and innumerable servants. My parents were remote, not only because of the long walks to their rooms but also because they carried on a very busy social life and were frequently away on trips. My older brother [Marshall Field IV] was sent to boarding school at the age of eight. My younger sister [Bettina] had an English nurse who wasn't on speaking terms with the French governess, and in the summers my brother had tutors who loathed them both, so life wasn't precisely what you'd call congenial . . . So many people told me that I should be like someone else, I ended not knowing who I was. If I sat down in the living room a footman would appear out of nowhere, plump up the cushion and erase the indentation I had made. Any impression I made was immediately wiped out. Many of my friends appear to have thrived on the type of upbringing I had, which was typical of a particular class at a particular time. I certainly didn't thrive."[29]

Barbara was just eight when her parents' marriage began to crumble. Barbara's mother Evelyn—called Evie—was a crashing snob (she actually had shrubbery moved at Caumsett so that she didn't have to see the servants), tempestuous, and imperious.[30] Author Louis Auchincloss remembered her as "very beautiful but also terrible; we used to call her 'poison Evie.'"[31] In 1930 Marshall and Evie divorced; Barbara felt adrift. Exiled from her beloved Caumsett, she disliked life at the gloomy New York City town house, where someone soon poisoned her beloved Cairn terrier. She felt abandoned by her father and, as she later admitted, was frightened of her mother, whom she saw only by appointment and who inexplicably took out her resentment over her failed marriage on her daughter.[32]

After graduating from the all-girls Brearley School Barbara reluctantly endured a debutante season that saw her parents publicly battle for her attention. In June 1936 Field gave his eldest daughter an elaborate debutante party at Caumsett. For the evening, the boxwood garden was transformed into a magical bower, with a turquoise crepe de chine canopy with a pink satin ceiling decorated with hundreds of flowers; the surrounding trees hung with some two thousand flickering Japanese lanterns. A forty-piece orchestra played as the thousand guests dined and danced. Barbara, wearing a silver lamé gown and white fur stole, looked lovely but slightly overwhelmed by the affair, which supposedly cost her father some $50,000.[33] Four months later Evie made Barbara go through a rival ball held at the Ritz-Carlton. This had a gold-and-silver theme, with doormen and waiters attired in specially created silver liveries and Barbara appearing in a complementary gown.[34]

Barbara was eager to marry and create the perfect home she had been denied. "I wanted to get away from a divided home," she admitted. "I married for the wrong motives and I made one of the first men who cared for me into something he had to be in my mind."[35] This was Anthony Bliss, a tall, patrician lawyer from a distinguished family whose father was chairman of the Metropolitan Opera in New York. There was a great society wedding on December 21, 1937, and a daughter, also named Barbara, was born on September 22, 1939. The marriage, though, soon faltered, and divorce followed in 1941. Barbara quickly wed again, this time to a physician, Robert Boggs; she later told her eldest daughter that she'd felt pressured into the marriage, as Boggs was in the navy and with World War II ongoing, the future seemed so uncertain. She gave birth to a son, Bobby, in 1943, as well as two more daughters, but once Boggs returned from the conflict, she realized that they had nothing in common.[36] Her entire life had been a series of highs and lows; suffering from depression, Barbara could never escape the crushing expectations that ringed her life.[37]

Ironically these same crippling expectations were also beginning to shadow the life of her daughter and namesake. Already planning to attend Sarah Lawrence and dabbling in operatic singing, the younger Barbara was caught between two worlds. There was the privileged way of life at her grandfather's Long Island estate, where, as she recalled, expectation came in the form of excelling at sports or after-dinner games like charades or twenty questions, living in society, and making an elite marriage.[38] And then there was the reality: there was no great fortune to back up the societal aspirations and in any case, as her daughter, Adelaide, recalls, the younger Barbara had more of a Bohemian spirit, yearning to break free yet uncertain of her footing.[39]

There had been six languid weeks in Italy before the Boggs family boarded *Andrea Doria*. Young Barbara Bliss recalled evenings at Lake Maggiore, where a hotel band serenaded them with "Arrivederci, Roma" and "Come Back to Sorrento." In Sienna, her family crowded the balcony of an Italian contessa to watch horses race around a medieval square, with young Barbara feeling ill at ease in a simple flowered cotton dress when their hostess wore black silk and a black lace mantilla on her head. And then there was Capri, where she first noticed her mother flirting openly with their Italian guide—"they were not discreet about the glances they'd exchanged," she remembered.[40] By the time they got on the *Doria*, Barbara Boggs and her husband, as she later wrote, "simply had a completely different way of looking at life . . . The whole relationship made me feel trapped."[41]

Also settling in to his First Class Cabin No. 5 on the Boat Deck was American-born Catholic priest Reverend Joseph Oppitz. After having to defend his doctoral thesis in Rome, Oppitz was anxious to return home. There had been a brief snag when Oppitz boarded and he was forced to change his cabin, but he didn't consider it an ill omen. After all, as he said, *Andrea Doria* had the latest safety technology and "it would be impossible for the ship to ever sink."[42]

Passage aboard the *Doria* was to be a honeymoon for the newly married Cecilia and John Pick. Boarding in Genoa, the couple traveled Cabin Class, though Cecilia—called Cissi—was undoubtedly the liner's most aristocratic passenger. Born in 1904, Cecilia de Piro came from an exalted Maltese family: in 1742 King Philip V of Spain raised the head of the family to the rank of marquis, and other titles, including Barons of Budach and Hereditary Nobles of Hungary, followed over the ensuing centuries. Igino de Piro, Cecilia's father, had become a British officer with the King's Liverpool Regiment and fought in the Boer War, taking part in the Siege of Ladysmith. As a third son, he never expected to become head of the family, but when one brother took holy orders and another died prematurely, Igino became Marquis de Piro and 7th Baron of Budach.[43]

Igino was stationed in Ireland when his wife, Nicolina Apap Bologna, herself the daughter of a Maltese aristocrat, gave birth to Cecilia, the second of the couple's four children. Beautiful and talented, Cecilia was brought up in Valletta, where she was deemed one of Malta's most eligible young ladies. In 1924 she married Marchese Nazzareno Charles Zimmermann Barbaro de San Giorgio, scion of a wealthy Maltese family. They had two sons, Charles and Edward, but the marriage was not a success. Nazzareno, says Cecilia's nephew, Nicholas, the current Marquis de Piro, "lived well beyond his means and mostly without her." He died young, but his widow was vibrant and graced many Maltese drawing rooms. Fluent in a number of languages, she was a gifted raconteur, an accomplished pianist, and enjoyed singing.[44]

During World War II, Malta was subject to aerial raids by German and Italian forces; Cecilia sent her two young sons off to the safety of an English boarding school, though she remained on the island, lending her active support to the British Institute and doing all she could for the Allied effort. In 1943, when the Italian Navy surrendered its Mediterranean forces, a British admiral asked Cecilia to join him as a translator; he also warned that she should wear "a formal dress." She arrived at the pier and went out with the admiral to his ship. Soon, the despondent Italians approached: as soon as these men spotted the elegantly dressed Cecilia, they began shouting, *"Bella! Bella!"* and blew symbolic kisses in her direction. Her charm had helped win over the vanquished Italians.[45]

After the war Cecilia's mother offered her the use of the family villa in Florence. Cecilia accepted and embarked on a restoration program while making herself popular in Florentine society. It was there that she first met John Pick, eight years her junior and a professor of English literature at Marquette University in Milwaukee, where he specialized in the works of Gerard Manley Hopkins. Romance soon blossomed, and in early summer 1956 the couple was married by the archbishop of Malta. Now, Cecilia boarded the *Doria* to start a new life with John in America, though she was scarcely traveling light: packed in steamer trunks that disappeared into the hold were some 240 wedding presents—"family heirlooms, sterling silver with an embossed crest for twelve, and silver table decorations." She brought three fur coats, three fur evening wraps, a collection of evening gowns and cocktail dresses, and a small fortune in jewelry: rings studded with diamonds and sapphires; two small diamond solitaires; bracelets of aquamarine, ruby, and gold; and a three-strand necklace of large pearls. "I intended to arrive as a glamour bride," she confessed.[46]

Twenty-six-year-old Tourist Class passenger Klaus Dorneich was one of the few German speakers on the liner. He had grown up in Freiburg with six brothers and sisters; with most of the city's infrastructure destroyed in World War II, Klaus attended a boarding school at St. Blasien, in the nearby Black Forest. After graduating from school, he spent some time in Indiana as a Fulbright exchange student and later was offered a position with Daimler-Benz of North America in Mexico, where the company planned to build an assembly plant. Because the Mexican government had not yet approved the project, he was to go to Guatemala and El Salvador to assist local agencies in organizing an automotive business. Before leaving from Genoa, he had been on business in Barcelona for a time and used the occasion to have a Spanish tailor make a white tuxedo dinner jacket especially for his voyage.[47] He decided to take *Andrea Doria* rather than fly. "I really wanted to go on the famous Italian ship," he later explained. "Trips by ship were so much cheaper than flights at that time."[48]

Andrea Doria made the first call of her voyage at four on the afternoon of July 17, this time at Cannes, which was a regular point of embarkation or departure. A number of excited passengers waited on the pier, none more imposing or controversial as Richardson Dilworth, the mayor of Philadelphia who, with his wife, Ann, was returning to America.

The fifty-seven-year-old Dilworth was a walking contradiction. A scion of privilege, formed by patrician influences, he dressed immaculately, spoke with a clipped upper-class accent, could debate in French, and greeted women with courtly bows.[49] But he was also a reforming brawler, a man of the people, and a champion of desegregation at a time when the issue divided America. In 1917 he'd left Yale and enlisted in the Sixth Marines; at the battle of Belleau Wood in France, his left arm was badly injured by exploding German shrapnel.[50] The injury got him a Purple Heart, "which is really no decoration if you're dumb enough to get hit," he lamented.[51]

Dilworth returned to America, graduated from Yale Law, married Elizabeth Brockie, and fathered four children, but the union unraveled under Richardson's career ambitions and his penchant for alcohol and other women. In 1935, he ran off to Havana with the beautiful and married Ann Kaufman Hill, granddaughter of Chicago millionaire Otto Young. Scandal followed when the pair divorced their respective spouses and married in 1935, but Dilworth shrugged off the criticism and flung himself into a political career, interrupted only briefly when he reenlisted in the US Marines during World War II.[52]

Dilworth had come from a staunchly Republican family, with a mother who insisted that Franklin Delano Roosevelt was insane; when he joined the Democratic Party, his mother accused him of being "a traitor to your class."[53] Dilworth was unfazed: in 1949 he became Philadelphia city treasurer; in 1951 he won the office of district attorney; and in 1956 he was finally elected the city's mayor. The campaign was ugly: his Republican opponent publicly hinted that Dilworth was too emotionally unstable to hold the post. To this, Dilworth declared, "Yes, I am an emotional man and I am a fighter. Do you think there would be any cities if there were not men to fight for them? I have had milk bottles thrown at my house. I have had threats of violence and threats of kidnapping of my family. I've had threats of libel suits and telephone calls at all hours of the night, and insults to my wife. Yes, I'll fight for the city because I love it, and if elected, I'll be the best damned Mayor it ever had."[54] In the end Dilworth won the race by more than 100,000 votes.

Dilworth took office on January 3, 1956, and immediately set about turning Philadelphia politics on its head. He implemented a new city charter that eliminated patronage jobs; tore down slums and replaced them with affordable housing; and promoted new parks including Independence Mall. He earned a record amount of hate mail by supporting desegregation and civil rights. "Why in the hell," wrote one constituent in what proved to be an unfortunately typical example, "don't you stop betraying your own people? We're sick of the Jews and the Niggers and the way you cater to them."[55] But Dilworth could reply in kind: "Drop dead, schmuck" was a favorite answer.[56]

The Dilworths lived in great style: their house was filled with eighteenth-century English furniture, Venetian paintings, and original drawings by Tiepolo—and always running in and out of the rooms, tripping up guests and generally causing havoc, were the couple's multitude of toy poodles: Montezuma, Cotton, Boom-Boom, Zsa Zsa—so famous that they even earned their own write-up in the *Philadelphia Daily News*.[57] Dilworth disliked the dogs—they were Ann's passion—but he put up with them to please her. He also left most of the parenting to his wife. Dilworth loved his children, but he treated them as miniature adults: they were sent out to campaign on street corners, and his idea of a family outing was to take them to rather age-inappropriate plays like *Cat on a Hot Tin Roof*.[58]

In 1956, when Ann inherited just over $1 million from her grandfather's trust, she decided to build a new house and take a trip to Europe.[59] "I work very hard at my job," Dilworth explained, "and it is a job that requires seven days of work each week. I have found that in order to perform my task with vim and enthusiasm it is important to take an occasional vacation."[60] As Philadelphia's mayor, Dilworth had also hoped to call on Monaco's new princess, the former actress Grace Kelly; the day that the Dilworths were to visit the palace, though, Prince Rainier summoned his wife to Paris, and so the mayor and his wife missed the pleasure of stopping in Monte Carlo for a royal luncheon.[61]

Disappointment was appeased somewhat when the Dilworths boarded *Andrea Doria* in Cannes. Their Upper Deck starboard Cabin No. 80 had a famous neighbor for the voyage, actress Ruth Roman, who quickly befriended the Dilworths and invited them to visit her in California.[62]

Roman had booked two starboard cabins on the Upper Deck, Nos. 82 and 84; one was for herself, and the other for her three-year-old son, Richard, called Dickie, and his nurse, Grace Els, described by Roman as "thin, gray-haired," and "a tower of strength."[63] Joining her on this trip was twenty-four-year-old fellow actress Janet Stewart, who had appeared with Roman in the 1951 film *Strangers on a Train*. Roman had sailed on *Andrea Doria* before, but those happier occasions seemed distant memories on this voyage: she was returning to America in the wake of her second divorce.

Born in 1923 to a family of Lithuanian-Jewish immigrants, Roman quit high school and took acting lessons in Boston before moving to New York and finally to Hollywood. In 1949 she landed a role as Kirk Douglas's character's wife, Emma, in Mark Robson's *Champion*.[64] Stardom followed: Ruth graced the cover of *Life* magazine in May 1950, which heralded her as a brilliant new actress with a welcome and contradictory combination of sexuality and wholesomeness, and played opposite both Randolph Scott and Gary Cooper in two westerns that year.[65] Her most famous role came in 1951, playing Anne Morton opposite Farley Granger in Alfred Hitchcock's 1951 film, *Strangers on a*

Train. By the end of the year, Ruth was receiving some five hundred fan letters a week.[66]

Ruth worked steadily; in 1955's *The Far Country*, she starred as Ronda Castle, James Stewart's character's love interest. Her own love life, though, was a complicated business. In 1940 the seventeen-year-old burgeoning starlet had married Jack Flaxman, divorcing him in less than a year. For a time she seemed to be seriously involved with Ronald Reagan, but on December 17, 1950, she married Mortimer Hall, whose family owned the *New York Post*. On November 12, 1952, Ruth gave birth to a son, Richard, whom the couple called Dickie. But by spring 1955 she'd left Hall and announced she was filing for divorce; they briefly reconciled, but in March 1956, on hearing that Hall was seeing actress Dorothy Malone, Ruth again filed for divorce.

Thure Peterson and his wife, Martha, had worried about reaching the pier in Cannes on time. The fifty-seven-year-old chiropractor and his fifty-five-year-old wife had spent the last month enjoying a European holiday for which they had planned and saved for twelve years.[67] Tall and imposing, Peterson had graduated from Carver College before starting a chiropractic practice and rising in the field to become president of the Chiropractic Institute of New York in 1950.[68] He'd married the pretty, petite former Martha "Marty" Larson—like himself the child of Scandinavian immigrants—and raised two daughters, Penny and Jane, in Upper Montclair, New Jersey.

The Petersons were determined to enjoy themselves on their trip. When they flew out of New York, they carried ten pieces of luggage, including new evening dresses that, with an eye to frugality, Martha had asked a seamstress friend to make. The couple visited the Swedish birthplaces of their parents and bought dolls and toys for their five grandchildren before an invitation came for Thure to speak at a European convention of chiropractors in Switzerland. The couple had planned to spend their last two weeks touring Italy, but Marty thought the Swiss appearance would advance her husband's career. Feeling guilty, Thure suggested that they extend their trip by two weeks. They had already spent $1,040 on their two First Class tickets for passage aboard *Andrea Doria* from Cannes on July 17, but Thure thought he could switch their reservations to her sister ship, *Cristoforo Colombo*, which was not due to leave Italy until two weeks later. The *Colombo*, though, was fully booked. Thure then decided to fly home and made reservations that would have placed them aboard a plane landing in New York City on July 26. But Marty had been looking forward to sailing aboard a liner— neither had taken an Atlantic voyage before. She was more than willing to give up an extra week in Italy for a week at sea. "Darling, let's forget the Italian tour altogether," she told her husband. "You're all tired out after the Switzerland lectures, anyway. And we're not as young as we used to be. The voyage home will give you a good chance to rest up." Although Thure was secretly worried he might be seasick, he didn't have the heart to disrupt his wife's much anticipated voyage, and so they kept their reservations aboard the *Doria*.[69]

The couple crammed all the sightseeing they could into their last week in Europe: to make the experience even more special, Thure hired a chauffeured limousine in France, which took them along the winding southern coast before depositing them at the pier in Cannes just before the *Doria* was to leave. They were happy with their Upper Deck cabin, No. 56 on the starboard side, though Marty was a bit disappointed: standing only five feet three inches, she found that she couldn't see out of the portholes. Since she couldn't enjoy the view, she took the inside bed.[70]

At the same time, Colonel Walter Jeffreys Carlin and his wife, Jeanette, were settling in to their nearby Upper Deck cabin. The seventy-five-year-old Carlin was a figure of some repute in Brooklyn, where he and his sixty-four-year-old, redheaded wife lived in a fashionable apartment at 35 Prospect Park West. Carlin had gained prominence during World War I, when he commanded the Forty-Seventh Regiment in France. After graduating from Columbia University and armed with a degree from the New York Law School, Carlin entered the legal profession and helped found the Lafayette National Bank. In later life, he gained fame as the most powerful figure in Brooklyn Democratic politics, maintaining important ties to officials and promoting rising young stars.[71]

Also from Brooklyn and boarding the *Doria* in Cannes, sixty-five-year-old liquor store owner Philip Trachtenberg settled into a First Class cabin with his wife, Arline, forty-nine. They had been in the midst of a European holiday when word came that her father was seriously ill. The couple had already booked passage home on the *Constitution*, but the illness, as Philip said, "caused us to seek a more speedy return to New York. So we had switched to the *Doria*." But Arline was nervous. "Phil," she told her husband once on board, "I have the strangest feeling about this ship. I have a premonition that something is going to happen." She was so upset that when the *Doria* arrived in Gibraltar, the Trachtenbergs tried to make airline reservations. The Italian Line, though, refused to refund their fares. Left with no option, Arline reluctantly agreed to continue aboard the *Doria*, though she remained convinced that some unknown disaster loomed on the horizon.[72]

Chapter Three

After leaving Cannes, *Andrea Doria* made a somewhat curious but regular detour on her westward voyages, sailing overnight from Cannes southeast, back to Italy, where she stopped at Naples on the morning of Wednesday, July 18. Here, she would take on a considerable number of passengers, along with mail and cargo. Standing at the ship's railing, Father Joseph Oppitz watched the comings and goings along the pier. As passengers were boarding, he spotted a group of Neapolitan craftsmen, each armed with a basket of goods, who climbed the gangplank to hawk their wares to those aboard the vessel. One man ran up to Oppitz, displayed his goods, and launched into his enthusiastic pitch: "Authentic gold rings, bracelets of pure silver, diamond earrings. Make your girlfriend happy!" Oppitz turned him down, saying he was a priest and had no girlfriend, but the merchant was not to be put off. "Even Americans have mothers!" he argued. "So buy something for your mother." When Oppitz again declined, the man lost his temper: "That's the trouble with you Americans!" he yelled. "You come over here and you don't respect our customs. And one of our customs is that if we do not make the first sale of the day, we will have bad luck. So you have to buy something!"

"Look, buddy," Oppitz said with finality, "if you don't stop bothering me, I'll have that cop throw you off this ship and then you'll really be in bad luck." In reply, the man let out with a string of expletives; as he was leaving, he shouted, "I hope you have bad luck on your way home!"[1]

Oppitz was far from the only Catholic priest aboard the liner: six others boarded in Naples, all Americans returning home. Thirty-year-old John Dolciamore was sharing First Class Upper Deck Cabin No. 58 with a fellow priest, thirty-three-year-old Richard Wojcik. Chicago natives, the two had graduated from Quigley Preparatory Seminary and the Seminary at the University of Saint Mary of the Lake in Mundelein before their ordinations. Dolciamore had been studying Canon Law at the Pontifical Gregorian University in Rome, where he earned a degree as a Licentiate before returning to Chicago to take up an appointment for the Archdiocese's Metropolitan Tribunal.[2] Music was Wojcik's passion. He'd earned a master's in Gregorian chant from Rome's Pontifical Institute of Sacred Music, and now carried his most treasured possession aboard the liner, a battered, much-annotated copy of *Liber Gradualis* full of ancient chants.[3] He had paid a steep $25 for the book and had spent fifteen years writing marginalia on its pages.[4]

The First Class tickets were a reward for years of diligent service from the Archdiocese of Chicago.[5] Also returning to Chicago, but sharing a Cabin Class stateroom on A Deck, were Reverend Raymond Goedert, twenty-eight, and Father Thomas Kelly, a few years younger. Both were tall, thin, dark, and boyish-looking—Kelly had, in fact, just been ordained the previous year.[6]

Goedert was one of twelve children; two of his brothers also became priests. Like his friends Dolciamore and Wojcik, he had studied at Quigley and at the seminary at the University of Saint Mary of the Lake before his ordination. He had spent the past two years in Rome, studying canon law at the Pontifical Gregorian University, living in a residence called Chicago House just off the exclusive Via Veneto. Here, Goedert recalls, "you wouldn't have known that a war had happened, but when we went out into the countryside there was still a lot of rubble in places." During his first year in Rome, coal was still scarce and the college had no heat: Goedert and his fellow priests sat through classes wrapped in overcoats and mufflers. He and his fellow priests had left Rome by train that July, arriving in Naples the day before the *Doria* sailed.[7]

Also traveling First Class was Father Paul Lambert, the fifty-six-year-old pastor of Saint Philomena Roman Catholic Church in Lansdowne,

Pennsylvania. Lambert, an immense man weighing nearly three hundred pounds, somehow seemed even bigger in his enormous black cassock; with his snowy white hair, he seemed the perfect Santa Claus. But Lambert was uneasy: "I'm scared to death of water," he candidly confessed.[8]

Life aboard *Andrea Doria* was absolute heaven for First Class passengers the Giffords. Clarence Gifford, forty-four and then president of the Rhode Island Hospital Trust in Providence, was returning to America with his family—wife, Priscilla; sons, sixteen-year-old Kilvert Dun (called Dun in the family), Charles (called Chad), and John (known as Jock); and nine-year-old daughter Priscilla (known as Bambi). At an early age, the couple introduced their children to cosmopolitan influences and international tastes. Clarence loved to spend weekends at Providence's Italian neighborhood of Federal Hill, bringing home vegetables, imported cheeses, veal, fresh fish, and olive oil; when Priscilla protested that she didn't know what to make of this assortment of foods still outside the mainstream of 1950s American culinary tastes, Clarence would lead her into the kitchen and together they would improvise a kind of Italian-American cuisine.[9]

In the early summer of 1956 the Giffords decided to take a long European holiday before Dun left for Harvard in the fall. They left New York on June 20 aboard *Queen Mary*. After visiting London, they moved on to the Continent, purchasing a yellow Volkswagen van in which they drove through Europe. They spent the next four weeks racing from one country to another: France, the Netherlands, Belgium, Switzerland, Austria, and finally Italy.[10]

When it came time to return to America, the Giffords booked passage on the *Andrea Doria*, although Bambi thought that her mother had wanted to sail on a British liner. But she was sure that, as "the newest boat, the flashiest," the *Doria* had a special appeal for her father.[11] On the *Doria* the family booked adjoining First Class cabins on the starboard side, No. 98 for Bambi and her parents, and No. 96 for the three sons.[12] Bambi herself thought that the liner was "fantastic, so over-the-top in everything. It wasn't the staterooms so much. They were just cabins. But the public spaces were amazing. They were Swedish hard-edge, with a lot of upholstery."[13]

Also switching their accommodations aboard *Andrea Doria* were Robert Young and his wife, Virginia, both forty-three, and their two children, fourteen-year-old Madge and eleven-year-old David. On boarding the liner shortly after four on the afternoon of July 18, Robert worried. Fearing that his wife might suffer from seasickness in First Class Upper Deck Cabin No. 56, Robert asked that they be moved to accommodations near the middle of the ship, where any rolling would be less noticeable.[14]

The Youngs had been living abroad for nearly four years, in Antwerp and in London. Born in Ceylon in 1912, Young had eventually moved to America, graduated from Tufts with a degree in marine engineering and naval architecture, and went to work for Bethlehem Steel in Fall River, Massachusetts. In 1937 he met and married Virginia; her daughter, Madge, recalls Virginia as "a typical woman of her day. She had gone to Radcliffe and had a degree in English, but she never did anything with it. She was content to be my father's helpmate. She liked being seen as his support."[15]

Shortly after getting married, Young joined the American Bureau of Shipping, which examined and classed ships for safety and insurance purposes. In 1942 Young moved his family to Portland, Maine, where he supervised construction of Liberty ships for use in World War II, providing a vital maritime contribution to the Allied victory. "They eluded submarines," Robert Young noted, "withstood air attacks, and floundered ruggedly through storms from the Arctic to the South Pacific to deliver the troops, weapons, and supplies which turned the fortunes of battle around the world.[16] In 1952, after a stint in South America, Young was appointed to head the Western European branch of the American Bureau of Shipping in Antwerp, Belgium. Madge remembers sailing to their new home aboard the *United States:* "She had beautiful lines and looked absolutely gorgeous, but the inside was really nothing to write home about. She had no warmth."[17]

In 1956 Young was due to have "home leave" from the company and decided to take the family back to America. "Before we left, my parents decided they wanted to go to Italy, which we'd never visited," Madge recalls. "We took the Orient Express and spent a few wonderful weeks wandering around. Unfortunately, being fourteen at the time, I didn't really appreciate the experience."[18] At the end of their holiday, they journeyed to Naples to board the *Doria*. "The era of great transatlantic passengers ships," Robert recalled, "was still at its height, and thus we could make a choice as to which of these magnificent floating palaces we would use for the ocean voyage."[19]

A trip to Europe had seemed the perfect use of an unexpected royalty check that had come to twenty-three-year-old Mike Stoller. Born in 1933, Stoller had studied piano as a way to escape from an occasionally difficult childhood. In 1950, after his family moved from New York to Los Angeles, Mike had met fellow seventeen-year-old Jerry Leiber. The latter termed Mike "a hipster. He was quiet and his cool depended on maintaining a certain reserve . . . He had a remarkable memory and could re-create almost anything he had ever heard."[20] Both shared a love of rhythm and blues and began composing songs, with Mike writing the music and Jerry the lyrics.

The pair's combined genius soon resulted in their first hit, 1952's "Hard Times," and they quickly followed up with "Kansas City" and with "Hound Dog," which became a hit when it was recorded by blues singer Big Mama Thornton the next year, as did "Smokey Joe's Cafe" by the Robins. Leiber and Stoller, said *Rolling Stone*, "initiated mainstream white America into the sensual and spiritual intimacies of urban black culture that fueled the birth of rock & roll."[21]

Mike first met Meryl Cohen when she came to buy one of his mother's paintings. One encounter led to another, as Mike discovered that Meryl was "a very caring and good person." They shared the same political views as well as a shared love of science fiction, and in March 1955 they married.[22]

In 1955, Mike and Jerry were surprised to receive a $5,000 royalty check from Capitol Records for their song "Bazoom (I Need Your Lovin')," which had been recorded by the Cheers; their song "Black Denim Trousers and Motorcycle Boots" was also on its way to becoming a hit—Edith Piaf had recently released her own cover version. Armed with this unexpected financial windfall, Mike and Meryl decided to take an extended trip to Europe. They flew out of Los Angeles on an SAS turbo-propeller that had to land twice for refueling until finally, after twenty-four hours, it landed in Copenhagen. They spent the next three months exploring Europe, visiting Amsterdam, Brussels, London, Dublin, and Paris before continuing on to a lengthy stay in Italy, Mike recording it all on his new movie camera.[23]

Mike and Meryl were pleasantly surprised at how far their money went in postwar Europe. Their pension in Venice had cost a mere two dollars a day, including meals, and they were able to explore more of the Continent than originally planned. On a ferry between Piraeus and Bari, Mike took particular note of the peculiar steering apparatus of the lifeboat: instead of regular oars, paddles were attached to metal pipes, which had to be pushed back and forth to propel the little vessel.[24] This observation would soon come in handy.

When it was time to return to America, Mike went to a local travel agent, who declared, "Take the *Andrea Doria*. She's beautiful. You'll never forget it."[25] Stoller was forced to agree once they boarded the *Doria* in Naples. He eagerly explored the Cabin Class public rooms on the Promenade Deck: the Lounge, with walls cloaked in pickled cherry set off by thin vertical strips of maple and reddish gold aluminum; the vinyl-walled Card Room and the Reading and Writing Room, with its decorative insets in embossed copper by Ettore Calvelli; and once he even slipped into the First Class rooms to investigate their design.[26] "The ship was beautiful," Mike recalls. "The public rooms were very attractive, even magnificent." But their Cabin Class Cabin, No. 23 on A Deck, was a disappointment. "There was an upper and lower berth but it was just a box, with no windows, so it was quite claustrophobic."[27]

Many of those who boarded in Naples were anxious to reunite with relatives already in America. Rosa Mastrincola was returning to America from an Italian holiday with her two children, nine-year-old Pat and eight-year-old Arlene. Her husband, Angelo, a second-generation American of Italian descent, had been a US soldier in World War II when he first met twenty-four-year-old Rosa in Naples. She was, her son, Pat, says, "absolutely beautiful, and they were immediately attracted to each other." Within six weeks of meeting, Angelo and Rosa were married. Angelo had to return to the United States, and not until 1946 did Rosa manage to join him in Haskell, New Jersey, where he worked as a builder.[28]

In the spring of 1956, Rosa wanted to go back to Italy to see her parents and show off her children; Angelo was unable to take an extended leave of absence, and so she set off with Pat and Arlene. "Mother absolutely insisted on taking the *Andrea Doria*," Pat recalls. On May 18, Angelo ushered his family aboard the vessel. It was mischievous Pat who, in record time, managed to cause an incident. "I'd never been on an ocean liner before, and I wanted to explore everything," he says. "The decks were very crowded with passengers and people seeing them off. There was an elderly woman on the Promenade Deck; it was a warm day, and she was trying to pull one of the big windows up. I went over to help her lift it and the damn thing came straight up so fast that I almost fell through it to the dock below. If I hadn't had my hands on the handle I'd have gone over. A man standing next to us was so startled that he dropped a slice of pizza on the shoulder of my father's new suit. My father erupted, and I took advantage of this to run off to do more exploring. I wanted to find our cabin, which was on C Deck. But of course I hadn't told anybody and no one knew where I had gone. As I was wandering around, loudspeakers were announcing my name, saying that I was lost. A crew member found me, grabbed me, and took me to our cabin, telling me to wait there. As soon as he was gone I wandered off again. The whole ship was in an uproar: the captain couldn't delay departure and so the *Andrea Doria* left the harbor with my father still aboard, searching for me—the captain told him they could put him off with the pilot boat. Finally, another crew member spotted me and hauled me up to the bridge, where my father was standing with Captain Calamai, who gave me an intimidating look. But it's a good thing the captain was there—I think my father would have beaten me to death for all the trouble I had caused if we'd been alone."[29]

Back in her native Italy, Rosa proudly showed off Pat and Arlene. "It was a very social time," Arlene recalls, "with lots of relatives, lots of gatherings, lots of food, and lots of presents."[30] And Pat remembers: "I was treated like a little king. My aunts, uncles, and relatives gave me anything I wanted." It did not take long for Pat to get himself into new trouble. His uncle ran a watch-repair shop, and while customers waited Pat would take their bicycles and ride off into the country without telling anyone. Finally, his exasperated relatives pooled their money and bought him a pricey beige Italian bicycle, which quickly became his prized possession. Before boarding the *Doria* in Naples, the family carefully wrapped the bicycle up in brown paper and carried it aboard the liner.[31]

Maria Varanelli Coscia was also returning to America after a holiday with her family in Italy. She had grown up in Carlantino, a tiny and remote mountain village in Foggia Province that was so isolated that it took hours to reach over winding and rutted roadways; even in the 1950s water was scarce and available only two hours a day from a communal pump. Born at the end of December 1900 in Argentina, where her parents had briefly gone after being denied entry to America, Maria Varanelli was one of six children; her parents were peasants who survived in Carlantino through meager farming and tending sheep. Their small house, with one large room and a loft above, had been built atop Roman ruins—columns could still be seen in the basement. Education gave way to survival: Maria never learned to read or write, and signed her name with an "X." Carlantino was a town of no opportunity and no future, and Maria was desperate to escape. In 1917, she boarded the liner *Canopic* and set sail from Naples to Boston with her two sisters Jenny and Antoinette. Accompanying them as chaperone was Raffaele Coscia, whom Maria married in 1919.

Maria and Raffaele settled in Bridgeport, Connecticut, with relatives before moving to New York City with their daughter Saveria (called Sadie), born in 1921: two more children followed—Aida (Ida) and Fortunato, called Fred in the family. Raffaele worked in a coat factory as a tailor while Maria kept their single-bedroom basement apartment in the Bronx. Gradually they carved out a frugal but comfortable life, purchasing a two-family house in the Bronx.

Maria was extremely sociable, recalls her granddaughter Renee Coscia, and loved to spend hours on her front porch, "talking to people who came walking by. When a supermarket opened up across the street, she knew everyone inside." During World War II, Raffaele heard that some prisoners of war from Carlantino were being held in New Jersey and somehow obtained permission for them to join the family in the Bronx for Sunday dinners. The couple purchased clothing and shoes for the men and one, Giacinto, soon became enamored with young Sadie.

Raffaele died of a cerebral hemorrhage in 1955, and Maria took the loss hard. Thinking that a trip back to see her mother and siblings in Italy would help her recover, friends and relatives talked her into a holiday in the summer of 1956. Standing just over five feet tall, a bit rotund, and with short black hair turning gray, Maria boarded the *Andrea Doria* in New York. "We went in and toured the ship before it left," Sadie recalls. "It was beautiful." Maria carried a special farewell gift that Sadie had made: a brassiere with pockets in which jewelry and other valuables could be concealed.[32]

Maria was happy to see her family in Carlantino but almost immediately she was homesick and decided to return home. She boarded the *Doria* in Naples and found the Tourist Class cabin she would share with a young woman she didn't know. The brassiere from Sadie came in handy: tucked inside the hidden pockets were three gold bracelets and other jewelry that she was bringing back as gifts for her family.[33]

Francesco and Alda Raimengia were also on a belated honeymoon voyage. Born in 1939, Alda grew up in Spigno Saturnia near Rome and first met Francesco, called Franco, when he was visiting relatives in Italy. A romance developed, and Alda readily agreed to become his wife and join him, his parents, and his two sisters in the Bronx. The couple married in January 1956 and began making plans for the move to America. "Franco wanted to travel in the best possible way," Alda recalls, and so he purchased two one-way Tourist Class tickets aboard the *Doria*. By the time they boarded the liner in Naples, Alda was four months pregnant with their first child.[34]

Paul Sergio was returning to America not only with his wife, Margaret, but also as caretaker to his sister-in-law Maria and four of her children, thirteen-year-old Giuseppe, ten-year-old Anna Maria, seven-year-old Margaret Domenica, and four-year-old Rocco. The two Sergio brothers, originally from Plati in Calabria, had met and married two sisters, Margaret and Maria Zappia. Paul and Margaret had moved to America in 1922, where he found success as a shoemaker in South Bend, Indiana. In December 1954 he had asked his younger brother Ross to join him in Indiana; Ross stayed with Paul and Margaret while working first as a cabinetmaker and then in a cousin's restaurant. In two years he had managed to save enough for his family to join him. Originally Maria had planned to bring her children to America on *Andrea Doria* in April, but Anna Maria failed to pass the physical examination; suspecting tuberculosis, immigration officials would not allow the family to travel. Only sixteen-year-old Anthony was able to make the voyage on the *Doria* while his mother and four siblings waited to receive permission to leave. Anthony was reluctant to travel by himself: very attached to his siblings, he had wanted to wait until they and their mother could all come together. But the ticket was already purchased, and so he joined three other young men in a shared Tourist Class cabin. His uncle and aunt met the *Doria* when it arrived in New York: they themselves were sailing on its return voyage to Italy, to visit Margaret's elderly mother. They put Anthony on a train bound for South Bend; luckily he found a man on board who also spoke Italian and was able to translate for him. This lack of English, his family knew, would be a stumbling block, and once he arrived in Indiana a cousin bought him a set of English language records and made Anthony listen to them for several hours a day; between these, television, and the radio, he quickly managed to pick up a basic vocabulary.[35]

By the end of Paul and Margaret's Italian holiday, Maria and her four remaining children had been cleared for travel to America. The entire family would travel back aboard the *Doria*, with Paul escorting not only his wife but also his sister-in-law and her four children. Paul and Margaret took a Tourist Class cabin on the port side of C Deck, while Maria and her children shared a family cabin, No. 656, on the deck's starboard side.[36] "How beautiful the children are," Paul commented to Maria as they all settled in for the voyage. "How lucky they are to be traveling to America so young, with their whole lives to live."[37] Their futures indeed seemed bright. Giuseppe, his brother Anthony recalls, "couldn't have cared less about school, but he was very gifted working with his hands." "I can't see myself sitting in a chair," he'd told his older brother. Anna Maria loved history and geography and wanted to one day design clothing; Margaret Domenica, Anthony says, "was very intelligent, the smartest of the lot, and hoped to be a teacher. Her school was surprised at how intelligent she was." Young Rocco probably missed his eldest brother, to whom he was very attached.[38]

Some emigrants had no relatives waiting in America: they were leaving Italy for the United States, hoping to start new lives and seize their share of the fabled American dream. Nineteen-year-old Melania Ansuini was immigrating from Perugia with her parents, Domenico and Giulia Ansuini, as well as her two brothers, fourteen-year-old Fillipo and ten-year-old Pasquale to live in California.[39] As she climbed the gangway, Melania was "impressed by the size of the *Andrea Doria* and its beauty."[40]

Most of Melania's attention, though, was directed to the small family walking up the gangway just in front of her: thirty-four-year-old radio and television technician Tullio Di Sandro; his wife, Filomena; and their four-year-old daughter, Norma. Two of Tullio's half brothers, Nicando and Severino, had emigrated to America in 1911, where they had successful careers in the building business. Emiddio, Tullio's father, had been a wealthy landowner in Abruzzo, but the Great Depression and the Second World War had decimated the family's fortunes. Tullio himself had spent much of the war in a German prison camp, and after marrying Filomena in 1951, he saw no future for them in Italy. But it took five years, during which Norma was born, to finally obtain their visas to emigrate.[41] "I noticed them right away," Melania remembers, "because Norma was so lively and beautifully dressed and adorable, and her parents obviously doted on her."[42]

Born in 1906, Nicola DiFiore boarded the *Doria* in Naples along with a distant cousin who shared the same name. He had first come to America in 1910, but when both of his parents died four years later he was sent back to Italy to be brought up by relatives. He'd had little luck with ships: during World War II, he survived the sinking of both military transports he was on in the Mediterranean. Now, he was leaving his village of Montazzoli in Abruzzo to visit his daughter Rita, whom he had not seen for five years, since she moved to Scotch Plains, New Jersey, on marrying Americo Checchio: it would be the first time that Nicola would see his two-year-old granddaughter, Marisa.[43]

Twenty-six-year-old Santino Porporino boarded the *Doria* in Naples with his wife, Antonietta, who was six months pregnant, and their two children, nearly two-year-old Giuseppe and seven-month-old Bruna. Antonietta's father, Benedette Margerita, who had fought with the American Army during World War I, had previously immigrated to New Jersey along with his sons, but it took five years—and the personal intervention of United States congressman Gordon Canfield—to win permission for the daughter's relocation. Antonietta was anxious to leave her village of Cetraro in Calabria: she'd previously been married but lost her husband in the war and suffered the loss of their only child, Federico, who fell from the balcony of their house when he was just six. Her first husband's family blamed Antonietta for the accident and were upset when she married again. Finally word came that Santino, Antonietta, and their two children had been approved for immigration: Benedette bought their Tourist Class tickets for the *Doria:* Antonietta thought that traveling on the beautiful ship was a good omen—her late husband's surname had been Andrea.[44]

Once aboard, the Porporino family followed the long corridors, hung with photographs of the Italian coast as a panacea to those emigrants reluctantly leaving their homeland for the new world, to reach their rooms.[45] They found themselves assigned to separate cabins: Antonietta and the two children housed in one, and Santino sharing another with several other men. He was careful to guard his accordion: Santino had stuffed it with jewelry and with money.[46] This separation of sexes in Tourist Class—even husbands from wives—was the Italian Line's usual practice, although exceptions were often made. But many families were surprised to find themselves on different sides, decks, or ends of the ship from their relatives, sharing accommodations with strangers, and with only curtains across the berths in place to lend some sort of privacy. The large, shared, multi-fixture common bathrooms could occasionally be perplexing. Young Pierette Domenica Burzio somehow locked herself into a Tourist Class women's bathroom and couldn't find a way to open the door. "I completely freaked out," she says. "I screamed and screamed, and finally a steward came and opened the door. When I walked out, a crowd of people who had gathered outside the door broke into applause."[47]

Fifteen-year-old Adalgisa Di Fabio had long dreamed of coming to America. Her small village in Abruzzo was beautiful but isolated, with no opportunities for an ambitious young woman. She'd lived through the uncertainties and hardships of the war: to avoid bombs her mother hid her and her sister in a little building in a nearby vineyard. In the years after the war, Adalgisa, called Ada, wanted nothing more than to leave her village. "It was a beautiful place, and I was quite happy, but for me, there was nothing. Boys could come and go and take jobs, but if you were a girl, the only acceptable future was making a living in the fields or by sewing, or joining a convent. We weren't even allowed to be around boys except for school or church." Two of her mother's brothers, Francesco and Antonio, had already gone to America, and after several pleading letters the former agreed to sponsor Ada to join him in New Jersey. "It took a few years to get all of the paperwork approved," she recalls, "and my father thought that he and my mother and sister could follow in a few years if everything worked out for me. I was so excited to leave and see what was beyond the mountains around us."[48]

When Ada arrived in Naples to board the *Doria* she was stunned: "This was the first time I had ever seen open water. I had never traveled before, never gone to the beach, never done anything like this by myself. It was a big adventure, but I felt like I could take care of myself. The scene at the dock was especially hard. All around families were separating, and fathers were saying goodbye to their wives and children. I kept telling myself that I was strong and would make it." She found her Tourist Class cabin and met the three other women whom would share it before returning to the deck for the ship's departure; she was surprised but also relieved to find a distant relative, Nella Massa, also traveling aboard the ship. "It was warm and beautiful as I stood at the railway. As we pulled away, I really felt like a whole new world was about to open for me: all of the things I really wanted in life were about to come true."[49]

Chapter Four

At half past ten on the morning of June 30, 1956, a United Airlines Douglas DC-7 crashed into a TWA Lockheed Super Constellation while flying through uncontrolled airspace some twenty-one thousand feet above the Grand Canyon. The DC-7's left wing sheared off the Constellation's vertical stabilizer and severed its tail assembly before the propeller of its left engine slashed through the fuselage. Both planes spiraled down into the canyon and disintegrated on impact, killing all 128 people aboard both instantly. It was the deadliest aviation disaster to date.

Ferdinand and Frances Thieriot were on holiday in Europe with their thirteen-year-old son, Peter, when the accident occurred. "My mother," recalled Peter, "hated to fly. That's all she needed to finish her off. They made this last minute thing to get on the *Andrea Doria*."[1] Now, at one on the afternoon of July 20, the trio watched as the liner arrived at Gibraltar, where they were scheduled to board her for the voyage home.

The Thieriots were akin to royalty in San Francisco, "the most family-conscious of all America's western cities," as Cleveland Amory noted.[2] They had been permanent fixtures in the city's society since Ferdinand's grandfather Michel de Young and his brother, Charles, had founded the *San Francisco Chronicle* in 1865, when the city was at the center of the Gold Rush. The paper made a name for itself by printing salacious details about affairs, rumored bribery, and allegations of corruption on the parts of the brothers' numerous political and civic enemies.[3] Violence followed: in 1880 an outraged reader shot and killed Charles as he sat at his editorial desk.[4] Four years later, Adolph Spreckels stormed into the *Chronicle* offices and shot Michel as revenge for an exposé against his father. Michel recovered and Spreckels got off—the *Chronicle*'s reputation was so bad that a jury deemed the shooting justified.[5] Years later, Adolph's wife, Alma—herself an indomitable figure in San Francisco society—offered a wry bit of understatement when she commented on Michel's daughters, "Those de Young girls are nice but we've never been close since my husband shot their father."[6]

Michel went on to run the *Chronicle* until his death in 1925, although there were frequent battles with William Randolph Hearst and his rival newspapers. What he most craved, though—social acceptance—was elusive. Michel sent his daughters off to European schools and donated large sums to civic and charitable institutions, but it was left to his descendants to conquer society. And conquer they did, making fashionable marriages into the Cameron and Tobin families, buying estates in the exclusive suburban enclaves of Hillsborough and Burlingame, and gradually appearing at the smartest and most important parties.[7]

In 1920, Michel's third daughter, Kathleen, who had married Ferdinand Thieriot, gave birth to a son, whom they called Ferdinand Melly Thieriot. After graduating from Princeton in 1941, Ferdinand studied geology and entered World War II, rising to the rank of major. On December 12, 1941, he married San Francisco society beauty Frances Harrison Dade, whom he had met on the French Riviera. She had been born in 1920 in the Philippines, where her father, Dr. Waller Dade, and his wife, Clara, ran a penal farm and served as chief of the Bureau of Prisons. Frances was, in fact, named after the governor of the Philippines, Francis Harrison, and her father was a descendant of Francis Langhorne Dade, who was killed in a battle with the Seminole Indians and after whom Dade County in Florida was named. After World War II ended, Ferdinand took a job as circulation manager at the *Chronicle*, and the couple made their home in Burlingame, outside of San Francisco, where they raised four sons, Peter, Nion, John, and George.[8]

Ferdinand, his son Peter recalls, "liked to garden and particularly liked azaleas. I used to work in the garden with him a lot." Although

Frances had a passion for tennis she—like many other socially prominent wives—carved out time for charitable pursuits, volunteering with
the Red Cross and at the Mills Hospital. She was also den mother to
Peter's Cub Scout troop.[9]

In 1956 the Thieriots were off to Europe. Ferdinand and Frances
apparently decided that it was too risky to leave thirteen-year-old Peter,
who had just finished St. Catherine's parochial school in Burlingame,
behind with his brothers. The last time they had done so, Peter had
terrorized the nanny so much that she had threatened to quit. They flew
to England, staying at a friend's farm in Somerset. Here Peter spent
several weeks working as a farmhand and learning to roll his own cigarettes before he and his parents visited Frances's mother and her second
husband in Biarritz and continued on to Spain to watch the running of
the bulls in Pamplona. "I think my parents enjoyed themselves on this
vacation," Peter recalls.[10]

The Thieriots had planned to return to America by plane, but then
word of the terrible accident over the Grand Canyon came and Frances
asked her husband to cancel their reservations and book passage on a
liner. They found that they could join the *Andrea Doria* at Gibraltar.
Ferdinand originally wanted one of the liner's four deluxe suites on
the Foyer Deck.[11] Each consisted of a bedroom with two beds, a separate sitting room with two folding berths, a baggage room for steamer
trunks, and two bathrooms. Starboard Suite Nos. 174–176 was probably
the *Doria*'s most famous room. Gio Ponti had hired Piero Fornasetti
to execute the decorative scheme, which took a rather hideous turn.
Known for his bold patterns and graphic designs, Fornasetti adorned
every inch of the suite with depictions of the Zodiac, constellations,
and astrological symbols, even on the ceilings and on the covers of the
toilets in startling blue, white, and gold.[12] It was all very modern, even
futuristic, but it left the eye exhausted.

With an eye to increased revenue, the Italian Line often broke up
these suites, renting the bedroom to one passenger and the sitting room
with its folding berths to another. Ferdinand Thieriot tried to book
Foyer Deck Deluxe Suite Nos. 178–180 on the starboard side; he found,
though, that Denver businessman Max Passante and his wife, Theresa,

had already taken No. 178, which ordinarily served as the suite's sitting room. And so Ferdinand and Frances took No. 180, modern yet a model of restraint compared to the Zodiac Suite, while Peter found himself accommodated in Foyer Deck Cabin No. 186, some fifty feet farther aft along the starboard side.[13]

On the cloudless morning of Friday, July 20, 1956, the Thieriots waited with their luggage, watching as the *Andrea Doria* finally appeared and dropped anchor in the harbor. A tender ferried them from Gibraltar out over the water to the waiting ship. As they approached the gleaming black hull, Ferdinand turned to Peter and pointed up at the second porthole forward of the open gangway doors on the Foyer Deck, saying that it belonged to their suite.[14]

Also floating out to the waiting liner with her mother, stepfather, and half sister, fourteen-year-old Linda Morgan was looking forward to the voyage. She'd been born in 1942 in Mexico City, where her father, Edward P. Morgan, worked as a journalist. In 1937 Edward Morgan, then in the early days of a storied career, had married twenty-two-year-old Jane Stolle, a former journalism major from the University of Washington.[15]

The start of World War II saw Morgan assigned to Europe; Jane and Linda remained in Mexico City. "Mom wasn't really good at being left by herself," Linda recalls. She soon met widowed *New York Times* reporter Camille Cianfarra, who'd been born in New York but brought up in Italy, where his journalist father worked for the *New York American* and for United Press. Called Cian by friends, he was, Linda remembers, "delightful, a great big hulking Italian, bombastic yet very gentle. He was very fair, extremely truthful, and very honorable as well as being quite funny."[16]

Jane married Cian when the Morgans divorced. "He totally accepted me as his daughter," Linda says. In 1946 Cianfarra was transferred to Rome, taking Jane and Linda with him. "It was right after the war," Linda says, "still occupied, and very grim. We rented a very big house next to a vineyard—vines even covered the windows. But coal was in such short supply that we could only ever heat two rooms." Venturing beyond the house, Linda was struck by "how many people on the street wore black. So many people had been killed, and the women who had lost their husbands were always in mourning."[17]

Linda was off to school, first at an establishment founded by Maria Montessori, then the American Overseas School, and finally to Rome's private Catholic Marymount International School. She also had a new half sister, Joan, born in 1949. The two girls were quite different. Joan, Linda says, "was kind of quiet, while I was boisterous and usually got into trouble. She was very bright and did well in school, while I just chugged along. She always wanted to hang out with me, which as a young girl I found a bit irritating. But she was very sweet, and we not only played together but we also shared a bedroom—I had to keep an eye on her as she had a habit of sleepwalking."[18]

In Rome Cian specialized in issues dealing with the Vatican. Linda remembers how he used his access to get his family an audience with Pope Pius XII. "I remember standing in line," says Linda, "waiting to go up, greet him, and get a blessing. At the end he gave you either a medal or a rosary. My turn came and the pope handed me a medal, but I really wanted a rosary, so I got back in line and went again. When I got to the pope, he gave me a funny look and said, 'Well, you've been here before!' But I said I really wanted a rosary, and he handed me one with a smile."[19]

During their time in Rome, Jane occasionally wrote articles on the Italian film industry for *The New York Times* but, as Linda recalls, "she had a lot of trouble learning languages, which kept her a bit isolated. At times she got rather depressed." Jane was always immaculately turned out and loved entertaining, but "Cian was so sophisticated that I think she sometimes felt like a bit of a country bumpkin. Cian, though, was wonderful to her, and she always said that he was the love of her life."[20]

In 1951 *The New York Times* reassigned Cianfarra to Madrid as their principal Spanish correspondent.[21] Linda adjusted easily, but in 1956 her mother and stepfather decided that she would attend boarding school in America; it would also be an opportunity to see her father, Edward Morgan, who had his own nightly news show on ABC Radio in New York City.[22] Passage on *Andrea Doria* was a compromise, after Cianfarra was unable to obtain accommodation on her sister ship. When the family boarded at Gibraltar, they were given two adjoining First Class cabins on the Upper Deck. Camille and Jane took No. 54, while Linda and Joan had No. 52. Linda's most prized possession was a small red autograph book, in which she'd already collected the signatures of Gregory Peck, John Steinbeck, and a number of other luminaries her mother had met and entertained.[23]

Before leaving Spain, Jane had interviewed Cary Grant and his wife, Betsy Drake, while visiting the set of his new film, *The Pride and the Passion.*[24] It was a surprise to find that Betsy Drake was also boarding the *Doria* at Gibraltar, but she smiled at the Cianfarras as she made her way to a First Class cabin on Boat Deck.

The smiles concealed Drake's inner turmoil: her life and her marriage were falling apart. Her grandfather had built the famous Drake Hotel in Chicago, and she grew up in privilege until the stock market crash of 1929 depleted the family's fortunes. After dropping out of the exclusive, all-girls Madeira School in McLean, Virginia, at seventeen, the pretty, blond Betsy decided to try her hand at acting. She moved to New York, worked briefly with director Elia Kazan at his Actors Studio, and finally gave her a part in his 1947 London play about race relations, *Deep Are the Roots.*[25]

Deep Are the Roots ended in the fall of 1947, and Betsy booked return passage to America aboard *Queen Mary.* Also aboard was Cary Grant, who had caught the play and been fascinated by the beautiful young Drake. He was famous, debonair, and utterly charming; he was also twenty years her senior and already twice divorced, first from actress Virginia Cherrill and then from heiress Barbara Hutton. One day during lunch on *Queen Mary,* Grant was sitting with actress Merle Oberon when he discreetly pointed to Betsy and asked to be introduced. "I hid in the nearest companionway," he recalled, while Oberon asked Betsy to join them.[26] They talked through the luncheon, then into the afternoon and evening; the next day Betsy and Cary were constantly together. By the time *Queen Mary* docked in New York, he was convinced that he was in love.[27]

Betsy was less certain about the whole thing: the disintegration of her parents' marriage had left her cynical about relationships, but Cary wouldn't be deterred. He got her a contract with RKO and starred opposite her in the 1948 comedy *Every Girl Should Be Married.*[28] "Betsy Drake," recalled Irene Mayer Selznick, "was an intelligent, studious, well-born woman of talent and dignity. She was a lady. But she had no comedic talent. She was a dramatic actress. My impression is she really wanted to be in the theater and only went to Hollywood because of Cary."[29]

More roles followed, and on Christmas Day 1949 Betsy and Cary married in a midnight ceremony, where Howard Hughes stood as best man.[30] Betsy wasn't interested in continuing to work, and Cary had agreed to devote himself to their marriage and not pursue his career. "I couldn't be an actress and a housewife, too," she explained.[31] The couple retreated to Palm Springs, where he had bought an estate, Las Palomas, but soon Betsy felt herself swallowed alive: "I drank white wine because Cary liked white wine," she later said. "And I ate well-done roast beef, even though I hated well-done meat."[32] It was a shock to find that the debonair Cary Grant of the screen was actually something of a bore in private life: he had few real interests, couldn't understand her passion for books, and preferred watching television to talking with her.[33]

The first signs of trouble came when Cary agreed to star in Alfred Hitchcock's *To Catch a Thief*. Betsy was especially upset that he'd be starring with Grace Kelly; hearing that Grace had a reputation for sleeping with her leading men, Betsy insisted on accompanying Cary to France when filming began. Things were so tense that they were barely speaking to each other.[34]

To Catch a Thief proved to be an enormous hit; despite his pledge, Cary soon signed on for another film, *The Pride and the Passion*, only telling Betsy once the contract was inked.[35] Unfortunately for Betsy, joining Cary for the Spanish shoot was Sophia Loren. Despite his own marriage and Loren's liaison with married director Carlo Ponti, it didn't take long for Cary to decide that he was in love with his costar. "We saw each other every night," Loren recalls; "we dined in romantic little restaurants on craggy hilltops to the accompaniment of flamenco guitars, drank the good Spanish wine and laughed and were serious and confessional and conspiratorial."[36] Cary was so smitten that he soon proposed marriage.[37]

It didn't take long for Betsy to hear the gossip about Grant and Loren, and she traveled to Spain to confront her husband. Things went from bad to worse when she saw Cary openly staring at Loren, and with his complaining to his wife about how sad and lonely he was when Sophia was away. It was too much for Betsy: she told Cary that she was returning to Hollywood to take a role in the upcoming film *Will Success Spoil Rock Hunter?* Rather than protest, he thought this was a splendid idea—a clear signal that the marriage was over. The next day, Betsy left Spain and traveled to Gibraltar, booking passage home aboard the *Andrea Doria*.[38]

"I had a terrible premonition that something was going to happen when I boarded the *Andrea Doria*," Betsy recalled, "but I thought it was going to be something that happened to Cary."[39] Accompanying her were several crates of furnishings she had purchased in Spain for Las Palomas; a manuscript for an autobiographical novel; and a quarter-million dollars in jewelry.[40]

Anchored in the shadow of the towering Rock of Gibraltar, *Andrea Doria* was temporarily besieged by a makeshift flotilla of small boats that had sped over the water and stopped along her shining black hull. They were full of vendors shouting for passengers to buy their wares: watches, shirts, blankets, perfume—all kinds of goods. Sailors on the *Doria* lowered baskets to the boats and once filled, hauled them back up on deck for the passengers to inspect: if someone wanted to purchase an item, they shouted back and forth with a boat over the price, sending the money back in the empty basket. Tenders also picked up letters and postcards that passengers had wanted to send to friends and relatives while aboard the *Doria*. Among those filling a canvas bag at Gibraltar was a letter from Tullio Di Sandro to his brother Mariano, in which he wrote warmly of their "truly wonderful journey . . . Norma is happy and is admired by the whole ship: everyone calls her the 'Beautiful Princess.' Who knows what future awaits her?"[41]

Finally, just after noon, the *Doria* let out a sharp blast of her whistle, signaling that she was about to leave—there had been no time for passengers to go ashore and explore the famous crag, with its Barbary apes. The little boats disappeared as the anchor broke the surface and, with a rumble, the liner's engines came to life. Within a few minutes *Andrea Doria* was on her way, her bow finally slicing through the open waters of the Atlantic as Europe receded against the eastern horizon.

Chapter Five

◆◆◆

After leaving Gibraltar, *Andrea Doria* headed west, out into the Atlantic. It was, Third Officer Eugenio Giannini said, "the beginning of the life of a city at sea."[1] This would be the *Doria*'s fifty-first westbound crossing. She carried 1,134 passengers, just shy of her total capacity of 1,241. There were 190 First Class passengers, 267 in Cabin Class, and 677 in Tourist Class. With a crew of 572, a total of 1,706 people were aboard, along with 401 tons of freight; 522 pieces of luggage; 1,754 bags of mail; and $2 million in furniture, olive oil, wine, fabrics, and assorted foods.[2]

Among these passengers were several who would make the voyage in *Andrea Doria*'s hospital. The liner's hospital on A Deck was the province of ship's physician Bruno Tortori-Donati; his assistant, Dr. Lorenzo Giannini; head nurse, Antonia Coretti; and a staff of four additional nurses.[3] Seventy-one-year-old Rosa Carola had been brought aboard the liner on a stretcher in Naples, suffering from terminal cancer of the larynx, a weak heart, and fluid around the lungs. Her daughter Margaret was also on the ship, sharing a Tourist Class cabin on A Deck with two women from Brooklyn, Christina Covino (who happened to be the grandmother of popular Italian-American singer Jerry Vale) and her sister Amelia Iazzetta (whose husband, Benvenuto, had taken a separate cabin). Also in the ship's hospital was sixty-five-year-old Mary Onder, who was returning to Pennsylvania after a disappointing visit to Italy. On her voyage in April, she had sailed on *Cristoforo Colombo* and fallen on the second day, fracturing her left thigh. A lengthy stay at a hospital in Genoa followed when the ship landed, but the injury was not properly set, and Mary was returning to America for better medical care.[4]

Thirty-five-year-old New Orleans native Robert Lee Hudson also spent much of the voyage in the *Doria*'s hospital. A sailor with the United States Merchant Marines, he had suffered two serious accidents while serving aboard the Stockard Steamship Company's freighter *Ocean Victory*. The first left him with two herniated discs in his back, while the second lacerated his right arm and hand, nearly severing his index finger. He was brought aboard the *Doria* at Gibraltar, to return to America for treatment.[5]

Andrea Doria carried nine automobiles in its air-conditioned garage on B Deck. In addition to the Volkswagen van used in Europe by the Gifford family, a Rolls-Royce belonging to a Miami couple returning from their honeymoon, and a red station wagon belonging to Barbara and Robert Boggs (it had, Barbara Bliss recalled, "stuck out like a sore thumb" as they drove it around Italy), the garage also held a new, experimental prototype automobile designed for the Chrysler Corporation and created by Italian manufacturer Ghia in Turin at a cost of some $150,000.[6] Called the Norseman, this was promoted as the most automated and technologically advanced car yet built, with a futuristic design, a cantilevered roof resting directly atop the windshield, and a retractable rear window.[7]

On the morning of Thursday, July 19, *Andrea Doria* held its one and only lifeboat drill: passengers had already embarked at Genoa, Cannes, and Naples, but the drill took place before collecting travelers from Gibraltar, who would have to rely on the printed notices hanging inside cabin doors, outlining evacuation routes, instructions on donning life jackets, and directing them to lifeboat stations. Several passengers later complained that the exercise had seemed confusing and perfunctory at best. A blast from *Andrea Doria*'s whistle that morning summoned the passengers to their various muster stations with the life jackets stowed in their cabins.[8] There seems to have been no consistency in the drill: Robert Young thought that it was professionally conducted, but his daughter, Madge, recalled that "it was kind of a joke. People treated it like a farce. Some had life jackets, and some held drinks in their hands." Even so, she thought that the exercise was "pretty standard for the era."[9] At some stations, a few passengers alleged, no officers or crew appeared.[10] At others, people seemed to treat it as "a sort of entertainment."[11]

Andrea Doria would take the southern route to New York, which meant she passed the Azores. This was usually a sunnier, calmer course than the northern one used by most liners, offering passengers opportunities to enjoy life on deck. For many, returning from European holidays or family reunions, the voyage was almost anticlimactic: all of the excitement was behind them as they anticipated landing and making their ways home. Temporary inhabitants of this floating hotel, most needed several days to settle in to life at sea, to get the layout of the ship set in their minds, to feel comfortable with the subtle roll of the waves beneath their feet, and to embrace all of the amenities available to them.

After the initial excitement of departure, passengers began appreciating the *Doria* itself. "The ship's decor was not as Old World as a ship like the *Queen Mary*," recalled Barbara Bliss, "but it still had a certain elegance and glamour."[12] Madge Young couldn't help comparing it— favorably—with the *United States*, on which she had traveled earlier. "*Andrea Doria* was a far more beautiful, more elegant ship," she recalls. The rooms were really splendid."[13] Priest John Dolciamore was struck by the bold colors used in the decoration of the ship—he'd never before seen so much blue and green mixed together. "It was state-of-the-art," he recalled. "There was nothing disappointing about it."[14] And Adalgisa Di Fabio was stunned by the ship's beauty. "I had never been on an ocean liner," she recalls, "and I was amazed at the decoration. Being on that ship was like a holiday. There was music all the time, and everyone dressed up in their best clothes. It seemed like a dream."[15]

Captain Calamai and his officers saw to the running of the ship, duties that allowed the reticent master to avoid most unwelcome social obligations. Still, at the beginning of every voyage, he had to meet with Chief Purser Francesco Ingianni to review the passenger list. It was Ingianni's task to point out any diplomats or aristocrats, celebrities, or particularly prominent passengers who demanded extra attention.

Inevitably there would be special invitations to private cocktail parties, tours of the bridge, and occasional concessions when Calamai had to dine at the Captain's Table and select those whom he would honor. It was always a delicate and often nerve-racking process involving protocol and the balancing of fragile egos.[16]

For most of the passengers, though, it was the extensive interior crew who catered to their needs, acting as efficiently as any staff at an exclusive hotel. At head was Chief Purser Ingianni, and his three assistants; below them were several hundred stewards and waiters; maids, cabin stewards, and cabin boys; butlers, barbers, and bartenders; and gymnasium instructors, two photographers, and switchboard and elevator operators.[17]

All of the proprieties of the era were in place on the *Doria:* male stewards served single male guests, and female stewards tended to ladies, while couples were attended by both sexes. Crews on Italian Line ships were known, recorded maritime historian John Malcolm Brinnin, for their "bemused demeanor . . . and pervasive sense of domestic intimacy this assured. Zest for a good table and white linen amenities of the nineteenth century gave even the most modern of Italian ships a combined air of opulence and hominess; and a characteristic open curiosity about everything human on the part of their staffs nicely checked the pretensions to aristocratic elegance the Italian Line's advertising encouraged . . . On an Italian ship a passenger pressing his call button would likely be greeted in a few moments by a stand in for Sophia Loren. As she stood poised on the threshold of his cabin, costumed in black, skin-tight poplin and frills of a sort once associated only with postcards depicting the raunchier side of domestic life in Paris, his signorina would address him with one enormously self assured stare."[18]

Early every morning, as passengers slept, the decks were cleaned as boys set up the teak chairs with their lap rugs, and stewards and maids filtered through the ship, polishing furniture and floors, washing sea spray from windows, and replacing flowers in vases. The ship's laundry hummed with humid activity. Every day maids and stewards collected soiled clothing and linens from passenger cabins: garments were carefully tagged to ensure that they were returned to their owners.

Although there were massive washing and drying machines and non-stop work that kept Giuseppina Battista and her staff of two pressers in a nearly perpetual state of activity, at least they did not have to worry about the ship's linens. The laundry only dealt with clothing from the passengers and the uniforms of the crew: *Andrea Doria* regularly carried some four thousand tablecloths, five thousand sheets, and twelve thousand towels, each sewn with the Italian Line logo. The ship's used linens were always off-loaded in New York or in Genoa to be laundered at an industrial facility and would be collected again when the liner returned.[19]

With clean linens in place, tables were set for breakfast. Some First Class passengers preferred to take their first meal of the day in their cabins—"you could have breakfast brought to your bed," recalls Bambi Gifford, "which mother loved."[20] Stewards filtered down corridors, pushing trolleys of trays laden with eggs and meats, fruit and pastries, and coffee, tea, and juices. From seven in the morning on, those who rose early could find buffets of coffee and tea, pastries, and a selection of meats at each of the liner's three lidos.[21]

For some passengers, the morning began with daily mass, held in the ship's Chapel on the Foyer Deck, where Monsignor Sebastiano Natta presided, usually assisted by one of the liner's inevitable priestly travelers. Situated in the center of the ship, the Chapel was open to all passengers, no matter their class, though for a liner that regularly carried a hefty number of Catholics it was surprisingly small. Eight wooden pews, four on each side of the central aisle, stood atop a floor of black and white diamonds facing the altar, allowing no more than several dozen to worship at any one time. Literature described the decoration, with dark wooden panels flanking the lower walls, as a mixture of Renaissance and Gothic styles. The altar, with its silver candlesticks and triptych mural depicting Virgin and Child flanked by saints, rested beneath an elaborate baldachino with scalloped edges and geometric designs.[22] Passengers slipping into the pews found special prayer cards asking for the protection of the ship and those she carried.[23]

Others spent mornings perusing the ship's newspaper *Corriere del Mare,* produced in Italian and English editions each day by Francesco

Bochino on Linotype machines in the *Doria*'s own printing office and briefly giving the latest news transmitted from shore. This would usually contain any updates to the list of passengers on board, helpful hints for travelers, advertisements for hotels and shops in New York City or Genoa (depending on whether it appeared during an eastbound or a westbound crossing) and an agenda of daily activities: games, contests, concerts, dances, films, and special receptions or dinners.[24]

Including—and more often, excluding—information in the paper was always a source of worry. Captain Raoul de Beaudéan of the *Ile de France* explained that a ship's newspaper had to account for "our unique position in the middle of a vast ocean, with a population consisting of all racial, national and religious groups. Indiscriminate dissemination of news involves the risk of troubling their peace of mind and arraying them against each other. Now, shouldn't they live in harmony for six days and isn't this existence on the margin of the world and its whirlpools one of the charms of life aboard ship? Why poison the happiness of this temporary community with alarming and inadequately verified news items?"[25]

The daily newspaper was but one source of information for the *Doria*'s passengers. On boarding, travelers had received little booklets containing a tentative passenger list; general information about meals and services available; plans of the ship to help them navigate the vessel; and even a guidebook to the works of art featured on the liner.[26] In addition, the print shop prepared programs for the passengers, deposited in their cabins during dinner and outlining the following day's activities. These listed the daily radio programs broadcast on the ship and sittings for meal times, as well as special activities; deck games and sports competitions that would take place that day; any concerts; titles and descriptions of the films that would be shown; and any entertainment that evening.[27]

Andrea Doria followed the tradition of most other liners: every effort was made to cater to passengers while ignoring the fact that they were actually at sea.[28] Instead of a voyage, passengers were surrounded by suggestions of a grand, cosmopolitan hotel. Glass-fronted vitrines and shops on the Foyer Deck displayed the latest in Italian fashion, art, and craftsmanship. Passengers could purchase decorative spoons; ashtrays and china adorned with the *Doria*'s name; crosses and rosaries; couture clothing, colorful scarves, and finely worked leather belts, handbags, and gloves; and jewelry and liquor.[29] The ship's Bank of Rome office and exchange, as well as the Purser's Office were conveniently nearby.[30]

In the mornings First and Cabin Class passengers might entrust their young children to the care of the liner's small contingent of babysitters, who presided over playrooms decorated with circus and animal murals and crowded with games, toys, slides, rocking horses, and other amusements meant to leave their parents unencumbered.[31] There was no such relief for parents traveling in Tourist Class, though the ship provided daily games, puppet shows, and cartoons and films (the works of Walt Disney were particularly popular). "They had silly horse racing games for passengers to bet on," recalls Pat Mastrincola, "skeet shooting, and shuffleboard, but I was too young to do any of those. My mother was always yelling at me to behave and pay attention, but I preferred to be a pain. I had grown up with woods behind our house and used to climb trees there, so I wandered around the ship, climbing over railings to Cabin Class, went up and down stairs, and got into places where I wasn't supposed to go. Once I made it to engine and generator rooms. After a day all of the crew members were well aware of me and used to chase me around the ship. As soon as they caught me, they'd escort me back to the cabin. I was always in trouble. I remember being in the lounge and climbing up on the back of a sofa. A crew member, probably tired of chasing me around, came up behind me and flicked his finger hard against my head so I fell. I wasn't hurt, but I was sure mad, and it didn't do a thing to stop my exploring." Soon, members of the *Doria*'s crew started calling Pat *"Il Peste"* ("The Plague").[32]

In contrast, Peter Thieriot confined himself to the tours conducted by members of the *Doria*'s crew. After befriending Chad Gifford, the two adventurous boys spent a good deal of time exploring the ship. Peter recalls being particularly impressed at the engine room—"three or four stories, a great big cavern, and so loud you couldn't hear yourself think."[33]

Passengers could compose letters and postcards to friends in the reading and writing rooms, play bridge and Scrabble in the card rooms, and enjoy leisurely conversation over drinks and cigarettes in the lounges. Some explored, inspecting the public rooms, the decks, and even areas ordinarily off-limits. Thure and Martha Peterson enjoyed their time on the ship and were delighted when Captain Calamai showed them the bridge and the radio room.[34]

"The weather was mostly sunny and warm" Father Oppitz recalled, "the waves were moderate and relatively calm, and we passengers were totally relaxed."[35] Passengers spent hours on deck lounging in rows of teak chairs they had reserved, their reading only intermittently interrupted by white-jacketed stewards offering coffee, tea, cocktails, and little sandwiches.[36]

Outdoor pursuits and healthy living were all the rage in 1956. "Games and sports aboard the ship," a booklet told passengers, "serve not only to pass the time, but also to keep the body in operation and to intensify the beneficial effect of sea air. Sport fights apathy, stimulates the appetite, strengthens the muscles, and tones the nervous system." Additionally, the booklet promised that "games and sports have the merit of breaking the ice between passengers, and creating a relaxed atmosphere of trust and general sympathy. The life on board wins over the reluctant, worries disappear, the heart opens, and the ship becomes friendly."[37]

Bambi Gifford discovered the kennel on the top deck. Missing her own dogs, she visited those belonging to the passengers, petting them through the wire cages. These dogs—or more precisely their owners— were a source of perpetual annoyance to the crew of most liners. Captain Raoul de Beaudéan recalled the trouble they caused on his *Ile de France*: "What has always annoyed me in regard to the transport of these little beasts is the extremely bad faith displayed by both the ship owner and the passengers. It ends up by dividing the canines into two distinct categories. The passenger who intends to travel with his faithful companion is advised in writing that the animal, while paying a tidy fee, will be housed in the kennel and entrusted to a crew member especially assigned to guard the shaggy beasts. Certain naive persons graciously comply with this ruling. But others—quite a few, particularly women—come aboard with the preconceived notion that no one could be so hardhearted as to separate them from their four footed friends. So there are two classes of dogs: those closeted behind the kennel barriers when they're not out for a promenade and the pampered pets whose promenade lasts all day long and ends up in their owner's bed, in contempt of rules."[38]

Several of the First Class teenagers found each other and began spending their days together: roughly the same age, Peter Thieriot, Madge Nickerson, and Linda Morgan passed the mornings and afternoons together on deck.[39] "*Andrea Doria* was magical," recalls Linda, "like a little village full of places to explore.[40] Linda found that she and Madge, in particular, "had a lot in common: she was an American living in England, and was also fourteen-years-old. Since we lived in Europe we could speak to each other in different languages."[41]

The liner's three swimming pools and their surrounding Lido decks were particular draws. All had been designed by Milanese architect Giulio Minoletti. The First Class Swimming Pool, Veranda Bar, and Lido were situated at the stern of the Lido Deck, with a terrace set above on the Sun Deck. The Cabin Class Swimming Pool, Veranda Bar, and Lido were one deck lower and farther back on the Boat Deck, while those for Tourist Class occupied the last sixth of the Promenade Deck. The square pools, decorated with colorful ceramic tiles by Lucio Fontana and rimmed by raised edges, were surrounded by tables and chairs shaded by large umbrellas, and sandboxes for the children—an innovation the crew largely despised as they were constantly cleaning and sweeping up the decks after playful afternoons.[42] Bars serving liquor helped ensure a lively, carefree atmosphere. *Andrea Doria* was not only the first liner to feature three open-air swimming pools but also the first to boast one for each class of passenger, further underlining the idea of luxury and the pleasures of Mediterranean living.[43]

Young Pierette Domenica Burzio recalled how different the chlorinated water smelled from the ponds to which she was accustomed.[44] Bars served drinks, and passengers sat at little tables set beneath the shade of umbrellas or lounged in deck chairs as others romped in the tiled pools. At noon stewards and waiters laid out a buffet: Linda,

Madge, and Peter usually had lunch by the First Class pool, wanting to enjoy the sunshine as much as possible.[45] Linda thought it was all "very magical," though several times Ruth Roman's young son, Dickie, interrupted the mood, "running about and making a lot of noise."[46] Melania Ansuini continued to note young Norma Di Sandro when she appeared on the Lido and in the public rooms—"she was very friendly, and attracted attention wherever she was."[47] While her brother explored the ship, Arlene Mastrincola soon learned to linger around the pool at lunch. "They always put out salami sandwiches along the bar," she says. "We were too short to be seen, and so all of us kids would go up to the bar, reach up, and take the sandwiches, which we thought was great fun."[48] For teenager Andrew Stevens, the First Class pool offered an opportunity for mischief as he went down the slide backward to cause the biggest possible splash: "All of the young ladies," he recalls, "would get upset."[49]

Passengers hung over the rails, watching the white ribbon of foam in the ship's long wake recede into the azure horizon. There were always games on deck: shuffleboard, bowling, tennis, and Ping-Pong. Mike Stoller was delighted to find himself crowned the Cabin Class Ping-Pong champion after a winning streak.[50] There was also trap shooting, something that appealed to Peter Thieriot, who won a trophy for his skills.[51] Those passengers less inclined to public activities could expend their energies on exercise bicycles and rowing machines in the gymnasium; relax in one of the spa's steam baths or at the hands of a masseuse, or bask in the ultraviolet rays of its sun lamps. And every afternoon ladies could indulge in bridge and canasta tournaments, where small souvenirs of the ship were awarded as prizes.[52]

Afternoon tea, served promptly at five in the lounges, followed another tradition: white-jacketed stewards pushed round little caddies laden with sandwiches, cakes, and pastries for the mainly female participants indulging in this more genteel pursuit.[53] The staid tradition somehow seemed out of place in the boldly decorated First Class Lounge, designed by Ponti and Zoncada and strewn with gray, brown, or purple overstuffed arm chairs and barrel-backs beneath a futuristic ceiling set with elongated geometric insets. An immense mural, *Legends of*

Italy, by Salvatore Fiume served as the focal point: composed of hundreds of pieces of hickory, cherry, myrtle, maple, and lemon woods, it wrapped the walls, its panels evoking a stylized Renaissance city and reinterpreting famous works by Cellini, da Vinci, Raphael, Donatello, Michelangelo, and other celebrated artists. At the rear of the room, the walls turned inward, forming an alcove: here stood a five-foot-tall bronze statue of the ship's namesake, Admiral Andrea Doria, clad in armor and cape, with his right hand resting atop the hilt of his sword. Above this hung a replica of his family crest, a magnificent piece of Renaissance silver that had for centuries graced his Genoa villa.[54]

By late afternoon people had begun disappearing to their cabins to prepare for dinner. *Andrea Doria* offered both a barbershop and a hairdressing and manicure salon, and both saw harried business as evening approached. A cocktail hour in the lounges usually preceded dinner. Children of First Class passengers had their own dining room, but other families dined together. Compared to many ocean liners, the *Doria*'s First Class Dining Room was almost a disappointment. Rather than sacrifice cabin space to aesthetic pretension, designer Antonio Ramelli kept the room a single story, its ceiling set with concealed lighting creating a slightly claustrophobic effect. "Low ceilings don't aid the appetite," the French Line had once sniffed, but by the time of the *Doria*'s creation the era of multistory, balconied dining rooms crowned with painted or leaded glass domes had passed into oblivion.[55] Lacking architectural elements, the room relied on an intricate wooden mosaic on the rear wall and the berry-colored chairs scattered across the pale blue linoleum floor to create interest.[56]

It was still a time when people dressed for dinner. For First Class passengers, this usually meant dinner jackets for the gentlemen and gowns for the ladies, a code reinforced on the printed daily itinerary, which offered "suggestions" as to appropriate dress for each evening. Peter Thieriot was surely not alone among the teenagers in finding the semiformality a nuisance.[57] There could be other difficulties as well: passengers were assigned tables, and thus found themselves bound to strangers for several hours a day. A dinner companion might be full of amusing anecdotes or droll observations, but they might also be loud, obnoxious, or otherwise disagreeable. One could discreetly ask to be moved to another table if the ordeal proved to be too much, but this always caused embarrassment.[58]

The *Andrea Doria*'s artistry, promised one advertisement, "extends to her great kitchens, where the art of flavoring a sauce according to some old world recipe or timing a two inch steak to perfection is an Epicurean's dream come true." The ship's culinary staff numbered some sixty people: a chef de cuisine oversaw a contingent of butchers, roasting chefs, sauciers, pastry chefs, ice cream chefs, bakers, confectioners, coffeemakers, and ice sculptors who turned out the lavish meals. Most had studied at the Istituto Marino Boccanegra, which specialized in training the hospitality staff serving aboard the ships of the Italian Line.[59]

Before every voyage the ship's enormous walk-in refrigeration and cold storage rooms were filled with some ninety tons of provisions: sides of beef, chickens, turkeys, duck, veal, lamb, ham, slabs of bacon; fresh fish packed in ice; and baskets of vegetables. On a typical nine-day crossing, the kitchen might make its way through fifty thousand eggs, fifteen hundred pounds of meat and fish, and two thousand pounds of fruits and vegetables. Then there were the beverages: one hundred and fifty pounds of coffee and tea a day, along with a hundred gallons of milk, two hundred gallons of wine, and an enormous amount of champagne, whiskey, beer, mineral water, and various sodas.[60]

Waiters and stewards directed passengers to the tables, where embossed and decorated menus stood atop white linen cloths bedecked with fresh flowers, and forks, knives, and spoons from the liner's twelve-thousand-piece silver-plated service from Broggi in Milan gleamed in the soft light. Menus became more complex with each ascending class, although the offerings were always substantial. Each dining room also had its own distinctive china patterns: ordinary First Class china, designed by the Italian firm of Richard Ginori, was trimmed in red or gold, or featured painted rims of a twisted rope, and bore the monogram of the Italian Line. There were separate services, decorated with colorful chinoiserie scenes, also used in First Class; dessert services by Ginori; and tea and coffee services from the firm of Schönwald. Tourist Class china was ringed with blue and silver, while Cabin Class china carried only a blue rim. Cut crystal goblets, tumblers, champagne flutes, water, cocktail glasses and wineglasses, and snifters also featured etched designs.[61]

"Overeating," wrote John Maxtone-Graham, "is the most popular Atlantic sport."[62] A typical dinner service might offer hors d'oeuvres including fruit cups, caviar, melba toast, smoked ham, olives and mushrooms, salami, sardines, cheeses and, as Bambi Gifford recalled, "shrimp cocktails in those cute stemmed glasses."[63] A soup course usually offered several choices: clear consommé, minestrone, a vegetable soup, or a cream-based soup. A pasta course followed, with a variety of sauces, before a selection of fish: fillets of sole, broiled sea bass, or salmon in sauce were common. Entrées might include roasted sirloin of beef, duck in orange sauce, pork, or roasted chicken or turkey; accompanying the entrées, passengers could choose from a variety of vegetables, including potatoes (mashed, boiled, roasted, or fried), cauliflower, roasted tomatoes, or sautéed endive. A cold buffet offered choices of roast lamb, turkey, chicken, ox tongue, ham, or roast pork, while salads might be mixed vegetables or various combinations of the green salads preferred by Americans. A round of various cheeses and crackers, along with fresh fruits, joined such favorites as pastries, cakes, crêpes suzette, soufflés, and ice creams for dessert.[64]

Culinary experiences aboard *Andrea Doria* could dazzle and bewilder, especially in their variety and in the constant waves of food. "There was always a wonderful selection for meals," recalls one passenger, "and everything looked and smelled splendid. The pastas alone were stunning."[65] Pierette Domenica Burzio, like many immigrants, boarded the *Doria* accustomed to simple fare like cheese, fried beans, and polenta. "On board the ship," she recalls, "the smells of the food were somehow strange yet appetizing," hinting at pleasures waiting to be discovered.[66] "It was more food than I had ever seen," remembers Adalgisa Di Fabio.[67]

Many First Class passengers flocked to the lounge after dinner, to wager on the mechanical horse races. A steward spun a wheel, and moved little wooden horses toward a finish line set out on the floor as passengers placed bets on who would win.[68] Peter Thieriot found the whole thing fascinating, as did young Bambi Gifford who, much to the anger of her brothers, won nine dollars one evening, along with a new Italian leather pocketbook.[69] Other competitions included memory contests, trivia games, and the awarding of the title of Miss Andrea Doria to one beauty from each of the three classes (voted on only by male passengers—females were excluded with the excuse that they could not possibly be impartial), which brought prizes of silver cups, commemorative china, and bottles of champagne.[70]

Once the games ended, passengers scattered for drinks and dancing. It was then, in the soft and subdued lighting of night, that the *Doria*'s First Class Ballroom and the adjacent Cocktail Lounge came to life. The Ballroom featured sofas and chairs of purple or silver, and waves of tables that circled the polished floor. One wall was adorned by Italian set designer and painter Pietro Zuffi with a modernist mural depicting Neptune presiding over a banquet; this contrasted with the parchment covering the other walls, which were accented with decorative strips of gold anodized aluminum and a sculpted, tiered ceiling whose yellow and pink mirrors refracted the concealed fluorescent lighting. Behind this, disposed in a U-shape around the funnel shaft, lay the First Class Cocktail Lounge on Promenade Deck, with an inset bar of deep blue fronted by a row of low-backed aluminum stools covered in blue leather against a curved wall of copper enameled in gold. Chairs covered in blue and yellow linen sprawled beneath a white ceiling crossed by gold aluminum panels set with concealed lighting strips, with Romano Rui providing two ceramic panels adorning the walnut veneered walls.[71]

Some evenings Dino Massa led the *Andrea Doria*'s orchestra, which provided a selection of current tunes and sentimental Italian songs as couples took to the ballroom floor. The ship also carried a supply of the latest records by popular artists to help fill in the gaps: on this voyage they included the foxtrot "Non Penserò Che A Te" and "How Bitter, How Sweet" by Peggy Lee.[72] There were also occasional concerts.

Barbara Bliss quickly befriended Dun Gifford and another teenage girl traveling in First Class, Nancy Coleman, and spent most evenings with them. Barbara thought that they "would have had more fun below in Cabin Class, with the college age kids traveling with knapsacks in large, boisterous groups," but the trio contented themselves with the lounge games and dancing to pass the evenings. Nearly seventeen, Barbara found herself attracted to the tall and handsome Dun, and a shipboard romance started to develop.[73]

There were also occasional concerts for Cabin and Tourist Class passengers, along with the screening of films in current release.[74] It was usually up to the chief purser and to Carlo Vitellozzi, the chief cinema operator, to pick appropriate titles. The selection usually included several recent films from Rome for the liner's Italian passengers, as well as a number of offerings from Hollywood. It was always a tricky business choosing which films to show: with priests, pious women, and children often present, the stories could not be too scandalous, the adult situations had to be kept to a minimum, and discreet cuts edited out language likely to offend.[75]

For Adalgisa Di Fabio, these evenings passed "like a dream, and I wondered if this was what life in America would be like for me. On July 21, I celebrated my sixteenth birthday on the ship and went dancing after dinner. These dances were completely new to me. Where I came from, girls weren't allowed to go dancing or meet boys—if you wanted to meet a boy you went to church." She was particularly taken with one fellow passenger, Anita Leone, who was traveling to America to be with her pregnant daughter. "She was the most beautiful woman I had ever seen. She was from Rome, and she always wore the most elegant tailored Italian dresses. I was so impressed by her. Even though I had on my best dress I felt like a peasant compared to her."[76]

The southern route across the Atlantic usually boasted fair weather and warm breezes in the summer, but on this particular voyage, almost as soon as *Andrea Doria* had passed the Azores, she encountered heavy seas and strong winds. The ship rolled and pitched its way westward. Brave First Class passengers could lounge in the ship's Winter Garden, with its enormous windows looking out over the bow, and peer through the thick rain pelting the liner to watch the incessant sprays crash over the *Doria*. The immense decorative ceramic panels by Florentine artist Guido Gambone based on Cubist designs and depicting "strange representations" of stylized people, animals, and mythological creatures, rattled on the Winter Garden's walls with every wave.[77]

Seasickness among passengers had always been treated as something of a joke by those who made their living on the sea, regarded with a kind of "bemused tolerance bordering on outright ridicule," as John Maxtone-Graham wrote. All manner of "cures" had been suggested over the decades, from drinking champagne to eating raw celery, staying in bed or exercising, none of which did much to alleviate the passengers' ailments.[78] By the 1950s, though, the synthetic antihistamine drug Dramamine provided most afflicted passengers with much-needed miraculous relief in the form of innocuous-looking, little round tablets.[79]

On the *Doria*, a third of the passengers seemed to disappear overnight, confined to their cabins as they prayed for the storm to pass. Speaking only Italian, Alda Raimengia had befriended several people who shared her table at breakfast, but as soon as the weather turned they had fled to their cabins. "Each time the boat would dip into the trough between waves," recalled Barbara Bliss, "my stomach would dip in tandem with it. The bartender, who was on duty even at ten in the morning, kept making me a mysterious concoction containing bitters. 'This fix you right up. Hold nose and drink, bella Signorina,' the bartender said as he pinched his own nose with his pinkie finger straight up in the air. The miracle cure didn't work. I stayed outside as much as possible where the fresh air seemed to help. I had persistent nausea the first three days of the trip."[80]

"I was so sick," Adalgisa Di Fabio recalls, "that I couldn't even get off my berth. The rolling seemed like it would never stop."[81] Young Pat Mastrincola wasn't seasick at all: "It was almost like being on a roller coaster," he says. "I wasn't scared at all, but one thing really bothered me. They kept the dining rooms open, and people would go in and eat, get sick, and then go back and eat more. The smell of vomit was disgusting."[82]

By Tuesday, July 24, the *Doria* had again entered calm seas and passengers who had abandoned the dining rooms gradually returned. Wednesday was to be the last full day at sea: *Andrea Doria* was due to arrive in New York City early on Thursday morning. Traditionally, the last night out saw the ship alive with entertainments, but given the schedule—and the fact that passengers would have to spend most of Wednesday evening packing—Captain Calamai switched his traditional farewell ball to Tuesday evening.[83]

Robert Young and his wife put in an appearance, as did Philip and Arline Trachtenberg.[84] The usually shy and retiring Calamai presided over this unavoidable maritime duty, and even seemed to enjoy himself as he exchanged a toast with the Trachtenbergs—"he was lighthearted and full of fun," Philip remembered.[85] He also visited passengers in Cabin and Tourist Class: Alda and Franco Raimengia were among those who proudly posed with the captain for souvenir photographs to commemorate the voyage.[86]

Soon the voyage would end. The bad weather was behind the *Doria,* and in less than forty hours tugboats would ease her into the Italian Line's berth at Pier 84. Still, a few of her passengers were uneasy. There was that odd feeling of impending catastrophe that Betsy Drake couldn't escape, and Arline Trachtenberg's sudden sense of fear that had led her to ask Philip to change their reservations when the ship anchored off Gibraltar. Other passengers harbored more concrete fears. Walter Lord's *A Night to Remember,* chronicling the sinking of *Titanic* in 1912, had just been published and was already one of the bestselling books of the year. It was one of two books that Mike Stoller had bought in Rome to read aboard ship (the other was a biography of Benvenuto Cellini).[87] It was perhaps a curious choice for an ocean voyage, but people on the *Doria* comforted themselves against such worries. Radar technology had improved to protect ships; the *Doria* was on a southern route during the summer, nowhere near the spring icebergs that had led to the disaster; and she was regarded as one of the safest ships afloat, boasting the latest equipment to ward off any unforeseen difficulties. Even the most nervous of passengers consoled themselves by dismissing their fears as unwarranted: soon they would be safely in New York.

Chapter Six

⋯

By Wednesday, July 25, *Andrea Doria* was twenty-four hours outside of New York City. Passengers awoke that morning to find the printed program for the final day at sea. They could join an exercise class, listen to the daily musical radio broadcast, or participate in deck games or skeet shooting. There would be a concert for Cabin Class passengers at three thirty, and two films were on offer: *La Fortuna di Essere Donna,* an Italian-language comedy starring Sophia Loren, Charles Boyer, and a young Marcello Mastroianni, and *Foxfire,* a western with Jane Russell and Jeff Chandler. Bingo and the usual horse-race game would follow dinner, and First and Cabin Classes would have dances and a cold buffet before passengers retired for the night.[1]

The *Doria*'s schedule called for her to arrive early the next morning. After the storm of the past few days, passengers welcomed the clear skies and sunny weather that Wednesday morning. But by early afternoon, as the *Doria* approached the East Coast of the United States, she began to encounter fog, intermittent wisps at first and then thick banks that only rarely dissipated. It was not an unexpected occurrence: when the cooler air of the Labrador Current met the warmer temperatures sweeping up from the southern Gulf Stream, mariners often had to contend with dense fogs that posed a danger to navigation. Fog not only diminished visibility but it also distorted sounds. Accidents off the Nantucket coast were not infrequent, especially as these waters were the most heavily traveled sea lanes on the North Atlantic, crossed by dozens of vessels sailing to and from New York.

As the afternoon lengthened, fog enveloped the *Andrea Doria* like a shroud. At two, when Thure Peterson first noticed it, the fog was still wispy; by half past four, when he looked out the porthole of his cabin, he could barely make out the ocean beyond. "This could delay us," he commented to his wife.[2] As the fog thickened, the *Doria's* whistle was turned on, sounding mournfully every one hundred seconds into the murky veil wrapping the ship.[3]

"The air was chilly and wet on our faces," recalled Barbara Bliss. "It was barely possible to see the person standing two feet away." Her stepfather, Robert Boggs, used his former rank as vice admiral in the US Navy to finagle a tour of the bridge that afternoon, and Barbara joined him. "During the twenty minutes we were up there on the bridge," Barbara later wrote, "Robert conversed politely with the captain and crew, who were focused on the radar since visual bearings were well-nigh impossible. As soon as we made our way back down the bolted metal-rung ladder to the passenger deck, Robert said, 'In this kind of fog, this damn ship is going much too fast. The captain's trying to make time and stay on schedule. We're going to hit another ship!'"[4]

"The fog," recalled Robert Young, "was vertically stratified, meaning that our course alternated between areas of dense fog and patches of clear air, so that we were playing an in again, out again, game."[5] Walking around the deck, Linda Morgan was stunned at how thick the fog bank was—"I feel like I'm in an envelope," she said to her sister, Joan. She couldn't see the other side of the ship.[6] Richardson and Ann Dilworth were also surprised—"it was impossible to see beyond the rails," he recalled. The mayor flagged down an officer and asked why they were traveling at full speed through such a fog, but the man assured him that there was nothing to worry about.[7]

With the *Andrea Doria* expected to arrive in New York City at eight the following morning, passengers spent Wednesday afternoon packing up most of their belongings. A bulletin earlier that day had advised: "Passengers are requested to have their baggage ready today at 3:30. At that time the cabin personnel will begin the transportation of the baggage from the cabins to the promenade deck to facilitate disembarkation. Tomorrow passengers will find their baggage on the pier under the initial of their names."[8] Throughout the day, stewards collected luggage and piled it along the starboard side of the Promenade Deck, where it could more easily be loaded onto conveyor belts as soon as the ship docked.[9] Passengers flocked to the Purser's Office, to retrieve valuables stored in the ship's safe; all across the ship, clothing was folded, suitcases loaded, and possessions packed away in anticipation of arrival.

As fog shrouded the westbound *Doria*, her passengers—packed and ready for landing the next morning—settled in to their last night at sea. Barbara Boggs visited the salon and had her hair done, but increasingly her mind was on her son, Bobby. He'd been complaining of a sore throat, and by the time the doctor arrived to look at him, he had a temperature of 103. There was nothing to be done except wait until they landed; before leaving for dinner, Barbara started to read a bedtime story to him, but Bobby quickly succumbed to sleep before she could finish.[10]

The last night of a voyage, at the best of times, was always a bit wistful, filled with nostalgia and a sense of anticlimax. On the *Andrea Doria*, though, many passengers felt something else, a sort of indefinable unease due to the fog and the constant sound of the ship's foghorn. As they strolled the deck on their way to dinner, Fathers Dolciamore and Wojcik found themselves discussing the fate of *Titanic*.[11] Others, though, felt oddly reassured. "The fog," recalled Father Oppitz, "became one of the topics of conversation, especially among those of us who had never experienced fog at sea. It was discussed not with any fear or apprehension, but rather with a sense of gratitude that we were on the *Andrea Doria*, a ship equipped with the very latest technology and a captain with many years of experience."[12]

Dusk came as passengers enjoyed the last dinner of the voyage. Linda Morgan had looked forward to the evening: her family had been invited to dine with Captain Calamai, and she hoped to get his signature in her autograph book. But when they entered the dining room, the maître d' pulled them aside. "I'm sorry," he told her stepfather, Camille Cianfarra, "the Captain will not be able to join you for dinner this evening.

He must remain on the bridge. Because of the fog."[13] "We were disappointed and even surprised that he didn't send a subordinate," Linda recalled.[14] The fog again became a subject of conversation. "Wouldn't it be fantastic," Cianfarra said to his family, "if the *Andrea Doria* crashed in the fog? Think of the exclusive we'd have for *The Times!*"[15] Thinking this might upset Linda and Joan, Jane turned to her daughters and assured them, "Don't worry, the Captain is doing his duty."[16] Near the end of the meal, Betsy Drake stopped by the table to say farewell: Jane, she warned, should get her jewels out of the purser's safe that night, to avoid the inevitable rush the following morning.[17]

Richardson Dilworth had arranged a small dinner party for his wife—it was Ann's fifty-fourth birthday.[18] A few tables away, Thure and Martha Peterson were also celebrating: he ordered a half bottle of champagne to mark the last night of their first ocean voyage.[19] The farewell dinner that followed was excellent: melon cocktail in marsala wine; appetizers of Parma ham, pâté of foie gras, stuffed olives, mushrooms in oil, and Waldorf salad; hot and cold beef broth and vichyssoise; Maine salmon in aspic and fillet of sole; roast beef with tomatoes, french fries, and bacon; roast capon; asparagus in hollandaise sauce; a cold buffet of roast lamb in mint sauce, chicken-and-celery salad, shrimp in mayonnaise, roast veal, and venison; and mint sherbet, fresh fruit, pastries, and a special farewell cake.[20]

After dinner passengers dispersed to enjoy their last hours at sea. Philip and Arline Trachtenberg passed the evening "bidding farewell to friends we had made on the Atlantic crossing." Everywhere he looked, Trachtenberg saw people "singing or dancing or joking or playing cards," and young lovers "smooching and holding hands and pledging undying devotion."[21] Many First Class passengers migrated to the lounge, where chairs had been lined up along the race course that the mechanical wooden horses would "run." The Giffords settled in to watch the game as well as the bingo match that would follow; Dun, looking smart in his gray flannel trousers, tweed jacket, and red tie, managed to maneuver himself into a chair between Barbara Bliss and Nancy Coleman. A waiter appeared, delivering Coca-Colas to the younger Giffords and crème de menthes for Dun and his parents.[22]

Camille Cianfarra proved to be lucky with both the horse race and at bingo: he won $95 at one of the latter games.[23] Young Bambi Gifford also won a bingo game—"she's always lucky," her brother Chad complained. The games came to an end at half past ten. Dun decided to stay up and asked Barbara and Nancy to join him, but his parents, Clarence and Priscilla, decided to take one last late-night stroll on deck before retiring. "You could hardly see across the deck," Clarence recalled, "so we only stayed out a few minutes. Priscilla didn't want her hair coming uncurled the night before landing." By the time Clarence and Priscilla had returned to the lounge, they found that Chad, Jock, and Bambi had raided the unattended tables for swizzle sticks, which came in different colors and had ANDREA DORIA printed along their sides. Collecting their younger children, the couple gradually made their way down to the cabins and the family, minus Dun, began preparing for bed. In their cabin, Chad and Jock counted up the precious swizzle sticks and started to undress.[24]

A few others briefly ventured out onto the decks. Lights shone like ghostly halos in the damp air, and the incessant foghorn only added to the eerie scene. Peering over the side, Andrew Stevens found he could no longer see the water below.[25] Madge Young joined her parents as they made a quick turn around the ship in the thick fog. "If they don't slow this thing down in a fog like this," Robert Young commented, in an echo of Robert Boggs's earlier remark, "something is going to happen."[26]

"Let's go to bed," Cianfarra told his family at half past ten.[27] Linda and Joan went to their cabin, No. 52; by the time Cianfarra and Jane looked in from Cabin No. 54 next door, Linda had already changed into yellow silk pajamas embroidered with Chinese characters. "No talking!" the parents warned the girls. "We have to get up early so you must get a good night's sleep."[28] The two girls had filled their beds with comfortable banks of extra pillows, which they had purchased in Spain.[29] For a moment, Linda glanced through her autograph book, then set it down on the nightstand between the beds and turned out the light.[30]

Thure Peterson was tired. At half past ten, he said to Martha, "Let's turn in." When they entered their Upper Deck cabin, No. 56, they found that the maid had already turned down their beds; she had placed his robe on Martha's inner bed, and Martha's white nightgown on his outer bed. "Do you want to switch beds for the final night?" Thure asked Martha. "No," she said, "you keep that one. I'll stay where I am." They undressed, and Martha changed while Thure, who slept in the nude, crawled beneath the covers of his bed. Martha picked up a book she had purchased in Denmark, but Thure turned off his light. After a few minutes, he heard Martha say quietly, "I can't keep my eyes open." By eleven she had also turned off her light.[31]

Peter Thieriot wanted to stay up, but his father reminded him that they all had to be up early the next morning. On reaching the Foyer Deck, Peter turned and started off down the corridor to his own cabin, away from Suite No. 180 occupied by his parents. "You go right to bed," his mother called. "We're going to have to get up at six."[32]

Other passengers also retreated to their cabins in anticipation of an early morning. Betsy Drake decided to read and went to her cabin on the Boat Deck. Richardson and Ann Dilworth turned in just after ten.[33] When they got to their cabin, No. 80 on the Upper Deck, he undressed and put his suit on a hanger; the mayor was about to hang it up when he thought, "There's no sense in packing them away in the wardrobe if we're going to get back into them so early tomorrow," and he left it at the foot of his bed.[34]

Wanting to dance, Dun Gifford, Barbara Bliss, and Nancy Coleman migrated to the ballroom, only to see the musicians pick up their instruments and move to the Belvedere Lounge above.[35] The trio lingered in the nearly empty room, with Dun sitting on a sofa between the two young ladies; with his parents absent, he started ordering stingers.[36] "One of the girls, I forget which, expressed a little anxiety," he recalled, "so I explained how radar works." He then pulled out a new leather-bound address book, embossed with ANDREA DORIA on the cover, which he had won the previous night at a dance contest, and asked the two young ladies to enter their addresses so that he could keep in touch.[37] Barbara noticed the piano and suggested that Nancy play while she sang.[38]

After his quick turn on deck, Andrew Stevens found his father in the First Class Reading and Writing Room on the Boat Deck, with its Cubist-style tapestry woven in Genoa after a design by Michael Rachlis and wooden ceiling adorned with geometric inserts.[39] Reverends Richard Wojcik and John Dolciamore had been ready to retire to their cabin when Father Paul Lambert, with whom they had frequently played Scrabble to pass the days aboard the ship, waved them down. "How about a farewell game tonight?" he quizzed. Wojcik was tired: "We plan on getting up pretty early tomorrow," he explained. "Maybe we should forget it for tonight." But Lambert, who was unnerved by the fog, pressed, and finally the two priests agreed to join him for a quick game in the First Class Card Room.[40] Here they found Barbara and Robert Boggs sipping cocktails and playing bridge.[41]

One deck below, a band played in the Cabin Class Ballroom, where a decorative painted mural by Felicita Frai alternated with panels of yellow parchment accented with gray.[42] Mike Stoller had hoped to go to bed early—"I wanted to go to sleep so I could get up early and take movies of the Statue of Liberty and try to imagine what my grandparents had experienced when they arrived in New York some sixty years before," he recalls. Meryl, though, had promised several young Italian ladies that she would join them in the ballroom, and so Mike reluctantly followed, watching as some shy Italian boys asked the ladies to dance. Bored, Mike ordered a glass of champagne and went off to see if there was a poker game in the adjacent Card Room.[43]

Cecilia Pick had been "terribly depressed" all afternoon—"I somehow felt that something awful was going to happen," she recalled.[44] Her spirits were buoyed after dinner, when she won nine dollars at bingo. Offering to buy her husband a drink with the proceeds, Cecilia led John to the Cabin Class Lounge—he had a beer, and she had a Strega. Finally she decided to return to their cabin. John lingered in the Lounge, saying, "I will be down in eight or ten minutes." Back in their stateroom, Cecilia started to get ready for bed. "I took off my jewelry and took off my watch," she wrote to her sister, "put my specs on to see the time, and then noticed that my brush and comb needed a wash, so

I went to the basin and started rinsing them out—I had already taken my belt off and unzipped my frock."[45]

First and Cabin Class passengers had bands to entertain them in their respective ballrooms; in the Tourist Class Lounge, it was left to a handful of amateur musicians to provide the entertainment as couples took to the floor to dance. By half past ten most of the families began returning to their cabins. The Sergios had enjoyed the dancing, and Paul's four nieces and nephews had especially relished the ice cream available in the adjoining Social Hall.[46] As Paul escorted Maria and her children to their cabins, Margaret Domenica and Rocco both tried to climb into his arms, begging to sleep in his cabin that night.[47] But Paul tucked them into their own berths, saying, "No, you've got to get your sleep tonight, you can't stay up late. We're going to dock in only a few hours. We'll see you in the morning."[48]

Adalgisa Di Fabio had given into temptation that night, and donned the special dress she had meant to save for the landing in New York when she went dancing in the Tourist Class Lounge. "Everyone seemed happy and excited for the next day," she recalls. Finally, just before eleven, her friend Nella Massa said, "We'd better go back to our cabins, since we're supposed to arrive at eight A.M." Ada reluctantly abandoned the lounge. Back in her cabin, "I took off my dress and folded it to wear the next morning and changed into a nightgown. I also put my passport and papers into my purse so that everything was prepared for the next day. Everything was very quiet. No one seemed to be in the hallways, and the people in my cabin were asleep."[49]

Maria Coscia decided to turn in early. She was just climbing into bed when one of the young women sharing her cabin started for the door. "Where are you going?" she asked.

"I'm going dancing!" the woman replied before exiting. Maria never saw her again.[50]

Excited and nervous about meeting her husband's family for the first time the following day, Alda Raimengia also decided to turn in early. Franco, though, wanted to collect a copy of their photograph with Captain Calamai and went off to obtain it. "Put the bolt on the door," he told Alda as he left their cabin, "and I'll knock when I come back down."[51] Santino Porporino had walked his wife and two young children to their cabin before retiring for the night. He was sitting on his berth looking through some photographs of his family when he felt a sudden stab of irrational worry, "as if something was going to happen." Pushing the thought aside, he climbed into bed but tossed and turned, haunted by images of his wife and children and a vague sense that he might not see them again.[52]

In one corner of the Tourist Class Lounge, Domenico Ansuini watched his beautiful daughter, Melania—"my parents were very old-fashioned," she recalls, "and so my dad went with me to the dances to keep an eye on things so that I would be okay."[53] Giovanni Vali, twenty-seven, had been visiting relatives in Sezze Romano, near Rome, and was returning to his home in Canada aboard the *Doria* when he first spotted Melania. "I guess I really loved her when I saw her for the first time," he recalled. That night, he asked her to dance and was delighted when she agreed; one dance turned into a second and then a third as the evening wore on.[54]

As Melania and Giovanni danced, her brother Fillipo went off to the Tourist Class Dining Room. A temporary screen had been erected and chairs arranged so that passengers could enjoy the 1955 movie *Foxfire*, in which a newlywed Amanda Lawrence (played by Jane Russell) joined her mining engineer husband, Jonathan Dartland (played by Jeff Chandler), looking for gold in an Arizona ghost town. Nicola DiFiore had wanted to go to bed but the prospect of meeting his new grand-daughter the next day left him too excited to sleep, and so he, too, took up a chair to watch the movie.[55] Rosa Mastrincola had put Arlene to bed in their cabin on A Deck before taking Pat to see the film. The nine-year-old had hoped for a western or a war movie, but *Foxfire* "was just some awful film that didn't hold my interest at all." A few minutes after eleven, he got up from his chair to pursue his favorite activity, exploring the ship.[56]

The last evening on the ship was winding down, but some First Class passengers lingered in the Belvedere Lounge, stylishly paneled in blond wood; ordinarily passengers could look out over the bow, but fog now concealed the view. Having said good night to her three-year-old son in the cabin he shared with his nurse, Grace Els, two decks below, Ruth Roman entered the room, wearing a tight sheath dress and high-heeled shoes, and sat at a table with fellow actress Janet Stewart, sipping a drink.[57] They listened as the band launched into the popular song "Arrivederci, Roma." It was 11:10 P.M.

Chapter Seven

At three on the afternoon of July 25, as the fog enveloping *Andrea Doria* thickened, Captain Calamai had ordered the usual precautions taken. A watch officer had been posted at one of the ship's two radar screens. The ship's fog whistle had been turned on, sounding mournfully every one hundred seconds into the murky veil wrapping the ship; the liner's twelve hydraulic watertight doors below A Deck had been closed, sealing her off into eleven watertight compartments. An additional lookout had been stationed on the bow and, finally, Calamai had reduced *Doria*'s speed from 23 to 21.8 knots.[1]

The Convention on the International Regulations for Preventing Collisions at Sea (SOLAS) dictated that "every vessel shall, in fog, mist, falling snow, heavy rainstorms, or any other conditions similarly restricting visibility go at a moderate speed, having careful regard to the existing circumstances and conditions."[2] Ostensibly this regulation dictated that a ship's speed should not exceed its ability to stop within half the distance of visibility. With visibility aboard the *Doria* almost nonexistent, this would, in practical terms, have brought her to a near standstill.[3] The slight reduction in speed ordered by Calamai ignored the regulation, but in this he was scarcely alone. Captains of passenger ships were under immense pressure to meet deadlines for arrival. In New York, 250 longshoremen would be waiting for the *Doria* at eight the following morning, and their pay of $2.50 an hour began when they arrived at the pier, whether the liner was there or not: a delay of several hours meant extra charges for the Italian Line and disruption of passenger schedules.[4] And then the ship had to be unloaded, cleaned, restocked with provisions from waiting trucks and vans, and refueled—all necessities scheduled well in advance. Late arrival would mean overtime pay for hundreds. Given these pressures, it is not surprising that a captain who slowed his liner to a crawl in a fog was the rare exception and not the rule. Calamai had made it a practice to do so only as his ship was entering heavily traveled waters like the approach to New York Harbor.[5] He also believed—like most captains of the day—that the ship's radar system offered all the advance warning needed to avert catastrophe.

As Calamai was ordering these precautions, another liner was just passing Fire Island, on its way to Europe. At half past eleven that Wednesday morning, the Swedish American Line's MV *Stockholm* had left New York City's Pier 97, bound for Gothenburg. All gleaming white except for her light yellow funnel, the 524-foot-long *Stockholm*, built in 1948, was the smallest liner running a regular North Atlantic route; she could carry just 548 passengers. She lacked the splendid public rooms and accommodations of the *Andrea Doria*, and could not compete with her elegant lines, but *Stockholm* did possess one formidable asset: her sharply raked bow, reinforced with two layers of inch-thick steel, meant that she could easily follow icebreakers required to keep the Swedish ports open in the frigid winters.[6]

This particular voyage was almost booked to capacity: 534 passengers and 208 members of the crew were under the care of sixty-three-year-old Captain Harry Gunnar Nordenson.[7] He had been born in Massachusetts to Swedish emigrants who returned to their native land when Nordenson was five. He had gone to sea at eighteen, studied at the Swedish Navigational College, and received his master's license in 1918 before joining the Swedish American Line two years later. He had a reputation as a stern disciplinarian who allowed no smoking on the bridge, did not mix with his officers, and kept conversation to a terse minimum.[8]

It was hot and humid when *Stockholm* left New York; as she sailed out into Long Island Sound, a fine haze hung against the eastern horizon.[9]

Nordenson took his usual course, heading east toward Nantucket at roughly 18 knots. But his usual course, meant to shave several hours off the voyage and save fuel, also set him some twenty miles north of the recommended route for eastbound (or outbound) ships and placed *Stockholm* in the path of incoming westward traffic in the congested area off Nantucket.[10] Mariners were not bound to this recommendation, but the Swedish American Line *had* signed the 1953 North Atlantic Track Agreement, which stipulated the southern route; by sailing in a northern lane Nordenson was violating this convention.[11]

Captain Calamai's attention was riveted on the bridge that Wednesday evening. He had gone back to his cabin at four that afternoon to do some paperwork and changed from his white summer uniform into his evening blue uniform before returning to the bridge.[12] At six he ordered the liner's backup radar, a Raytheon radar screen, switched on and manned.[13] At half past seven he ordered his dinner brought to the bridge: some soup, a small cutlet, and an apple.[14] The sun set at a little past eight: by this time the fog was so thick that visibility was a mere mile and a half; at times, even this diminished, and it was barely possible to see the bow from the bridge.[15]

At eight the watch was changed, with First Officer Luigi Oneto and Junior Second Officer Guido Badano relieved of duty. In their place came Second Senior Officer Curzio Franchini and Junior Third Officer Eugenio Giannini. At thirty-six, Franchini was the more experienced of the pair. Tall and thin, he'd been at sea for eighteen years, serving in the Italian Navy during the war and joining the *Doria*'s crew the previous autumn. Eight years younger, Giannini was short and blond and had graduated from the Italian Naval Academy six months earlier, after serving aboard various ships since 1949. Both Franchini and Giannini held master's licenses.[16] Franchini manned the first radar screen, while Giannini took over the Raytheon radarscope screen.

Calamai refused an offer to be relieved: he planned to remain on the bridge while his vessel cleared the fog. This was a diligence practiced by seasoned mariners in these particular waters, and especially during the summer, as Raoul de Beaudéan, captain of the *Ile de France,* explained: assaulted by conflicting warm southern and cold northern currents, the area was a "boiling kettle . . . from Hatteras to Newfoundland," and produced "an unending and formidable fog, in which ships move without being able to see further than their sides." At such times, whether in fog or even anticipating fog a seasoned captain would remain, as Calamai did now, "on his feet until the danger is completely over. And this can last several days so that it is impossible for him to get a real rest despite his fatigue."[17]

At approximately 9:20 that night, Giannini's radar screen showed a blip some dozen miles distant. Franchini took the information and signals and plotted the respective positions using loran, a long-range navigational system that checked radio signal distances.[18] This determined that the blip belonged to the *Nantucket Lightship,* a vessel permanently anchored in the southern shoals off Nantucket Island to provide signals to approaching maritime traffic.[19] Twenty minutes later, Captain Calamai ordered a slight change of course to port, from 267 degrees to 261 degrees to enable the *Doria* to pass at least a mile south of the stationary vessel.[20] At 10:20, the lookout stationed at the bow reported hearing a foghorn as they passed the *Nantucket Lightship.*[21]

At 10:46 another blip appeared on Franchini's screen, some seventeen miles ahead and some 4 degrees starboard; if maintained, this course would seemingly bring whatever it was roughly a mile north, off the *Doria's* starboard side.[22] "I think it is unusual for a ship to be coming eastbound in these waters," Franchini said. Calamai agreed, and again ordered a change in course as his ship neared Nantucket.[23] Radar gave no indication of the other vessel's size: because ships of significant size weren't supposed to be traveling on this eastward track, Captain Calamai believed that the approaching vessel was probably nothing more than a small fishing trawler returning to Nantucket; as such it would pose no risk.[24]

The International Regulations for Preventing Collisions at Sea stipulated that two ships approaching each other should steer starboard, to enable a port-to-port passage. Calamai decided that to do so—for what he believed to be nothing more than a fishing boat—would imperil both vessels, with the *Doria* deliberately crossing into the oncoming ship's path and thus bringing them closer to each other, whereas if both vessels maintained their current courses they would pass safely. There was another danger to starboard—the shoals of Nantucket, with shallow water and the possibility of grounding. Unfortunately there was no bridge-to-bridge communication at the time, nor any regulation stipulating that either ship make radio contact with the other.[25]

Aboard *Stockholm*, Captain Nordenson ordered a change to take his vessel several miles south of the *Nantucket Lightship*.[26] *Stockholm* was running at 18.5 knots—full speed—on what her crew later claimed was still a clear sea. At ten, Nordenson retired to his cabin, leaving orders with Third Officer Johan-Ernst Carstens-Johannsen that he was to be called if the ship encountered any fog.[27]

Nordenson's departure left twenty-six-year-old Carstens, as he was called, in charge of *Stockholm*. He had come on duty at half past eight that evening to relieve Senior Second Officer Lars Enestrom. Carstens had attended the Swedish Navigational College, received his master's license in 1953, and served aboard several ships before joining the Swedish American Line.[28] He had come to *Stockholm* just two months earlier from the liner *Kungsholm*, and tonight would be his first time taking sole charge of the bridge. Carstens had been up since six that morning, having supervised the loading of baggage and boarding of passengers in New York; perhaps this contributed to the errors he would make that night.[29]

Carstens had three seamen under his command that night: fellow Swedes Sten Johansson and Ingemar Bjorkman, and Danish-born seaman Peder Larsen who, according to the practice of the Swedish American Line, regularly rotated positions throughout their watch between service in the crow's nest, manning the helm, and acting as standby to the officer on watch. In this the Swedish American Line differed from most other companies, which usually kept two officers on the bridge at all times, one in overall charge and one to monitor radar. The lack of a second officer on *Stockholm*'s bridge meant that all responsibilities fell to Carstens: he was expected to maintain the watch, monitor the radar, take regular radio direction readings, plot the ship's course, and ensure that *Stockholm* maintained her track without deviation. These duties necessarily divided his energies and focus; if he had to leave the bridge and check anything in the chart room behind the wheelhouse, temporary care of *Stockholm* was in the hands of these three seamen.[30]

A few minutes after ten, Carstens said that he took *Stockholm*'s position based on radio signals received from Block Island and from the *Nantucket Lightship*. He must have heard the broadcast coming from the *Lightship:* four dashes a minute, followed by two minutes of silence, indicating dense fog ahead. Yet the inexperienced Carstens was apparently unaware of the signal's meaning.[31] At 10:10 P.M. Carstens ordered a slight change of course south, from 089 degrees to 091 degrees, although he later claimed that he had not done this until 10:30 P.M. At 10:40 Larsen took *Stockholm*'s helm. This was his first voyage on *Stockholm*, which he had joined eleven days earlier. Less than twelve hours out of New York, Larsen quickly proved himself a less than reliable helmsman. Not only was he unaccustomed to the position, but he also had the disconcerting habit of letting his mind wander and allowing the ship to drift off course.[32] From this point on, *Stockholm* began veering a few degrees to port and then to starboard.[33] As Carstens later admitted, he "found it difficult to cope" with Larsen's erratic handling of the helm.[34]

Although Carstens had graduated from the Swedish Navigational College and had his master's license, he had received no specialized instructions in the use of *Stockholm*'s radar. He had had to learn the basics himself by reading the manual in his spare time.[35] This placed him at a disadvantage; he later admitted that he had trouble adjusting the brightness level on the screen, which rendered the images as indistinct blurs.[36] Additionally, unlike the *Doria*, *Stockholm* did not have a Gyro repeater attached to its radar screen. Carstens thus had to rely on the error-prone Larsen for correct course headings unless he left the bridge to personally check the coordinates; any mistake by Larsen thus led to an incorrect plotting on *Stockholm*.[37]

There would later be questions about Carstens's recollection of certain times and events on *Stockholm*'s bridge that night. Among them was what time *Stockholm*'s radar first picked up another approaching vessel, which he estimated some twelve miles distant and slightly to port of the Swedish liner. Carstens first maintained that they had spotted the approaching ship at 11:00 P.M., and that it had been some ten miles ahead and 2 degrees to port; later, when shown that the relative speeds of the two ships in question made this distance impossible, Carstens suggested that he had only approximated the time.[38]

Carstens maintained that plotting suggested the other ship was steering away from *Stockholm*'s direct course and that they would pass safely if perilously close. There was a standing order aboard *Stockholm* that she should not get within a mile of another ship at sea, yet Carstens now estimated the vessels would likely meet somewhere between a half mile to a mile of each other. Carstens ignored Nordenson's instructions that he was to be called if they came within a mile of another vessel, perhaps fearing the notoriously stern captain, or perhaps because he was simply reluctant to admit any shortcoming in his own navigational abilities.

When radar indicated that the ships were fewer than five miles apart, Carstens took his binoculars out onto the bridge wing and scanned the horizon but saw nothing. This should have been a warning: something must be obscuring his view of the approaching vessel. However, Carstens had not navigated alone in fog. Apparently he never considered the possibility that an unseen bank of fog might be cloaking the other ship's lights. Although failure to see the lights suggested caution, Carstens did not reduce *Stockholm*'s speed nor did he deem the situation serious enough to summon Nordenson to the bridge as he had been instructed to do.[39] At 11:07 P.M., Carstens later testified, a lookout on *Stockholm* saw the red light of another ship. Carstens decided that a 20-degree starboard turn would increase the passing distance, and ordered the helmsman to change course. He did not mark this change in course with the required blast from *Stockholm*'s whistle.

On the bridge of the *Andrea Doria*, Calamai continued to watch the other vessel's approach. There was still no reason to worry. Franchini switched the radar from a range of twenty to eight miles, to show a more accurate view of the situation, and after reviewing the screen, reported that the other ship was about seven miles ahead and would likely pass the *Doria* about a mile off her starboard side.[40] Giulio Visciano was at the *Doria*'s helm as the minutes ticked by. At 11:05, to increase the distance between the two vessels, Calamai ordered the *Doria* turned 4 degrees to port and thus away from the oncoming ship.[41]

The minutes ticked by. Calamai stood on the bridge wing, scanning the fog-bound ocean through his binoculars, but he could not see any approaching lights.[42] It was Giannini who first spotted a faint glow through his binoculars, just off the starboard side. He ran to Calamai, but the captain had also just spotted the lights. At the same time, the bridge phone rang: it was Salvatore Colace on the bow, reporting that he had seen approaching lights to starboard. Franchini, who answered the call, said, "We are seeing lights, too."[43]

The ghostly lights, haloed by fog, continued to loom ever closer out of the darkness. Giannini couldn't understand why the other vessel wasn't sounding its foghorn—"Why don't we hear her?" he said. "Why doesn't she whistle?"[44] Everything was quiet; the officers could feel the low rumble of the *Doria*'s engines as she swung to port. Giannini watched the lights through his binoculars. Every ship carries a green light on the starboard side, a red light on the port side, a white light on the foremast, and another white light higher on a mast behind the wheelhouse. By observing the position of these lights, mariners can follow any turns made by an approaching vessel. At first, the *Doria*'s officers saw that the lower mast light of the other ship was to the right of the upper light; then, suddenly, the lights began to switch positions, indicating that the other vessel was turning. Now, through the fog, they could see the faint red glow of the other ship's port light. She had not only turned but had turned directly into the *Doria*'s path. "All of a sudden," Calamai later explained, "we saw that the ship was swinging to her starboard, heading toward us. Because the other ship was definitely turning to starboard, any turn by us to that side would have been unavailing and more dangerous."[45] It was 11:10, and just a mile separated the two vessels.

"She is coming right at us!" Giannini shouted. Calamai quickly ordered the helm put hard to port, hoping he could turn his vessel out of the path of the oncoming ship.[46]

"What about the engines?" Franchini cried out. But Calamai decided his best option was to try to outrun the other ship, and he answered,

"No, let them be! We need all the speed we've got now!"[47] Calamai sounded the *Doria*'s siren twice.[48] The seconds ticked by as the nearly seven-hundred-foot-long *Andrea Doria* began a hard swing to port in a desperate attempt to avoid a collision. But it took time for the *Doria* to turn, and she continued her forward motion even as her bow started to swing left. No one aboard the Italian liner could do anything but watch in disbelief as the other vessel plowed on straight toward her.

At 11:11, at a speed of 18.5 knots, *Stockholm* slashed into the *Andrea Doria*'s starboard side. The Italian liner shook and shuddered at the impact as a deafening screech of twisting metal filled the night. *Stockholm*'s tapered, reinforced bow sliced into the *Doria* just aft of the bridge, penetrating some forty feet into the ship and demolishing all in its path. A horrible cacophony of death and destruction shattered the stunned silence: shards of broken glass tumbled through the air, ceilings collapsed, bulkheads were crushed, timber shattered, and metal tore away in jagged shears. Screams from within the hull pierced the night as the liner continued forward. Showers of angry sparks burst like fireworks against the darkness; the insulation between hull and interior caught fire and thick clouds of noxious, white smoke began wafting through the ship.[49] These developments triggered the ship's internal sprinkler system, with water raining down from ceilings and seawater entering from below.

Still moving ahead and to port at near full speed, the Italian liner briefly dragged the Swedish ship forward as *Stockholm*'s bow remained lodged in the *Doria*'s hull. Perhaps thirty seconds passed, during which *Stockholm* began an astern maneuver. As the *Doria* continued to shake and shudder, *Stockholm* ripped away from her, tearing out at an angle and leaving an arc of death and destruction in her wake. She scraped back along the *Doria*'s starboard hull, grinding and crashing against plating, beams and portholes, her path marked by showers of sparks cascading into the night.[50] It was all over in less than two minutes.

Standing on the starboard bridge wing, a stunned Captain Calamai watched as *Stockholm* slid away from his ship and floated off like some avenging phantom that had appeared suddenly, brought chaos, and now receded into the swirling fog. Captain Calamai could feel the *Doria* shift beneath his feet, as an inrush of water sent her into an immediate starboard list. Looking down from the bridge wing, he could see the terrible gash in his liner's side: a dark abyss illuminated here and there by the amber glow of flames, an open wound now spilling luggage, furniture, ruined walls, broken ceilings, and torn beams into the churning sea below.[51]

Chapter Eight

◆••◆

Death came to the *Doria*. First Class passenger Walter Carlin was standing in the bathroom at the end of the corridor of Upper Deck Cabin No. 46, brushing his teeth, when the sudden jolt knocked him to the floor. There was a flash of heat and smoke as he quickly scrambled to his feet and ran back to help his wife, Jeanette, who had been in bed reading. As he reached the cabin, though, he stopped short: an immense hole gaped in the starboard wall and the floor where Jeanette's bed had been a few seconds earlier was now gone. Looking out into the dark, Carlin could barely discern a receding mass of white steel as *Stockholm*'s bow pulled away.[1]

Carlin's was not the only Upper Deck cabin demolished: at least seven others were also smashed by *Stockholm*'s bow. The entire starboard stretch aft from Cabin No. 42 to No. 58 was impacted. Thure Peterson was just drifting off to sleep when a deafening crash of ripping steel, shattered wood, and exploding glass filled Cabin No. 56. From his bed against the starboard wall, he saw something he couldn't process. There was a glint of white, massive and moving, that in an instant had torn into the cabin, destroying everything in its path: only later did he realize that it was *Stockholm*'s bow. He felt himself moving suddenly through the air before blacking out.[2]

Cabin No. 52 was crushed: young Joan Cianfarra was killed in her bed, while her half sister, Linda Morgan, disappeared through the gaping hole where the outer wall had once been. *Stockholm*'s bow had continued its tearing motion, ripping into No. 54, occupied by Camille and Jane Cianfarra, twisting through the Petersons' cabin, No. 56, and pushing the wreckage of both cabins into No. 58, shared by Reverends Dolciamore and Wojcik. The collision hurled both Camille and Jane into the ruins of Cabin No. 56. Jane landed atop Martha Peterson, still in her bed, while Cian was thrown in a pile of twisted steel and broken wood into the corridor leading to the main passage.[3] Badly injured, Jane briefly came to only to hear Cian moaning in the dark, "It's better to be dead than to live like this."[4]

Directly below this, the same area on the Foyer Deck was crushed. The *Stockholm*'s bow plunged into Deluxe Suite 178–180, tearing away walls, ceilings, floors, fittings, and passengers in a great, grinding symphony of horror. In No. 180 Ferdinand and Frances Thieriot were killed in the devastation. On A Deck, the collision tore into First Class Cabin Nos. 202–238, and the destruction continued down through B and C Decks. Thousands of gallons of seawater cascaded into compartments and down corridors, trapping many. Collapsed bulkheads, ceilings, and jammed doorways prevented escape.[5]

For others, the collision came in less deadly form. Dun Gifford, sitting on a sofa between Barbara Bliss and Nancy Coleman and facing the tall starboard windows of the First Class Ballroom and the Winter Garden beyond, saw a blur of light. "I had a sense of something," he said, "I don't know what, outside those windows across from us."[6] Immediately he thought of a lighthouse, but then muttered, "A lighthouse in the middle of the ocean?"[7] Then came the sound—"tearing, grinding, snapping metal." He held tightly to each of the girls' hands as the lights flickered off and then on and the floor tilted away to starboard at a precarious angle.[8]

"The jolt was followed by a loud crunching, grinding, scraping noise that must have lasted for at least twenty seconds," Barbara Bliss recalled.[9]

"Bottles were thrown around," Dun remembered, and he and the girls tumbled over a glass-topped coffee table; when the lights flickered back on, he saw that they had all been cut and were bleeding.[10]

"Oh my God!" Barbara shouted. "We've run aground!"

"To hell we have!" Dun answered. "We've hit another ship! Get up, you two. I know where our life stations are, and I'll drop each of you with your parents before I find my own."[11]

"All of a sudden there was an explosion, like a firecracker," recalled Ruth Roman. "I knew something had happened, but I didn't know what."[12] She later described the "crashing, crushing impact" of the collision, followed by "shouts in the night" as *Andrea Doria* lurched to starboard. She immediately thought of her young son, Dickie, who was in Upper Deck Cabin No. 82 with his nanny, Grace Els, and ran out of the Belvedere Lounge, kicking off her shoes as she went—"on a listing ship high heels are absolutely no help," she said. "A sailor grabbed at me, fearing perhaps that I had panicked."[13] "I have to get my son!" she shouted and pushed him away.[14] Roman's tight sheath evening dress hampered her movements; she paused only for a moment, ripping it up the back so that she could run before continuing to her son.[15]

Andrew Stevens felt rather than heard the collision as he was bidding his father good night in the First Class Reading and Writing Room. The shaking threw his father, Archie, out of his chair while Andrew fell to the floor.[16] Almost immediately, smoke began pouring through the vents.[17] Just aft of the Belvedere Lounge, Barbara and Robert Boggs were playing bridge in the First Class Card Room when the collision came. "We were thrown from our seats," she recalled.[18] Sitting nearby, Father John Dolciamore was playing Scrabble with fellow priests Richard Wojcik and Paul Lambert. Dolciamore remembered "a crunch, a sort of grinding noise" that marked the collision.[19] He could hear shouts coming from the Belvedere Lounge.[20] To Wojcik, "it was as if someone was kicking the back of your chair." As the ship began to list to starboard, a siren rang out.[21] "Don't get excited," a steward told the men, "everything is all right."[22]

Most of *Andrea Doria*'s First Class passengers were in their cabins when the collision came. Philip Trachtenberg recalled "a mighty roar, as though a boiler had exploded, followed by the ripping, grinding eruption of steel girders and bulkheads. Splinters of shattered glass slashed through the air. Great billows of heavy, black smoke poured from gaping gashes in the wall of the stateroom; lights flickered and grew dim." Then, after a few seconds, there was another "thundering rumble" from within the hull, accompanied by "the sudden, sickening odor of burning paint. For an eternity of six seconds there was no sound at all. Nothing moved. Then, as I staggered to my feet, the *Doria* dipped crazily over on her starboard side. I knew then that disaster had struck."[23]

"My mother and brother were asleep," recalls Madge Young. She was standing at the bathroom sink, wearing knee-length blue seersucker pajamas, when she heard "a terrible loud crash, and then a bang. It knocked me sideways, and I fell into the bathtub." When she managed to stumble back into the family's cabin, she saw her father shaking her brother, David, awake: somehow he had slept through the collision. Her mother, attired in a sheer nylon nightgown, reached for a coat while her father grabbed four life jackets from the cabinet and quickly tied them on his family. "We have to go!" he urged.[24] Madge was confused: "I thought, What a big do Daddy is making out of this whole thing," she recalls. "But I thought it would be fun to wear the life jackets with pajamas."[25] As he opened the cabin door, Madge saw "a lot of thick white smoke in the hallway," but even this failed to scare her: "To me it was just a bit of excitement; I didn't have any sense of danger, though obviously my father knew that something serious had happened."[26]

Having left Dun in the First Class Ballroom, the rest of the Gifford family had gone to their staterooms: Clarence, Priscilla, and Bambi in No. 98 and Jock and Chad in No. 96, which they shared with Dun. Suffering from an ulcer, Clarence phoned the steward for a glass of milk; Priscilla had already changed into a nightgown, and Bambi was pulling off her dress when the steward arrived. Clarence had just set it on the dresser and taken off his jacket when the collision came.[27] Bambi recalls "a horrible wrenching noise. I thought it couldn't be another boat, but that we must have hit rocks somewhere."[28] The glass of milk slipped from the top of the dresser to the floor and shattered amid a "terrible grinding and snapping of metal, followed by a terrific screeching of metal and then another huge bump." All three Giffords stumbled.[29]

In the adjacent cabin Jock and Chad had just finished counting their collection of swizzle sticks. Jock stripped down to his underwear and climbed into the top bunk, while Chad was removing his tie when the liner shook. The impact threw Jock to the floor.[30] In a few seconds the boys stumbled from their cabin into the corridor, which was filled with smoke; both thought there must have been an explosion. "We just knew we had to get out of there as fast as we could," Jock remembered. Just then their father flung open his own stateroom door. Clarence saw his fellow passengers in the corridor, looking "stunned and bewildered. There was excited talk but I heard no screams or hysterical outcries." When he saw his sons Clarence ordered them to get their life jackets; the two boys rushed back to their cabin, where Jock quickly pulled on a pair of pants and a shirt before grabbing a life jacket. Chad looked down at the nightstand and thought he should grab his wristwatch. "But when I reached for the watch I was so excited I just picked up three or four swizzle sticks and ran." Back in No. 98, Priscilla quickly pulled Bambi's dress back down over her head and grabbed a cloth coat and a wicker purse. As Clarence ushered them out into the corridor, he looked back and saw the shattered glass on the carpet. "Dammit," he thought, "I've got to remember to sweep that up before we come back or Priscilla will cut her feet."[31]

Richardson Dilworth and his wife, Ann, were asleep in their cabin when they were jolted awake and literally knocked out of their beds. "We must have hit an iceberg," Ann said. "It's like the *Titanic*."[32] Dilworth was confused: "At first we didn't know what happened," he recalled. "We heard people running outside in the hall. There was smoke in the hall, so we knew it must be something pretty serious."[33] "We'd better get upstairs!" Dilworth told his wife. He paused at the foot of his bed, trying to decide which shoes to put on when Ann shouted, "For Christ's sake, we've got to get out of here!"[34] They put on their life jackets and ran out into the corridor, but the ship was listing so badly that they found they were forced to crawl along the passageway toward the staircase.[35]

"I was just getting ready for bed," Betsy Drake recalled, "when all of a sudden there was a big bang. Everything flew across the room."[36]

Her cabin was on the port side, but she felt the ship "lurch to the side with a great noise. People were screaming, and I was standing there with nothing on. I might just as easily have run out that way, but I managed to get dressed."[37] Wearing a fashionable suit, she remembered to grab her jewels—some $250,000 worth of diamonds, pearls, and other gems that Cary Grant had given to her—before leaving the cabin.[38] As she stepped out into the corridor, a crew member spotted her and helped her with her life jacket before Drake made her way to the port deck.[39]

Hearing the crash, Nora Kovach and Istvan Rabovsky immediately jumped out of their beds and ran for their cabin door, only to find it stuck. Istvan finally managed to pull it open, but the corridor beyond was filled with smoke. Grabbing his wife's hand, he led Nora out into a crowd surging toward the staircase.[40]

In the Cabin Class Lounge, Mike Stoller was returning to Meryl when he glanced out the windows and saw an object "like a letter opener" pass by the side of the ship. "There was a loud crunching sound, with metal torn and glass being shattered," he says. As the shuddering ceased and the floor tilted beneath him, a boy ran into the room, shouting that there had been a collision with another ship. "A lot of worried conversations broke out as people stood up," he recalls; he heard more than one mention of an iceberg. "Since I'd been reading *A Night to Remember,* my own thoughts briefly went that way." He knew immediately that he needed to get to their cabin and retrieve life jackets.[41]

Cecilia Pick was standing at the washbasin of her cabin when the collision came. "All of a sudden," she said, "there was a frightful thud. I opened the cabin door and there was a terrible odor of fumes and gas and the sounds of cracking woodwork."[42] The jolt startled priests and cabinmates Raymond Goedert and Thomas Kelly. In the first minute following the impact, as they tried to sort out what had happened, they could hear people running in the corridor; when they looked out, they saw that most of them had their life jackets on. Kelly had not yet undressed and still wore his black clerical outfit, but Goedert hastily pulled on a pair of pants and tied a life jacket over his white T-shirt before leaving the cabin. Once in the corridor, they found themselves swept along in the panicked human wave pushing toward the staircase that would take them to the lifeboats above.[43]

In the Tourist Class Dining Room, the collision came as the movie *Foxfire* was playing out on screen. People stumbled, fell from their chairs, and crashed into one another as the lights flickered out and then came back on. Sitting with his cousin, Nicola DiFiore recalled the collision "like a driver slamming on the brakes of a moving vehicle." He was thrown from his chair as the ship took an immediate list to starboard.[44]

Pat Mastrincola had abandoned the chair alongside his mother after growing bored with the film. "I saw a waiter standing behind the portable screen, so I decided to wander off to bother him." Just as he walked behind the canvas, though, he sensed the ship making a sudden turn. "What the hell are they doing?" he thought. "This isn't normal." The crash came within a few seconds; after "a horrible, jarring noise," the floor lurched and rows of dishes on the shelves behind Pat crashed to the floor "like a noisy avalanche. Everything seemed to tip over. The screen fell over, and it and everything else, me included, began sliding across the floor toward the wall. It was like all hell had broken loose." When he finally stopped, Pat looked back and saw his mother, Rosa, clinging to a dividing trellis to avoid falling. Agile as a monkey, he scampered back across the listing floor to her side. "My baby! My baby!" she was screaming.

"It's okay, Mom," Pat assured her. "I'm here!"

"No, not you!" Rosa answered. "Arlene!" And suddenly Pat remembered that his eight-year-old sister, Arlene, had gone to bed alone in their cabin on A Deck. "It was just instinct that led me to try to go down to the cabin for Arlene," he recalls. Pat crawled toward the main entrance that would take him to the corridors and staircases leading to their cabin but found his way blocked: "In a panic everyone had pushed against the doors, trying to escape. Since I was small, I managed to get down low and push my way through their legs and out into the hallway."[45]

Klaus Dorneich was sitting in the Tourist Class Lounge when "a mighty shudder traveled through the ship, as though its forward motion had been stopped by a great force, followed by a bursting crash. The floor of the hall rolled heavily." People fell, bottles of liquor crashed to the floor, and glass shattered as the ship listed to starboard. Looking out, Dorneich "saw the lights of another ship skim by within arm's reach" through the fog. Within a few moments, everyone started pushing toward the doors, "a shrieking mass . . . wildly seeking a sound footing."[46]

Giovanni Vali was in the middle of his third consecutive dance with Melania Ansuini when the collision occurred. As dancers stumbled, furniture turned over, the ship listed, and the lights flickered, Melania screamed, "Don't leave!"[47] But Giovanni promised to return with her family, and set off for their cabin.[48]

Melania's family was scattered: her father had been in the ballroom, but her brother Fillipo was in the Tourist Class Dining Room to watch *Foxfire* and her mother had taken her ten-year-old brother, Pasquale, who was suffering from a mild case of seasickness, below to their cabin. "I heard and felt the crash," Pasquale, called Pat, remembers. In a panic his mother reached for the door, but it was jammed. Finally she managed to yank it open and, grabbing a single life jacket, pushed Pat, wearing his underwear and a T-shirt, out into the corridor as they fought their way toward the staircase.[49]

Maria Coscia was just drifting off to sleep when the collision shook her awake. She jumped from her bed, terrified and not knowing what had happened. The lights flickered off and then came back on as she dressed: she was in such a hurry that she put her padded brassiere, stuffed with jewelry, on backward before grabbing her purse, and fleeing out into the corridor.[50]

Alda Raimengia was sitting up in her berth, awaiting her husband Franco's return, when she felt "a big jolt. I could see my glass of water sliding across the bedside table. The door of the cabin flew open, and I got up and looked out." The corridor beyond was suddenly filled with puzzled people; she followed them as far as the staircase, then stopped, sitting down on one of the risers to await her husband's return. In just a few minutes Franco appeared and quickly took her back to their cabin so that Alda could change out of her nightgown and retrieve her jewelry. They grabbed two life jackets and plunged back into the crowded corridor, joining the rush of people desperate to get to the upper deck.[51]

"I was just getting ready to climb into my upper berth," recalls Adalgisa Di Fabio, "when there was a very, very loud noise, like a big explosion. The ship suddenly tilted on its side. I didn't understand what had happened but I knew it was something big, and it was not good. I woke my roommates to leave the cabin. I grabbed my best dress and my shoes and held them to my chest as we left the cabin. At first there was no one in the hallway, but I knew I wanted to get out of there."[52]

After saying good night, Santino and Antonietta Porporino had gone to their respective cabins. Santino was just drifting off to sleep "when I heard a collision, a big explosion." Jumping out of his berth, and clad only in his undershorts, he ran out into the corridor, racing to his wife and children in No. 376, just three cabins away. Antonietta had put their two young children to bed and retired for the night when "a screeching sound" jolted her awake. She was immediately flung off her bed into a pool of cold water that was rushing into the cabin. When Santino kicked open the cabin door, he found his wife in her satin nightgown, standing helplessly in a foot of water. He grabbed Antonietta, Joe, and Bruna and hustled them out into the corridor, along with Antonietta's roommate, who had struck her head and was bleeding from her wound. By now the corridor was filled with "panicked people screaming, crying, shoving, and pulling hair" as they tried to get up to the deck.[53]

Tullio and Filomena Di Sandro had retired early, after tucking four-year-old Norma into her bed. The collision awoke them—"a violent bump," Tullio recalled as their cabin seemed to vibrate and a loud tearing sound filled the previously still night. Tullio jumped out of bed and switched on the light; both he and his wife at first thought that the engines had failed before Tullio decided that they must have hit something. "I thought instinctively of the *Titanic*," he remembered, "but it was not the time of year for icebergs." When he opened the cabin door and looked out, the passage was empty, but within a minute the couple heard "excited voices and the first screams of fright." As the cabin lights flickered off and on, Tullio pulled on a shirt while Filomena put on one of his T-shirts over her nightgown. He then bent down and picked up the still sleeping Norma. By now the corridor was "tilted and full of people screaming with fright and pain. I prayed and shouted to my neighbors to be calm to avoid greater danger."[54]

One by one and in terrified groups, the confused and shocked passengers began fighting their ways toward the lifeboats.

Chapter Nine

―――・●・―――

W ithin a minute of the collision Captain Calamai ran back into the bridge: the *Doria* was still moving forward at near full speed and he ordered the engines stopped.[1] The first thing to be done was to determine the extent of damage to his ship. The Swedish liner had penetrated some forty feet into the *Doria*, ripping through seven of her eleven decks and creating both a vertical and a horizontal V-shaped swath of destruction matching the taper of *Stockholm*'s bow.

Below the passenger decks, *Stockholm*'s bow inflicted devastating damage. "The penetration of *Stockholm* into the *Andrea Doria*," says naval architect William Garzke, "occurred at a vulnerable portion of the hull. SOLAS regulations required that the closest longitudinal bulkhead to the shell be spaced at a distance of twenty percent of a ship's beam. The reinforced bow of *Stockholm* penetrated beyond that point."[2] In the area of the collision, the bow ruptured the *Doria*'s starboard fuel and oil tanks, resulting in asymmetrical flooding that created a serious starboard list. The deep tanks containing fuel oil ran along both the starboard and port sides of the double bottom. The collision opened five of these tanks to the sea. The portside fuel tanks still contained fuel for *Doria* to return to Italy; in emergencies they could be filled with water to provide additional ballast, but this was not customarily done. Now only half-filled, they created an imbalance as water rushed into the starboard tanks, resulting in an immediate starboard list.[3] At some point during the collision, the *Doria*'s keel was also damaged, perhaps by the initial collision or by the twisting motion of the *Stockholm* as she gradually freed herself from the bowels of the Italian liner.[4] As *Stockholm* slid along the *Doria*'s starboard side, she likely caused further damage, breaking portholes and weakening some of the riveted plating, leading to additional flooding on the starboard side.[5]

Most of the damage was concentrated in the fourth of the *Doria*'s eleven watertight compartments, but water also entered from damage extending aft of the collision area. The air-conditioned garage on B Deck quickly flooded while, as Garzke noted, "the forward diesel generator room, located just aft of the collision area, also started to flood through an access tunnel linking the generator room to a small pump room in the deep tank compartment which had been breached. The generator room, containing five diesel generators that provided most of the liner with electric power, flooded slowly despite effort to control it. Unfortunately, the transverse bulkhead at the double bottom level did not have a watertight door, as the tunnel bulkheads were protected by longitudinal bulkheads further outboard that had been breached by the bow of *Stockholm*. That main transverse bulkhead also had been damaged in the collision."[6] *Stockholm* had smashed directly into a watertight bulkhead separating the third and fourth compartments, and in twisting out of the *Doria* had likely opened another, the fifth compartment, to the sea.[7]

Andrea Doria had been designed to remain afloat with any two watertight compartments flooded. The 1948 requirements laid down in the SOLAS regulations governing merchant vessels had not envisioned a scenario such as the *Doria* now faced: it was believed that no danger existed in any breach above waterline. Watertight bulkheads did not extend above A Deck. *Stockholm*'s bow had ripped a gash extending two decks beyond this, to the Foyer and Upper Decks. The 1948 SOLAS guidelines were based on a penetration of only 20 percent of the ship's beam; *Stockholm*'s reinforced bow for ice transit in the Baltic penetrated to within 30 percent of the *Doria*'s hull, causing damage no maritime authority or regulation had ever anticipated.[8]

In designing the *Doria*, naval architects and engineers had anticipated a possible list of 7 degrees if any one compartment had been flooded;

if by some misfortune two compartments were breached, this might result in a 15-degree list. To ensure safety, the naval architects at Ansaldo designed the *Doria* with an added margin of 5 degrees: she could therefore list up to 20 degrees without danger of continued flooding.[9] With three compartments seemingly opened to the sea, and the still half-empty port deep tanks being reserve buoyancy, the Italian liner soon developed a 22-degree list. This meant that, as water flooded the liner, it would inevitably reach the tops of the watertight bulkheads on the starboard side; slowly, inexorably, it would spill over, seeping through hallways, down staircases, and along rooms, downflooding one compartment after another along the starboard side until the stability of the *Doria* was fatally compromised from free-surface effects and she would finally capsize once all stability was lost. The Italian liner was doomed.

Calamai now faced every captain's worst nightmare. He had no idea how much time he had to keep the ship afloat: if the ship rolled over and suddenly capsized, as seemed possible, hundreds might be killed. He quickly wrote out a distress message. Third Officer Antonio Donato ran to the radio room behind the wheelhouse, where at 11:20 P.M. operator Carlo Bussi tapped out the call: "SOS de ICEH [*Andrea Doria*'s call sign] SOS" along with her position and a plea: "We need immediate assistance."[10]

Message dispatched, Calamai immediately recalled his experience in World War II, when he had saved the torpedoed battleship *Caio Duilio* by running it into shallow waters in November 1940. He now wondered if he could beach the *Doria*. The nearest shoals were twenty-two miles away. He pushed the telegraph to slow ahead but, after a short rumble from somewhere below, the *Doria*'s engines shuddered to a stop. When Calamai rang Chief Engineer Alcisio Chiappori for a report, he learned that water was rising toward the generators, threatening to short-circuit them; the sea was already in the engine room, and the pump controls were flooded. Only the port engine was operable.[11] The *Doria* was effectively dead in the water.

At the same time, Calamai ordered Second Officer Badano to have the crew take charge of both the port and starboard lifeboats. They began removing the tarps covering the boats and set about freeing them from their stocks. The boats were designed to swing out as their davits pivoted over the edge of the deck, allowing for them to be lowered to the Promenade Deck below, where they could be loaded as passengers easily stepped from deck to boat once the enormous floor-to-ceiling sliding windows were opened.

At least this was how the evacuation was supposed to go. It didn't take long for Calamai to realize that the usual procedures were now impossible to perform. Badano soon reported back to Calamai: the port davits, designed to operate with lists up to 15 degrees, now could not swing out with the *Doria* at a 22-degree starboard list. This meant that none of the lifeboats on the port side could be lowered: even if the crew could somehow manage to physically push them over the liner's side, which had proved impossible in the few attempts already made, the boats would then hang inboard at uneven angles along the tilting port hull. Passengers would have to somehow climb up into the unstable lifeboats before they could be lowered; even then, the loaded lifeboats would scrape sideways along the hull as if being let down the steep slope of a mountain. The smallest mistake, the merest lurch of the *Doria,* the unequal distribution or shifting of weight—anything could cause a lifeboat to overturn. Passengers wouldn't just be spilled out into the sea below but hurled against the side of the hull, perhaps crushed if the boat swung farther to starboard, and almost certainly suffer traumatic, possibly fatal injuries. Half the *Doria*'s lifeboats were useless.[12]

Ironically almost the exact same scenario had played itself out forty-one-years earlier, after *Lusitania* was struck by a German torpedo. The day before the disaster, *Lusitania*'s lifeboats had been swung out on their davits so that they cleared the railing. Within minutes of the torpedo striking the Cunard liner, *Lusitania* took on a perilous list to starboard, leaving most of the portside lifeboats useless.[13]

The *Doria*'s list also posed serious problems with the starboard boats: they could be lowered but by the time they reached the level of the Promenade Deck they hung out too far away from the ship, leaving a dangerous gap. It would be impossible for crew to load them at the Promenade Deck: it was likely that many passengers would miss their footing and tumble into the sea, or that the crew would lose control of the lifeboats and accidentally spill their passengers. The only safe way to use the starboard boats was to first lower them, empty, to the water and then, using ropes or ladders, fill them with descending passengers.

Like Edward Smith, captain of the ill-fated *Titanic* before him, Calamai faced a crisis: he had 1,706 people on board his ship, and room in the operable lifeboats for only 1,004.[14] This situation now shaped Calamai's decisions. In such a disaster, regulations called for the ringing of alarms to signal abandon ship; when Badano asked if he should sound the alarm, though, Calamai replied, "No, no. We have only half the lifeboats."[15] "Inasmuch as only the lifeboats at starboard were available," Calamai later explained, "and there was no immediate danger according to our estimation, the prescribed order of abandon ship was not given with the siren in order not to create confusion and panic among the passengers."[16] It was now eleven thirty, just twenty minutes after the collision.

Calamai did order Badano, who spoke English well, to use the ship's loudspeaker to make two announcements. The first was addressed to the crew, in Italian: "Personnel to abandon ship stations."[17] Unlike most shipping companies, the Italian Line did not assign passengers to individual lifeboats but instead to muster stations in case of emergency.[18] This was the second announcement. "Passengers must go to their muster stations wearing their life jackets and keep calm," Badano repeated in both Italian and in English.[19]

What passengers heard—or did not hear—soon became the subject of much controversy. There is no doubt that the announcements were made, but within forty-eight hours of the disaster, a group of ninety survivors released a statement asserting: "No instructions were received by public address system or by word of mouth from the crew that danger was imminent."[20]

Passengers later gave conflicting accounts of this announcement, which only added to the sense of confusion immediately after the disaster and led to erroneous charges that the loudspeakers had been silent. There was no consensus on the issue. Alda Raimengia "definitely" heard announcements that night, but cannot recall what language they were in.[21] Philadelphia Mayor Richardson Dilworth, too, recalled the loud-speakers "blaring out harsh commands," but like Alda he was unable to say in what language they had been: he remembered only the words "Abandon ship."[22] These were also the only two words that Tullio Di Sandro could recall.[23] Father Richard Wojcik recalled announcements "first in Italian and then in English, telling passengers to go to their rooms, get their life jackets, and go to a lifeboat station."[24] Wojcik's fellow priests Fathers Raymond Goedert and John Dolciamore had different recollections. Dolciamore recalled that the announcement ordered passengers to retrieve their life jackets from their cabins.[25] Goedert, though, remembers hearing no instructions in English—"No one was telling us what to do or where to go," he recalls.[26]

Many passengers could recall only the Italian language announcements.[27] All Cecilia Pick heard were the words "Keep calm" some fifteen minutes after the collision. "From then onward," she wrote, "we were not told a thing or given any instructions."[28] Dun Gifford, too, remembered the only announcements as being in Italian and asking a fellow passenger to translate for him.[29] His sister, Bambi, agreed that the only announcements she heard were in Italian.[30] Barbara Boggs remembered "waiting to hear something over the loudspeaker system and hearing nothing except the crew talking to each other in Italian, not knowing if help was on the way and feeling the ship listing more and more every minute."[31]

Barbara Bliss wrote of "unintelligible announcements in Italian . . . garbled by static like a New York subway."[32] Robert Young, too, heard only announcements being given in Italian. Many other passengers heard nothing in either language and complained that the *Doria*'s crew either ignored their pleas or had seemingly disappeared. Klaus Dorneich vividly recalls how "the loudspeaker remained silent."[33] "The worst part of the night," remembers Adalgisa Di Fabio, "was that no one told us anything."[34] And Mike Stoller recalled: "During the hours we were waiting for help, we didn't hear any directions."[35]

"Captain Calamai," wrote Robert Young later, "has been criticized for not sounding the general alarm. Whether to do so or not was a difficult decision for him to make. I personally believe he made the right one, because had he sounded it an uncontrollable panic could have ensued."[36]

Memory is a fragile thing. A crisis hones senses in some people while overwhelming senses in others. In the chaos of that moment aboard *Andrea Doria*, it is certain that a few passengers, surrounded by panicked and noisy crowds, failed to hear the announcements when they were made. It is also true that the collision shorted out electrical systems and may have rendered some of the loudspeakers inoperable.[37] There is no reason to doubt that Badano made the announcements, but the ensuing confusion might have been avoided had they been repeated throughout the long hours of waiting. The lapse, though, was understandable. Captain Calamai was too consumed with attempting to save his passengers to worry about keeping them informed of developments. In hindsight it might have been better had the passengers at least been told that another ship had collided with the *Doria* and that preparations for safe evacuation of the liner were under way. Without this information, most passengers heard only speculation and vague rumors and had no idea that a larger rescue was under way.

And a rescue effort was under way within minutes of the *Doria*'s initial SOS. The urgent radio message was quickly received and acknowledged, first by radio in South Chatham, Massachusetts, then by the Mackay (New Jersey) shore station, and finally by the Coast Guard station at East Moriches on Long Island.[38] At 11:25, East Moriches, in turn, transmitted the message (as well as an SOS radio message from *Stockholm*) to Third Coast Guard District Headquarters in New York City, which relayed the request across airwaves: orders from New York and from Coast Guard Headquarters in Boston set in motion what was to become the largest maritime rescue in peacetime.[39] In all, six Coast Guard vessels began racing toward the stricken liner. The 322-foot seaplane tender *Yakutat* and the cutter *Campbell* quickly departed Cape Cod; the 254-foot cutter *Owasco* left from New London, Connecticut; and from New Bedford came the 125-foot cutter *Legare*. Two vessels set out from Woods Hole, Massachusetts: the cutter *Evergreen* and the buoy tender *Hornbeam*.[40]

Fifteen miles southeast from the *Doria*, the 390-foot United Fruit

Company freighter *Cape Ann* was on its way to New York from Bremerhaven, Germany, when its radio operator picked up the SOS call from the Italian liner at 11:23. Its captain, Joseph Boyd, altered course and radioed that he was on his way.[41] The *Doria* quickly cabled back, asking how many lifeboats the *Cape Ann* had. The response was two. To this, the *Doria* answered, "Danger immediate. Need boats to evacuate 1,000 passengers and 500 crew. We need boats."[42] Despite the heavy surrounding fog enveloping the ship, Boyd ordered *Cape Ann* ahead at her full speed of 14 knots; by some miracle, she actually made 17 knots that night.[43]

The second vessel to answer the *Doria*'s cry for help was the US Navy's *Private William H. Thomas,* a converted troop transport that had served during World War II as USS *Rixey* before being renamed and used to carry American soldiers back to New York from postings in Italy.[44] *Thomas* was nineteen miles away from the *Doria* and in a deep fog when the SOS was received.[45] Also answering the call was the 306-foot US Navy destroyer-turned-training-ship *Edward H. Allen* and the 425-foot Tidewater Oil Company tanker *Robert E. Hopkins,* on its way to Corpus Christi, whose captain, René Blanc, had assured the *Doria* that his ship was on her way as early as 11:21.[46]

But by far the most reassuring answer to the *Doria*'s SOS came from the French liner *Ile de France*. She'd left New York City earlier that same day, carrying 940 passengers and a crew of 826 on her way to Le Havre. Time hadn't been terribly kind to the once-glamorous floating palace: "modernized" in a 1950s style grafted onto her 1920s art deco rooms, stripped of her third funnel, and now adorned with her name spelled out in garish lights atop her superstructure, she'd lost her elegant luster. But she had two things going for her that night: she was big—739 feet—and she was fast. Baron Raoul de Beaudéan, the *Ile*'s venerable, aristocratic captain, was on her bridge, chain-smoking as his liner raced east. For the past half hour the *Ile* had been plowing through a fog bank of "exceptional intensity," as Beaudéan recalled, so thick "we could not see the bow from the bridge."[47] The fog was so dense, he said, that even the mast "had also disappeared . . . I had never seen anything like it."[48] It is worth noting that all the ships in the area reported thick fog: indeed, the United States Weather Bureau estimated that visibility in the area was "probably less than a mile."[49] Only Carstens aboard *Stockholm* would claim otherwise.

At 11:30 that night, *Ile de France* Radio Officer Pierre Allanet raced onto the bridge with the *Andrea Doria*'s SOS and call for assistance, relayed as a general alert by an unidentified ship.[50] The news seemed incredible. The *Ile* was forty-four miles east of the Italian liner by Beaudéan's calculations. He could turn his vessel around and race to the stricken *Doria* but this would be a costly move in terms of fuel consumption and schedule delays: if there really was a disaster, rescue efforts might involve not hours but several days of disruption. According to the 1948 SOLAS regulations regarding safety at sea, ships receiving an SOS from another vessel were not obligated to provide assistance if other, closer ships were also answering the call. "A modern vessel is quite solid, after all," Beaudéan reasoned. "I know very well that it isn't common practice to clutter the air waves with fictional alarms but I would like to have a few more details."[51] He had Allanet radio the Italian liner for more information: no answer was forthcoming—unknown to Beaudéan the *Doria*'s generators had lost their power. The French captain then decided to ask the *Stockholm* if she couldn't provide immediate aid given that she was on the scene: the Swedish liner swiftly replied that her seaworthiness after the collision hadn't yet been determined and therefore couldn't risk her own lifeboats.[52]

This news convinced Beaudéan to act. At 11:54 he cabled to the *Doria:* "I am going to assist you. Will reach your position 5:45 GMT [1:45 AM]. Are you sinking? What kind of assistance do you need?"[53] Again there was no reply, but the *Cape Ann* radioed the French liner: "*Andrea Doria* wants to disembark 1,500 passengers and crew. Strongly suggest you have all your lifeboats ready to assist."[54]

At midnight Beaudéan ordered the *Ile de France* swung around and began racing at 22 knots—his top speed—toward the stricken liner.[55] The sleeping passengers were to be left undisturbed as the French crew began preparing for the worst: Staff Captain Christian Pettre was to supervise as lifeboats were uncovered and prepared for lowering to rescue the *Doria*'s passengers; Michel Delafon, the liner's doctor, readied his infirmary to treat the injured; and Chief Purser Tournyol Du Clos and his stewards noiselessly moved through the now bright public rooms, setting up piles of blankets and tables that would offer survivors food and drinks.[56]

On *Stockholm*, the collision had sent Captain Nordenson racing for the bridge. He found Carstens ashen and shaking. "We collided with another ship," he muttered, adding that he'd ordered the engines astern and closed the watertight doors. Nordenson asked Carstens why he hadn't been called earlier if they were in fog as they neared another vessel; although the fog was so thick that Nordenson initially took the outline of the distant *Andrea Doria* for the Swedish liner *Kungsholm*, Carstens insisted that conditions had been clear.[57] Second Officer Lars Enestrom saw that the other ship's course hadn't been entered on the plotting board; Carstens claimed that he had plotted the positions but erased the data in the few minutes that had elapsed following the collision. Enestrom thought Cartsens was in shock.[58] Nordenson then asked Carstens to plot the location of the ship they had hit using radar; Carstens did so but his calculations were off by some five miles.[59]

Nordenson ordered Enestrom to evaluate the damage. Enestrom, soon joined by a small rescue party, crept through the fog across the bow: he could barely see the moon overhead. In the collision the first upper seventy-five feet of the bow had been compressed, ripped, or torn away: the first watertight compartment was essentially gone. Twelve crew cabins had been destroyed, taking with them the bodies of two young crew members, seventeen-year-old Kenneth Jonasson and eighteen-year-old Sune Steen.[60] The chain locker had been torn open: in the force of the collision, the two seven-hundred-foot-long anchor chains had jogged loose and quickly unwound, carrying nineteen-year-old kitchen boy Evert Svensson with them as they smashed into the seabed some three hundred feet below.[61] They also left *Stockholm* essentially anchored in place: shortly after the collision, the *Doria* began to drift with the tide and came within a third of a mile of the Swedish liner. Nordenson could only watch as the larger vessels loomed toward his own ship before miraculously passing at a safe distance.[62] Had the two ships collided a second time, events that night would have taken an even more disastrous turn.

The rescue party on *Stockholm* heard moans and cries for help coming from the wreckage. Menacing tendrils of twisted steel reached out in the night, illuminated only by the sickly hues of pale green emergency lights. Finally they located five members of *Stockholm*'s crew and, using acetylene torches, managed to free them and carry them to the infirmary. Painter Sven Ahlm's injuries were relatively minor, but his roommate, messboy Karl Osterberg, soon died of a fractured skull. Thirty-year-old seaman Alf Johannson had also suffered a fractured skull and the collision had crushed his legs, leaving jagged bones jutting out from the shredded remnants of his pants; twenty-one-year-old pantry boy Lars Falk had a broken neck and fractured skull, and blood was oozing from his mouth. Crew member Wilhelm Gustavsson had been found in a crumpled heap, one leg broken, face bloody, and an eyeball hanging from the socket.[63]

It was *Stockholm* crew member Bernabe Polanco Garcia who, on the remnants of the foredeck, first detected a faint moan coming from behind a gunwale near the crushed bow. As he neared the area, he heard a cry in Spanish, "I want my mama!"[64] On the other side of the gunwale Garcia found Linda Morgan. She had been asleep on the *Doria* when a "crashing and banging" filled the night.[65] She passed out as the *Stockholm*'s prow destroyed her cabin. Somehow, the tangled steel had pierced the mattress of her bed; when the twisted bow pivoted out of the ruined cabin, it pulled the mattress—and Linda on it—out of the *Doria*. Both mattress and unconscious girl had landed on *Stockholm*'s foredeck, where the gunwale had protected her from further harm.[66]

Linda awoke "outside, under stars, with ocean all around me. I was totally confused. Had the roof of my cabin disappeared?" She couldn't move her left arm; she heard an unseen woman moaning and then began crying out in Spanish. It was a stroke of luck that Garcia, the only member of *Stockholm*'s crew from Spain, heard her. "My name is Barnabe Polanco Garcia," the stunned man told her. "You are hurt. I will take you to the infirmary."[67] As Garcia lifted her up, he saw the crumpled body of a red-haired woman snagged in the wreckage of the bow some fifty feet away: thinking that she was Linda's mother, he said nothing to the girl.[68]

Stockholm's chief purser, Curt Dawe, was in the infirmary when Garcia entered with Linda. Thinking that she was a passenger on the Swedish liner, he asked, "What's your name?"

"Linda Morgan," she answered in English. "Where's my mother? Do you know where my mother is?"[69]

Dawe looked at the passenger manifest: there was no Linda Morgan. She then suggested, "Look under Linda Cianfarra, my stepfather's name." Again there was no listing. "Where do you come from?" Dawe asked. "Madrid," Linda answered. Dawe was still perplexed.[70] Finally, Linda asked, "Isn't this the *Andrea Doria*?"[71] Dawe suddenly realized what had happened. "No, this is the *Stockholm*," he told her.[72]

A quick examination suggested that Linda had broken her left arm and fractured her knees. Fearing that she might have internal injuries, a doctor forced her to drink warm salt water, thinking that if she vomited he could spot any blood.[73] Finally, they laid her on a couch and gave her a shot of morphine to ease her pain.[74]

Garcia, meanwhile, had gone back to the ruined bow, where he had spotted the woman he assumed to be the girl's mother in the wreckage. He carefully crawled along the twisted deck but she was out of his reach.[75] Aware that she had been moaning and might still be alive, *Stockholm* crew member Valdemar Trasbo tried again. After an agonizingly perilous journey across the wreckage, Trasbo finally reached the woman, who was sitting upright, now silent and motionless against a piece of twisted steel.[76] He could see the gold ring on her left hand, set with a large blue stone: unknown to him, he had found Jeanette Carlin, pulled—like Linda—from her cabin on the *Doria* in the wreckage of *Stockholm*'s bow. Trasbo gently grabbed her arm and started to pull her toward him: he was horrified when the arm tore away from the torso. Trasbo dropped it and quickly reached for her hair: it, too, tore away in great tufts.[77] Thoroughly unnerved and sure that she was dead, Trasbo finally retreated.

In the meantime, an assessment of *Stockholm* brought reassuring news. Although the collision had torn away the first watertight compartment, the Swedish liner was built to remain afloat with a single compartment flooded; the watertight bulkhead that had separated the first and second compartments was now holding fast, essentially acting as a new watertight bow to prevent further flooding. Pumps were keeping any list to a minimum.[78] *Stockholm* was unlikely to sink. Hearing this, Nordenson finally took to the *Stockholm*'s public address system just after midnight: "We have collided with the Italian passenger ship *Andrea Doria*. But there is no danger. There is nothing to worry about."[79]

There was plenty to worry about, though, on the *Doria*. Just after midnight, Badano called the engine room and relayed Calamai's orders: "You must stabilize the ship by any means possible." The heroic engine room crew had been trying to do just that for the last fifty minutes. The ventilation system had been turned off to save power for the lights and radio; the bowels of the *Doria*, filled with a rising mixture of machine oil and thousands of tons of seawater washing against hot machinery, became saunas. The ever-increasing starboard list made it nearly impossible to work: crew clung to ropes strung across the compartment to keep their balance. But the pumps could not keep up with the inrush of water.[80]

At twelve fifteen, the *Doria* had radioed to the *Stockholm*: "You are only one mile from us. Please if possible come immediately to pick up our passengers." To this, *Stockholm* replied: "Here badly damaged. The whole bow crushed. No. 1 filled with water. Have to stay in our present position. If you can lower your boats we can pick you up."[81] The *Doria* radioed back in desperation: "You have to row to us." *Stockholm* again insisted: "Lower your lifeboats. We can pick you up."[82] Only now did the *Doria* fully explain her situation: "We are bending [listing] too much. Impossible to put boats over side. Please send lifeboats immediately."[83]

Nordenson, having determined that *Stockholm* was in no immediate danger, finally radioed back, telling Calamai that he would start sending his lifeboats in another forty minutes, as soon as they could be readied. *Stockholm* carried three motor launches and eight lifeboats: Nordenson decided to keep four of his regular lifeboats in reserve, in case the condition of his ship suddenly worsened.[84] Waiting helplessly, Calamai ordered flares fired from his bridge to guide would-be rescuers. They streaked into the night, hovering momentarily in the murky mist before bursting and cascading down like fireworks against the dark sky.[85]

Chapter Ten

—◆◦◆—

A few of the *Doria* passengers were lucky: in the immediate aftermath of the collision, Betsy Drake had calmly dressed and left her cabin. In the corridor, a man she had met on the ship spotted her, took her arm, and escorted her up to the deck, saying, "Perhaps we'd do better if we stayed together." In "a state of shock," she accepted his arm and made her way out to the port side of the boat.[1]

Fellow actress Ruth Roman endured a more difficult trek. Having reached her cabin and roused her son, Dickie, and his nurse, Grace Els, she grabbed three life jackets and some blankets and began the climb back up the tilting staircase to the deck above.[2] Reaching the top of the Grand Staircase, she took Dickie on her lap and sat down next to Grace Els, building a barricade of life jackets and blankets "so they would not slip and roll down the deck." She was surprised at how calm she was as a waiter came around with some milk he had heated for the small children. "I put my arms over my head and thought, I may have to swim with Dickie; I'll need all my strength. Then restlessly sitting up, I spotted a deflated party balloon on the deck. I blew it up, gave it to Dickie and told him that we were going on a picnic. As I stood there Dickie held the balloon in one hand, waved to me with the other. 'Picnic!' he called. 'Picnic!'"[3]

For the Dilworths, reaching the upper decks was a struggle: "You couldn't walk because the ship had such a bad list," Richardson recalled. "We had to crawl on our hands and knees through the corridors."[4] The floors were slick with water and machine oil—the mayor likened them to "a toboggan run."[5] Passengers around them slid and crashed into each other and against walls as they struggled to keep their footing, and many "got badly bruised."[6] They finally came out on the starboard deck, near the stern, and waited. Soon, though, crew members began ordering passengers to the port side. It took all of their strength. Once safely on the port deck the couple could do nothing but sit "shivering in the cloak of fog, holding on desperately to the rails."[7]

Andrew Stevens ran to his cabin, grabbed his life jacket and his passport, and made his way to the First Class Lounge, his assigned muster station, where he found both of his parents with several hundred other anxious passengers. They braced themselves against walls and furniture and waited, but they never saw a single member of the crew.[8] Finally, when the list began to send plants and other fittings sliding across the floor, they decided they would be safer out on the open deck. Despite the list and the absence of any instructions, Andrew wasn't particularly worried: "The ship was twice as long as a football field, and you felt pretty secure." But reality soon intruded when a dazed Walter Carlin wandered onto the deck. Jeanette, he said, had simply disappeared when their cabin was demolished. "She's gone," he kept repeating, "she's just gone."[9] Some shipboard acquaintances helped him into a deck chair, listening as Carlin sobbed, "I want to recover Jeanette's body. I'll offer a reward. I'll pay anything."[10]

Instinctively most of the *Doria*'s passengers made their ways to the higher, port side of the ship. After quickly dressing, Philip and Arline Trachtenberg had rushed from their cabin into a corridor, where, "frantic passengers were running in every direction. Most of them wore only their night clothes." Trachtenberg stopped a steward to ask what had happened. "One of the elevators jammed," the man said. "I looked at him. How ludicrous can you get, I thought. The most modern ocean liner afloat had suddenly taken a 25-degree list because an elevator had jammed?" Ascending to the upper decks was an ordeal: the Trachtenbergs had to slowly pull themselves up the tilting Grand Staircase using the handrails. When they finally reached the port side of the Upper Deck, Trachtenberg recalled, "there was every sign of panic. No

Actress and previous passenger Joan Crawford sitting with Captain Calamai beneath the statue of Admiral Andrea Doria. *Courtesy of Cathy Crawford Lelonde.*

Barbara Field, later Boggs, at the time of her debut, with her father, Marshall Field III, at his Long Island estate of Caumsett. *Courtesy of Adelaide Mestre.*

John and Cecilia Pick on the day of their wedding in 1956. John Pick is kissing the ring of the Archbishop of Malta, who had performed the marriage ceremony. *Courtesy of Nicholas, Marquis de Piro.*

Klaus Dorneich. *Courtesy of Klaus Dorneich.*

The actress Ruth Roman. *Authors' collection.*

Reverend Raymond Goedert.
Courtesy of The Archdiocese of Chicago's Joseph Cardinal Bernadin Archives and Records Center.

The Young Family, three months after the wreck, aboard the SS *America*. From left: David, Robert, Virginia, and Madge. *Courtesy of Madge Young Nickerson.*

The Mastrincola Family. From left: Pat, Rosa, Angelo, and Arlene. *Courtesy of Pat Mastrincola and Arlene Meisner.*

Maria Coscia, shown here some ten months after she escaped the *Andrea Doria*, on the marriage of her son Fred in May 1957. She is escorted by her son-in-law, Joseph Pedone. *Courtesy of Renee Coscia.*

Francesco (Franco) and Alda Raimengia, 1956. *Courtesy of Alda Raimengia.*

The Sergios' passport photo. Maria is shown in the middle, surrounded by her children. Clockwise from lower left: Margaret Domenica, Anna Maria, Giuseppe, and Rocco. *Courtesy of Tony Sergio.*

Giovanni and Melania Vali, shown in their Bay Area restaurant a few years after the *Andrea Doria*'s last voyage. The restaurant's walls featured newspaper articles covering the tragedy. *Courtesy of Melania Ansuini Vali.*

Tullio Di Sandro, shown with his little daughter Norma, on July 22, 1954 in Milan. *Courtesy of Ermanno di Sandro.*

Nicola DiFiore, reunited with his family. From left: his wife, Concetta DiFiore, Nicola with his granddaughter Marisa Checchio Angelozzi, his daughter Nicolina DiFiore Nizzardo, and his friends Anthony and Amerina Importico. *Courtesy of Daniela Sellinger.*

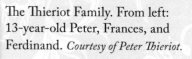
The Thieriot Family. From left: 13-year-old Peter, Frances, and Ferdinand. *Courtesy of Peter Thieriot.*

Joan Cianfarra and her half-sister Linda Morgan, circa 1956. *Courtesy of Linda Hardberger.*

Jane and Camille Cianfarra in Vatican Square. *Courtesy of Linda Hardberger.*

Pat Mastrincola, wearing a white sweater, at the side of the Tourist Class Pool on board the *Andrea Doria.* *Courtesy of Pat Mastrincola.*

Passengers taking the sea air on the First Class Promenade. *Courtesy of Michael Poirier.*

The rescue at night, taken from the deck of the *Ile de France*, showing passengers and survivors watching from the liner. *Courtesy of Dana Hall/OceanGate.*

The damaged bow of the *Stockholm*. *Courtesy of Dana Hall/OceanGate.*

The *Andrea Doria* at around 10 A.M. on July 26, 1956. *Courtesy of The Mariners' Museum and Park. Photograph P0001.003-01--PB17126.*

The portside lifeboats break away from the ship in the final moments of the *Andrea Doria*. *Courtesy of The Mariners' Museum and Park. Photograph P0001.003/01--PB17134.*

The *Stockholm* with accompanying tugboat heads for New York with her damaged bow clearly seen. *Courtesy of The Mariners' Museum and Park. Photograph P0001.003/01--PB17131.*

Eight-year-old Pierette Simpson arrives in Detroit after surviving the wreck. From left: Pierette's grand-mother Domenica Burzio; her mother, Vivian Massa; Pierette. *Courtesy of Pierette Simpson.*

one seemed to know what to do. Men were shouting and women were wringing their hands. Children were whimpering and clutching at their mothers." Fog hung over everything—"a dank, gloomy, impenetrable curtain. It was impossible to see beyond it. The scene on deck was unreal. Yellow life jackets covered nightgowns, pajamas, dinner jackets and evening dresses. One man was naked except for a pair of shorts. A middle aged woman stood by the rail, nibbling on a bottle of Scotch. A few feet away a man with a rose in his lapel calmly smoked a cigar." Everyone seemed to wonder what to do—"Where's the crew?" Trachtenberg heard shouted. "Isn't the crew supposed to put the boats over?" Trachtenberg looked around and spotted "a steward sitting in a deck chair. He had propped the chair so it wouldn't slide. He had nothing to say nor did he move."[11]

In contrast Madge Young remembered no panic as her family left their cabin and made their way to the Promenade Deck: "Nobody talked or screamed or pushed," she wrote. "Everything was done orderly and in silence." They had planned to go to their muster station but once they reached the deck they saw people "pouring out of the main lounge and ballroom onto the glass enclosed deck so we followed them."[12] Along with her parents and her brother, Madge grabbed the railings "so we wouldn't slide across the deck. It was July so it wasn't cold; in fact it was warm, and my mother was dying from heat in her big coat, but she couldn't take it off since she only had on a sheer nightgown. 'From now on I travel only with flannel,'" Virginia said.[13]

Barbara Boggs and her husband had been playing bridge when *Stockholm* hit the *Doria*, while twelve-year-old Bobby, suffering from what he thinks was a case of the mumps, had been asleep in their Upper Deck cabin.[14] "We didn't stop to speak or pause to think," Barbara later said. "Our first thought was to get Robert out of his room and we went down as fast as we could. The ship listed heavily and instantly, so it was difficult to move on the stairways and through the corridors. The place was filled with oil-smoke and steam."[15]

When Barbara finally reached their cabin and opened the door, she saw her son, Bobby, on the floor. In treating his illness, *Andrea Doria*'s doctor had given him a strong sedative and the young boy had slept through not only the collision but also being thrown out of his bed. "We awakened him, grabbed our life preservers and rushed frantically to find our daughter," Barbara later wrote.[16]

"My dad carried me on his back like a fireman," Bobby recalls, "and down a corridor to get to the stairs. I remember seeing wreckage in the hall."[17] Finally, the family found daughter, Barbara, in the First Class Lounge—"Thank heaven she had the sense to go to our lifeboat station, figuring we would probably bring her life preserver," her mother wrote.[18]

Barbara Bliss was startled to see her stepfather "carrying Bobby, half-asleep, over his shoulder like a sack of potatoes." Her mother handed her one of the life jackets they had taken from their cabin.[19] Along with the other passengers, the Boggs family soon wandered out to the port side of the Promenade Deck. "The toughest part," Barbara Boggs said, "was the endless wait, lying flat on the tilting promenade deck, trying not to kick the heads of the people stacked up at your feet, waiting to hear something over the loudspeaker system and hearing nothing . . . Now and then the *Doria* blew long blasts. I heard a woman scream and then a slap followed."[20]

Clarence and Priscilla Gifford also began the frantic race to their muster station. "The trip down the passageway wasn't easy," Priscilla recalled. "There was an awful pitch to the ship and we had to walk in the angle between the floor and the bulkhead, sort of in the gutter, and brace ourselves as best we could."[21] Bambi remembers hearing screams and the "sharp, acrid smell of electric shorts," as she followed her parents up the tilted staircase. "We all went like rats to the high side of the ship."[22]

Dun Gifford met his parents at the top of the Grand Staircase; because of the heavy smoke wafting up from below he was sure there had been an explosion. They ran to the port side. "I had been there a minute or two when I realized that I didn't have a life jacket and I knew I wanted one," Dun recalled. "So I beat it back to the cabin. I was scared but I knew I had to have a jacket. I slid across the cabin floor and bumped against the outside bulkhead because of the slope. There was a porthole in the cabin but I didn't waste any time looking out. The weirdness of the scene was brought home to me by the way the clothes in our closet hung. There were two jackets and I grabbed them both and beat it."[23]

"At first we stood around in groups and tried to discuss what it might have been," Clarence Gifford remembered. "But we discovered quickly that it was tiring to try and stand on a sharply sloping deck. So we sat down and braced ourselves." Priscilla found the list "the most terrible part of it. It's hard to describe how tiring it was. People had to throw away their shoes to get a better grip on the deck." As she struggled to keep hold, Priscilla promised herself, "If we ever went on another trip I wouldn't let us go together so if anything like this happened again we wouldn't all be lost." Chad, Dun, and Jock all lay down on the sloping deck, with their heads hanging over the side. "As long as I could see the water I knew I could swim for it if I had to," Jock remembered, "and I felt better."[24]

Priests John Dolciamore and Richard Wojcik had quickly left the First Class Card Room and run two decks below to reach their cabin, No. 58 on the Upper Deck. When Wojcik opened the door he was stunned: the outer wall of the cabin was gone and he could see the night sky through the ragged opening. "If I had been in bed I would have been cut in two," he later said.[25] "Don't come in!" he warned Dolciamore as smoke began to fill the corridor.[26] Wojcik was able to reach into the closet and retrieve their life jackets before backing out: he had no idea that Thure Peterson had been pushed through the wall of Cabin No. 56 into No. 58 and now lay injured and unconscious in the wreckage. The two priests made their way back up to their muster station, clinging to the stair rails and pulling themselves up along the wall, on the Promenade Deck.[27]

Fellow priests Raymond Goedert and Tom Kelly had grabbed life jackets and left their cabin immediately after the collision. Goedert recalls how the list made it extremely difficult to ascend the staircase. Finally they came out onto the port side, joining a crowd of confused and nervous fellow passengers outside their assigned muster station. "All of the evacuation plans sounded good in practice," he says, "but there was no follow through in the actual disaster. We sat there, in the fog, on a listing ship, facing the real possibility of death. It was very unreal."[28] After a few minutes, Kelly decided, "If I'm going to go down I want to do something worthwhile."[29] He began asking some of the male passengers to join him in going below and retrieving life jackets from empty cabins. Some refused, but three finally agreed. Kelly had formerly worked as a lifeguard instructor and was a strong swimmer, but the list worried him: at any moment, he knew, the *Doria* might suddenly capsize, trapping him below. Still, he pushed on, ignoring the jewels and money he saw in cabins as he collected life jackets and brought them back to passengers above. The list, the panicked passengers still pushing up from below, the smoke, and the rising water made each attempt increasingly difficult. After his fourth trip, Kelly collapsed on the deck, completely exhausted.[30]

Somehow, Peter Thieriot slept through both the collision and the first rush of passengers to the decks above. He awoke and, still half-asleep, wondered why he found it difficult to stay in his bed: it seemed to be at an odd angle. He got up and peered through a porthole: the water seemed closer to the window. But his mother had said, "Every once in a while you get in a storm at sea. Waves slosh over the bow and against the porthole. Don't worry about it." Peter returned to his bed, "not giving it a helluva lot of thought." But his bed was still at an odd angle, and "there wasn't any rocking and rolling" to suggest a storm. Finally, he got up again, opened his cabin door, and looked out. The First Class Foyer beyond was a shambles: chairs and tables were overturned and lay on the floor, broken glass was everywhere, and a mannequin, still clad in an elegant Italian ensemble, had crashed through one of the vitrine windows. "It looked like a bunch of drunks had been out there partying," Peter recalls. As he stood in his cabin doorway, a man spotted him and said, "You'd better put your life jacket on."[31]

Something was obviously wrong. Peter later told Jock Gifford that he'd picked up the telephone in his room and tried to call his parents' cabin but there had been no answer.[32] Peter wanted to find his parents, whose cabin lay down the corridor, past the First Class Foyer. He went as far as he could but recalls "the corridor was blocked—the bulkhead had been pushed in, so that the hallway tapered to a V." He then tried to approach from the port side, around the Chapel and down a hallway that led to his parents' suite only to find that it, too, was blocked by a wall that had been pushed in.[33]

"I was never, never afraid," Peter later said. "I don't attribute that to any courage or anything. I was just too young to know what was going on." He finally went up on deck, hoping to find his parents but had no luck. Max Passante, who with his wife had shared the other half of Ferdinand and Frances Thieriot's luxury suite, saw Peter and reassured him that his parents would soon find him.[34] But Passante, who had tried to reach his cabin and retrieve life jackets, had seen the damage inflicted in the collision: he was sure that the elder Thieriots were dead.[35]

Peter stayed with Passante on the Promenade Deck, but his eyes searched the crowd of passengers for any sign of his parents. "I can't understand where my parents are," he said. "I'm sure they'd come to find me . . . I'm going to look for them." Peter wandered over the liner, looking in the Belvedere Lounge and other rooms before finally wondering if his father was below, helping people from their cabins. This time he took a circuitous route that he hoped would lead him to his parents' cabin. Finding this approach blocked, he went down to A Deck and stopped when he saw that some two feet of water had already flooded the starboard corridors. Reluctantly, he turned and made his way back to the Promenade Deck.[36]

Mike and Meryl Stoller had rushed to the port side of the Boat Deck, clinging to the rails. "We've got to have our life jackets," Mike told her. "I'm going down to get them."[37] One of Meryl's shipboard friends, the wife of a US Navy officer, was standing next to them and heard his plan: she handed Mike the key to her cabin, asking if he could also retrieve her life jacket.[38] Mike managed to reach his cabin on A Deck: the corridor was awash with a mixture of machine oil and seawater. "I saw some women sitting in this mess, praying with rosaries, while others were just screaming."[39] He found his cabin door ajar. "I saw Meryl's jewelry in there," he recalls, "but I didn't take the time to grab it or a large number of rolls of color film I had taken while going around Europe on our three-month trip." He stumbled down the corridor, holding the life jackets in one hand and trying to brace himself against the tilting wall with the other.[40] Throughout, "sirens were blasting and people were screaming."[41] He decided against going to the other woman's cabin, which was on the opposite side of the ship, as the list seemed so bad that he feared the *Doria* might capsize at any moment: instead he'd just give her his own jacket and try to swim for it.[42] As he made his way back up the staircase, he felt a sudden jerk on his arm and turned to find a teenage boy trying to grab one of his life jackets. Stoller kept his hold on the precious jackets; soon another man, standing with his wife, son, and daughter, stopped Mike and begged him for the jackets. "They're not for me!" Mike said, and managed to push his way past them.[43]

Mike had been gone for only fifteen minutes, but by the time he returned, Meryl, convinced that he had become trapped below, was hysterical, standing at the railings and screaming his name over and over again.[44] "I shook her by the shoulders and slapped her on the cheek," he recalls. "She calmed down."[45] But now she began sobbing, "I wish I had been on one of those planes over the Grand Canyon," referring to the crash of the two passenger planes several weeks earlier. "Then I would have died quickly," she explained. "I wouldn't have to stand here waiting."[46] And waiting was all they could do: "We just stood there," Mike recalls, "holding on to the railing behind us while others leaned against the metal bulkhead opposite. Minutes were turning into hours."[47] "I considered praying," he recalls. "But being an atheist that seemed a waste of time."[48]

Immediately after the collision, Cecilia Pick ran from her cabin into the corridor and raced toward the staircase, all the while screaming her husband's name. She finally met him at the top—"we fell into each other's arms," she recalled. They came out onto the port side of the Promenade Deck and "clung to railings on the side that was up until the strain in our arms was insupportable, and then slid down and huddled against the lounge wall."[49]

First and Cabin Class passengers had reached the decks first. After some minutes, though, their ranks swelled as those in Tourist Class finally began appearing from below. Until this time there had been more confusion than panic, but the sight of these passengers cemented the growing sense that the *Doria* was in a desperate situation. Many of them, Dun Gifford recalled, "were injured, bloody, or covered with black oil. It was terrifying."[50] Philip Trachtenberg heard many mumbling, "desperate to be understood. It was Italian and I didn't understand. Most of them were old, many had been injured when the stampede for safety had started. Some limped. Others had to be helped. They slumped to the deck like tired animals. Even in the dark and the fog I could see the fright in their eyes." A nearby steward told Trachtenberg what they were saying: "It was terrible down there. The men fought with the women. Children and old people were crushed and trampled on the stairways. There was no order at all. Oil and water was up to their shoulders. Some of those who got shoved down didn't come up. It was everyone for himself. Some of them had no life jackets and others had three. They pulled them off each others' backs."[51]

Madge Young saw people tearing down curtains in the public rooms "to use as blankets for the children, whose clothes were all a sopping wet, oily mess."[52] Santino Porporino was one of the grateful recipients. He had rushed out of his cabin wearing only his boxer shorts, desperate to reach his pregnant wife, Antonietta, and their two young children, Giuseppe and Bruna.[53] There was "complete panic," he later said, "with people crying, screaming, shoving, and pulling hair to get on deck."[54] By the time he finally got his family to the Upper Deck, Santino had lost his voice. A *Doria* crew member saw him standing on deck, clad only in his underwear, and quickly retrieved a set of beige-and-plaid drapes from a First Class cabin, which Santino wrapped around his waist. Santino looked and looked but he could find no life jackets or life preservers anywhere on deck.[55] Peering out into the foggy night, he muttered to himself, "We're dead, we're dead, we're dead."[56]

Melania Ansuini remained with her father while Giovanni Vali ran off to round up her mother and two brothers. As he ran along the crowded corridors, he kept trying cabin doors until he found one that was unlocked; entering, he grabbed three life jackets and then continued on, finally meeting Giulia and Pasquale in the hallway. He quickly steered them up to be reunited with the rest of the family and joined them in waiting on the port side near the stern of the liner.[57] Nearby stood Tullio and Filomena Di Sandro, the former holding his four-year-old daughter, Norma, in his arms. Tullio had led them through "long corridors, tilted and full of people screaming with fright and pain," and awash with "heavy oil and water," until they finally reached the deck near the stern. Now, they stood in the fog, "praying and begging for help, while the ship became more and more inclined, until one struggled to stand up or sit down."[58]

Nicola DiFiore had lost his cousin in the ensuing chaos; when he reached the top deck, the list was so bad that he clung tightly to the railing to avoid falling.[59] Alda and Franco Raimengia found the deck "very slanted and very slippery. There were suitcases and trunks sliding and flying around from the piles of luggage that had already been placed for disembarkation in the morning."[60] Klaus Dorneich saw what happened to the unfortunates on the starboard side whose grips were not as secure, as people "slid across the slippery deck and crashed into the opposite railing. Shrieks of fear and cries for help were mixed with groans of the injured. The universal panic mounted from minute to minute. The people cried constantly for help, but the loudspeaker remained silent."[61]

Adalgisa Di Fabio, still clad in her nightgown and carrying her best dress and shoes, faced a precarious trip up the staircase. When she first saw how tilted it was—"almost on its side"—she hesitated, but "as I did, I smelled smoke and oil and finally decided I had to get out of there." She crawled up to the landing, stood, turned, and again clambered along on her knees, one hand holding on to her dress and shoes and the other clinging to the handrail to keep from tumbling back down. Once she finally reached the top, she pulled her dress on over her nightgown, put on her shoes, and made her way to the Tourist Class Lounge under the flicker of lights that dimmed and disappeared only to shine again a few seconds later.

The lounge looked very different than the room where Ada had been dancing just an hour before: "All of the furniture had slid across the floor and was piled up on one side," she recalls. At first the room seemed deserted, but then a voice cut through the creaking moans coming from within the ship: "Where's your life jacket?" She turned and saw Father

Thomas Kelly, who had frequently joined in celebrating mass on the ship. He quickly took off his own life jacket and tied it around Ada. "As he did that I kept thinking how stupid I had been not to have taken the life jackets from the cabinet in our cabin. But when you're sixteen you think you know it all, and I didn't stop to think."

The young priest led Ada out of the room: below, there had been confusion, those flickering lights, the unsettling list, and the waves of smoke filtering down corridors, but it wasn't until the young woman walked onto the deck that she felt the terror of the night. "Families were screaming and crying: a lot of the husbands on the ship were in different cabins than their wives and children, and people were shouting out names of missing relatives and slipping across decks moist from the fog and the water." She quickly found Nella and they made their ways to the stern, standing on the higher port side, "holding on to the railings, looking out into the fog. I spent four hours there, waiting to die."[62]

Nine-year-old Pat Mastrincola was on his own perilous adventure. After pushing his way through the legs of passengers crowding the exit from the Tourist Class Dining Room, he set off to his family's cabin to rescue his sister, Arlene. He raced down the listing staircase to A Deck, fighting against the crowd of people pushing upward to reach the decks above: "They were banged up or covered in oil," he recalls. "There was a lot of panic inside the ship: it wasn't like *Titanic*, where people had hours to wonder what was going to happen. You knew from the list of the ship that you were in trouble." The terrified passengers pushed him aside and knocked him down, but Pat always managed to scramble back up and keep going.

"Thick, white smoke" filled the corridor leading to their cabin, making it impossible to see clearly. The smoke was so dense that Pat got lost; finally he spotted a box on the wall with a red cross and a glass case with a fire hose—familiar landmarks that told him to turn right. "It was difficult walking—the floor didn't look right and the ceiling didn't look right, being tilted." When he finally flung open the cabin door, he was surprised to see Arlene, calmly asleep on the floor after the list sent her rolling out of her upper berth—"how she slept through that I don't know," Pat says. He grabbed her and shook her awake, shouting, "Arlene, get up! The ship is sinking!"[63]

"Maybe because I slept through it," Arlene muses, "the collision wasn't as traumatic for me as for others." But Pat's words, and the terrified look on his face, unsettled the drowsy young girl.[64] She started to scream and ran for the cabin door; behind her, Pat struggled to retrieve life jackets from the cabinet before finally joining Arlene in the hall. As they rushed down the corridor, Pat recalls passing an open cabin door: inside, three Italian women sat on their beds, praying. Dragging them by their arms into the passageway, he shouted, "Come on! Let's go! We've got to get up to the top."[65]

Clad only in her underwear, Arlene hadn't stopped with her brother: suddenly aware that she was alone, she quit running and waited at the bottom of the staircase. Soon her mother appeared, fighting her way down the listing staircase, and in a moment Pat had reached them. Arlene thought her mother was in shock, and again it was nine-year-old Pat who took charge of the situation, pushing and urging them back up to the decks above.[66] They finally reached the Tourist Class Lido area near the stern and found an area just in front of the port fantail where they could brace themselves on a bench. Here, as Pat remembers, "we waited and waited along with everyone else. No lifeboats were being lowered from our side, and we couldn't see what was happening on the other side of the ship, so we didn't know that people were leaving. But there wasn't anywhere else to go."[67]

Sitting in the swirling fog, Arlene remembers thinking, "Where are the people who are supposed to save us?" Even so, she wasn't worried. "Children were more innocent and naïve back them," she says. "I remembered all of the positive stories and television shows and they always had a happy ending, so I never expected not to be saved."[68] Pat was a little more realistic, though even in the uncertain situation he discovered a moment of levity. "At one point," he remembers, "the same crew member who had hit me on the head in the lounge a few days earlier came out on deck, sprinkling bags of flour or sugar to cover the oil so that people could stand. But he slipped, and slid across the deck. He hit the raised side of the swimming pool, bounced off it, then careened over into a pile of deck chairs and fell through them before hitting the railing with a thunk." Though bloody, the man wasn't seriously injured, and the impish Pat said to himself, "You got yours, mister!"[69]

Physician Bruno Tortori-Donati and his assistant, Dr. Lorenzo Giannini, had rushed to the *Doria*'s infirmary on A Deck in the wake of the collision. "It is nothing, nothing," Tortori-Donati had tried to assure the two passengers under his care, "nothing, a little explosion in the engine room." Tortori-Donati was on his way to the bridge when he heard the announcement summoning passengers to their muster stations; he quickly returned to the hospital, knowing that he and Giannini had to evacuate sixty-five-year-old Mary Onder, who had a fractured left thigh, and seventy-one-year-old Rosa Carola, suffering from terminal cancer and a weak heart. Joseph Onder had rushed to the infirmary to be with his wife, and he now helped two nurses place Mary on a stretcher and carry her through the ship, up three listing staircases, and out onto the Promenade Deck. Safely moving the fragile Carola proved more difficult. Tortori-Donati and nurse Antonia Coretti placed the sedated Carola on a stretcher and began the arduous journey toward the Promenade Deck, but she began gasping for breath and went into cardiac arrest during the move. They set her down, and the doctor used a syringe to inject digitalis into her heart before administering another dose of morphine and using a needle to withdraw some fluid around her heart. When she had stabilized they resumed their journey, but while maneuvering up the staircase Carola again gasped and her heart stopped a second time. Tortori-Donati gave her another injection of digitalis and waited for her to rally before continuing the ascent. It took them an hour to safely bring her up to the Promenade Deck.[70]

Paul and Margaret Sergio had tried to rush from their portside cabin on C Deck to the starboard room occupied by her sister, Maria, and her four young children. "My sister, my sister!" Margaret sobbed. But a steward blocked their way to the starboard corridor. "There's no way you can get in there," he warned. "They'll be all right. They'll go up another stairway toward the front of the ship." Margaret stood rooted to the spot, at least until the rising water began lapping at her feet.[71] Finally Paul led her to the staircase: after spilling over the starboard tops of the bulkheads, water mixed with machine oil had already begun cascading down the staircase to flood the *Doria*'s lowest passenger deck. It took the Sergios an exhausting ninety minutes to climb the five flights of stairs needed to reach the Promenade Deck.[72]

But on deck there was no sign of Maria or her children. Paul tried to reach their cabin once more: by the time he got to C Deck, the entire starboard corridor was flooded. He knew that his sister-in-law and her children must be dead, drowned in their cabin, which had been almost in direct line of *Stockholm*'s lethal bow. Returning to Margaret, Paul couldn't tell her the truth: instead, he said that a sailor "told me that passengers from Maria's section were safe."[73]

Chapter Eleven

Unaware of what was happening, most of *Doria*'s passengers clustered on her port side, waiting for any news or instruction. Philip Trachtenberg saw several fellow passengers attempting to free one of the port lifeboats and joined them. "We struggled with the ropes and the blocks," he said. "We couldn't budge it."[1]

At first—at least for many of the First Class passengers—there was only a vague sense of unease mingled with curiosity. Madge Young wasn't at all afraid: "I had no idea that anything was serious; my father did, but he wasn't communicating that to us to keep us calm. I was most interested in trying to find my friends, but my parents kept pulling me back."[2] Her brother, David, was initially upset but, she recalled, he "quieted down with the idea that he might be going the rest of the way to New York on a destroyer or a helicopter."[3] Ann Dilworth remembered sitting in the dark, "shivering in the cloak of fog, holding on desperately to the rails . . . There was a deathly quiet, as if the ship already were gone, and all of us with it."[4]

"Mom and Dad were really good about not being panicky," recalls Bambi Gifford.[5] Priscilla Gifford tried to divert her youngest children's attention from the chaos on deck: "She had us talk about our favorite country," Bambi recalls, "our favorite hotel, our favorite meal, our favorite city. It worked for a while as we tried to state why we liked what we liked best. I, of course, picked Venice, as it was so magical."[6] But then Bambi remembered the dogs in the kennel aboard the ship and asked her mother what would happen to them; after Priscilla assured her that someone would rescue them, the young girl finally settled into a fitful sleep.[7] In fact, in the panic of that night, and consumed with rescuing passengers, it seems that the crew forgot about the unfortunate dogs and that they went down with the ship.

Barbara Boggs admitted that the collision "terrified me, and I'll guarantee you it terrified everyone else as much."[8] Her thoughts turned to the past: while some aboard the *Doria* had been enjoying *A Night to Remember,* Barbara had a more personal link to the *Titanic* tragedy. In April 1912, her mother, Evelyn, had been aboard RMS *Carpathia* when it sailed from New York. Early on the morning of April 15, Evelyn had been stunned to learn that her cousins were suddenly also aboard the vessel. They were among the passengers who had survived the sinking of *Titanic* a few hours earlier and who had been rescued by *Carpathia.* Now, she could only pray that fate would be as kind to her family gathered on the *Doria*'s sloping deck.

From time to time, Barbara "looked over the edge of the deck and couldn't conceive of jumping from where we were—it was about three stories high. We decided that my husband would hang on to Bobby and [her daughter] Barbara and I would hang on to each other if we had to go into the ocean. I was afraid the water would be cold—cold water takes my breath away. My mouth was so dry I could barely breathe already. . . . The strangest, most disconnected thoughts flash through your mind when you believe you are about to die and have considerable time to think about it. I thought of our two children at home, who were at camp, and the fact that they would be orphans. My husband and I never flew on the same plane, for the very reason that we didn't want them to be orphans, and now look, because we had decided to come home by boat, these two children were not only going to be orphans but were going to be minus one brother and sister as well. . . . I thought of so many things I had meant to do and cursed myself for not having done more of them. And there were so many things I wanted to do. Life had suddenly become infinitely precious and desirable."[9]

"I sat between Dun and my parents," Barbara Bliss recalled. "We watched as panic quickly began to spread all around us like an oil-slick fire, fueled by the rumor that the *Doria*'s lifeboats couldn't be launched because the ship was tipping so fast and at such a steep angle. . . . We sat on deck in the pitch black, with out knees drawn to our chins, heels braced against the severe angle. We would stay like this for what seemed hours."[10]

"After a while," recalled Dun Gifford, "you sensed that people were striving to control their fear because they stopped talking about what had happened or what might happen and began to find subjects to take their minds off our trouble. Barbara Bliss was at my left and mother at my right. Barbara and I tried singing. We sang 'With a Little Bit of Luck' from *My Fair Lady* and that got some response."[11] Madge Young remembers that it "was all great fun" when people started singing "It's a Long, Long Way to Tipperary."[12] Philip Trachtenberg heard the strains of "Home on the Range" and "My Old Kentucky Home" from somewhere on deck, while Mike Stoller, clustered against the Cabin Class Gymnasium on the port side of the Boat Deck, recalls launching in to "Shine on Harvest Moon" and other songs to help calm nerves.[13] Young Pat Mastrincola found it absurd: "I thought that they were all drunk," he remembers.[14]

Gradually the singing died out, and an uneasy quiet settled over the passengers gathered on the *Doria*'s decks. Other sounds replaced the hopeful songs: the tumble of furniture sliding across the polished floors; the clang of abandoned musical instruments cascading through the Belvedere Lounge; the crash of china and the shattering of glass; and dull thuds as accumulated luggage gradually slipped across the Promenade Deck. And, from somewhere within the ship, below them, passengers could hear "loud, creaking noises . . . a cacophony of mysterious sounds . . . brief ones, like thuds, bursts and slams, and longer ones that seemed to resound for several minutes," as Pierette Domenica Burzio recalls.[15]

As the minutes ticked by, the sense of unease and worry grew. Clarence Gifford went off with a small group of male passengers to see what they could learn. "I remember they came back and said things looked pretty grim," Dun Gifford recalled.[16] Clarence was worried about the list: "If the bottom swung out too far it might not have been possible for us to have jumped without hitting it. I thought that maybe we ought to prepare for jumping." With the smell of fuel oil in the air, Dun remembered fearing an explosion: people standing on deck would light cigarettes and just as quickly someone would angrily tell them to put them out. "The ship was listing more and more," he said. "I could tell because I watched the angle of the curtains in the lounge and it widened. The ship didn't settle over gradually. It did it in little tiny, perceptible lurches. And these caused fear."[17] "We all thought we were going to die." he later said.[18]

Betsy Drake recalled, "For two hours I clung to the post on the high side of the ship." As she waited, she began praying and "suddenly I felt quite good."[19] But for most passengers the waiting became an ordeal, with many reflecting on what they were sure was impending death. "I think everyone grew resigned to his fate," said Philip Trachtenberg. "I know I was. If help did come it would never find us in this fog. It was just a matter of time . . . The minutes dragged on. The agony lay in the waiting, the silence, the mystery of what lurked behind the fog, the fear of the dark and the swirling waters below. I wondered what the end would be like. How it would feel when the water closed around me? Would it be slow? Should I just close my eyes and leap in the water? Would I relax—or would I clench my teeth and hold my breath and fight until the very end?"[20]

Adalgisa Di Fabio remembers: "I spent hours at a railing on the port side near the stern, waiting to die. I wasn't thinking about myself. I had no regrets about going to America. The thing that worried me was thinking about my mother and father and my *nonna*. I might drown, but I was more concerned about their suffering if I did. I don't remember ever crying: the life jacket gave me a sense of peace. I was there, accepting what was happening to me. I wonder what it feels like to drown? I asked myself as I waited. People kept slipping across the decks: they were moist from the fog and the water."[21]

Mike and Meryl Stoller remained near the Cabin Class Gymnasium on the Boat Deck with some twenty other passengers; their views were restricted and no one had any idea what was taking place in other parts of the ship.[22] "Occasionally we would look up at the lifeboats just dangling there, useless because of the heavy list," Mike recalls. "Someone in our group tried to reassure us by saying, 'Maybe they can pump the water out and right the ship.' As if in response a young fellow in our group who was an engineer sadly shook his head. I said to myself, This is it. We remained on the boat deck, even though our muster station was on the promenade deck; at least we were near lifeboats (should they become operable) and on the outside of the ship."[23]

As Barbara Bliss sat on the darkened deck, Dun Gifford "leaned over and kissed me tenderly on the cheek" and ominously wished her luck.

"What do you mean?" she asked. "They're going to pull another ship alongside and we'll walk across a gangplank to the other ship."

"That's not going to be possible," Dun warned, "because of the list."[24]

Sebastiano Natta, *Andrea Doria*'s chaplain, had made his way down to the Foyer Deck following the collision, intent on reaching the Chapel, which sat amidships. The starboard passage was blocked; he finally went to the port side and made his way in to the Chapel, taking the silver ciborium containing the consecrated Holy Eucharist from the altar before returning to the Boat Deck. Here, he began breaking the wafers into small pieces in an effort to make them last, administering communion to those Catholic passengers who stopped him.[25]

Natta refused to give any general absolution, as he wasn't convinced the danger was imminent enough to discard church rules.[26] The American priests traveling aboard the *Doria*, though, had no such hesitations. "Anyone who wants to should quietly make an act of contrition," Father Thomas Kelly called out, "then I will give you absolution."[27] Soon fellow priests Paul Lambert, Richard Wojcik, John Dolciamore, and Raymond Goedert followed suit, crawling across the decks, hearing confessions, holding hands, and leading passengers in the Rosary. "You simply be a priest," Wojcik recalled. "You think of others and take care of their needs."[28] "The people appeared to have been strengthened by the Rosary and the confessions," said Dolciamore. "There seemed to be less crying than before."[29] Wojcik remembered how "everyone talked in low tones; a heavy quiet hung in the air."[30]

Watching these scenes, Dun Gifford was "amazed at how this helped the distress of the people who received it. Those who received it, if they had been crying, stopped crying. All of them seemed strengthened. But to us non-Catholics it seemed to lower our morale a little in some way."[31] Peter Thieriot had led a small group in saying the Rosary. At the end, he retreated to an isolated bench only to see that someone, rather than risk going below to use the facilities, had defecated on it.[32]

Finally Natta administered Communion to everyone he could reach. Lambert watched him at the railing as he hurled the silver ciborium and the last remaining wafers into the sea: having been consecrated, they could not be left on a sinking ship.[33] Seeing this, Goedert suddenly began to lose hope. Later he said: "I think we kid ourselves as priests. We talk of the joy and happiness of Heaven. I was faced with the prospect and found that I was not all that happy to go. I was willing to wait."[34]

Some ninety minutes after the collision, the first of the vessels responding to the *Doria*'s SOS finally arrived at the scene. This was the four-hundred-foot-long freighter *Cape Ann*. Joseph Boyd, her captain, had raced through the night; he ordered the crew to prepare her two lifeboats, each capable of holding forty people, for lowering and set stations to treat any wounded.[35] The single-funneled freighter slowed as she neared the scene: the fog was so thick that, although Boyd could see the faint lights of both the *Doria* and the *Stockholm* shimmering in the distance, he couldn't tell which ship was which. He telegraphed *Stockholm*, and adjusted his approach, stopping his engines when *Cape Ann* was still some distance from the stricken *Doria*: in this fog he didn't dare go closer and risk hitting any lifeboats or stray passengers. It took some time to safely maneuver *Cape Ann* into place: at 1:05 she finally lowered her two lifeboats.[36] As he waited on the bridge, and despite the distance between his ship and the stricken liner, Boyd could hear distant screams and cries for help through the fog.[37]

The list aboard *Andrea Doria* had grown to 27 degrees.[38] With no way to successfully launch the portside lifeboats, Calamai told Third Officer Eugenio Giannini, "Go get the passengers on the port side and bring them to the lifeboats on the starboard side. Go by way of the stern."[39] Giannini set off, but it would take him an hour to traverse the length of the starboard side to the stern and make his way to the port side of the dangerously listing vessel. Most passengers had gone to the higher port side of the liner; some remained on starboard despite members of the crew directing them to port. They now saw the crew's unsettling efforts to launch the eight starboard lifeboats. The starboard boats all bore odd numbers. No. 1 could hold fifty-eight passengers, while No. 3 had a motor and could carry seventy. Both jammed in their davits and had to be pushed free even as other starboard boats were lowered into the water.[40]

What happened next soon became a point of embarrassment and lingering controversy. Evacuating the *Doria*'s passengers according to the usual procedure would, even under ideal conditions, be a precarious operation; now Captain Calamai had to wrestle with a set of potentially deadly complications. Even for the young and fit, descending by ropes or by netting strung from the starboard side over the railing to the boats below was precarious; for the elderly or infirm, it was a nightmare. Anticipating a host of problems, Captain Calamai—after consulting with Staff Captain Magagnini—decided that all of the starboard boats should be lowered with five extra crew members aboard, so that adequate manpower would be ready to render assistance. This was the plan, but it soon went awry. The vast majority of the liner's crew were service personnel: waiters, cooks, stewards, and kitchen boys. While the officers and sailors remained to help passengers, many members of the service personnel panicked: some jumped into the ocean and waited to be picked up by the lifeboats as they entered the water; others crowded past passengers and pushed their ways into the precious spaces. And, inevitably, some sailors beyond the numbers Calamai had specified also took seats in their desperation to abandon ship.[41]

In this case it was easy to differentiate between passengers and crew. Passengers wore brightly colored, sleeveless padded orange life jackets stamped with ITALIA, while the jackets for the crew, most of who wore their uniforms, were gray. At twelve forty-five that Thursday morning, the first three lifeboats from the *Doria* arrived at the *Stockholm*. "We saw them quite clearly from *Stockholm*'s bridge," Carstens recalled, "but to help them maneuver we aimed a spotlight toward the boats. The A deck's opening, which was located on the port side, lay only a couple of meters above water level. There it would be fastest and easiest to help the passengers in the lifeboats aboard. Our people who stood there waiting to help them onto *Stockholm* were amazed to see that the big lifeboats . . . were only half full and most of the occupants were men wearing the gray jackets of the ship's crew. *Stockholm*'s crewmen were furious. Such conduct ran in the face of good seamanship, even if these were not sailors in the ordinary sense but service personnel."[42]

These three boats could carry among them a total of 146 passengers. Most now held less than half that number.[43] The first boat held forty *Doria* crew members and only four passengers even though half the seats were empty.[44] More crew members sat in the second lifeboat; only the third boat contained an apparently equal mixture of crew and passengers.[45] Over the next few hours, *Stockholm* would take on 234 members of the *Doria*'s crew and 311 passengers.[46]

Officers on the *Doria* slowly began preparing for the evacuation of the ship's passengers. Ropes and fire hoses were secured and hurled over the starboard side, down which the passengers could descend to lifeboats waiting in the water. Aware that this would be a time-consuming process, Third Officer Giannini hit on another strategy. He directed sailors to remove the nets covering the swimming pools and hang them over the starboard side: these, along with some cargo nets, thus formed makeshift Jacob's ladders, providing footing and handholds and making the descent easier.[47]

Shortly after one that morning, as Philip Trachtenberg recalled, "the fog had vanished. The stars blinked down from a clear, cloudless sky. A full moon turned the night into day."[48] The fog lifted just as the US Navy transport *Private William H. Thomas* arrived at the scene. "A thing like that would happen once in a lifetime," commented her captain, John Shea. "If the fog hadn't lifted when it did it would have been bad." With visibility at the scene now increased to several miles, Shea maneuvered the *Thomas* as close to the stricken *Doria* as he dared and ordered his two motorized lifeboats into the water to rescue passengers.[49]

On the *Doria*, Jock Gifford was watching the clock in the First Class Lounge; at half past one, he recalled, "word passed from person to person that boats were being loaded on the other side and that women and children were wanted first."[50] "There is no reason to be scared or frightened because now there are plenty of boats," Giannini told a group on the port side of the Promenade Deck. "You must keep quiet and calm. Everyone will be rescued."[51] Some were skeptical: "I had to convince them, explaining in Italian and English, that there were truly lifeboats on the starboard side," Giannini said.[52] The bartender in the Cabin Class Lounge gave a similar message to a group of passengers: "There are boats coming to our rescue. If you will just be quiet and come in an orderly manner I will lead you out."[53]

This was easier said than done. The list made getting from port to starboard a difficult maneuver: often passengers had to descend tilting staircases, cross rooms, and then climb back up on the starboard side: in some places ropes were stretched across decks and rooms to provide extra support while, in others, people went hand-in-hand, attempting to keep each other from slipping.[54] A grim, determined silence fell over the ship as people began to traverse the liner: moisture from the fog and hundreds of bare feet dripping water and machine oil had left decks and floors slick. The previous afternoon, stewards had filled the starboard side of the Promenade and Boat Decks with baggage from passengers' cabins, in anticipation of arrival and unloading in New York Thursday morning: now, it had all slid across the teak decks, jamming against the railings in unstable mountains that had to be scaled or circled to reach the railing.

Bambi Gifford remembers crossing the liner from port to starboard as "very frightening."[55] "People were sliding. Some people fell in. . . . You had to hold on to people to make your way across the deck."[56] The Giffords had to go along the edge of the deck to the First Class Lounge, cross the room to reach the Grand Staircase, and make their ways up to the Boat Deck. "We all grabbed something firm and we sort of handed the women and children along, one by one," Clarence Gifford recalled. "That's where a lot of people got hurt," Priscilla Gifford said. "They couldn't hold on to the rail in the lounge, and they tumbled right across the width of the lounge. I had Bambi in one hand with my handbag and held on with the other. But I didn't have enough strength and I went sprawling. Except for some bruises, though, we were all right." When she finally reached the starboard side, Priscilla tossed her purse aside so that she could get a better grip on her daughter. "Oh, Mother!" Bambi objected. "Your pocketbook and your money!" Jock reached out and retrieved it for her.[57]

A steward told Barbara Boggs and her children to follow him to the other side of the liner. Young Bobby at first refused to leave his father, until Boggs told him, "You must take care of your mother and your sister."[58] The trip from the *Doria*'s port to her starboard side was a grueling trek: "We had to crawl up the sloping deck and slide along a corridor," recalled Mrs. Boggs. "It was frightfully slippery, and many people fell and suffered broken bones."[59] "My mother, brother, and I," remembered Barbara Bliss, "with the guidance of our cabin steward, slipped and slid our way up the oil-slicked stairs and down a passageway to our destination. We had to sit down and slide, just as if we were on a slide in a kindergarten playground. The surface was cold and chafed our bare skin where our dresses rode up. I remember wetting my pants."[60] When they finally reached the starboard railing, Barbara Boggs said, "there was our waiter from the Dining Saloon. He gave us our first word of cheer I had heard, telling us that there was a ship standing by."[61]

Philip Trachtenberg and his wife, Arline, "slowly made our way down and across the beam of the boat, slipping, sliding, banging into things." The starboard deck "was like hitting the giant slide at Coney Island . . . Oil slick and vomit were everywhere. It was impossible to stand up without holding onto the rail or one of the cables."[62]

Richardson and Ann Dilworth made their ways from port to starboard via the stern, crawling on their hands and knees because it was impossible to stand. It took them some ninety minutes to cross the Promenade Deck. At one point, Dilworth tried to help his wife but "instead I did her harm." As she began to slide on the deck, he reached out for her shoulder but instead caught her foot: Ann spun around and slid away from him, crashing down and through a glass door. Richardson slid down after her: Ann had suffered a gash on her head, bruises, and had a black right eye but remarkably was otherwise unharmed.[63]

"They stretched some ropes across the deck so we could get to the starboard side," says Pat Mastrincola. "We had to hang on them, go down a flight of tilted stairs, then grab another rope stretched across the inside of the ship. At the end of that, we had another climb back up to the deck before we finally reached the starboard railing."[64] His sister, Arlene, remembers how her mother stood in front of her, arms outstretched to form a protective cradle and prevent her falling over the side.[65]

By now the list on the *Doria* had grown to 33 degrees.[66] "The small bell over the outdoor swimming pool," says Klaus Dorneich, "hung so slanting that I realized the dangerous list of the ship."[67] Across the waves, Captain Nordenson had finally decided to send his own lifeboats to the *Doria*. He took to the ship's public announcement system: "This is the captain speaking. As I have said before we have collided with another ship. Now we are going to launch our lifeboats. But they are not for us. They are to pick up survivors from the other ship. There is no danger on the *Stockholm*."[68] Nordenson sent all three of his motorized boats: No. 7, the first to leave, was under the command of Second Officer Lars Enestrom; Junior Second Officer Sven Abenius took charge of No. 8, while Carstens received the captain's permission to take out No. 1. Each boat carried a few sailors to assist in the rescue.[69] Carstens thought it was about half past one when he finally left *Stockholm*.[70]

Some two miles of ocean now separated the *Doria* from the *Stockholm*.[71] Carstens estimated that the trip to the Italian liner took some thirty minutes. "The weather was very good," he later said. "As almost always on the North Atlantic, there were swells but these were gentle swells that would not disturb the rescue work." As he went, he saw that "the ocean around us was littered with diverse objects that had fallen out of the big hole on the starboard side close to the bridge after the collision."[72]

Enestrom was the first to reach the *Doria*. He maneuvered Boat No. 7 around the stern, where he saw ropes and netting hanging over the starboard side. As soon as his boat was spotted, the ropes were alive with frantic figures desperate to leave the sinking ship. The first down was a man dressed in the white jacket of one of the *Doria*'s stewards; he climbed into the boat without a word.[73] *Stockholm* crew member William Johnson, manning one of the Swedish liner's boats, vividly recalled the scene as he came alongside the *Doria*: "We saw crew members from that ship (no doubt as inexperienced as I was) fighting with passengers for places in the lifeboats."[74] Next came more men wearing the gray life jackets of the *Doria's* crew. Seeing this, one of the *Doria's* officers standing on the deck above shouted, "Women and children first!" Soon, a steady stream of passengers began descending down the ropes and nets; a few, unwilling to wait, panicked and jumped. Enestrom watched as one woman hurled herself over the railing above and plunged down into the sea; he tried to reach her, but the current carried her away as she screamed for help.[75] Others rushed the ropes and netting, fighting with their fellow passengers and kicking them off into the water below.[76] Panicked parents began tossing their children over the liner's side: Enestrom and his small crew picked them out of the water, then grabbed blankets and stretched them taut, trying to catch the boys and girls as they came over the side of the looming vessel.[77]

The list of the *Doria* was so severe that to the *Stockholm's* men it seemed as if she might capsize any minute. By this time the port propeller had risen out of the water and was clearly visible as the lifeboats swung around the liner. From the boats below, the scene above was horrific: hundreds of people pressed against the railings, screaming and shouting for help. More and more jumped into the black sea, risking injury as they hurtled into a surface awash with dangerous debris; the Swedish sailors managed to pull most in, their bodies weighted down by waterlogged clothing, which was often covered in greasy machine oil.[78]

Carstens remembered "the terrible sounds that could be heard from afar in clamorous contrast to the stillness of the sea. There were cries and lamentations and prayers and from the officers' attempts to use loud commands to impose some kind of order on the prevailing confusion. We also heard the often recurring splashes as people leaped into the water for fear that *Andrea Doria* would suddenly capsize and pull everyone with her down into the deep." He maneuvered his boat around the stern and past the port propeller; just then a swell pushed it against the hull, breaking the rudder. Several of the passengers taken aboard, Carstens saw, "were covered with blood and smeared with oil." When his boat was full, he turned about for the return journey back to *Stockholm*, using an oar to steer in place of the damaged rudder.[79]

Santino Porporino got his pregnant wife, Antonietta, and his two young children to the starboard side of the Boat Deck; as they waited, he stepped away to search for life jackets. When he turned around, his family was gone. Members of the crew had tied ropes around young Joe and Bruna and lowered them down to one of *Stockholm*'s boats; when it came time for Antonietta to go, the sailors had to retie the rope beneath her arms to avoid putting pressure on her stomach. Santino ran to the railing: "I saw that they were in the boat already."[80]

Ruth Roman finally abandoned her place at the top of the Grand Staircase: "The boat was listing so badly that I had to take my son on my lap and slide down the side of the deck to the lifeboats," she said.[81] Nicola DiFiore helped Ruth and her son get to the railing, where she handed Dickie to Giuliano Pirelli, a twenty-three-year-old officer cadet aboard the *Doria;* Pirelli tied the boy to his back before descending down a rope ladder to *Stockholm*'s Boat No. 3.[82] Roman followed over the railing; she was halfway down the ladder when the lifeboat pulled away from the side of the ship. "As I stood there," she recalled, "Dickie still held his balloon in one hand and waved to me with the other. 'Picnic!' he called. 'Picnic!'" Despite her screams to stop, the lifeboat continued to move away from the *Doria;* Roman finally climbed back up the ladder to the deck.[83]

Giovanni Vali ushered Melania Ansuini and her family to the starboard side—"it took forever to cross down to the lower side," Melania recalls, "because it was foggy and wet and slippery. There were suitcases and furniture in the way that moved and slid around, and we also had to get by all the other people. It was noisy and everyone was yelling and screaming."[84] As she clung to the railing, Melania heard someone shout, "Save yourselves, those who can!"[85]

They saw a boat approach—it was Sven Abenius, who maneuvered Boat No. 8 from *Stockholm* toward the *Doria*. He watched as a middle-aged woman, Julia Greco, attempted to navigate her way down one of the ropes; she lost her grip and fell with a loud thud into the bottom of the boat. She had broken her back in the fall.[86]

A few minutes later Abenius witnessed another tragedy. Tullio and Filomena Di Sandro had gathered at the starboard railing. "I looked over the rail and saw a lifeboat in the water," Tullio later said, "about fifteen feet below."[87] It has always been said that Tullio called out to the boat below that he was going to toss his daughter, Norma, over the side so that the sailors could catch her in their outstretched blankets. The Swedish crew, supposedly, did not understand his Italian, did nothing, and let Norma fall.[88] In fact, Melania Ansuini saw Giovanni Vali help Tullio, with Norma clinging sleepily to his back, over the edge: "When Tullio was lowering himself," she says, someone nearby also leaped over the side, "bumping into the child."[89] Norma plunged into the night, striking her head on the side of the boat with a sickening thud before careening unconscious into the bottom of No. 8; she would later succumb to her injuries.

Chapter Twelve

———— ◆•◆ ————

After arriving on the scene at 1:23 Thursday morning, the United States Naval Ship *Private William H. Thomas* had put her two motorized lifeboats into the water and, together with *Cape Ann* and *Stockholm,* joined the process of picking up passengers from the stricken *Doria* and ferrying them back across the water to safety. "Many," recalled *Thomas* crew member Ernie Melby, "were hysterical, others knelt down on our deck and prayed. Many kissed the deck in their joy of having been rescued." He particularly noted a young woman as she came aboard his ship: "She was very beautiful and wearing a stunning pure white evening gown. At first glance it looked like she was perfectly dressed for a lavish party, and the gown looked perfectly clean. Then the bottom of her gown caught my eye. It was stained with fuel and wet up to her knees."[1]

The efforts came as water continued to wash through the *Doria*'s engine room. As it crept along the lower decks, it began shorting the circuits, rendering the pumps useless; with the air-conditioning turned off to save power, the engine room was like a steam bath. There was no hope: at 2:00 A.M., with the encroaching water perilously near the three diesel and two turbine generators, the chief engineer shut them down. The *Doria* lost her power and was suddenly plunged into darkness. Engineers shifted the circuits to the emergency, battery-powered generator on A Deck; this could only supply the emergency lights and the lifeboat davits.[2]

The emergency lights shone ghostly amber halos across the liner. Just as it seemed the end was near, though, the *Ile de France* arrived. When the *Ile* was eight miles from *Doria*'s radioed position, Beaudéan slowed his engines and began drifting toward the scene. With most of the fog now lifted, the sky above was full of stars and the moon shone silver on the water. His searchlights caught an eerie tableau: the stricken *Doria*, listing heavily to starboard, surrounded at a distance by the pallid hull of *Stockholm* and the brightly lit *Cape Ann* and *Thomas*.[3] "Despite the danger," Beaudéan recalled, he ordered the *Ile*'s engines stopped and allowed his ship to drift to within a mile of the wounded *Doria*.[4]

It was 2:00 A.M. as the *Ile de France* came to a stop. "Light up our name!" Beaudéan ordered, "the funnels, the decks! Light up everything, quickly!"[5] In an instant the *Ile de France*'s public rooms and decks were illuminated; her searchlights swept across the water; floodlights washed her orange and black funnels; and the gaudy letters spelling out her name in electric lights between the two funnels glowed against the night.[6]

This was a moment of high drama. "Probably about an hour after we arrived on the scene," remembered Ernie Melby aboard the *Thomas*, "I spotted a huge dark shadow approaching, almost entirely unlit. A lone white light was visible on the mast, and a red running light glowed faintly on the port side. It quickly came between our ship and the *Andrea Doria* and we could feel the vibrations as the huge ship backed down full astern and came to a stop. Then, every light on that ship must have been turned on. Huge lighted letters spelled out *Ile de France* and even the sea around it was lit up. This was truly a theatrical production on a grand scale in what was a life and death drama."[7]

"God, what a sight that was!" Barbara Boggs recalled of the *Ile de France*'s appearance.[8] Her son, Bobby, vividly remembers seeing "this gorgeous ship suddenly come up, with all of her wonderful lights lit."[9] "It looks like a Hollywood movie set," Father Wojcik said of this sudden burst of light.[10] Bambi Gifford thought the glowing letters spelling out the French liner's name "almost looked like an amusement park sign."[11] For Raymond Goedert, the brightly illuminated ship "came out of the darkness, like salvation. It was a beautiful sight."[12] "Everyone cheered and cried," remembers Pat Mastrincola.[13] It was, said Philip Trachtenberg, "the most encouraging sight" of the night: "She stood out there on the murky waters as a solid symbol of everything we wanted: life, warmth and security."[14]

The French liner's loading door on the port side of C Deck, some fifteen feet above the waterline, was opened, and rope ladders and harnesses were draped over the hull; above, ten of *Ile de France*'s lifeboats as well as a motorized tender—each capable of holding ninety passengers—were soon in the water.[15] Standing on the bridge wing, Beaudéan could distinctly hear "a confused clamor, a mixture of anguished wails and indistinct cries for help" coming from across the water. "The last poignant drama of all these people in the grip of panic and fear, wildly searching the darkness for a ray of hope, raises a lump in our throat." An anxious Beaudéan watched as his flotilla of lifeboats slowly left the *Ile* and headed toward the *Doria*. "If the wreck capsizes," he thought, it "will crush them under its enormous weight, dragging rescuers and rescued to their deaths."[16]

After the sickening scene of Norma Di Sandro landing against the side of a lifeboat, her father immediately dove into the water. But the boat drew away as his attention was temporarily diverted by a scream. Giovanni Vali had urged the Ansuinis to climb down into the lifeboat: the rope ended some twenty-five-feet above the water, and seeing that they would have to jump into the ocean, the Ansuinis hesitated. Vali decided to go first and show them that there was nothing to fear. Down he went with a splash, narrowly avoiding hitting the lifeboat whose crew pulled him from the water. Melania remained frozen at the railing.[17] "Come down!" Vali shouted at her.[18] She finally grabbed the rope and swung over the side but lost her grip and with a scream fell into the water so hard that the wind was knocked out of her.[19] "As I was about to drown," she says, "someone pulled me up by putting his arms under my back, carrying me to the lifeboat. It was Tullio who saved me, taking me to the boat with courage and the strength of despair."[20] "I could see her, real close, lying on her back almost all under water," Vali recalled. He leaned out and, together with Tullio, heaved her into a lifeboat, "almost like a sack of potatoes," Vali said. "When she came to, she was crying about her family. We didn't know they were safe until we all met again on the liner *Ile de France*."[21]

On the *Doria*'s starboard side, recalled Philip Trachtenberg, "Women and children were being herded to one of two Jacob's ladders that were over the side, but they couldn't be used. Most of the men were doing their best to help. But others were jumping over the side or sliding down ropes and nets. Ever so slowly the line to the ladder moved. The men had formed a human chain and along it we passed the women and children. The closer they came to the rail the more was their anguish and anxiety. Most of the women were past middle age. When they reached the rail and were told to climb onto the ladder they froze with horror. 'I can't do it, I can't do it!' they yelled. 'I'll be killed.' But even as they screeched they were lifted bodily over the side and pushed down the swaying ladder. It was the only thing to do."[22]

"We sort of handed the women and children along, one by one," said Clarence Gifford. "Some of the people surprised me the way they really pitched in on that job. There was one fellow I remember. I'll never try to judge people again from what they seem. He had annoyed me some days earlier, because he insisted on keeping his deck chair near where the children had their slide into the swimming pool. And he wouldn't move and the kids were afraid to ask him." But the man "did more work that night" in helping passengers "than anyone else."[23]

"All around us people were trying to get into the boats," said Dun Gifford. "People actually fell trying to get down. A woman's arm was broken. It was not a pretty sight, not orderly at all."[24] Klaus Dorneich joined forces with several fellow passengers at the stern to help in the rescue. Although ropes and netting had been put over the railing along most of the starboard side, there were only makeshift efforts at the stern. Dorneich's friend Gustav Schmidt "had an idea—we cut the ropes from the awnings which had been fastened to the railings as a shelter from rain and wind. One child after the other was bound up like a package and lowered; most of them lost their balance and were lowered head-first to the sailors below. The people applauded—none of the little ones were harmed." The two passengers flung a few ropes over the stern and helped women down them toward the water but then they spotted an elderly and heavy blind man: they tied ropes around him and "with great care we lifted him over the railing. Halfway to safety the cord broke—and he crashed into the boat below where he lay bleeding."[25]

Arline Trachtenberg's turn came when a lifeboat from the *Cape Ann* pulled up alongside the *Doria*'s starboard side. "I won't go without my husband!" she shouted as she was pushed toward the railing. "You'll go now, or you won't go at all!" a crew member answered, grabbing her and pushing her over the side to the ropes and down to the safety of the waiting lifeboat. "I was happy that she had made it," Philip Trachtenberg said, "but I was wondering if I would ever see her again. I didn't think any of us men who formed the human chain would make it. The *Doria* was sinking too fast."[26] Nora Kovach used her agility as a ballerina to easily maneuver down a rope to a waiting lifeboat; she would later reunite with Istvan aboard the *Ile de France*.[27]

Although boats from the *Cape Ann,* the *Thomas,* and *Stockholm* continued to collect and ferry passengers across the water to safety, it was the *Ile de France* that took the greatest number of *Andrea Doria* survivors. Someone told Betsy Drake that passengers were being taken off on the starboard side: barefoot, she slipped and slid as she made her way from port to starboard, only to find that she was one deck too high. She finally managed to get to a spot where a lifeboat was taking passengers descending a rope ladder. "How I got down there I'll never know," she said. "There are portions of the night that I can't remember." Drake settled into one of the *Ile de France*'s lifeboats and looked back as it pulled away. "It was an unbelievable sight," she recalled. "It was [a] balmy night. I looked at the big ship, lying at a crazy angle with the searchlights playing. I could scarcely believe it."[28] After being separated from her young son, Ruth Roman had climbed back up the rope and waited on the *Doria*'s sloping deck until a lifeboat from the French liner pulled up. Roman again descended, followed by Dickie's nurse, Grace Els, and by her fellow actress Janet Stewart.[29]

Clarence Gifford ushered his wife and children to the railing just as Roman disappeared over the side. "I don't think it really hit me until then," Bambi remembers. Getting down the rope ladder, she says, "was easy for me: I was a little monkey then, but it was harder for some of the older people. It was very oily and dirty, and oil got all over us." Dun held back: "I wanted to stay with the men," he said. "It was women and children first, but I considered myself a man." But his father insisted with these ominous words, "You're going. You're the man of the family now."[30]

"The ship was heeling well over," Dun recalled, "and the ladder was swinging back and forth. The smokestack and masts were way over your head. I remember thinking, This is the moment the sucker is going to roll. We're going to go down in that big whirlpool." Jock was surprised to find that the lifeboat "was already half-full of crew members."[31] Clarence Gifford, Bambi recalled, stood at the railing above, waving at his family as the lifeboat pulled away. "Mother, I know, was distraught but very stoic." Bambi found herself sitting on her brother Jock's lap, next to Ruth Roman, "who was crying and carrying on" about being separated from her son.[32] "I was more scared on the lifeboat," Priscilla Gifford said, "than at any other time. I knew the boat was overloaded, and on top of that the ship leaned over us at an alarming angle. I kept feeling that it would roll over us at any moment. By this time I knew what had happened because people in the lifeboat pointed out the hole in the *Doria*'s side. We were loading right beside it. It was a terrible looking sight."[33]

Andrew Stevens was standing on deck with his parents when a group of fellow passengers asked him to help rescue an elderly woman on the port side. Too terrified to move, she resisted all calls to cross to starboard and enter a lifeboat. Stevens and the other men convinced her to leave, and led her across the ship and up two flights of stairs so that she could leave the liner. "I helped her over the rail," he recalls, "where a crewman handed her into the waiting lifeboats." By the time he finished this task, though, Stevens found that his parents had disappeared: a steward told him that his mother had gotten into one of the lifeboats sent by the *Ile de France* and that his father had gone to the port side. Stevens set off to find him.[34]

Watching her fellow passengers evacuate the ship, Barbara Boggs hesitated for a moment: "They would panic halfway down a rope ladder and be unable to go either up or down. Some people were jumping into the water and swimming to the lifeboats. . . . I panicked, but inside myself only. I couldn't show it on account of the children, and I knew also that if one person let go there would be mass hysteria."[35] Sailors tied a rope around twelve-year-old Bobby and lowered him down to a lifeboat from the *Ile de France:* "My mother and I," Barbara Bliss remembered, "were expected to climb down the rope ladder. At the end of the rope there was still at least a ten foot drop to the water, under which the lifeboat rose and fell on huge swells. The French crew, standing upright in the rocking boat, urged me to jump into their waiting arms. That was the one moment, before letting go of the rope, that I felt real fear. But I had no choice. With people crowding down on top of me, I felt my fingers slip and I was suspended in space, hurtling to the waiting arms of the French crew below. Finally, in the safety of the lifeboat, I looked up at my mother, who was about to descend the ladder. I saw her take off her gold watch and let it drop in the water. She never understood why she did that."[36]

"They literally jammed the lifeboat full of people," Barbara said, "and it took close to an hour because of the difficulty in handling the elderly and children. Some of them cried and declared that they couldn't make it, but they did, with help. Some people jumped from the deck above. We picked up one man who had jumped from the bridge." Soon the overcrowded boat was on its way to the *Ile de France.*[37] "I was torn between pity for those in the water," Barbara recalled, "and self-preservation."[38]

Ann Dilworth reluctantly followed over the railing and descended to a lifeboat below. "She just looked at me as we parted," her husband said. "She didn't cry. She didn't say anything."[39] Robert Young kissed his wife and children goodbye as they prepared to leave the *Doria;* his daughter, Madge, thought it "felt funny. I didn't think there was any danger of anything happening." A rope ladder stretched from the rail some fifty feet down to a lifeboat; a pile of abandoned shoes lay on the deck nearby. "David went first," Madge recalls, "then Mummy and myself. At the top of the ladder, just before we climbed down, there was a pile of shoes on the deck that people had taken off because it was easier to go down barefoot."[40] "Descending the rope ladder, Madge says, "was the scariest moment of the night. I felt like turning around and going right back up. A crew member held one end, and the other end dangled below, where another person in the boat held on to it. The boat was riding up and down in the swells, so it didn't seem very stable."[41] The boat was full, "but as we looked up people kept coming over the side. The ship was listing so badly by now that it felt as though it would roll over on top of us any minute." Madge took a seat next to Ann Dilworth—her "head was bleeding through a bandage and her life jacket was soaked in blood," she recalled. "She looked so weak that I don't see how she climbed down the rope ladder." As people continued to climb over the railing, some of those in the lifeboat frantically called out, "Enough! Enough!" As the boat pulled away, Madge saw the hole in the Doria's hull.[42]

By the time the Mastrincolas reached the starboard side, the Doria's increasing list had reduced the distance between the railing and the lifeboats to some thirty-five feet. A sailor at the railing told Rosa and the other women that they should throw their purses over the side so that their hands were free during the descent; Rosa opened up her purse, took out a gold watch and put it on her wrist, and then reluctantly tossed her handbag containing her money and the family's passports, into the night.[43]

Pat watched as his mother shepherded Arlene toward the railing, but the young girl froze.[44] "I was terrified to slide down it," Arlene says. People behind her began yelling, "Go! Go! Go!"[45] Rosa thought that if she went down first and showed that it wasn't dangerous her daughter would quickly follow, but Arlene remained frozen in place. "People," Pat recalls, "were yelling, 'Throw her over the side!' Finally she went down. I was the last to go. I thought I'd be really clever and slide down the rope and spin my way down in a spiral, but about halfway down, the back of my life jacket got caught on something sticking out from the side of the ship. I let go of the rope and was just hanging there off the side of the ship, trying to reach the rope when a man saw me and went to the deck below, where he could reach up and unhook me. I finally made it to the boat. The last thing I remember seeing was my bike: it had been wrapped in brown paper and was sitting out on deck with other luggage, waiting to be unloaded the next morning. I stuck my face against the glass of a window and kept my eye on it as I slid down the rope into the lifeboat."[46]

When Rosa settled into the lifeboat, she was surprised to see that her handbag had landed in the bottom, and she quickly reclaimed it.[47] "It was fairly warm and I was comfortable," Pat says of the night. "I don't remember being cold, but I never touched the water." Reunited with her children, Rosa said, "Thank God we're all saved." But one of the crew pointed at the listing liner and flatly told her, "Lady, if this thing rolls over you're not saved!" As the lifeboat pulled away, Pat saw a man leap over the railing above and plunge into the ocean. "The water was full of wreckage and furniture and he must have hit something because he wasn't moving when he bobbed back up."[48] The ride across the water to the *Ile de France*, Arlene says, "was rough" as swells buffeted their lifeboat.[49] Several of the passengers got sick, and soon "the whole bottom of the lifeboat was full of vomit," Pat recalls. The smell made him sick: "I thought, Let me go back to the *Andrea Doria*!"[50]

Nicola DiFiore assisted several other passengers, tying ropes around children and lowering them to waiting lifeboats. But the list was so severe that he lost his footing and fell hard, injuring his back. He was finally able to inch his way down a rope and into one of the lifeboats from *Ile de France*.[51] Paul Sergio spent an hour trying to convince his wife, Margaret, to leave the *Doria*, but she still refused to go without her sister, Maria. Finally, as she stood crying on deck, a sailor grabbed her and pushed her toward the railing. "Go down!" her husband, Paul, shouted. "Save yourself! At least one of us has got to be alive for the family. I'll stay here and wait." Protesting and kicking, Margaret was finally forced over the side and down into a lifeboat from the *Ile de France*.[52]

Alda Raimengia had slipped on a pair of high-heeled shoes before leaving her cabin; now, as a sailor ushered her toward the railing, he warned her to take them off so that she could easily climb down the rope ladder. The descent "wasn't particularly difficult," she recalls, and she and Franco entered one of the *Doria*'s lifeboats that soon carried them to the *Cape Ann*.[53] Maria Coscia threw her purse over the side of the ship into a waiting lifeboat, but hesitated as she stood at the railing, afraid of the descent. "Lady, if you want to stay here and die," a man shouted, "go ahead! Let the rest of us go!" Several people pushed ahead and descended into the boat, which pulled away, taking Maria's purse with it. As she stood at the railing, Maria watched as a woman went down the rope with a child clinging to her back. "If that woman can do it," Maria said she later thought, "I can, too." And so Maria grabbed the rope and descended into a lifeboat from the *Ile de France*.[54] Adalgisa Di Fabio crossed from port to starboard, sliding down the deck, and finally reached the ropes hanging over the rails. "A line of people waited to go down them. I remember hesitating a little when whoever was guiding us down told me to go next. I'd spent a lot of time climbing trees and I was physically fit but I was still scared. Finally, though, they said that the next person was waiting for me to go, so I grabbed the rope with both hands, held on tight, and slid down toward the lifeboat. Two young girls, already in the boat, reached up, grabbed my legs, and pulled me in. The lifeboat was already full but they found a place for me and Nella. As soon as [Nella] got into the boat she passed out, but they quickly revived her. It was hard to see much of anything through the fog but finally we came to the *Ile de France*."[55]

An hour passed as desperate passengers evacuated the *Doria*. Around three, Peter Thieriot joined a group of passengers making their way from port to starboard; when he came out on deck he saw some *Doria* crew members take an inflatable raft, toss it into the water, and then jump in after it.[56] He was still reluctant to leave, but Max Passante continued to assure Peter that his parents must have taken an earlier lifeboat. Peter wasn't convinced: "I knew my parents weren't about to set one foot off that ship without me," he says.[57] But finally he approached the railing: by this time, the list was so great that only a few feet separated the deck from the lifeboat sent by the *Ile de France*.[58] As the lifeboat pulled away, Peter looked back at the *Doria* and saw the gaping hole in her starboard side. When the Thieriots had boarded in Gibraltar, Peter's father had identified the doors to the First Class Foyer for him and counted over the portholes to show his son the suite he and Frances would occupy. Now, Peter found himself doing the same thing, looking at the Foyer Deck doors and counting portholes. "When I counted over the right number of portholes," he said, "there wasn't any ship." It was like a punch to the gut—"I can remember the visceral sensation in my stomach." Shock set in: Peter "knew what I had seen and the significance of it," as *Doria* gradually retreated into the night.[59]

Mike and Meryl Stoller remained with the group of some twenty passengers who had gathered on the port side of the Boat Deck; in their sheltered position against the walls of the Cabin Class Gymnasium, they had no idea what was taking place elsewhere on the ship.[60] But finally, Mike recalls, "we saw people in lifeboats heading toward the *Ile de France* and realized that they were getting off the *Andrea Doria*."[61] Crossing from port to starboard was difficult: the group linked hands and formed a human chain, slowly snaking its way across the listing vessel; the situation seemed so precarious that even this little group worried that adding their collective weight to the starboard side might literally tip the balance and cause the *Doria* to capsize.[62]

A crew member tied a rope around Meryl and urged her toward the railing. But when faced with the prospect of climbing down the rope ladder to a lifeboat sent by the *Cape Ann,* she was seized with panic. "I can't move!" she shouted.

"Get going!" Mike yelled.

"If I'm going to die I'd rather die where I am!" she sobbed.[63]

The passengers already in the boat began shouting, "Leave them! Leave them!" "I knew we had to hurry," Mike recalls, "so I told Meryl that I'd step on her fingers if she didn't move quickly enough." Finally she went down the ladder, and Mike joined her in the lifeboat. Getting away quickly seemed important: if the *Doria* rolled, she would crush the escaping passengers.[64] Mike thought there must be seventy people in the boat, all anxious to flee, but they faced a new problem: the lifeboat had a broken rudder, and had to be rowed with paddles pushed back and forth on metal pipes.[65] "After swaying out of control for a while," Mike says, "we pulled away. I was so relieved to be out from under that leaning mass of twisted metal over our heads that I could have rowed all the way to New York."[66]

Shortly after three in the morning, Cecilia Pick felt the *Doria* give a perceptible shudder beneath her feet. "Chaos or no chaos," she said to her husband, John, "we are getting out of this." They were still in their sheltered position on the portside Promenade Deck, and decided to cross the liner by way of the stern. "The angle," she recalled, "was by then so steep that it was impossible to stand or walk. I crawled, fell, and pulled John, who was still trying to observe order. We both had to take off shoes and stockings, and still slipped." At the starboard railing, they found nets and ropes hanging into the sea. Cecilia saw several passengers leap into the ocean: she was ready to follow but John stopped her and insisted that they descend using the ropes. John went first, and Cecilia followed, sliding down some fifty feet into one of *Stockholm*'s waiting lifeboats. "I am no acrobat," she wrote later to her sister, "and there were exertions and excitements mixed with fear that the ship was going to give her last lurch—as she was heaving over every minute."[67]

Andrew Stevens finally found his father, and they made their way to the starboard railing. They took off their shoes and socks before grabbing a rope that swung out over the side to a lifeboat from the *Ile de France* below. "It was tricky timing the release of the rope to jump into the waiting lifeboat but we both made it," Stevens remembers.[68] The most unnerving part, Stevens says, was sitting in the lifeboat, waiting to pull away, as the listing *Doria* loomed over their heads. Finally, the lifeboat set off across the water.[69]

Most of the women were now gone: clusters remained on the port side and at the stern, but on the starboard side men began entering the boats. Italian immigrant Chiaromonte Miriello spotted the Philadelphia mayor on deck: "There was a lot of confusion . . . I looked around, wondering what to do, and saw a tall man—a man in rumpled clothes but I knew he was a *sindaco*—a man of authority. He was calm and confident and he quieted some who seemed about to panic. He helped them to the lifeboats."[70] Dilworth thought that it was about four that morning when he finally entered one of the *Ile de France*'s lifeboats.[71] "I pride myself on keeping fit," the mayor later declared, "but let me say I had a terrible time getting down those ladders myself. But by the time our boat pulled away, the boat deck was a mere ten feet above the water. Normally it would have been about a hundred feet."[72]

"The moon still shone," Philip Trachtenberg recalled, "and the glaring searchlight from the canted bridge of the *Doria* cut an eerie path through the mist that rose in wisps from the rolling Atlantic swells. Here was peace and beauty and tragedy and disaster all rolled into one." Finally a sailor directed Trachtenberg to climb over the side and down a rope ladder to a waiting lifeboat. "Now," he said, "I knew why the women screamed, why the kids were terrified. . . . This was like being lowered over the side of the Empire State Building. Step by step I went down as the ladder swung back and forth from the tilted hull. Halfway down I stopped, horrified. There, directly in front of me, was the gaping wound in the side of the *Doria*. By the reflection of the moon and the searchlights on the water I could see the twisted shambles of the staterooms and the passageways." Peering into the hole, he saw that "bunks where people had been sleeping were crushed and broken like matchboxes . . . Steel bulkheads were twisted, hideous arms grasping out into the shadows. Walls, partitions, doorways, were sandwiched together. Floors and girders were ripped as though some giant can opener had torn them apart." The horrific sight paralyzed Trachtenberg: "I felt sick to my stomach. A wave of revulsion swept over me. The presence of death overpowering." He continued his descent, seeing how "waves rolled in and out of the ugly hole in the side of the *Doria*. There was the bubbling sound of air fighting its way to the surface. Gleaming black oil gurgled up as though from an underground spring. Pieces of bed linen, blankets, smashed tables and chairs, life jackets, all kinds of clothing, floated about. The water made a lapping, hollow sound as it sloshed the debris in and out of the crevices, and inch by inch it rose higher." Finally Trachtenberg dropped into the lifeboat, "like a sack of sawdust. As I started to pick myself up I discovered the swill in the bottom of the boat. It was a combination of oil, sea water and vomit."[73]

With the *Doria*'s list increasing, Klaus Dorneich and Gustav Schmidt decided to leave the ship. They found a place in one of *Stockholm*'s lifeboats but the voyage across the water was difficult. "The waves became higher, and the sight was dim because of the fog." It was almost dawn by the time they reached *Stockholm*, "all seasick and scantily clad."[74] Waiting for his turn to descend a rope ladder to a lifeboat, Robert Young saw Father Paul Lambert approach the railing, then suddenly freeze.[75] For several hours Lambert's fellow priests Wojcik and Dolciamore had tried to persuade their colleague to leave the ship. Lambert continued to protest that he couldn't swim but eventually the two priests got him to the railing only for Lambert to be stricken with panic.[76] Young and another passenger grabbed Lambert's hands and pried them loose from the railing as sailors urged him to climb down the rope ladder as they held it in place.[77] But when Lambert finally placed his foot on the ladder, his 300-pound girth yanked the ropes loose from the sailors' hands: for a few terrifying minutes, Lambert spun in the air until crew in the lifeboat below grabbed the bottom of the ladder and the priest made his way down into the waiting vessel.[78] As soon as Lambert was safe, Wojcik and Dolciamore followed, settling into one of the lifeboats sent by the *Ile de France;* by this time, Dolciamore recalled, the *Doria's* starboard Promenade Deck was just ten feet from the water.[79] As they pulled away, Wojcik looked back. "It was like a movie," he later said, and it almost seemed as the *Andrea Doria* "was sleeping on its side."[80]

Fellow priests Raymond Goedert and Thomas Kelly also recognized that the time to leave the ship had come. Goedert tied his shoes to his life jacket and joined Kelly as they struggled to cross the Promenade Deck from port to starboard, over piles of deck chairs and around the stern to reach a rope ladder. Both climbed down into a boat sent by *Stockholm.*[81] As Kelly took his seat, the sailor manning the lifeboat said, "Good evening, Sir, we're the ones who sank you!"[82]

Robert Boggs had drifted toward the stern after seeing his family off the *Doria.* A sailor had tried to convince him to go over the starboard side, but the doctor, who had been in the navy, thought that it was safer not to place himself directly under the listing hull. He found a cargo net at the stern and quickly descended to one of the *Ile de France's* lifeboats.[83]

Throughout the night and into the dawn hours, this makeshift flotilla of lifeboats ferried passengers from the *Doria* across the water; sweeping searchlights from the Italian liner, from the *Ile de France,* and from other vessels sliced through the darkness, briefly illuminating the grim tableaux. Among the last to leave was Thure Peterson, who had spent the night engaged in the agonized effort to save his wife, Martha. He had awoken in darkness and immense pain some minutes after the collision, unaware that he'd been pushed through the ruined wall separating his own cabin, No. 56 and No. 58 behind it. A dim gray light spilled across the twisted remains, and everything seemed eerily quiet: through the hole where the wall of No. 58 had once been, Peterson could hear the sound of waves breaking against the liner's side below. Then, there was a low, pitiful moan. "Marty, Marty, are you all right?" Peterson called out.[84]

The answer came from the darkness: "My legs," Martha whimpered back. "They're caught."

"Don't move!" Peterson warned. "Just don't move! Help will be coming."

"There seems to be someone here with me," Martha muttered before lapsing into silence.[85]

It took all of Peterson's effort to free himself of the splintered wood and broken furniture trapping him against the wall. Finally he stumbled to his feet: he could feel blood flowing from wounds to his head, back, chest, and abdomen. He tried to find Martha's bed, but something was wrong: the bed wasn't where it was supposed to be. He kept calling out for Martha, but her answers were muffled; Peterson sliced his bare feet open on the shards of glass as he felt his way in the dark. It was not until reaching the washbasin that he realized he was no longer in his own cabin: the layout was reversed. He finally managed to find the door and enter the main passenger corridor. As he did, he looked back: the door plate read NO. 58.[86]

Peterson had locked the door of No. 56 when he and Martha had turned in. The bottom panel, though, was splintered, and he managed to knock through it, crawling in the dark on his hands and knees into what remained of the corridor leading to the cabin. As he reached forward, his hand landed on a cold face: it was Camille Cianfarra, who had died from his injuries. Peterson kept calling out to Martha: an answer came from the ruined cabin ahead. But he found a pile of wreckage blocking his access: in the darkness, the only thing Peterson could see clearly was that the cabin's outer wall and much of the floor was missing; if the wreckage fell loose, it would send Martha tumbling into the sea. Peterson moved back down the corridor to the passage and reentered Cabin No. 58; the wall separating 56 and 58 was torn back at the bottom, and he managed to pull aside a small section and crawl beneath it to reach his wife. In the pallid light filtering through the missing outer wall, Peterson finally saw Martha. "Mrs. Cianfarra is with me," she told him. Both were trapped in wreckage, and neither could move.[87]

"My husband was in the other cabin," Jane muttered. "I think he's dead." Peterson realized that he had encountered his body in the cabin corridor. But rather than say anything upsetting, Peterson assured the two women, "Don't move. I'll go for help."[88]

Peterson crawled back beneath the shattered wall into No. 58 and went toward the main passage. Only then did he realize that he was naked. He ripped down the maroon-and-beige curtains that hung across the baggage closet and wrapped them around his waist before staggering on bloody feet down the hall and making a difficult ascent up the Grand Staircase. When he finally came out on the Promenade Deck and asked for help, twenty-five-year-old Raymond Waite, studying for the priesthood at Saint Charles Borromeo Seminary in Philadelphia, volunteered to assist him. Peterson led him back down to the Upper Deck, into Cabin No. 58, and beneath the sheared wall into No. 56. "I've got someone to help," Peterson told the two trapped women. But Martha said, "Don't bother about me. Help Mrs. Cianfarra first." The two men tried to lift the wreckage, but it would not move. They crawled back into No. 58. Here, out of Jane's hearing, Peterson told Waite that he was sure Camille Cianfarra was dead in the corridor leading to No. 56 and asked the seminarian to give him the last rites. Since he was not yet ordained, Waite entered Cabin No. 56's corridor and knelt down by Cianfarra's body, offering prayers for the dead.[89]

Peterson once again climbed the Grand Staircase. At the top, coming out on the Promenade Deck, he spotted Cabin Class waiter Giovanni Rovelli handing out life jackets to panicked passengers. Forty-eight and with a wife and son in Genoa, Rovelli had completed a long day and retired to his shared crew cabin when the collision came. Rovelli had worried about the fog all day and into the night; a few years earlier, in a similar fog, he'd survived the collision of two ships in Norway. By the time he finally retired, Rovelli read for only a few minutes before exhaustion forced him to turn off the light. But within a few minutes the collision jolted him awake, and he quickly dressed and ran for the deck.[90]

"I need help," Peterson implored. "My wife and another woman are trapped." Together with First Class waiter Pietro Nanni, Rovelli followed him back to the wreckage of Cabin No. 56. Nanni had a flashlight, and now shone it as Peterson crawled back beneath the wall separating 58 from 56, followed by Rovelli; Nanni could not follow—not enough floor remained in the ruined cabin—and so he handed off the flashlight and returned to the Promenade Deck above. The flashlight's beam now revealed the horrible reality. Both Martha and Jane wore nightgowns covered in blood. Martha lay on her ruined bed, her back bent around the corner of the elevator shaft, with her head hanging down a few feet above the shattered floor. Wreckage held Jane in a half-sitting position atop her, with one of her legs trapped in the springs of a ruined mattress. Both were in great pain, and after Martha complained she could not feel her lower body, Peterson was sure that her back and legs had been broken.[91]

Peterson needed something to cut through the springs holding Jane atop his wife before he could attempt to free Martha, but he also wanted a doctor. Left in the cabin, Rovelli tried to pull more of the wreckage loose, but it was impossible. After assuring Martha and Jane that he would be back soon, Rovelli went back to the Promenade Deck, falling and slicing open his leg as he made his way to the paint locker to retrieve a jack to use on the wreckage. But the jack wasn't there, and so Rovelli returned to the ruins of Cabin No. 56.[92]

The half-naked Peterson, meanwhile, found *Andrea Doria*'s head physician, Bruno Tortori-Donati, and his assistant, Lorenzo Giannini, on the Promenade Deck and asked for morphine for his injured wife and for Jane. Tortori-Donati, in the midst of safely evacuating passengers from his hospital, refused to hand over any morphine but said that he would come below to see the injured women when he could.[93] Not willing to wait, Peterson decided to ask Captain Calamai for help. He struggled up three decks to reach the bridge, where he found Calamai surprisingly calm. After Peterson explained the situation, the captain assured him that he would send help to No. 56.[94]

When Peterson returned to No. 56, he found that Waite had located a pair of pants for him to wear in place of the curtains still wrapped around his waist. In his absence Rovelli had propped up the opening in the wall separating it from No. 58 with a piece of wreckage and cleared away as much of the jumble of metal and wood as he could. The two men managed to free Jane's right leg easily, but her left was still enmeshed in the coils of the ruined mattress. Both women were moaning in pain, but Peterson told them that the captain was sending help.[95]

"Darling, how will they ever get me out of here?" Martha asked. "Why don't you save Mrs. Cianfarra and yourselves?" Minutes ticked by until Dr. Tortori-Donati shouted from the passage. He had brought the morphine with him but made no move to crawl into the ruined cabin and tend to the injured women. Seeing his hesitation, a frustrated Peterson said, "Fix a double injection. I'll give it to them myself." Peterson took the hypodermic and crawled back into the cabin, giving Martha and Jane injections in their arms. "We need wire cutters, scissors, pliers," Rovelli said, "anything to cut the mattresses and the bed springs. And we must get a jack to lift the debris off your wife." Once again Peterson set off: this time he climbed up to the radio room, where the operator directed him to a drawer with two pair of wire cutters. As he left the radio room Peterson glanced at the clock on the wall: it read 1:12 A.M.[96]

By the time he returned to the ruins of No. 56, Peterson found that Rovelli, too, had retrieved some tools—a large carving knife, a pair of scissors, and, most ominously, a bone saw from the ship's infirmary. With these and the wire cutters, Peterson and Rovelli began the laborious task of slicing away at the wreckage. Finally, all that held Jane in place atop Martha was a piece of broken laminated paneling. "This is going to hurt," Rovelli warned, "but we must move it to get you out." Jane closed her eyes, and the men managed to tear the wood away and finally free her. Rovelli lifted her from the ruined bed. Holding on with her one good arm, Jane clung to his back as he struggled to crawl with her beneath the ruined wall into No. 58. Peterson spread a blanket on the floor, and Rovelli gently placed Jane on it. The two men were able to carry her down the passage and to the bottom of the Grand Staircase, but the list made it impossible for them to ascend without fear of dropping her. Peterson again made the exhausting climb to the Promenade Deck and returned with three fellow passengers and a crew member who, together with Rovelli, carried Jane up the staircase.[97] As they placed her on the deck, Jane kept begging the men to rescue her husband, Cian, and her two children.[98] Waiting to be lowered into a lifeboat, Jane asked a passing steward if she could have a drink of water. "I'm sorry, lady," he replied. "I can't help you. There is no water now."[99] Finally, she was lowered into a lifeboat from the *Ile de France*.

While still on deck, Rovelli searched in vain for a hydraulic jack. Finally he called out to a sailor in one of the *Thomas*'s lifeboats, "I must have a jack, a big jack! There's a woman, she's trapped! We must get it quick." When Rovelli returned to the cabin, he told Peterson that he'd asked for a jack but couldn't be certain that one would be sent. He urged the chiropractor to once again ask the captain for help.[100]

Peterson was exhausted as he climbed through the sharply listing ship, pulling himself up the five flights of stairs to reach the bridge, only to find that Calamai was elsewhere. Peterson staggered off in search of the doctors, finding them on the Promenade Bridge tending to injured passengers. But when he asked for another dose of morphine, one of the men said, "We must keep all we can for the seriously wounded."

"In God's name," Peterson shot back, "don't you think my wife is seriously injured?" He finally got another injection, but when he returned and gave it to Martha, she moaned, "Darling, I'll never make it. Why don't you save yourself?"[101]

Peterson refused to abandon the fight to save her. Leaving Martha's side, the chiropractor made yet another exhausting, difficult trip up to the bridge. This time Captain Calamai was there. After Peterson again asked for help, Calamai ordered a crew member to take a fire ax and accompany him back to the ruined cabin. These efforts were futile:

the blows of the ax only pushed wreckage onto Martha's immobile body. When she screamed, the man gave up and left.[102]

"Can't you please put me out of my misery?" Martha begged her husband. Peterson and Rovelli raced back to the almost empty Promenade Deck for help; as they paused at the railing, Rovelli heard a shout from the water: "Are you the fellow who was looking for a jack?" The sailor from *Thomas* had found one and ferried it back to the *Doria*, but getting it aboard the sinking liner took some doing: it weighed 150 pounds, and it took fifteen minutes to pull it up by rope. The fight was not yet over: Peterson and Rovelli had to get the jack down the listing stairs and push it along the corridor to Cabin No. 56. Getting the jack in place was almost impossible, and even then the six-foot-long handle could not be manipulated in such a tight space. Peterson grabbed the ax on the floor of the main passage, broke off the handle, and told Rovelli to use it on the jack.[103]

Just as he began to pump the jack using the makeshift handle, Rovelli heard Martha moan, "Oh, darling, I think I'm going . . . I'm going." In the gray light, Rovelli saw blood seeping from her mouth. "Doctor," he yelled back down the corridor, "I think your wife's dead." Peterson crawled down the corridor to the ruined bed, put his head on her chest for a moment, and then held her left wrist before finally clasping her hand in his. "Marty's dead," he said quietly.[104]

"Why couldn't it have been me?" Rovelli cried. "I'm nobody." Peterson kissed Martha's lips, took a pearl ring from her left hand and pushed it onto one of his fingers, and covered his wife with cushions. With bowed shoulders, Peterson walked back up to the Promenade Deck and climbed into a lifeboat at four thirty. Only as it pulled away, and he looked back at the hole in the ship's side where his wife's corpse lay, did he finally burst into tears.[105]

Chapter Thirteen

A s the long, uncertain night edged toward dawn, lifeboats continued racing from the injured *Doria* to the flotilla of rescue ships
that lay silently in the gray light. On *Stockholm*, two doctors and five
nurses who had been traveling on the Swedish liner volunteered their
services to the ship's own small medical crew, and officers cleared out
of seven cabins near the infirmary so that the injured could be treated
and rest in private.[1]

Many of the rescued passengers were horrified to see their lifeboats
approach the damaged *Stockholm*. The ship loomed white against the
waning night: the only sound, as Klaus Dorneich recalls, was steel in
her ruined bow, "pounding rhythmically against an iron plate as though
it were beating the time to this symphony of horror."[2]

Without shoes, and wearing only a light summer dress of cotton,
Cecilia Pick shivered in her lifeboat. "It was cold and horrid," she wrote.
"Once in the lifeboats we bumped and bounced on the Atlantic for
about one-and-a-half hours, as we had to look for another lifeboat that
had gone astray. . . . I only had a light summer sleeveless dress on."
When they finally arrived at *Stockholm*, the Picks found three other
lifeboats waiting at the ladder; Cecilia and John had to step across them
to reach the side of the liner.[3] "As my wife was being helped aboard the
Stockholm," Pick said, "she fainted."[4] Crew members carried her to the
infirmary, but she had temporarily succumbed to nothing more serious
than exhaustion.

Once aboard *Stockholm*, rescued passengers drifted in shocked silence through the corridors, the injured to the infirmary or to the Tourist Class Dining Room, where tables covered with blankets served as temporary beds, and the rest to the Tourist Class Lounge, where they were offered sandwiches, coffee, water, and tea.[5] Stewards on the Swedish liner had rounded up what they deemed necessities—blankets, extra clothing, and cigarettes—and handed them out as passengers filtered through the lounge.[6] "The staff crew of the *Stockholm* did their best," recalls Klaus Dorneich. "Everybody was intensely concerned with the shipwrecked." He thought the lounge "resembled a camp. Stunned and crowded, the passengers of the *Andrea Doria* sat there—the shock of the past experience plainly inscribed on their faces."[7]

It did not take long for the issue of the behavior of some of the *Doria*'s crew to again become a point of contention. "The Swedish crew members," said Cecilia Pick, "told us that the first lifeboat to arrive was filled with nothing but *Doria* crew members."[8] The atmosphere was embittered. Members of *Stockholm*'s crew manning the buffet tables found themselves handing over sandwiches and drinks to several hundred men wearing the white stewards' jackets of the Italian Line or carrying the gray life jackets issued to the *Doria*'s crew.[9] Apparently the Swedish crew expected their rescued Italian counterparts to help serve the *Doria*'s passengers; they were surprised when some refused, saying that they, too, should be treated as survivors.[10] It was clearly too much for some of the passengers: waiting in line for food, one commented, "Perhaps the *Andrea Doria* crew members should be served first since so many of them got here before us."[11] Cecilia Pick echoed this sentiment: "The complete disgrace," she wrote, "was that the crew all seemed to have got aboard before us. I could have murdered each member of the crew, who even on the *Stockholm* behaved abominably, not taking the least care of us passengers, pushing their way to eat first . . . and appropriating cushions and blankets without bothering whether any of us passengers had any."[12]

If there was scattered anger at the behavior of some of the *Doria*'s crew, most of the Italian liner's passengers agreed that *Stockholm*'s passengers and crew more than atoned for it, sharing food, cabins, and clothing. The latter contributions were especially welcome as people smeared with oil, sat huddled beneath blankets, many still dressed only in underwear or nightgowns. Gösta Ekspong, a physics professor at Stockholm University, was traveling home with his wife when they spotted Santino Porporino, still clad only in the pair of First Class curtains pulled from a cabin on the *Doria*, huddled with his pregnant wife and two young children. The Swedish couple immediately pulled the family aside and gave them clothing out of their own luggage.[13]

On the *Ile de France,* two doctors and ten nurses waited to treat the injured.[14] When the lifeboat carrying Madge Young, her mother, and her brother, David, pulled alongside the liner, heads appeared along the railing above, shouting down questions in French. Since Madge knew the language, she helped translate. Loading doors some twenty feet above the lifeboat were opened, and a rope ladder unfurled. One lady, who was injured, insisted that she was too weak to make the climb, and she had to be fitted into a harness and hauled up to the opening. When Madge prepared to climb the rope ladder, someone shouted down that she should take off her life jacket first; she reluctantly did so, having wanted to keep it as a souvenir. "By the time I got to the top of the ladder and inside, there was no one in sight," she recalled. "I walked down a long hallway. It sure felt better to be walking on level decks again."[15]

Pat Mastrincola found his arrival at the *Ile de France* somewhat less welcoming. "They had a rope ladder hanging from the open gangway and I was ready to climb up, but someone put a jacket around me and they suddenly hauled me up like a sack of potatoes. I didn't go ten steps on the ship before they patted me down—I don't know what they were looking for."[16] Slowly the rescued passengers came aboard: the Dilworths; the Giffords; Peter Thieriot; the Stevens family; Fathers Dolciamore and Wojcik; the shattered Di Sandros; Adalgisa Di Fabio; and a visibly shaken Ruth Roman, still wearing her torn and oil-stained evening gown.[17] One passenger on the *Ile de France* caught sight of her, "utterly beautiful" but her face marked with fear: "This was an ordinary woman, who was very afraid and worried to death about her son."[18]

Andrew Heiskell, who worked as a publisher at *Life* magazine, was asleep with his family on the *Ile de France* when he awoke and realized the ship had stopped; seeing what was going on, he grabbed a note-book, a pen, and his camera, also waking *Life* magazine photographer Loomis Dean, who was traveling for an assignment in Paris. Armed with cameras, both men stood along the deck, shooting photographs of the stricken, spotlit *Andrea Doria;* the contingent of lifeboats as they slid over the dark water; and the dazed faces of rescued passengers as they continued to come aboard the French liner.[19]

"I was proud of our children in the lifeboat," Barbara Boggs recalled. "Barbara was trying to help a woman with a badly cut head and Bobby, who was scrunched up on my lap, yelled, 'Well, at least we don't have to go through customs!' a comment which made everyone laugh." When their lifeboat came alongside the *Ile de France,* Barbara hesitated at the rope ladder—"it looked awfully long and high and although the sea was comparatively calm there was quite a swell that involved a bit of expert timing. The sailors on the lifeboat tied a rope around Bobby to his utter disgust. Of all of us, he was probably the last one who would have fallen between the lifeboat and the *Ile de France.* When I stepped aboard the *Ile de France* a sailor kissed me on both cheeks and said, *'Eh bien, Madame, c'est fini, n'est-ce-pas, et tout va bien.'* I said nothing—I was afraid I would break down and cry."[20] Standing in the gangway door, Andrew Heiskell spotted Barbara Boggs as she arrived; they knew each other from New York, and he now greeted her with a jaunty "My God, Barbara, what have you done to your hair?"[21]

As on the *Stockholm,* stewards waited with blankets and stood behind tables offering food and beverages. As survivors made their ways down the line, nuns handed the adults a ration of three donated cigarettes per person.[22] Stewards had been frantically rushing about the Promenade Deck, setting up hundreds of chairs and equipping each with a pillow and one of the ship's wool blankets.[23] Arlene Mastrincola was "struck by the beauty of the *Ile de France*" and took in everything with wonder; less pleasing were the blankets they received. "It wasn't all that cold," she says, but she remembers thinking that "the blankets were rough and scratchy." She later realized this was probably because she was still walking around in her underwear, and that this was the best the crew members could do at the time.[24]

Captain Beaudéan ventured out from the bridge to look over the scene. He saw "half-naked people—without shoes, numb with cold—who had escaped from the *Doria* by improvised means often incompatible with their age and physical stamina, painfully climbed the few rungs of the ladder which separated them from salvation. Then they collapsed on deck, having reached the goal toward which they had strained with all their nerves."[25]

Most of those traveling aboard the *Ile de France* had no idea of what was taking place until dawn approached. Lester Sinness, a senior vice president of DuPont, awoke at half past four that morning and suddenly realized that the ship was no longer moving. "About this time," he wrote, "muffled cries came through the portholes and I scrambled out of my bunk to take a look. The fog had completely lifted and the sea was bathed in moonlight. Only thirty yards from the ship I saw a lifeboat filled with people clad in orange life belts." At first he thought that the *Ile de France* was sinking; looking out again, he saw "a brilliantly lighted passenger ship about a quarter of a mile off the port stern, listing so heavily to starboard that it looked as though she would go under momentarily. In the path of the many dancing lights on the water I saw fifteen or twenty lifeboats either coming to the *Ile* fully loaded or returning for another load." Dressing quickly, he went up to the Promenade Deck and found the teak chairs "filled with very scantily clad people . . . Some were sitting glassy-eyed, some were sobbing, and many were jabbering in Italian at no one in particular. Many were smeared with oil."[26]

"Early in the morning," Pat Mastrincola recalls, "I remember some people coming out onto the deck. They looked at us and asked us to get out of their deck chairs. They didn't know what had happened until the crew said there was a ship sinking."[27] Families separated during the rescue desperately sought missing relatives. "My mother didn't lie down," Barbara Bliss later wrote. "After she settled Bobby in a deckchair [*sic*] and saw that he'd fallen asleep, I watched her anxiously pacing the deck."

"What if something happens to Robert?" Barbara Boggs cried. "I went through this during the war and now it's happening again."

"I'm sure he's all right, Mummy," her daughter answered.[28] Robert Boggs finally arrived on the *Ile de France* and found his wife huddled with Bobby. When *Doria*'s main physician, Bruno Tortori-Donati, spotted the boy on the deck, he came up to him and jokingly said, "I thought I told you to stay in bed, young man!"[29]

On seeing his father finally come aboard the *Ile*, Dun Gifford ran to him. "Neither of us could say anything," he remembered. "We just held each other."[30] Robert Young, too, soon found his wife and children on the French liner. "Daddy," recalled Madge Young, "came walking down the deck toward us. Mummy ran to him as she had been worried about him ever since we left him. I just said, 'Hi, Daddy' as he walked up. Mummy couldn't understand why I wasn't the least bit worried about him."[31] Although he came aboard the *Ile de France* with his father, Andrew Stevens had no idea what had happened to his mother. Then, as they walked along the deck, they spotted Heiskell, who was a previous acquaintance. "He told us where we could find her on the ship," Stevens remembers. "It was a joyous reunion."[32]

But not all families had such happy moments. Tullio and Filomena Di Sandro had no idea where their daughter, Norma, was. Melania Ansuini saw them on the *Ile de France*, "standing at the rail with their arms around each other, looking absolutely bereft."[33] They had, Tullio said, "searched everywhere for the child, but could not find her."[34]

Captain Beaudéan visited his ship's infirmary to check on the injured survivors. It was here, he wrote, "that all the horror of this drama is most apparent. Every ward, male, female, and isolation, is filled. Not a single cot is available. The faces of the overworked doctors, orderlies and nurses are drawn with fatigue." Among them was Jane Cianfarra. The captain thought that she looked gravely injured, with "horrible fractures" and a face covered "with violet-colored contusions." Having heard Cian die immediately after the crash, she was convinced that both Linda and Joan had also perished in the collision. When the captain bent down and asked if she was in great pain, she burst into tears, sobbing that she had lost her husband and her two children.[35] The usually genial Beaudéan could think of nothing to say and quickly left the room.[36]

A passenger traveling aboard the *Ile de France* allowed Ruth Roman use of his cabin. There she took off her torn and oil-stained evening gown and exchanged it for borrowed clothing: a white polo shirt and a pair of men's trousers.[37] Lists of survivors were being assembled on all the rescue ships, a slow, laborious process and one not entirely free from mistakes. Ruth knew that her young son, Dickie, had been taken away in a lifeboat, but she wasn't sure which vessel had picked him up. After wandering through the bedraggled crowd of survivors on the *Ile de France,* Ruth was sure he must be on another ship. As the morning wore on, passengers and survivors alike crowded around a few small portable radios: one transmission mentioned a Richard Hall aboard *Stockholm,* and for the first time Ruth felt a sense of relief.[38]

"Since dawn," Beaudéan wrote, "the survivors have been sending reassuring telegrams to their next of kin on both sides of the ocean. In addition, and this is the most tragic aspect, families separated during the rescue operation are now trying to locate each other from ship to ship. Urgent messages demand names which at the moment none of us can comply with any certainty . . . It should be easy to understand that it was impossible to have each survivor fill out a questionnaire upon arriving on board. Most of them were scarcely able to stand on their feet. Now they are scattered pell-mell throughout the ship, guests of those who have offered them hospitality, so that it becomes a herculean task to locate them all and question them in order to present a minimum identification to the American authorities. However this is precisely the task my clerks have set for themselves and in their praise I must say that they did a remarkable job."[39]

There were a few bright spots in the tragedy's wake: sitting on the deck wrapped in blankets, Giovanni Vali exchanged addresses with Melania Ansuini and promised to stay in touch.[40] But, for others, there was an uncertain numbness. Peter Thieriot had searched the *Ile de France* for his parents: by coincidence he discovered that a girl he had dated was aboard and her mother gave him ten dollars, but of his parents nothing was to be seen.[41] Madge Young had found her friend Dorothy Bollinger, who had also been traveling on *Andrea Doria,* aboard the *Ile de France,* and the two of them wandered the deck, happily greeting friends from the *Andrea Doria* until they saw Peter. The young boy, Dorothy said, was crying "a little" as he spoke to them.[42] Peter explained that his parents had been in "a different part of the ship" and that he "was worried about them because he had not seen them yet," Madge remembers. "We told him that his parents were probably on another ship."[43] But Jock Gifford, who had also befriended Peter aboard the *Doria,* was more realistic when he found the boy sitting alone. Peter explained his frantic efforts to locate his parents. "I think he knew all the time," said Jock, that his parents were dead.[44] Barbara Boggs found him sitting silently on deck, and swept in to look after Peter until they arrived in New York.[45]

As Beaudéan made the rounds of the Promenade Deck, he saw that "people still in the throes of shock are asleep in outfits made decent only through the charity of everyone aboard. But shoes are rare and most of the clothing consists of light gray woolen blankets whose color, while not detracting from their quality, adds nothing to their elegance. . . . Expressions of gratitude are offered in all languages. Unprepared for these demonstrations I stammer amiably. I try to speak Italian with authentic Americans. Some laughter, already a sign of convalescence, is heard here and there."[46]

Early rising passengers were stunned at the sight awaiting them on the *Ile de France*'s deck. "Where did all these people come from?" asked one startled man as he walked out onto the Promenade Deck.[47] Some passengers, on learning of the disaster, offered the rescued their cabins. One elderly man appeared briefly at the *Ile de France*'s Purser's Office and silently handed over a note: "My wife and I are very comfortably established in our deck chairs . . . We had not unpacked anything but an overnight bag, which is all we shall need for the time being; we have moved the rest of our baggage out of the way, and our cabin is quite ready for another tenant. Please offer it, with our warmest sympathy, to someone whose need is greater than ours."[48]

As they awoke, the *Ile de France*'s passengers also began donating clothing to the survivors. Later that morning, Arlene Mastrincola and her mother were invited into one of the shops on the *Ile* along with several other women and allowed to select whatever articles of clothing they needed. "I was so excited!" Arlene recalls. "I finally had some clothes."[49]

Joan Crawford's two youngest daughters, Cathy and Cindy, had enjoyed their previous voyage on *Andrea Doria* and the elaborate birthday dinner menu they had planned. Now, by a strange coincidence, they were aboard the *Ile de France*, on their way to join their mother, who was scheduled to film a new movie in England. They learned of the disaster when Mrs. Howell, their nanny, woke them that morning.[50] "I had often told them," Joan wrote, "when you give something of your own, give the best. They learned that lesson only too well. On the *Ile de France*, as soon as the twins woke up in the morning and heard that there were children on board without any clothes, they handed over their pretty lace-trimmed underthings." It was a generous gesture, though as Joan wryly noted, the "recipients would probably have preferred warm wool coats."[51]

Dawn gradually chased away the night, revealing the quartet of ships spaced out across the water: the *Stockholm*, its bow a mass of twisted and smashed steel; the *Cape Ann*, black hull gleaming in the rising sun; and the *Thomas*, decks lined with survivors. At the center lay the crippled *Doria*. The Italian liner, said Hans Hinrichs, a writer traveling aboard the *Ile de France*, was "never more beautiful than she was in the blue gray light of early dawn. The tiles of her three swimming pools sparkled as the sun, red and fiery, rose and overpowered the soft yellow of the moon at the opposite end of the sky."[52]

"The *Doria*," recalled Father John Dolciamore, "was slipping further on her side."[53] "We had drifted now," wrote Madge Young, "and were within about 500 yards of the *Doria*. We could see everything quite clearly: the three swimming pools, the slides on our swimming pool, and the sun deck where we had spent many sunny days. It all looked deserted and miniature. We could see water pouring over the deck from the swimming pools."[54] Even though the liner's situation looked dire, Madge says, "I still didn't think the *Andrea Doria* would actually sink. It just seemed impossible."[55]

Mike and Meryl Stoller reached the *Cape Ann* shortly before dawn. Their lifeboat swung around the bow in order to approach the ladder

leading to the platform at the side of the hull; as it did so, water from
Cape Ann's bulge pumps poured down, nearly swamping the lifeboat.
Standing on deck above, a sailor looked down and said, "What the fuck
are you people doing?" It snapped Meryl out of her worried state. "Gee,"
she called out, "it's great to hear a real American voice!"[56] The couple
ascended the ladder, to find an "enormous breakfast of scrambled eggs
and bacon" awaiting them. Realizing that he was finally safe, Mike
"felt as if I had been reborn. I finally managed to exhale all the air I
had been holding in my lungs for three or four hours, and when I did
I burst into tears."[57]

Cape Ann had been the first rescue ship to arrive on the scene: now, it
became the first to leave. She had taken 129 survivors aboard, including
nine who were seriously injured. At half past four that morning, she
pulled up her lifeboats and signaled that she was leaving for New York.
With a blast of her siren she steamed off in the soft golden light.

Stockholm, too, had taken on hundreds of survivors. Captain Nordenson worried about her seaworthiness. While there was no immediate
danger, Nordenson did not want to make the return voyage to New
York without an escort, in case the bulkhead in the smashed bow gave
way and his vessel began sinking. At two thirty, Nordenson cabled the
Ile de France: "Our foreship damaged. Our No. 1 hold flooded. Otherwise ship tight. Will try to proceed to New York at slow speed. If you
are going to New York with passengers from *Andrea Doria* could we as
a precaution keep company?"[58]

Captain Beaudéan, though, did not want to prolong his journey. "I
myself would have to return to New York," the captain later wrote.
"My unexpected guests are too numerous to envisage any other solution
more appropriate to the demands of our schedule. But we are 180 miles
away from New York and if we have to drag along at a speed of five or
six knots, we will not get there for a day and a half. Thus the next sailing
of the *Ile de France* from Le Havre can no longer be planned without a
delay. Now I know by radio that other ships have responded to the distress signals and are actually in the vicinity. Among them there surely
must be one which is in less of a hurry than we are and is headed for
New York and can provide the necessary escort."[59]

Shortly after receiving *Stockholm*'s request, Beaudéan radioed back: "Will proceed to New York full speed when all are rescued. Please ask another ship. My schedule is imperative."[60] "I was seized with remorse upon re-reading it later," the French captain admitted. "Nothing is perfect in this poor world, and the best disciplined mind has its weaknesses, especially when the fatigue of a particularly harassing night weighs on one's shoulders. This reply had an involuntary dryness, intensified by the awkward use of a foreign language."[61]

By now *Andrea Doria* had lost all communications. As dawn came, *Ile de France* signaled: "I intend to return full speed to New York as soon as you will release me. Are you abandoning ship or do you stay on board with party? Please let me know your intentions. How many persons have you still more or less to evacuate?"[62] Calamai used his Morse lamp to reply: "If *Thomas* remains at our assistance until Coast Guard ships arrive here you can proceed your trip. Thanks."[63] The *Ile de France*, in turn, radioed, "No more help needed. All passengers rescued. Proceeding to New York full speed."[64]

It took the crew nearly an hour to pull up and secure all of the *Ile de France*'s lifeboats. "We are about 1000 feet from the apparently deserted wreck," Beaudéan recorded. "Some whaleboats, which probably carried crew members remaining under Captain Calamai's orders, cruise around it."[65] At six fifteen, Captain Beaudéan ordered the liner's engines started. In a last tribute to the dying *Doria*, the *Ile de France* circled the stricken vessel three times, letting out long, mournful blasts from her whistle and dipping her flag as she passed.[66] Ritual completed, the *Ile de France* steamed west, carrying 177 members of the *Doria*'s crew and 576 of her rescued passengers.

Chapter Fourteen

—◆◆◆—

It had been a night of high drama on *Andrea Doria*'s bridge. At some point, as the rescue operations were getting under way, Captain Calamai seemed to have recognized that his ship might sink. He ordered the ship's logs be saved, although there is no agreement on precisely when he did this: various sources place it anywhere between 1:40 and 2:30 A.M.[1] Calamai asked First Deck Officer Luigi Oneto and Officer Cadet Mario Maracci to retrieve the documents but did not supervise their efforts.[2]

An investigation of the collision would surely take place, during which certain papers would have to be produced. These included the course graph recorders, which captured the *Doria*'s movements; radio logs; engine room logs; the ship's general logs; the ship's cipher book; and the ship's NATO instruction manuals (to be used if a war erupted while the liner was at sea).[3] Maracci had to crawl across the tilting chart room floor and grab at the jumble of papers that had fallen in the list; Badano tore off the last twelve hours of the course graph recorder and handed it to Maracci. "Did you take everything?" Badano asked Maracci.

"I am full of papers," came his reply.[4]

Badano—and Calamai—thus assumed that everything had been saved and, in the middle of ongoing efforts to save the passengers and keep the *Doria* afloat, no one thought to double-check. In fact, Maracci had retrieved only the accounting and crew logs, along with the course graph recorder. The *Doria*'s general, radio, and engine room logs went down with the ship. This later became a point of contention. After the sinking the Italian Line publicly stated that all the logs had been saved; they were forced to amend this when they realized that Maracci had neglected to retrieve the missing documents, which only fed a public perception that they were attempting to conceal information damaging to Captain Calamai.[5]

Calamai still held out hope that the *Doria* might be saved. His idea was that tugboats might be able to tow the stricken vessel to Nantucket, where it could be safely beached. At 2:38 A.M, with the *Doria*'s emergency generator weakening and her list approaching 33 degrees, Calamai asked *Stockholm* to send out a radio message on his behalf: "We need immediately tugboats for assistance." Soon replies came that United States Coast Guard vessels were speeding to the scene but would likely not arrive for at least another three to four hours.[6]

At 3:00 A.M., aware of *Stockholm*'s damaged bow, Calamai radioed the Swedish liner, "If you are in bad condition you can proceed to New York and many thanks for assistance. Other ships stay here and one should keep watch for me."[7] But *Stockholm* was still stuck in place by her anchor chains, a situation that could not safely be remedied until the rescue was complete and dawn had come. The Swedish liner would remain. At 3:50 A.M., alerted to his injured crew and rescued passengers, Nordenson cabled for Coast Guard assistance: "Have three serious casualties aboard our ship from *Andrea Doria* who need immediate attention. Please investigate. If possible send helicopter to our position."[8]

Shortly after four that morning, Staff Captain Magagnini told Calamai, "We have checked all parts of the ship to which we have access. All passengers have been disembarked in the lifeboats."[9] But Magagnini was mistaken: at least several passengers were left on the ship, amazingly still asleep or trapped in their cabins. No search was undertaken.[10]

Three women shared Cabin No. 230 on the starboard side of A Deck in Tourist Class: Margaret Carola, and sisters Amelia Iazzetta and Christina Covino. Amelia's husband, Benvenuto, had shared a different cabin with Luigi Carola, Margaret's father. After the collision, both men ran to Cabin No. 230, which was situated at the end of a small passageway off the main corridor. They found the corridor full of smoke and awash with creeping water.[11] But when they tried to open the door they found that it was stuck, apparently jammed when the wall bent. "I could hear them yelling in their cabin," Benvenuto later said. At that moment, several stewards ran down the smoke-filled corridor. When Carola asked them down to help rescue the women, one shot back, "We have to think of ourselves!" and fled.[12] Another grabbed Iazzetta and Carola, shouting, "Go up!" and pushing them toward the staircase; he promised to send someone to help rescue the trapped passengers.[13]

Help eventually arrived, but not for those trapped in Cabin No. 230. Captain Calamai later said that he had dispatched crew members down to A Deck to rescue the trapped women. Although the exact circumstances remain murky, apparently the crew ran into the corridor on A Deck and heard a woman scream, "Help me! Someone please help me!" It was Alba Wells, shouting from the door of Cabin No. 236. Her young daughter was trapped, with her right hand wedged between the wreckage of an upper berth and the bent cabin wall. She was freed— and the crew returned to the decks above, never venturing the twenty-odd feet forward and into the corridor, at the end of which was No. 230. They either assumed that they had been sent to rescue someone in 236, or were unwilling to risk being caught in the rising water on a perilously listing ship.[14] The women trapped in No. 230 had been alive after the collision; they might have remained alive until late that morning, when the ship began to capsize and water flooded the starboard length of A Deck.

It is possible that other passengers were also trapped aboard alive the *Doria*. Certainly thirty-five-year-old merchant seaman Robert Hudson escaped any searches. He had spent part of the voyage in the ship's infirmary, where doctors tended to his injured back and right hand, but on Wednesday night he had returned to his assigned cabin on A Deck and, sedated by painkillers, had slept through the collision and the ensuing rescue.[15]

Hudson awoke in a daze. He couldn't understand why it was so hard to sit up in his berth. The light switch didn't work: Hudson grabbed a cigarette lighter and used its flame to look at his watch, which read five fifteen. He then saw that the door to his cabin was open; when he jumped from his berth he discovered that the cabin floor was covered with a mixture of water and machine oil. "Is anybody there?" he shouted into the corridor. "Anybody there, please?" But the ship seemed deserted. Realizing that the *Doria* was listing dangerously, he knew he had to flee, and he ran out clad only in his boxer shorts. Moving down the corridor, bare feet straddling the tilted wall and the floor, was an ordeal.[16] "I'll never make it," he thought. "She's going under. She can't possibly stay afloat." After an hour, he finally reached the Tourist Class staircase and climbed up to the Promenade Deck.[17]

For a moment Hudson stood on the deck: in the early-morning light he could see jumbles of deck chairs, and rope ladders and netting hanging over the side. As he tried to get his bearings, a wave washed over the starboard side of the deck and swept him into the sea. Hudson swam back to the side of the hull, grabbing one of the swimming pool nets that had been used as makeshift rope ladders and surveying the scene. In the distance he spotted a lifeboat and shouted, "Help me! Help me! Over here!" No one seemed to notice him. Another wave knocked him against the hull and threatened to overwhelm him. Hudson washed back and forth for nearly an hour, certain that the *Doria* was about to sink and pull him under.[18]

Just after six that morning, destroyer escort USS *Edward H. Allen* and the Tidewater Oil Company tanker *Robert E. Hopkins* arrived on the scene. It was a lifeboat dispatched by the *Hopkins* that finally spotted Hudson at half past seven that morning and pulled him in.[19] Hudson was the last person—and the last passenger—off of the *Doria*, and the only one rescued by the *Hopkins*.[20]

As this drama played itself out, another emotional scene had engulfed the *Doria's* bridge. With the arrival of dawn, Captain Calamai turned fatalistic. "If you are saved," he said to Guido Badano, "maybe you can reach Genoa and see my family. Tell them I did everything I could."[21]

"What are you saying?" Badano asked. "The *Ile de France* is close by. We will be saved. If I go back to Genoa, you will go back to Genoa."[22]

Captain Calamai remained silent. He had apparently decided that it was best to follow tradition and go down with his ship. The collision, the passengers who had perished, the loss of *Andrea Doria*—it would all rest heavily on his shoulders, subsuming every successful command, every heroic action, every previous uneventful voyage. The shame of it all apparently seemed too much to bear. For Calamai, an honorable death was apparently preferable to a life clouded with guilt and accusations of negligence.

Calamai ordered the crew to abandon ship; he asked for volunteers to remain behind with him until the Coast Guard arrived, still hoping that the *Doria* might be towed to shallow water. At first a large contingent of some forty men stayed, but within an hour their number had fallen to twenty and then to twelve. Those who now stood with Calamai on the bridge in the dim morning light included most of the ship's most senior officers, including Staff Captain Magagnini, Chief Officer Luigi Oneto, First Officer Carlo Kirn, Third Officers Donato and Giannini, and Officer Cadets Maracci and Giovanni Conte.[23]

No one knew how long the *Doria* would last, but it seemed a forgone conclusion that she would soon roll over onto her starboard side and capsize. The minutes ticked by. Finally Magagnini told Calamai, "It is senseless to stay aboard, *Comandante*, a senseless risk of life. We can wait for the tugs in the lifeboats."[24]

Calamai again refused to leave, saying that Magagnini and the others could go. "If you stay we will stay with you," Magagnini told the captain.[25] Three lifeboats waited next to the *Doria*'s starboard, bobbing serenely on the gentle waves.[26] At half past five, the officers finally decided to leave. Calamai joined the little group as they struggled from the bridge to the Boat Deck, where a rope ladder hung over the side. One by one, the officers climbed down the ropes: as he settled into a lifeboat, Magagnini looked up and saw Calamai still standing at the railing. He seemed lost, vacantly watching the scene, not wanting to abandon his ship.[27]

"Come down!" Magagnini shouted up to Calamai. But the captain had again decided to go down with his ship. "Go!" Calamai shouted back. "Go away! I remain!"

"Either you come down," Magagnini yelled back, "or we'll all come up!"

Calamai resisted. "Go! I'll wait for the tugs. If need be I'll swim out to you. Go!"

Magagnini decided that the only way to convince Calamai was to place his own life in peril. He started back up the rope ladder to rejoin the captain. Only when Calamai saw that his officers might again board the *Doria* and go down with the ship did he finally act. Reluctantly, he grabbed the rope ladder and descended to the lifeboat.[28]

At half past seven, two helicopters, one sent from Otis Air Force Base at Falmouth and piloted by Lieutenant Claude Hesse, and the other from the Coast Guard station in Salem and piloted by James Keiffer, arrived at the scene to evacuate the most seriously injured passengers and crew aboard *Stockholm*. It was only moderately windy, but any attempt at landing on *Stockholm*'s narrow deck seemed too dangerous.[29] They decided to hover over the vessel and bring the injured up in stretcher baskets. Klaus Dorneich watched as, "like a huge bumblebee," the yellow Coast Guard helicopter came low over the foredeck, "lowered a wire-rope basket with which one after the other of the wounded on board were removed."[30]

Norma Di Sandro was the first to be airlifted. The little girl had not regained consciousness after reaching the *Stockholm*, and no one had any idea who she was: the only possible clue to identity seemed to be a tiny gold bracelet, with a ram's horn, that hung on her left wrist.[31] The medical crew aboard *Stockholm* had attached a tag to her nightgown: "Italian child, recommended treatment at nearest surgical clinic, consequence of fractured cranium." She was hoisted to the hovering helicopter. Next came *Stockholm* crew member Alf Johannson, who was also in a coma and who died a few hours later. Three other injured *Stockholm* crew members were also taken off the ship: Lars Falk, who had a broken neck and fractured skull; Wilhelm Gustavsson, with his missing left eye and fractured collarbone; and Arne Smedberg, with a concussion and broken leg.[32] Soon the injured were on their way to Nantucket, where another Coast Guard plane waited to take them to Boston's Brighton Marine Hospital.

After eight that morning, more vessels began arriving at the scene, including the cutters *Owasco* and *Campbell;* the watch standing ship *Yakutat;* the Coast Guard buoy tender *Hornbeam;* and the Coast Guard cutter *Evergreen.*[33] Calamai and his officers had remained in the *Doria*'s lifeboat No. 11, watching the scene from a distance. Silence reigned: no one wanted to speak as they stared at the proud Italian liner gradually and inexorably slipping farther over onto her starboard side.

At half past eight Calamai declined to board the *Edward H. Allen*, saying he wished to wait in the lifeboat for the requested tugs: clearly he thought that he would be returning to his vessel to help guide her to shallow waters. When the *Hornbeam* arrived on the scene, Calamai finally left the lifeboat and climbed aboard to confer with the captain. But when Coast Guard Headquarters in Boston was asked about the possibility of towing the Italian liner, they were instructed that none of their vessels should attempt such a dangerous effort; instead the Italian Line was contacting a commercial towing company to see if they might help save the ship.[34]

This back-and-forth was for naught. By 9:45 that morning, the *Doria*'s list had increased to nearly 50 degrees; above, planes circled the wreck, with photographers and newsmen shooting the dramatic scene as the red along the bottom of *Doria*'s port side and hull shone against the blue ocean. Most of the starboard side had disappeared, and oily waves began washing over the decks as her superstructure met the ocean; water shot up in angry geysers as air trapped in the liner began its escape. The funnel was almost parallel to the sea: bystanders could now look straight into its black void.

As the *Doria* slipped deeper, the onrush of water swept through her elegant rooms, smashing finely veneered panels, breaking partitions, shattering fluorescent lights, and capturing Ponti's colorful furniture in an inexorable swirl of destruction. Ceramics, statuary, and china crashed against walls that had now become floors. By ten, the ship had turned completely on its starboard side, with waves washing over the bow; as water cascaded into the bow, its weight pulled the *Doria* down slightly, and her stern rose out of the sea: her rudder and port propeller dripped and glistened in the sunshine. It took another minute to bring the *Doria*'s funnel level with the sea: water rushed in, pulling her farther down and over as she began to capsize.

Captain Calamai and his officers stood against the rails of the *Hornbeam*, watching this scene unfold. No one spoke, and only Badano's muffled sobs broke the silence.[35] On *Stockholm*, the rescued passengers and crew also lined the railings facing the *Doria*, "silently and passionately watching the incredible event before us," as Klaus Dorneich recalls.[36]

By 10:02, the white funnel, with its red and green bands, had disappeared beneath the surface. The flooding now seemed to accelerate. The bow was gone, and the ocean began closing over the bridge; the blue ceramic tiles lining the now-empty three swimming pools at the stern gleamed in the sunlight. The ocean continued its merciless conquest, seizing the liner in its unrelenting grasp and pulling it downward. By 10:05, the starboard half of the ship was underwater; her stern still hovered out of the sea as the ocean now began refilling the empty swimming pools.

As the minutes ticked by, water began washing along the port side, ripping several of the unused lifeboats from their davits. Escaping air from the interior of the ship rippled and bubbled to the surface in an ever increasing boil that mingled deck chairs, clothing, and machine oil in a terrible cauldron of destruction. Then, as the sea churned around her, the remaining length of the *Doria* slipped beneath the surface: for a moment, she seemed to hesitate as the sun struck her stern and illuminated the bronze letters of her name for the last time. Then, the stern, too, slipped from sight. It was 10:09 A.M., Thursday, July 26, eleven hours after the collision. "There was a light sun," Guido Badano recalled, "and the ship sparkled as she sank."[37]

Beneath the cloudless blue sky, the sea continued to boil for fifteen minutes as air from the now lost liner continued rising to the surface. Then, the tumult subsided: all that was left was a long, languid stretch of machine oil shimmering like a rainbow, in which bobbed the flotsam and jetsam of the great Italian liner: a few empty lifeboats; life jackets;

broken furniture; luggage; debris from the shattered cabins; pieces of clothing; and odd shoes that had been abandoned on deck.

On *Hornbeam* Calamai turned from the scene in shock. He made his way to the radio room and wrote a terse cable to be sent to the Italian Line: "*Doria* sank 10:09."[38]

Chapter Fifteen

A NDREA DORIA AND STOCKHOLM COLLIDE, ran the headline in *The New York Times* on Thursday, July 26. ALL SAVED, it added.[1] Unfortunately, this early optimism was misplaced. In the first days after the tragedy, the press focused largely on dramatic stories of the collision and aftermath as newspapers recounted "the swift, herculean mass rescue operations on sea and air that became a Dunkirk-like tableau of precision and effectiveness."[2] Only after the initial shock subsided did the press begin to pick apart what had happened and question the reasons behind the catastrophe.

It had been forty-four years since the *Titanic* disaster. Radar, radio communications, and navigational advances had seemingly ensured that such tragedies could no longer occur. The collision between the *Doria* and *Stockholm* shattered this complacent trust. Modern technology, as soon became apparent, was still subject to human interpretation and error.

News of the collision first reached the *Doria*'s home port of Genoa early on the morning of July 26. Captain Calamai's wife, Anna, happened to be out doing her morning shopping when she saw a newspaper announcing that her husband's ship had sunk after a collision. She rushed back to her house in tears, ignoring the small crowd that had begun gathering outside: her eldest daughter, Marina, was on her way to London, but she told fourteen-year-old Silvia of the disaster.[3]

"I had to gather my strength to inform my husband's aged mother," the captain's wife said. "I did so, and told a white lie when I assured her that he was safe. My heart kept coming up in my throat because I wasn't sure at all. I spent five hours of torture, minute by minute, as I followed the succession of events by radio and frequent calls to the officers of the Italia Company. I alternated frantic calls with prayer. I don't remember how many prayers I offered and how many supplications I made. I do remember invoking God's intercession to avoid loss of life and spare my Piero. I knew my husband's temperament and his dedication to the navy code of honor. I knew he would go down into the sea with his ship unless he were ordered to leave it by someone high up."[4]

Hundreds of people thronged the Piazza de Ferrari outside the office of the Italian Line, waiting for news.[5] When the sinking was finally confirmed, it was as if Genoa had lost a part of itself. *Andrea Doria* had been born there, built there, sailed in triumph from there to carry the spirit of a revived Italy across the globe. The people of Genoa had watched her rise at Ansaldo, cheered her on her maiden voyage, and rejoiced at her celebrated reception. "When a ship like this sinks," reported one newspaper, "all the city weeps."[6] "A piece of Italy is gone," reported *Corriere della Sera*. The *Doria,* the newspaper said, had "been the perfect concentration of the best of Italy, a synthesis of its noblest qualities . . . serious, brilliant, powerful, true, tenacious, and smart."[7] "The great marine disaster which has stricken Italy and so many of God's creatures," said Pope Pius XII, "raises a deep and painful echo with our earth. We share the suffering of all."[8] Loss of the *Doria*, declared President Giovanni Gronchi, "plunges the whole Italian nation into sadness."[9]

Word of the disaster began to spread among passengers' families on the morning of July 26. In the Bronx, Maria Coscia's family had spent the previous day planning a party to welcome her home. On the morning of July 27, Maria's son Fortunato, called Fred, awoke early and went off to the corner store to get the day's newspaper. He saw the headlines about the *Doria* and ran back home, slamming the paper down on the kitchen table in front of his startled sister Sadie and sobbing, "Mama's not coming home!" "Everyone," Fred's daughter, Renee says, "was in a panic. They knew my grandmother was not athletic or a physical risk-taker, and could not imagine her being able to survive the crash." Fred spent the next few hours on the telephone to no avail: finally, he and some other relatives decided that they would find out more from *The New York Times* and set off for the newspaper.[10]

Edward Morgan had arrived in New York City from Washington, DC, late the previous evening, so that he could meet his daughter, Linda, when she arrived on *Andrea Doria* with her mother, Jane Cianfarra. At five that Thursday morning the telephone in his hotel room rang. "We didn't want to wake you up before," explained Francis Littlejohn, Morgan's director at ABC News, "because everything was so confused, but it's all right now. The *Andrea Doria* and *Stockholm* have collided off Nantucket in a fog and the *Doria* is in a bad way but the *Ile de France* has just radioed that everybody has been rescued. Nobody has been lost. I'll call you back if I get anything more."[11]

Morgan was stunned but relieved. As the morning wore on, though, and the initial, hopeful reports gave way to more accurate news about the tragedy, the broadcaster grew increasingly uneasy. He rang *The New York Times*, thinking that surely Linda's stepfather, Camille Cianfarra, would have recognized this journalistic coup and called in with an eyewitness report, but no one at the paper had heard from him. This worried Morgan even more. He next tried United Press and the Associated Press to see if they had heard from Cianfarra or had any list of survivors that included Linda, but no one could help him.[12]

Even as the world began to learn of the disaster, the drama at the scene continued. At 11:00 A.M., Captain Calamai and his officers left *Hornbeam*, traveling in the same lifeboat that had brought them to the vessel. In order to reach New York sooner, they boarded the *Allen*. Once Calamai was aboard, he disappeared into the captain's cabin to compose an initial report on what had happened. Already he had received a message relayed from the Italian Line through their offices in New York: he was not to make any public statements or grant any interviews until Italian officials first debriefed him.[13]

The *Allen* left in its wake oil-slicked waters strewn with wreckage. Nearby vessels retrieved luggage floating in the ocean that still bore tags for Ruth Roman and Betsy Drake. An odd assortment of relics found their ways onto the decks of the cutters *Yakutat* and *Legare,* including deck chairs, a cocktail table, and three of the *Doria*'s empty lifeboats. The other boats from the *Doria*'s starboard side bobbed, unoccupied, in the water along with the port boats that had broken away, circled now and then by flashes of white as sharks passed by. Rather than retrieve the lifeboats, *Yakutat* and *Legare* shot at them with their deck guns, hoping to eliminate them as potential navigational hazards. But, as if these last remnants of the *Doria* were trying to protest the loss of the great vessel, the lifeboats refused to sink. Round after round split the silence of the ocean: it took a full fifteen minutes before the shattered little boats finally sank beneath the waves.[14]

As *Ile de France, Cape Ann, Thomas,* and *Allen* steamed west toward New York City, preparations were under way to receive survivors and respond to their immediate needs. The Italian Treasury advanced ten million lire (approximately $163,000) in emergency funds for passengers.[15] Both the Italian and the Swedish American Lines booked blocks of rooms for survivors at several New York City hotels and arranged for meal vouchers, while crew members were to be given rooms at the Manhattan Seamen's Church Institute.[16] Catholic Relief Services began collecting donations of clothing, shoes, personal items, and money to distribute to arriving survivors, and the Travelers Aid Society dispatched representatives to meet the rescue ships.[17] Department stores throughout the city set up booths on the pier, filled with donated clothing and shoes. The Red Cross was especially active, dispatching representatives to meet the incoming ships and offering more than $100,000 in emergency aid to the survivors.[18]

Realizing that many of the survivors had likely lost their passports, visas, and identification papers in hastily abandoning the *Doria,* the United States State Department announced that the usual inspections and presentation of documents for foreign arrivals wouldn't be necessary. The usual health inspections were also waived.[19]

As these preparations were under way, the armada of rescue ships and their traumatized passengers were approaching New York. On *Ile de France* many of the shell-shocked survivors sat dazed in deck chairs, while others thronged the radio room, hoping to send messages to friends and relatives. "Not a single officer was seen by any of the survivors I talked to," wrote *Ile de France* passenger Lester Sinness, "and all those survivors were uniformly bitter about the crew."[20]

Just after seven, Fathers John Dolciamore and Richard Wojcik arranged an impromptu mass for survivors in the ship's ballroom. In these years before the Second Vatican Council, strict fasts were in place for those who received the Eucharist. Many of the survivors had been given food, coffee, tea, or medicine aboard the ship and now worried that if they participated in communion they would violate Church law. Wojcik assured them that, under the circumstances, they could ignore the rules. "There are no laws now," he said. When he finally returned to Chicago, Wojcik explained his actions to Cardinal Samuel Stritch. "You did well," the cardinal assured him, but added, "don't do it again."[21]

Maria Coscia was desperate to let her family know that she had survived, but she assumed that she would be charged for sending a telegram from the *Ile de France* and she had no money with her. Early that morning, she walked into the lounge and up to a table where several elegantly dressed ladies were playing cards. "I came from *Andrea Doria*," she said in her broken English, "and I'd like to let my family know that I'm safe and well. Would you mind making a collection for me to pay for a telegram?"

"I'm not making any collection," one of the ladies said as she stood. She took Maria by the arm and led her to her cabin, gave her a sweater to put over her water- and oil-stained nightgown, and then escorted her to the Purser's Office, where she helped dictate and paid for the telegram. It was Fred's fiancée, who had arrived at the house in the Bronx on hearing of the catastrophe, who first learned the good news.[22]

Lounging in a deck chair, Madge Young awoke from a short nap to brilliant sunshine. The girl sitting next to her gave her a look of triumph as she announced the fate of *Andrea Doria*: "She sank! See, I told you she would!"[23] Madge was stunned: she had been certain that the ship would somehow survive. She had spent the morning with her reunited family, clad in their odd assortment of donated clothing. Her father, Robert, got a khaki shirt and a pair of black pants from one of the waiters aboard the *Ile de France*, but "couldn't find any shoes to fit him, and so was wandering around barefoot." He eventually went below to one of the men's bathrooms to shower and there encountered one of the *Ile de France*'s passengers; the gentleman had slept late and had, with no idea of the drama that had taken place, eyed the oddly dressed Young with curiosity. When Young told him what had happened and explained why he was barefoot, the man gave him his bedroom slippers to wear.[24]

Barbara Bliss found Dun Gifford on the *Ile*'s deck—"we were both still much too full of adrenaline to settle down on a deck chair," she later wrote. They wandered over the liner, exploring some of the public rooms before coming upon "a seven-foot stack of deck chairs in a corner that we were able to clamber up on and find a little privacy under some blankets as we collapsed in exhaustion. We kissed and caressed each other under a blanket with a kind of desperation until we fell asleep on our uncomfortable perch. Somehow our parents never looked for us, and we came down for breakfast around eleven with the ship's horn blasting and people crowding the rails with the excitement of coming into the port of New York."[25]

Survivors aboard the *Ile de France* were handed notices prior to landing: "Due to the unusual circumstances of your arrival, we are dispensing with all formal immigration proceedings. However we ask you for your name and address." As the vessel neared New York, officials asked the disheveled passengers, most of who had only the (often borrowed) clothes on their backs, if they had anything to declare. Madge Young recalls that her mother presented bundles of her family's pajamas, and that officials duly marked them.[26]

It was late afternoon when the *Ile de France* steamed past the Ambrose Light and into the channel leading past Sandy Hook to New York City. Survivors lined the deck, watching as the distant towers of Manhattan appeared ever closer on the horizon, their glass walls gleaming in the golden light. Through the Narrows she went: as she neared, the water was increasingly clogged with hundreds of smaller ships that had come to greet her: tugboats, fireboats, and a flotilla of tenders, yachts, ferries, and even canoes. "We passed the Statue of Liberty," says Adalgisa Di Fabio, "but I didn't know what that was. The thing I most remember is that it was like a celebration: there were boats everywhere around us, escorting us, including fireboats shooting water into the sky. Everyone stood on deck, watching as we approached New York City."[27] It was a moment Barbara Boggs would never forget: "People lined the shores for miles; every boat blew her whistle and raised and lowered her flags. Helicopters hovered overhead taking pictures. I was leaning against the railing of the Promenade Deck with Bobby, and for the first time I cried. Bobby, still clad in his oil stained pajamas, said, 'What is there to cry about now, for heaven's sake?'"[28]

"As we steamed in—the first rescue ship to reach shore—we were greeted by every ship, from tugs to liners," says Madge Young. "They all gave us three blasts, which we returned. The noise was deafening. We really were being welcomed."[29] It was, she says, "quite a memorable reception."[30] "The *Ile*," remembered Captain Beaudéan, "had probably not received such a welcome since her maiden voyage."[31]

Captain Beaudéan had thought he could safely disembark his rescued passengers and quickly turn around, sailing back out of New York that same evening. But, as he recalled, the French Line "politely asks if I have gone crazy. Relief organizations, the Red Cross, families of the victims, the press, radio and television are waiting. . . . Under no circumstances could we disappoint them."[32] He would be expected to play to the press and emphasize his heroic role in the rescue.

It was five when tugboats finally eased the *Ile de France* to her berth at Pier 88 on Manhattan's west side. The whole of the pier and the length of the flanking streets were jammed with thousands of people. Some were anxious friends and relatives desperately hoping to see their loved ones; others simply wanted to witness the unfolding drama of this modern maritime disaster. Reporters, cameramen, and newsreels pushed against flimsy police barricades, eager to record the triumph and tragedy of an event that had captured the attention of the world. The Italian Line had called in a number of translators. Rose Calvelli, who ordinarily worked for the New York City branch of the Bank of Rome, was one of those who volunteered to greet the incoming arrivals and offer her services. Amid shouts, tears, and cries of joy, she recalls, the rescued passengers began leaving the *Ile de France*. "Most of them had shocked faces, and were very quiet as they came off. They looked very sad, some wrapped in blankets and others only half-clothed. A few people pushed but most just shuffled along. We did the best we could, directing them to help and trying to answer questions. I especially remember one girl, about sixteen, who was carried on a stretcher down the gangway. A white sheet covered her up to the waist; she held a religious medal in her hands and just stared off into space."[33]

Edward Morgan had managed to get himself aboard a Coast Guard cutter that had taken him out to *Ile de France* before the liner reached its berth in New York. But he found that "survivor lists were incomplete. Someone had heard that Mrs. Cianfarra was aboard, gravely injured. I found her in the sick bay, swathed in bandages."

"Cian is dead!" Jane told her former husband. "I heard him die. Where are the children?"

Morgan tried to reassure her: perhaps Cian was alive, and both Linda and Joan were probably aboard another one of the rescue ships. He went off to the Purser's Office and scanned the list of those rescued: "No familiar names. I trudged the decks. No familiar faces." Still, he said nothing and returned to Jane, accompanying her as she and fifty-six other injured passengers were carried on stretchers down the gangway and loaded into ambulances to be taken to local hospitals.[34]

"Many of survivors," one newspaper reported, "who had behaved admirably throughout the collision and rescue at sea, completely lost their self-control and turned into a pushing, milling, shrieking mob at the narrow entrance of the gangway in their eagerness to get off. Fights broke out, women pulled hair and tore at each others' dresses, and a number of women fainted in the hour-long crush. New York policemen waiting on the pier tried to control them."[35]

A shaken Thure Peterson walked alone, head bowed as he spoke of his wife, Martha: "She went down with the ship."[36] In contrast, Richardson and Ann Dilworth seemed almost genial as they disembarked, met by his press secretary, who struggled to control the couple's two poodles he had brought from Philadelphia to greet them.[37] The newsmen recognized Betsy Drake, who managed to tell them, "I still don't believe it happened."[38] Her friend Judith Balaban Kanter heard about the collision and rushed to New York to meet the actress. "I drove in from the country," Kanter recalled, "with some things of mine, because if Betsy was there, in all likelihood she was going to be without luggage." She was startled that Betsy's hair "was very neatly combed. Since she never wore much makeup, she didn't look much different from when she wore the minimum amount. She was wearing a charming little silk suit with a little pin on the lapel. It was all adorable except that on her feet were huge, bulky white sweat socks loaned to her by a sailor. Betsy had lost her shoes."[39]

Married to a minor Sicilian aristocrat, Eleanor Castaliogni had been at the Pierre Hotel with her grandson Larry Russell when word of the collision came: they were due to sail on the *Doria* on her return trip to Italy. Now, Eleanor and her grandson rushed to Pier 88 and watched the scene. Eleanor was surprised to see Ruth Roman appear—they were friends from Beverly Hills. The press engulfed the actress: Ruth was shivering and distraught as she tried to answer questions. Seeing this, Eleanor swept forward, took off her own mink coat, wrapped it around the actress's shoulders, and quickly took her away from the mob.[40]

Charles Thieriot met his nephew Peter as the young boy came off the ship and quickly took him to his house on Long Island.[41] Evie Field Suarez, Barbara Boggs's imperious mother, also waited at the pier: she collected her daughter, son-in-law, and young Barbara and Bobby and drove them back to their house on Long Island.[42]

"At the bottom of the gangway," recalls Madge Young, "people were expediting us through the red tape rather quickly, probably because officials wanted to speak to my father, given his expertise with the American Bureau of Shipping. But there was still a lot of shoving going on, especially from members of the media." She remembers one reporter rushing up to her mother, shoving a microphone in her face, and shouting, "Do you consider this a miracle?" Disgusted, she shot back, "Go away!" and pushed her way past the crowd.[43] Robert Young ushered his family into a taxi, and they fled to the privacy of a Manhattan hotel, where friends and relatives soon arrived with clothing.[44] Richard Wojcik's mother had come to New York to meet him; she had gone to bed early the previous night and had no idea that anything had happened to the *Doria* until she arrived at the pier and a reporter told her that the liner was gone. "How could they crash with so much water out there?" she asked. She was greatly relieved when she saw her son come down the gangway.[45]

Maria Coscia's family had rushed to the pier, waiting for her arrival. Her son, Fred, climbed a pole to get a better view. "I see Mama!" he shouted when Maria finally appeared on the gangway. Her nightgown was water-stained, her legs covered in oil smears, and her hands and arms marked with ugly rope burns, but she was alive, and still carried the three gold bracelets in her padded brassiere. They had to wait for her to go through the Red Cross checkpoints before they could hustle her away from the *Ile de France* and the crowd of reporters. Back at her home in the Bronx, her daughter Sadie filled a bathtub with warm water. By the time Maria was done bathing, the tub was black with grease and machine oil.[46]

The name "Nicola DiFiore" had appeared on a list of survivors, but none of his relatives knew if this meant the older man or his young cousin of the same name. Rita Checchio, waiting to see her father for the first time in five years and show him the granddaughter he had never met, raced from her home in New Jersey to witness the *Ile de France*'s arrival. Scanning faces among the disembarking survivors, she finally spotted her father, unshaven and looking tired, descending the gangway. In a few minutes, Nicola was holding two-year-old Marisa, tears streaming down his face as his daughter whisked him away from the crowd.[47]

Angelo Mastrincola first learned of the disaster when he saw a report of the collision in his morning newspaper. Throughout the day lists of survivors were being assembled, with constant updates on the radio and on local television stations. Angelo rushed to Manhattan's Pier 88 as the *Ile de France* arrived and searched the crowds for his family. "There were people everywhere," Arlene recalls, "and we walked around and around until we saw my father, together with my uncle Lou and aunt Antonietta. My father looked terrible, like he was sick with worry." All Arlene wanted was a bath; she was covered with dirt and machine oil.[48] Her brother, Pat, took the excitement in stride: he was still mourning the loss of his new Italian bicycle.[49]

Adalgisa Di Fabio had stood anxiously at the railing of the *Ile de France* as she steamed into New York. "I was so eager to meet my uncle Francesco and my aunt Tomassina, and then I looked down at myself. My beautiful dress was covered in oil, and ripped up one side. I wasn't thinking about what I had gone through, just that I looked like a wreck." As she came down the gangway to the pier, she says, her most vivid memory was seeing a Red Cross station "piled high with doughnuts. There were tons of people waiting and crowding around but finally I heard my name called out. My two uncles and my aunt had driven in a car from Elizabeth, New Jersey, to New York to get me."[50]

Seventeen-year-old Anthony Sergio had been coming home with his cousins Thursday morning after watching a Chicago Cubs baseball game the previous night when the car radio blasted an alert that *Andrea Doria* had been in a collision and sank. He didn't know enough English yet to understand, and his cousins silently agreed to say nothing until they arrived home. There, Anthony found his father, Ross, who swept him up in his arms and said, "We are alone now. Mama and the others are all gone." Ross and his cousin Tony immediately set off by car for New York. They arrived in time to see Paul and Margaret disembark from *Ile de France;* she was in a state of shock, sobbing as Paul explained their futile efforts to save Maria and her four children.[51]

A similarly heartrending scene took place as a frantic Tullio and Filomena Di Sandro left the *Ile de France.* They had spent all day in a fruitless search among the survivors on board looking for their daughter, Norma. A reporter noticed them, Filomena "beautiful but very, very pale" and Tullio, "composed and serious" but his eyes red and swollen from crying. "We have lost our little girl, the only one we have," Tullio said. Norma, Tullio explained, had been wearing a gold bracelet with a ram's horn trinket on it.[52] It took several hours to learn that a young girl wearing such a bracelet had been airlifted early that morning from *Stockholm* and taken to Brighton Marine Hospital in Boston. Though still unconscious, she was alive.[53] Reading this bulletin, the journalist rushed back to the pier and found the Di Sandros still waiting for the next rescue ship to arrive. "I have found your daughter!" he shouted.

"She is at the hospital."[54] He ushered the couple to his car, saying that he would drive them up to Boston.[55]

In all, *Ile de France* had rescued 743 survivors: 576 passengers and 177 members of *Andrea Doria*'s crew.[56] More survivors arrived aboard the US Navy ship *Private William H. Thomas,* which docked at the Brooklyn Army Terminal with 112 passengers and 46 members of the *Doria*'s crew.[57] Among those on board was Arline Trachtenberg. She was forever grateful to the *Thomas*'s crew but had one minor complaint: for dinner that Thursday, the mess served spaghetti. "For nearly a week," she said, "I had eaten nothing but Italian food. I would have given anything for an old fashioned American meal."[58]

Cape Ann also arrived in New York City that Thursday night, carrying ninety-one passengers and thirty-eight members of the *Doria*'s crew.[59] When Mike and Meryl Stoller finally left *Cape Ann,* his writing partner, Jerry Leiber, stood waiting on the pier. He had brought some extra clothing and welcome piece of good news: "We have a smash hit!"

"You're kidding?" Mike asked. "'Hound Dog' and Big Mama Thornton?"

"No," Leiber replied, "some white kid named Elvis Presley."[60]

Alda Raimengia remembers "there was chaos on the pier when we arrived in New York." In the ensuing confusion, Franco's family, who had come from the Bronx to meet them, failed to spot them, and because Alda reported that she was four months pregnant, Red Cross officials insisted that she be examined at a local hospital. The woman who shared her room tried to question her, but Alda didn't understand English. But the next morning a newspaper arrived with a large photograph of the crippled *Doria*. Alda held it up for the woman to see and pointed first at it and then at herself, in an effort to explain why she was there. Luckily Franco soon appeared, and the couple dispatched telegrams to relatives back in Italy to let them know that they had survived. These came as a blessing, especially for Alda's family—"I came from a very small town with no real television reception to speak of at that time, but my brother had a radio headset so that he could hear the news every day," she recalls. "My family were listening to a nighttime radio show of music and entertainment, and then there was a break with the news of the *Andrea Doria*."[61]

Edward H. Allen was the last ship carrying survivors, including Captain Calamai and his senior officers, to arrive that Thursday night in New York. As soon as the ship docked, officials from the Italian Line and their lawyers rushed aboard. Members of the press had gathered en masse on the pier to question the captain, and Calamai's employer wanted to ensure that he delivered nothing more than general remarks. When Captain Calamai, still in his blue uniform, finally descended the gangway at 11:30 P.M., he faced a bewildering storm of flashbulbs, television cameras, and pushing microphones as he read from a prepared statement. "With the absolute certainty that no passengers were still on board the vessel, having reached such a list that to remain longer on board would have meant nothing else but a useless sacrifice of human lives, the Chief Engineer having already confirmed to me that nothing more could be done inasmuch as only emergency dynamo and pump were still working, having consulted the Staff Captain and the officers present, I gave the order to embark on the last boat. We left in order of rank. When the last officer had left, I too embarked."[62]

Calamai's brother happened to be living in New York at the time. His daughter Angela ushered her uncle Piero into a car and spirited him off to their apartment: reporters waited outside, and so she took the captain in a rear entrance. Captain Calamai, she recalled, "didn't say much. My feeling was that he was more sorry they didn't let him go down with the boat, because that was the classical way, and I think that hurt him more than anything—that he couldn't do what he thought he should."[63]

One last drama played itself out that Thursday night. Edward Morgan had seen his former wife, Jane Cianfarra, safely delivered to St. Clare's Hospital, where her broken right leg and ankle, along with her fractured right hand, could be properly treated. He still had no idea what had happened to their daughter, Linda, although the fact that her name had not appeared on any of the lists of survivors seemed to indicate the worst. Still, he phoned Francis Littlejohn, his director at ABC, and said he'd be there shortly to do his regular nightly radio broadcast.[64]

Morgan had just gotten into the studio when a reporter from *The New York Times* called, asking if he had a photograph of Linda that they could use. When Morgan asked why they wanted a picture, the reporter told him, "Of course, you know she and Joan and Cian are dead."

"Who the hell said so?" Morgan demanded. "I've just come off the *Ile de France*, and I couldn't find anybody to confirm anything."

"Well," the man told him, *New York Times* reporter Harrison Salisbury had "found the doctor who rescued your ex-wife and he saw the bodies."[65]

Stunned, Morgan put down the phone. He was due on air in just a few minutes. Although Littlejohn argued that he should skip the broadcast, Morgan swallowed his grief and sat before his microphone:

"Good evening," Morgan began. "Here is the shape of the news. Tonight it is the shape of disaster." He spoke of "the main story, the story around the world tonight, the story of the sinking of the *Andrea Doria* . . . About seventeen hundred persons were picked up from the *Andrea Doria* in the fog of early morning. Conflicting reports say that about five or six people were killed and hundreds injured. There is no conclusive count yet. . . . This is a jumbled story, a story told in the faces of the persons that you see on the ship. Perhaps the best way to tell it, from notes and from memory, is just to jog down through the notes informally as I go. Take for instance, a particular case: the case of a person who had persons, relatives, aboard the *Andrea Doria* and was notified this morning about five o'clock that the two ships, the *Andrea Doria* and the *Stockholm*, had collided in the fog last night. There is the numbing, the wait, the confusion, the conflicting reports. And then in the afternoon the news that correspondents would be picked up by the Coast Guard and taken down the harbor to board the *Ile de France*. . . . The afternoon in New York City was warm and humid, with a gauze of cotton cloud on the sky, and as the Coast Guard tugboat, which was ironically named *Nevasink*, went down New York Harbor toward Gravesend Bay, the afternoon was alive with activity. . . . A lump comes in one's throat as one sees this vessel, a vessel of mercy. . . . Customs and Immigration officials were put aboard from another tug, appropriately first. As we push under the starboard side, one looks up and sees a line—a necklace of faces—looking down from the rail. Somebody wants to know who are the passengers and who are the survivors. Soon one is able to tell. Here a shirttail sticking out. Here a nightshirt. Here a bandaged head. . . . But there were other people. There was Camille Cianfarra, the Madrid correspondent of the *New York Times,* his wife, Jane, and his stepchild and another child. Where were they, I asked. I was told that Mrs. Cianfarra was badly hurt. . . . One finds her. She is badly hurt but she is not on the critical list. She has multiple fractures and cuts. She asks about her husband. It is reported but it is not confirmed that Camille Cianfarra of the *New York Times* is among the dead. The children may be aboard another ship. It is not proved. It is not certain. . . . Slowly, little by little, torturously for the persons who don't know, happily for the persons who do, the whole pieces of the disaster will be fitted together."[66]

Morgan never once mentioned that his daughter, Linda, had been aboard the *Doria,* or that he had just learned that she had died before he went on air—it "seemed improper, as if I would be soliciting condolences in a public place," he later explained. As if holding out for a miracle, he returned to his hotel and rang the rescued Thure Peterson, who had told Harrison Salisbury of *The New York Times* that he had seen Linda's body in the wreckage of the ruined cabin on the *Doria.* "I apologize for bothering you," Morgan said, aware that Thure had lost his wife, Martha, "but I need your confirmation that Linda and Joan are dead."

"There is no doubt of it," Peterson said. "I saw their bodies." Why Peterson thought this is not known, but he seemed sincere in his belief.[67]

Though distraught, Morgan found "a certain comfort in an end to the doubt." He took a cab to St. Clare's to break the news to Jane. When he entered her hospital room, he found that Betsy Drake had come to visit her. "The girls had such an utterly happy time on the voyage," Betsy said in condolence. "You can remember that." Not until he was on his way back to the hotel did the enormity of the situation hit Morgan. Finally realizing that he had lost his daughter, he broke into sobs.[68]

Chapter Sixteen

———◆◆◆———

As the *Ile de France, Cape Ann, Thomas, Hornbeam,* and *Allen* left the scene of *Andrea Doria*'s sinking throughout Thursday morning, *Stockholm* remained, still stuck in place by the massive anchor chains loosed in the collision. Enestrom and Chief Officer Gustav Kallback tried to burn through the chains with acetylene torches: this was a nerve-racking task as they hung over the ruined and twisted bow, surrounded by the knifelike edges of steel plating and perilously clinging to ropes to avoid plunging some seventy feet into the sea. In the mass of wreckage they found a cocktail shaker from the *Doria* and Linda Morgan's little red autograph book.[1]

It took several tries to cut through the links. Standing on deck, Father Raymond Goedert watched the scene. Finally, the torches cut through the links, but the chains still hung over the wrecked bow and into the sea; Nordenson started *Stockholm*'s engines and began moving his ship in an effort to free it. Suddenly the entire ship seemed to shudder; in a terrible roar of metal tearing and twisting, almost seventy feet of the smashed and ruined bow, still attached to the chains, tore loose and crashed into the sea amid plumes of white water.[2] Goedert saw the mass of steel tear away and plunge into the ocean; as it did so, he saw a body float past.[3] Those closest to the wreckage saw that it was a woman, almost certainly Jeanette Carlin, who had been spotted trapped in the twisted metal hours earlier. Soon, the water was filled with blood, as sharks set upon the corpse.[4]

Finally, *Stockholm*, too, left the scene late that Thursday, headed back to New York.

Stockholm was under way when another tragedy struck. Fifty-year-old Carl Watres and his wife, Lillian, had been rescued from the *Doria*. "He just felt badly," recalled a friend, "and told us he was going to see the ship's doctor." Even this effort proved too exhausting: he collapsed into a deck chair.[5] Father Tom Kelly, sitting nearby, heard him moan: Watres fell out of the chair and onto the deck, having suffered a fatal heart attack.[6] "He never had heart trouble," Lillian later said bitterly. "But he wore himself out trying to help other passengers off the ship." To the press, she complained that, had the *Doria*'s crew acted appropriately in the rescue, her husband would still be alive.[7]

Stockholm kept its speed at a slow 8 knots, with Nordenson worried that a faster pace might further damage the ship's shredded bow and risk even greater disaster.[8] This meant that the voyage back to New York took an extra day—time the survivors passed often uncomfortably on the Swedish liner. As on the other rescue ships, survivors crowded the Purser's Office, filling out telegram forms to assure family and friends that they were safe, and added their names to lists that were radioed back and forth between the vessels in an attempt to compile a complete registry. Unfortunately many of these messages were apparently never sent. Klaus Dorneich recalls that he sent a telegram to his parents in Freiburg, Germany, that day from the *Stockholm*'s cable room, but they only learned that he had survived when, on landing in New York, he dispatched another telegram to them.[9] "I remember thinking how important it was to get news to the survivors' families as soon as possible, and in an organized way," says Raymond Goedert. He, too, sent a telegram to his parents, but they never received it.[10]

Passengers tried to adjust as best they could: most decided to spend that Thursday night sleeping on deck, uncertain that *Stockholm* was truly seaworthy and unwilling to risk being trapped inside the liner if disaster befell her: many still wore their life jackets as they dozed fitfully. Anticipating their departure, the Porporinos exchanged addresses with Professor Gösta Ekspong and his wife, Inga—the Swedish couple noted down the information, adding a description: "Italian family with two half-naked children on board *Stockholm* from *Andrea Doria*."[11]

Finally, *Stockholm* reached New York Harbor that Friday afternoon. Her battered bow stunned the crowds that gathered along the piers to watch her entrance—no one could understand how she was still afloat. The tangle of twisted and flattened steel hung perilously over the water: on the port side, only the last four letters of her name remained to be seen.[12] As four tugs eased *Stockholm* into her berth at Pier 97, the crowd of reporters and anxious relatives surged against the barricades. *Doria* survivors stood along the *Stockholm*'s railing; some shouted greetings but many were subdued—"Here there was none of the gay hand waving seen when a ship usually returns to port," newspapers reported.[13]

Among those waiting on the pier was Ruth Roman, desperate to see her son, Dickie. Newsreels and press photographers captured the scene as the boy, standing at *Stockholm*'s railing, spotted his mother and shouted out, "Mommy!" Ruth burst into tears, and shouted back, "Everything's all right now, it's all right!"[14] She ran to her son and swept him up into her arms, assuring him, "Miss Els is all right!"[15]

Cecilia Pick left the *Stockholm* in her dirty and tattered dress. "Look at me!" she exclaimed to a reporter. "I'm feeling like something the cat dragged in. Like I'd been left in brine for twenty-four hours." She tried to make light of the situation—"I'm arriving like a pioneer," she declared.[16]

Raymond Goedert's parents and one of his brothers waited on the pier: not having received a telegram from him, they had met each successive rescue ship the previous day, hoping to finally see the young priest.[17] Pat Margherita had been on his way to work the previous morning when he heard a radio report that *Andrea Doria* had sank, but there was no word of his sister, Antonietta Porporino, or her family. He quickly turned around, collected their father, Benedette, from Paterson, New Jersey, and drove to New York City. Late Thursday word finally came that Antonietta, her husband, Santino; and "a child" had survived and were arriving on *Stockholm* the next day. "They were going crazy thinking that one of us children had been killed," says Joe Porporino. When they were finally reunited, and it was obvious everyone had survived, Benedette was relieved but angry that the death of one of his grandchildren had been reported.[18]

Klaus Dorneich faced an onslaught of reporters as he disembarked from *Stockholm*. He boarded one of the waiting buses, which took survivors to Pier 84, where the Italian Line had arranged to process passengers and provide them with any immediate necessities. Officials gave him fifty dollars in cash and some blank prepaid telegram forms, so that he could notify his family that he was safe, before ushering him to a hotel, where the Italian Line had reserved and paid for a number of rooms for survivors. There, representatives of the American Red Cross waited with additional help, including vouchers for Macy's and Gimbels that allowed survivors to shop free of charge for new clothes, necessary toiletries, and replacement luggage.[19]

Efforts by the Red Cross did not end at the piers. Officials helped survivors arrange transportation to their intended destinations, and provided enough money to cover thirty days of rent as well as the purchase of "minimum household furnishings for immigrants who lost their furnishings aboard the *Andrea Doria* or who lost funds that were to have been used for the purchase of furnishings." They sent letters to local chapters across the country, noting that "immigrants on the *Andrea Doria* have had a terrifying experience and a sad introduction to a new country" and suggested that churches adopt families and provide financial and spiritual assistance.[20]

The last of the rescue ships had come in, but dramas continued playing out across New York City. Edward Morgan had drifted off into an agonized sleep Thursday evening, convinced that his daughter, Linda, had perished in the collision. But Friday morning another telephone call stunned him. "*The Times* just phoned," Morgan's editor at ABC Francis Littlejohn said. "They have a list of survivors coming in on the *Stockholm* and the name Linda Morgan is on it. Probably a mistake but the ship is docking now and you'd better go down and find out."[21]

Morgan thought that it must be "a cruel joke," especially after Thure Peterson had assured him the previous evening that he'd seen Linda's body in the wreckage. Arriving at the pier, Morgan saw the "hideous wound of tangled steel" that had once been *Stockholm*'s bow. This time, he was unable to board the ship and had to wait until her officers began disembarking to question them about Linda. Finally, Morgan cornered *Stockholm*'s Purser Curt Dawe, who stunned him by saying that Linda was indeed alive. "You ought to know where we found your daughter," Dawe said. "In the wreckage on the bow." Badly injured, the young girl had already been taken off the ship and was on her way to Roosevelt Hospital.[22]

Linda remembers being carried off *Stockholm* aboard a stretcher: "The press was all around us asking questions," she says.[23] In great pain, and in a daze from the morphine administered to her aboard the Swedish liner, she managed to mumble a few words: "I don't know what happened to my mother, sister, or father. I was thrown out of my cabin—I think—on a pile of stuff. A Spanish man helped me. I don't know what else happened."[24] There was no peace once she was on her way to the hospital: "The ambulance sound was frightening and I was scared of all that was happening, still not comprehending anything."[25]

Morgan, meanwhile, had another frantic taxi ride across town. When he arrived at Roosevelt he was told that Linda had instead been taken to St. Vincent's Hospital. Back to a cab he raced: "The drive downtown seemed like a trip across the continent," Morgan recalled. He arrived at St. Vincent's just as Linda was being wheeled into the radiology department for X-rays prior to surgery to treat her fractured legs and right arm.[26] On learning of Morgan's arrival, a nurse halted the process briefly, telling Linda, "Your father is coming to see you." Linda "assumed they meant my stepfather, Camille. When my father walked into the room I was disappointed. I didn't know him well, and I wanted to see the family who had tucked me into bed a few days earlier. But I hid my disappointment."[27]

"Oh, Daddy," Linda asked her father, "where is Joan?" Thoroughly unnerved by his experiences of the last twenty-four hours and aware that he had already received erroneous information, Morgan apparently said nothing, but he did tell Linda that her mother had been rescued and was in another hospital. Once Linda was wheeled away, Morgan raced to the telephone and rang Jane's room at St. Clare's

Hospital. "Linda is alive," he told his former wife. "I am with her now."[28]

As dusk fell across Manhattan, Morgan once again returned to the ABC studio to make his nightly broadcast. The previous night, he had made no mention of the fact that his daughter had been aboard the *Doria* and was presumed dead; now, the joy of her survival burst forth as Morgan once again took to the airwaves:

"How does a reporter cover a story in which he himself is partly involved? Especially a story that touches emotions springing from the very roots of being, the emotions that are now the lovely flower of life, now the hard, piercing cactus of death . . . Within the space of twenty-four hours this reporter has been pushed down the elevator shaft of the subbasement of despair and raised again to the heights of incredible joy, washed, one suspects, with a slightly extravagant rivulet of some heavenly champagne. Last night, as far as the world at large was concerned, a girl, age fourteen, nationality American, was dead. She happens to be this reporter's daughter. She had been killed, according to the incontrovertible evidence of an eyewitness, by the crash of the liner Stockholm *into the very stateroom on the* Andrea Doria *which her stepfather,* New York Times *correspondent Camille Cianfarra, and her mother, Jane Cianfarra, occupied. Linda and her half sister, Joan, were sleeping in their cabin just forward of the Cianfarras. But Linda is not dead. One can only deduce that the impact hurled her from her bunk into the wreckage of the bow of the* Stockholm, *where she was found, alive, painfully but not critically hurt. . . . There is something sacred I feel about the mystery of life which in the alchemy of the unknown enables people, as they face the supposed tragedy of death, their own or that of another. It makes other things seem so petty and unimportant . . . Through all this incredible blackness and sunshine I kept remembering what a wonderful human being from Philadelphia named C. Jared Ingersoll once told me in recounting how he kept right on going after the death of his wife and then his son. 'I try to live fully,' he said, 'so that when my luck changes there will be little room for regret or recrimination over time lost or*

misspent.' This reporter hopes tonight he has learned that lesson well enough to teach it with tenderness to a girl young enough to grow with it into a full blossom that will give joy to others for her very living. Perhaps, perhaps, she has learned it already herself."[29]

But not every story had a happy ending. After landing in New York aboard the *Ile de France*, Tullio and Filomena Di Sandro had raced through the night across Connecticut, Rhode Island, and Massachusetts, hoping desperately to reach their hospitalized daughter, Norma, in Boston. Police escorts even shepherded them part of the way. The couple arrived at Brighton Marine Hospital at three fifteen on the morning of July 27. "My baby daughter!" Filomena cried out on seeing the unconscious Norma before fainting. When she came to, doctors explained that they had already performed surgery to relieve pressure on the brain caused when Norma's head hit the side of one of *Stockholm*'s lifeboats. "We've done everything we can," a physician assured the parents. "All we can do now is wait and hope she wakes up."[30] She never did: at nine fifteen that Friday night, shortly after Edward Morgan had shared the jubilant news of his daughter Linda's miraculous survival, Norma Di Sandro died without ever regaining consciousness.

A week later, clad in a white gown and holding a Bible in her tiny hands, Norma was buried—at Red Cross expense—at St. Francis Cemetery in Pawtucket, Rhode Island.[31] A month earlier, Tullio's half brother in Rhode Island had registered Norma for school; now, the classmates she would never know appeared at the service, all dressed in white. Norma was buried beneath a monument adorned with a Madonna and St. Joseph flanking a little girl clutching a lily as a symbol of eternal purity.[32]

Chapter Seventeen

⎯⎯•◆•⎯⎯

Exactly one week after *Andrea Doria* was lost, on August 2, Cardinal Francis Spellman presided over a requiem mass for the victims at New York City's immense St. Patrick's Cathedral. Captain Calamai emerged from seclusion to attend the service. After his brief statement on arriving in New York, he had largely disappeared from public view, though he did put in an appearance at Manhattan's Hotel Governor Clinton, where most of the *Doria's* surviving crew members were given temporary lodging. "I, as well as you," the captain told the assembled crew, "have a broken heart. You did all that you should have done to save the passengers and I thank you all." In reply, the crew had shouted, "Long live our Captain!"[1]

Italian Line officials and lawyers kept Calamai isolated: they wanted no further public statements about the collision. Now, he joined some four hundred members of the vanished liner's crew. A large black cat-afalque stood before the steps to the altar, flanked by lighted tapers burning in tall candelabra on either side. Twenty-five Italian-American priests joined the cardinal in celebrating mass: all wore black.[2] Many survivors, along with relatives of the dead, filled the cathedral, among them Klaus Dorneich. The Te Deum, as he recalls, was "unforgettable" as it "sounded throughout this impressive cathedral in the midst of Manhattan."[3]

In one way the service marked an end to the period of public mourning, but tendrils of the tragedy continued to unravel and grow as the weeks passed. "No matter how far we press against the outer limits of time and space with the science and engineering we take for granted," read an editorial in the *New York Post*, "there will always come a time when the ultimate test faces us in stark and simple terms: man against nature with nothing to aid him but his fellow man. Wednesday night was such a time. The original dispatches that all aboard were safe and/or accounted for were much too slick and easy to be believed. It is only now, when one tragic epic story begins to break down into two thousand short stories that courage and valor take shape in a manner one can recognize and thrill to."[4]

The first twenty-four hours after the disaster had passed in a kind of stunned disbelief that such a thing could happen in the modern age between two liners each equipped with the latest technology. There had been dramatic stories of uncertainty and tales of heroic rescue. But with the arrival of the *Ile de France* and then the *Thomas,* survivors began relating shockingly different stories that portrayed the *Doria*'s crew as, at best, negligent and at worst, cowardly.

Things had taken an ugly turn when *Cape Ann* arrived in New York. During the voyage, Meryl Stoller had heard an American sailor aboard the ship recount how, when they first dispatched their lifeboat to the stricken liner, members of *Andrea Doria*'s crew had tried to descend first; the Americans had threatened the men with their oars, insisting that the passengers be saved first. This only added to the sense of resentment: Mike and Meryl had heard no announcements and had received no assistance from the *Doria*'s crew. Others shared this bitterness, and one man finally suggested that the survivors write a statement, outlining what they saw as negligence on the part of the Italian sailors.[5]

"It is our intent to show that there existed a state of complete negligence on the part of the crew and the officers toward its obligations and responsibilities to the safety of the passengers of the ship," the statement began. It charged that passengers had not been told of their muster stations, and that "no instructions were received" that "lifebelts should be donned." Passengers, it said, "acted on their own initiative." The crew "assumed no posts or took any organized action at any time during the entire period of the emergency," although the statement praised "a small number of crew members who worked alongside of the passengers, as individuals. In aiding the abandoning of the ship, we give these men recognition as individuals, carrying a private sense of responsibility." It ended: "It is our firm belief," the statement finished, "that the above mentioned facts constitute abhorrent disregard for the fundamental responsibilities of the officers and crew of the ship for the safety of the passengers in their care."[6]

All but one of the surviving passengers on *Cape Ann* signed the statement. Alda Raimengia put her name to the document but later regretted it.[7] Mike Stoller wondered if some of the Italian passengers who did so had thought that they were adding their names to a list of survivors.[8] This is possible, but many who signed clearly understood the statement, which was passed on to the media even before *Cape Ann* docked.

This statement quickly loomed large in the *Doria* story. While some of the allegations—no lifeboat drills and no announcements—were erroneous, others were not so easily dismissed. The allegations received widespread publicity and helped cement opinions about the *Doria's* crew, which many survivors were only too happy to share with members of the media who greeted them along the piers.

More anger had spilled when *Stockholm* arrived in New York. One of the Swedish stewards complained that most of those in the first boats from *Andrea Doria* had been "kitchen help" from the Italian liner.[9] "Right after the crash," said Lillian Watres, "crewmen in our First Class area got out bottles of whiskey, which they passed around among themselves and started drinking. Then they disappeared. I asked the head steward where I should go. He said, 'Anywhere,' and ran off."[10] "It had been a pleasant trip," she later commented. "We enjoyed Italy. But I lost my love for Italians that night."[11]

"As far as any help went," Barbara Boggs wrote, "the crew, by and large, might as well have been playing pinochle."[12] "The Italian crew," said Chad Gifford, "by all means did not show an example of maritime leadership, to say the least." His brother Jock added, "It was the passengers that were taking the leadership positions." And their father, Clarence, declared, "There was not too much organization in the rescue."[13] Klaus Dorneich said, "Of the ship's personnel, nothing was to be seen so far on our deck. A few sailors had dropped long ropes down the side and had then disappeared."[14] Mike Stoller, too, complained that "the crew was nowhere to be found."[15] Cecilia Pick was particularly bitter when it came to her experiences—"as usual and traditional," she wrote to her sister, "the Italian crew were first off . . . I do want to stress how awful the behavior of the officers was, particularly in not giving assistance or any orders."[16]

Some attempted to downplay any complaints at the time. Philadelphia mayor Richardson Dilworth, for example, sent the Italian Line an open letter: "I want to tell you that both my wife and I have nothing but good to say about the beautiful ship *Andrea Doria* and about the conduct of the crew as we saw it the night of the accident. . . . Both the stewards who were helping the passengers from the deck, and the men who were manning the boats, certainly did an outstanding job."[17] Later, and privately, Dilworth is said to have been more equivocal, condemning much of the crew's behavior as "atrocious."[18]

The criticism became a rolling, self-fulfilling prophecy. Contrary voices were often drowned out—and there were indeed contrary voices. One survivor offered: "There are just no words to describe the courage of the crew of the *Andrea Doria*."[19] Another praised the *Doria*'s crew as "wonderful and very helpful throughout."[20] "I think the crew did a great job in getting people off the ship," says Pat Mastrincola. "I wouldn't be here if not for them. Some of the waiters and kitchen crew left before passengers, but they had no loyalty to us, while the crew felt responsible."[21]

When Captain Calamai had arrived in New York late on the night of July 26, the narrative of negligence had already taken hold. The bewildered captain was met by a barrage of shouted questions, asking about the collision and the behavior of the crew. The Italian Line's lawyers had forbidden Calamai to address anything touching on the collision, but he was so infuriated by the charges against his crew that he briefly engaged. When asked if the *Doria*'s first lifeboats reaching *Stockholm* had principally carried members of his crew, Calamai said, "I deny it! I deny it!"[22] In a few words, Calamai said: "The search and rescue was made possible because of the discipline and calm of the passengers and the sense of duty of my crew," before officials from the Italian Line hustled him away from the mob and into a waiting car.[23]

Understandably these accusations caused resentment among the *Doria*'s crew. "We worked so hard to save so many lives," Cadet Mario Maracci told a reporter. "Perhaps they didn't understand. The passengers were highly excitable, fighting among themselves. They made it difficult."[24] Sebastiano Natta, the *Doria*'s chaplain, made a similar statement: "The men," he said, "performed in the best tradition of the sea. They were courageous to the point of death in aiding passengers to escape unharmed."[25]

A propaganda war was being waged across the pages of America's newspapers, one in which the Italians were reluctant to join. At first, others took up the cause. The August 2 issue of *The Pilot*, published by the National Maritime Union of America, interviewed crew members from *Cape Ann*. All denied seeing any cowardice by the *Doria*'s crew.[26] The following day, a letter from a survivor appeared in *The New York Times* defending the *Doria*'s crew: "I regret that some . . . of my rescued companions on the rescue ship *Cape Ann* chose to criticize the officers and crew of the *Andrea Doria* in terms that are, for the most part, untrue, and for the remaining part display the petitioners' inability to think when suffering from shock and fatigue. . . . What I witnessed in the hours I spent on the stricken ship following the crash and during my rescue by an Italian crew and an Italian-manned lifeboat have me cause to admire the actions and behavior of the officers and crew of the *Andrea Doria* and to be grateful to them. They met the crisis with courage and intelligence, more than fulfilling their responsibilities and obligations."[27]

Such isolated letters did little to arrest the growing public perception that the *Doria*'s crew had behaved in a cowardly manner. On August 6, therefore, the Italian Line issued a press release:

Officials of the Italian Line, indignant at the unwarranted criticism leveled at the crew of the Andrea Doria, *praised the action of the*

officers and crew in effecting a rescue for more than 1,650 passengers,
an operation unprecedented in maritime history. They pointed out
that lists of survivors showed that nearly all the dead, missing and
unaccounted for were berthed in cabins situated in the area that was
pierced by the prow of the Stockholm. . . . *They demonstrated evidence*
that passengers who were on the Doria *almost to the last attest to the*
fact that none of the ship's crew were guilty of neglect of duty. Back
and rested from the nightmare at sea, Andrea Doria *passengers rallied*
to the defense of the crew. Survivors who had blasted the crew on
television called in to say they had spoken in haste; others claimed to
have been misquoted in newspapers. From far and wide letters came
into the Italian Line office on New York's State Street, attesting that
the crew had, in fact, acted in the true tradition of the sea.[28]

Such accusations of negligence were scarcely new to maritime di-
sasters. Indeed, it had all happened before, in more overt and deadly
fashion. In the 1898 sinking of the French ocean liner *La Bourgogne,*
crew members used axes, knives, and oars to keep passengers away
from the places that they themselves took in the few available lifeboats.
There were even reports that surviving passengers in the water had their
fingers or hands hacked off by crew members when they tried to climb
into the bobbing lifeboats.

Survivors of the *Lusitania* disaster in 1915 suffered a more benign
neglect. Life jackets were in short supply, but many passengers complained that crew members quickly grabbed the few readily available
and refused to hand them over. There seemed to be complete chaos
when it came to the frantic evacuation of the doomed liner—there was
"no discipline or order," complained passenger Charles Lauriat, and "no
officers taking charge."[29] The end result was that only 39 percent of the
passengers survived, compared to 42 percent of the *Lusitania*'s crew.[30]

History is rarely composed of black and white: nuanced shades of
gray shape context and suggest answers more complex than simplistic
readings wholly condemning the *Doria*'s crew, on one side, or dismissing complaints outright, on the other. Many survivors were naturally
in shock after the disaster, and the anger that spilled out was not al-

ways justified; the reflexive Italian defense, driven by nationalistic sentiments, was often equally less than compelling. The controversy only gained momentum, as the charges "cast a stigma upon the integrity of not only the *Andrea Doria* crew and the Italian Line but the seamen everywhere," as one author commented.[31]

It is futile to attack the experience of many passengers who felt themselves abandoned or ignored by the liner's crew during these tormented hours. Much of the criticism, though, stemmed from the fact that most passengers had gathered on the port side while the majority of the crew focused their efforts on the starboard side, launching lifeboats and working on ropes and netting down which they hoped to evacuate the liner. They were thus largely invisible for many hours. There was also possible confusion over the colors of the life jackets, gray for the crew and orange for the passengers. It was not always safe to make assumptions: "I did see quite a few crew members giving their life jackets to passengers who had been unable to get their own," said Robert Young, who thus noted, "a lifeboat loaded with people wearing gray life jackets did not necessarily mean that they were all crew members."[32] Mike Stoller was among those who received a life jacket from a crew member. But some passengers, like Dun Gifford, also handed orange jackets to crew members who did not have one.

Despite Calamai's denials, it is true that the majority of those in the liner's first three lifeboats to reach *Stockholm* were members of the *Doria*'s crew. Even Osvaldo Magagnini was forced to admit this uncomfortable fact: "The rescue statistics were bad for us," he said. "Not all men are the same."[33]

In the case of the *Doria*'s crew, two things become apparent. The first is that many of the reports alleging cowardice were undoubtedly, as the *Doria*'s Third Officer Eugenio Giannini said, "distorted." But not all, and here the distinction between the liner's officers and able-bodied seamen and its service personnel helps clarify the issue. The small minority attached to the *Doria* who fled the ship, especially those in the first three lifeboats to reach *Stockholm*, were waiters, stewards, or members of the kitchen crew. This Giannini admitted, saying, "One can't expect every staff member out of 532 to display optimal courage."[34]

In the heat of the moment, in terror and facing the ordeal of rescue, it is natural that most passengers who offered up complaints about the *Doria*'s crew made no such delineations. Few understood why a waiter who served their dinner should feel any less responsible for their safety than an officer attired in a crisp uniform. Once the allegations reached the newspapers, most of the public lumped them all together, whether steward or senior officer. The resulting press simply tarred the valiant members of the crew with the same brush that should have been reserved for the small number of service personnel who placed the value of their own lives above the needs of the passengers.

In the wake of the tragedy survivors faced incessant demands from the press as they tried to come to terms with the emotional impact of the disaster. It had all unfolded with chilling randomness: decisions to take a last stroll around deck, play a game of Scrabble, or nurse a final drink had saved some lives, while early bedtimes had claimed others. The trauma was often unseen, unsuspected. "At the time I didn't think I had really been affected by the sinking," says Madge Young. "Being fourteen, I had no thought that we'd ever been in real danger, and I certainly had no idea that the ship would actually sink. I didn't lose anyone. I can't say that I had any real nightmares, but after the sinking I started having the same dream, over and over. I'd be in the ocean drowning, and then the next thing, I'd be in an elevator and the doors would open and I'd walk out. As soon as those doors opened, I knew everything was going to be okay."[35]

On Saturday, July 28, Madge and her mother went to St. Vincent's Hospital to visit Linda Morgan. "She'd just had an operation, and so I didn't stay long," Madge recalls.[36] "I thought to myself, Lucky for them," Linda says, "they didn't get hurt at all." She asked them to sign her little red autograph book, which had been returned to her after being discovered in the wreckage of *Stockholm*'s bow.[37] Bernabe Polanco Garcia, the Stockholm crew member who had rescued her, also came to see Linda, bringing her three carnations and adding his name to her autograph book.[38]

It would take nearly two months, and several operations, before Linda's shattered legs were repaired and she was finally released. She wanted to see her mother, but Jane—herself confined to another hospital for her fractured leg and hand—was, like her daughter, temporarily immobilized by casts and in traction.[39] In the first few days, Linda remembers, "I had no true privacy. . . . There was pandemonium all around me as the press was in and out of my room constantly for interviews and photographs. My father, being a broadcaster, believed the media should have easy access to my story and me. I admit that I enjoyed the attention I was getting while I was awake but the nights were disturbing. I would wake up from nightmares feeling frightened and disoriented."[40]

After a few days, Edward Morgan finally told Linda that both her stepfather and her half sister had perished. "It was almost too much for me to comprehend," she recalls. "I was very close to my stepdad, who had raised me since the age of two." As for Joan, "I wished I had told her that I loved her. But instead I recalled the fights we had had, and I felt remorseful." Linda would gradually recover, but by the end of that summer, she had grown to hate the constant media attention, of "being reminded of how I had lain on top of that giant heap of twisted steel and had been spared being dropped into the ocean within moments."[41]

Richardson and Ann Dilworth returned to Philadelphia, where the controversial mayor suddenly found himself hailed as a hero. Never one to miss an opportunity, he invited reporters into his living room and enthralled them with an account of the disaster. A photographer managed not only to record Ann's still blackened eye but also the mayor, looking distinctly unkempt, hair askew and barefoot as he perched on the edge of a sofa whose springs stuck out of the bottom. When the photo appeared, Dilworth received offers from a number of upholsterers and furniture stores, each eager to replace the decrepit sofa.[42] A few weeks later, Dilworth was again in the limelight when he welcomed fellow survivors Nora Kovach and Istvan Rabovsky, who had just made a triumphant and much publicized appearance on Ed Sullivan's television show, to Philadelphia and presented them with a key to the city.[43]

"We all had trouble calming down," Barbara Bliss recalled of returning to her Long Island home. "I remember running back and forth from my bedroom to my mother's, chatting incessantly. I wanted to have a turn on the telephone, but before I could pick up the receiver, another concerned friend or relative would be calling." There was a brief escape when they went to their summer house on Martha's Vineyard the following week. One day Dun Gifford sailed over from his parents' summer house on Nantucket and he and Barbara shared stories of how debris from the wreck—deck chairs, life jackets, and assorted flotsam—kept washing up on their beaches. This "eerie" sense gave way to panic when Barbara watched a television program on the disaster. "I began to get short of breath," she wrote, "and my heart started to beat very fast. When I saw the live footage of the ship going down, I began crying uncontrollably."[44]

The family had another jolt just a few weeks after the *Doria* was lost. Barbara Boggs's father, Marshall Field III, and his wife, Ruth, were on holiday in Maine when their yacht *Corisande II* struck a submerged rock and began sinking. Field and his wife had to cling to the side of the ship and clamber atop a nearby reef to avoid drowning. It was an unwelcome reminder of a trauma whose memory would never fade away.[45]

Some survivors seemed able to quickly put the disaster behind them, at least in emotional terms. Klaus Dorneich had little lingering trauma from that night at sea. Over the next week, he faced the ordeal of filing separate claims on his lost luggage; American Express travelers' checks; going to the German consulate to seek a replacement for his passport and more cash loans; and obtaining a new ticket on Air France. Late that Friday, a reporter working for a German magazine sought him out and obtained an interview. A few hours later, Klaus went off to Long Island to spend the weekend with the family of a former exchange student he had befriended at the University of Freiburg. "There was a celebration dinner," he recalls, "and half the neighborhood gathered to congratulate me on my lucky rescue. From all of this I was so excited that I hardly could sleep that night, but rather used the time to punch on a borrowed typewriter my first report that I had already written as a draft on the stationery of first class lounge still on board the *Stockholm* days before." He was delighted to sell his firsthand account to several German magazines and newspapers, which gave him some much appreciated additional money. He visited some friends in St. Louis before finally leaving for Mexico City.[46]

Many survivors, though, were not as fortunate in their experiences. A thread of psychological scars ran just beneath the surface, barely understood and often ignored as people struggled to readjust to life in the days after the disaster. Returning to Chicago, Father Richard Wojcik found his oratorical skills in demand as he was repeatedly asked to speak about the *Doria*. He didn't mind, and nothing seemed wrong as he relived the experience, but he soon found himself unable to sleep and spent nights pacing back and forth.[47]

When the Mastrincola family finally returned home, all that young Arlene wanted was a bath—"I felt filthy," she says. There were relatives in and out of the house for the next few days, along with a constant stream of reporters. "Everyone wanted to know all about it," Arlene remembers.[48] "We were like celebrities," Pat recalls. "I thought this was really nice, and they took pictures of me kissing my sister and put them in the paper. But after the third day or so they were writing all kinds of crap, including that I was a girl, so I finally took to fleeing the house and climbing a pine tree in our backyard to hide whenever they showed up." Then Pat began having nightmares: "I would be so scared I wouldn't open my eyes, and my father would come in and make me open them—once I saw the square windows of our house I knew I was okay. If I'd have seen portholes I would have lost it."[49]

Adalgisa Di Fabio spent the Friday after the collision shopping with her aunt to temporarily replace the wardrobe she had lost on the *Doria*. She drifted through these days without much thought about the ordeal she had undergone, at least until the telephone rang in her uncle Francesco's house one day. The caller explained that she was the daughter of *Doria* passenger Anita Leone, whose elegant clothing and polished manner had so impressed Adalgisa aboard the liner. Now, Adalgisa learned that Anita had perished in the collision. "That's when I realized everything that had happened and it suddenly all caught up with me,"

Adalgisa says. "I began having nightmares. I went to bed and would wake up screaming. It was the worst thing: my aunt would rush in and sleep with me."[50]

After departing the *Ile de France*, Melania Ansuini and her family spent several weeks with family in Philadelphia before taking a train across America to San Jose, California, where they had planned to settle with relatives. The nightmares came and went—Melania dreamed that she was "surrounded by impassable tanks of water" and could not escape. But they gradually faded, at least until the day when one of her cousins took her on an excursion. She had no idea where they were going when suddenly their car came to a headland above Carmel. As soon as Melania saw that they were headed for the beach—and the water—"I felt my heart begin to sink."[51]

Cecilia Pick tried to be philosophical. After arriving in New York, she and John had gone to stay with his family. Sitting down to write a letter to her sister, she inexplicably found herself "suffering from a strange form of shock, which is intense contraction of all the neck muscles and nerves, which practically makes me pass out; it occurs about three times a day, and I feel like dying so am under treatment." Still, she tried to be optimistic: "Perhaps I was altogether too happy; however God spared us to each other." Her new husband, Cecilia declared, "is just the most wonderful person; he too is suffering from shock and exposure but tries to control his feelings for my sake and we try also to console each other for our mutual losses, and pray and have prayed so much that I am sure God will give us strength and courage." Care packages began arriving from friends—"it really is difficult to conceive that one has just nothing, as when one was born. Everything went, absolutely everything, and I try not to think as it is very upsetting." She ended by imploring her sister to send some money and "a few items of clothing, which might make life brighter."[52]

For those who had lost relatives aboard the *Doria*, the first week after the collision was a time of pain and grief. Charles Thieriot had met his nephew Peter as the young boy came off the *Ile de France* and quickly took him to his house on Long Island. "The main problem was keeping him away from newsstands," he recalled, not wanting Peter to see any reports about his parents until the facts were certain. After a few days, though, he finally faced the inevitable. "No question about it," he told Peter, "your parents are dead. They died instantly, and there was no lingering pain." Having seen the hole in the *Doria*'s side where his parents' cabin had been, Peter had instinctively known that his parents were gone, but not until his uncle said the words did the reality finally hit him. "I cried," Peter says, "not because of the surprise, but because someone had put it on the table."[53]

Ross Sergio, as his son Anthony recalls, tried to act as normally as possible, but it was obvious that he was holding everything inside. Having lost his mother and four siblings, Anthony wanted only to return to Italy. He avoided going to church, and although friends and relatives tried to comfort him by saying, "They're in a better place," he would argue bitterly. "I didn't want to hear anything about anything," he recalls. The disaster had left his aunt Margaret completely shattered; like her nephew, she no longer wanted to leave the house to attend church. Anthony thought that she had simply lost the will to live. As for Paul, he carried his own guilt, never able to forgive himself for not having allowed his youngest niece and nephew to stay in his cabin that fatal night.[54]

"It was so unnecessary," said Christina Covino's daughter. She could not get beyond the horrific idea that her mother and her aunt Amelia Iazzetta had likely been alive for hours after the collision and had drowned when no help came to rescue them from their cabin. "It was so uncalled for. The family hasn't been the same since. We cry every day, every single day. We just can't get over it—that our mother is at the bottom of the sea."[55]

In all, forty-six people had died aboard *Andrea Doria*, and five members of *Stockholm*'s crew also perished. It was a miracle that the casualty numbers were so low, though there were three additional victims. The first was Carl Watres, who had suffered his fatal heart attack aboard *Stockholm* after exhausting himself in the rescue efforts. The death of Norma Di Sandro on the evening of July 27 added to the list. The last of the casualties directly caused by the collision was forty-eight-year-old Angelina Greco, who had broken her back during the evacuation when she fell into a lifeboat from *Ile de France*. She lingered in a hospital for six months, in great pain, before finally succumbing to her injuries.

Chapter Eighteen

◆•◆

"Do you think you are to blame for the collision?" a reporter had asked Captain Nordenson when *Stockholm* arrived in New York on July 27. The Swedish captain demurred: "I don't think I should answer that question." As reporters continued with their questions, Charles Haight, a lawyer from the firm of Haight, Gardner and Poor that represented the Swedish American Line, intervened and ended the press conference: the issue, he declared, would be settled in the legal process.[1]

A formal inquiry into the collision was inevitable. Within twenty-four hours of the *Doria*'s loss, the United States House of Representatives Committee on Merchant Marine and Fisheries announced that they were commissioning an investigation into the sinking. While this would involve an expert review of the circumstances surrounding the disaster, it was doomed to be cursory at best: the House committee had no authority to compel testimony or demand cooperation from two foreign-based shipping lines.[2]

The Italian Line hoped to settle the issue quickly. Harold Kennedy, their lawyer in New York, wrote a memorandum to the Swedish American Line's New York lawyer Charles Haight: "This is a mutual fault case. For the good of the industry let us settle it now 50/50 and worry about the details some other time." Haight's reply was abrupt: "Your offer is refused. You are solely at fault."[3]

On August 6, the press picked up the Swedish American Line's allegations. Among other things, these asserted that *Andrea Doria* had suddenly turned into the path of *Stockholm* and thus caused the collision; that the Italian liner had failed to maintain a proper lookout; that *Andrea Doria*'s speed in the fog was reckless; that her radar equipment had been faulty and not properly manned; and that her captain and crew had been negligent in their handling of the ship.[4] A formal letter outlined these complaints. If the Italian Line did not agree in advance to limit the Swedish American Line's liability for actual losses and claims by passengers, the Swedes threatened to go to court and assert that the *Doria* sank not because of the collision but because it was inherently unseaworthy; lacked necessary stability; and that her pumps had not been used properly after the collision. It also claimed that "many of the deaths and injuries were not proximately caused by the collision but on the contrary by the bad behavior of the crew of the *Doria* following the collision, which was the result of lack of discipline, inadequate emergency drills and emotional instability."[5]

This salvo, in what had become an ongoing propaganda war waged in the press, signaled that the Swedish American Line was on the attack. The Italian Line fought back, pointing out that Nordenson's decision to steer *Stockholm* on a course some twenty miles north of the recommended eastbound course, as well as her final turn to starboard, had caused the collision.[6] Under these circumstances, neither shipping line could reach a mutual settlement, and both ended up suing each other. The Italian Line asked for $30 million to cover the loss of the *Doria*, while the Swedes asked for $2 million to cover the cost of replacing *Stockholm*'s bow and loss of revenue.[7]

A preliminary inquest began on September 19, 1956, in the United States District Court for the Southern District in New York, presided over by Federal Judge Lawrence E. Walsh, who was assisted by four attorneys (Simon Rifkind, Louis Loeb, Benjamin Matthews, and Mark MacLay) charged with assembling the evidence.[8] In addition to testimony from the two captains and members of their crew, the inquest examined data preserved in the course recorders from both ships.

Reporters crowded the courtroom to watch the proceedings. Carstens was the first witness. Charles Haight, representing the Swedish American Line, treated him with extreme care and allowed a visibly nervous

Carstens to give his version of events without interruption, including his contention that it had been "about 11 P.M." when he had first observed the *Doria* on *Stockholm*'s radar.[9] Even under friendly questioning, Carstens couldn't explain why the "Night Order Pad" containing Nordenson's instructions to him had gone missing.[10] He next confessed that instead of following the rules in *Stockholm*'s navigation instruction book outlining the use of radar and plotting to evaluate the speed of an oncoming vessel, he had made an educated guess; although he insisted that he had plotted three times that night, he had only recorded having done so once.[11]

Eugene Underwood, representing the Italian Line, was more forceful, and under his cross-examination Carstens began making damaging admissions. Just before the collision he had answered a telephone call from the lookout, which took his attention away from the radar and from the view.[12] He acknowledged that as he turned *Stockholm* to starboard (and toward the *Doria*) he had not sounded the required siren alert, which might have warned Captain Calamai of his intentions.[13] He was also forced to admit that Larsen, the helmsman on *Stockholm*, was "more interested in surrounding things than in the compass" and that he often veered off course.[14]

Carstens gave most of his testimony in Swedish, though as he became increasingly agitated by Underwood's cross-examination he began shouting answers in English. Carstens first claimed that *Stockholm* had not been in a fog and that visibility was clear that night. Underwood pointed out that ordinary visibility at sea meant that Carstens should have been able to see the *Doria*'s lights at a distance of no more than five miles, yet the young officer insisted that he had not observed the Italian liner until less than two miles separated them. If there was no fog, Underwood demanded, "What do you think obscured her lights?"[15]

"I'm also wondering about that," Carstens replied. Under continued questioning, Carstens admitted that "something, maybe a fog bank," had obscured the *Doria* that night.[16] Finally, he conceded that a bank of fog had prevented him from seeing the Italian liner.[17]

At several damaging points in Carstens's testimony, Haight jumped up and shouted objections.[18] But he could not save Carstens when

Underwood began pressing the young Swedish officer on his claim that he had first spotted the *Doria* at 11:00 P.M. that night and that she had been some twelve miles away. The collision occurred less than ten minutes later. The *Doria* was traveling at 21.8 knots, and the *Stockholm* at 18.5: it was impossible for the ships to cover the distance separating them, even at their top speeds. This alone proved that the *Doria* had been some five miles from *Stockholm* when Carstens had first spotted her.[19] Faced with this uncomfortable fact, Carstens changed his story, claiming that 11:00 P.M. had only been an estimate on his part.[20]

Captain Nordenson's testimony scarcely went better for the Swedish American Line: on the third day, when asked to explain how Carstens had made such significant errors in plotting, Nordenson said nothing, then murmured, "I do not feel well." He was admitted to a local hospital, to be treated for a small blood clot in the brain, and the proceedings were postponed.[21] There was little sympathy from Underwood when the Swedish captain returned. Nordenson admitted that he was sailing north of the recommended outbound track to save time and fuel, and had not reduced his ship's speed despite the area being known for fog.[22]

When Captain Calamai finally took the stand, he seemed to carry the weight of the disaster on his shoulders. He explained that he had avoided executing the required port-to-port passing maneuver "because I considered that the two ships were going green-to-green [starboard-to-starboard]."[23] A turn to port would have taken the *Doria* directly into *Stockholm*'s path.

The hearings in New York City were in temporary recess when the House committee on Merchant Marine and Fisheries issued its report on December 21, 1956. Penned by retired US Vice Admiral E. L. Cochrane, Rear Admiral H. C. Shepheard, Coast Guard Commodore E. M. Webster, and H. L. Steward, emeritus professor of mechanical and marine engineering at Yale University, this raised "serious questions as to whether the ships were being operated in accordance with the precepts of good seamanship and the provisions of the International Convention for Safety of Life at Sea."[24] It noted that *Stockholm* was traveling twenty miles north of the recommended course for eastbound traffic, and asserted that "the data made available by use of radar obviously was not properly utilized to prevent collision. The *Andrea Doria–Stockholm* collision would have been prevented if the information provided by radar had been properly used."[25]

The report made no overt assessment of blame, but it did focus on the claims made by lawyers for the Swedish American Line that the *Doria* had not been entirely seaworthy at the time of the collision and that this contributed to her loss. The liner, the report stated, "met the subdivision requirements of the 1948 Safety of Life at Sea Convention by a very narrow margin. It is stated in the Stability Report (prepared by Ansaldo) that the ship also could meet the stability requirements of the 1948 convention provided she was kept ballasted with substantial and specified quantities of liquids in her various tanks. It does not appear possible to account for the behavior of the ship immediately following the collision on July 25, 1956 except on the assumption that she was not in fact ballasted in accordance with this information at that time."[26] In essence, the report claimed, Captain Calamai's decision not to fill the empty port fuel oil tanks with seawater as additional ballast had directly contributed to the liner's immediate list and ultimate loss.

This was a red herring. Most captains refrained from filling their fuel oil tanks with seawater because it combined to create a noxious sludge that would need to be discharged before a vessel could be refueled. A captain couldn't simply dump the mixture into the harbor: rather, it had to be pumped out once in port. Such a procedure was costly and time-consuming and, as previously noted, the *Doria* was never designed to take on seawater as ballast except in an emergency.[27]

In 1956 damage to the *Doria* could only be guessed at, as the report admitted, but it insisted that the known or presumed flooding caused by the collision was not sufficient "to account for the list taken unless the actual stability of the ship before damage was low, perhaps only one third of the amount indicated as required in the Stability Report."[28] In fact, as later expeditions to the wreck would reveal, the Italian liner had suffered far more damage than anyone had previously suspected. Diver Peter Gimbel was the first to record the devastation in 1981. Swimming along in the generator room, he saw that the main transverse bulkhead separating it from the access tunnel had been crushed.[29] As he continued, he suddenly found himself outside of the hull: Gimbel had unknowingly exited through a gash he estimated at eighty feet, which had left the *Doria* "split open like a ripe watermelon."[30] *Stockholm* had penetrated into the *Doria*'s bottom and the compartment forward of the deep tanks, and gone much deeper into the ship than was usual in most collisions; she had also pivoted within the hull, smashing and tearing away in a devastating arc that may have breached the keel and possibly left a third compartment open to the sea.[31] All of this damage made *Andrea Doria*'s sinking inevitable.

The Italian Line quickly rebutted the claims about the *Doria*'s stability and ballasting, but the issue refused to go away. At the request of lawyers representing the Swedish American Line, naval architects carried out an inspection of the *Doria*'s sister ship, *Cristoforo Colombo*, in the autumn of 1956. Their report suggested two reasons for the *Doria*'s rapid list and eventual loss. The first was the fact that her watertight bulkheads only extended as high as A Deck, which allowed an onrush of water once the sea level reached their tops. The second was the absence of a watertight door in an internal access tunnel adjacent to the generator room, which they suggested had led to accelerated flooding.[32]

Then there was a memorandum, sent to Charles Haight from the Swedish embassy in Rome, concerning the *Doria*'s construction and stability. This has been taken quite seriously, though no authoritative name has ever been publicly attached to the charges: rather, they have only been described as having come "from an Italian source which is considered more reliable than most," not exactly instilling a sense of veracity about the claims.[33]

The memorandum made a number of charges, including that the *Doria* "had serious design defects. The drawings and design plans were made up very carelessly by inexperienced Italian technicians and approved no less carelessly without checking by the engineers in the Italian shipping registry (Registro Italiano Navale, RIN) and by corrupt officials in the Ministry of the Merchant Marine." With this bit of unsubstantiated gossip used to tarnish Italian officials, the memorandum went on to assert that the ship was inherently unstable and could not right herself if she encountered a list of more than 19 degrees (a claim disproved by the fact that, during her maiden voyage, the *Doria* had taken a list of 28 degrees in a heavy storm and recovered). Engineers at Ansaldo, the report insisted, had been aware of such problems but had been forced into silence "to avoid a scandal."[34]

Though heavy on innuendo and lacking any named sources, this memorandum was taken seriously. As the House of Representatives report noted, *Andrea Doria* fully met the 1948 requirements under the Safety of Life at Sea Convention; the margin might have been minimal to avoid what were deemed unnecessary costs, but in this case Italian Line was no different from other shipping companies.[35] The lack of a watertight door at the access tunnel undoubtedly accelerated the flow of water but did not doom the ship, as has often been said.[36] As to ballasting, the Italian Line was able to produce the original stability recommendations. These revealed that the fuel tanks were never meant to take on seawater as additional ballast except in extreme emergencies; loss of fuel during a voyage was to be countered by filling the forward peak tank and the ship's double bottom.[37] In essence, while the empty port fuel tanks might have contributed to the ship's list after the collision, Captain Calamai had no reason to fill them with seawater as they were emptied during the voyage.

In 1912 *Titanic* sank two hours and forty minutes after colliding with an iceberg; in 1915, *Lusitania* sank within eighteen minutes of being struck by a torpedo. *Andrea Doria* lasted eleven hours before capsizing. All things considered, her lingering death was mute testament to the integrity of her design.

But without knowing the extensive damage to the *Doria*, most authorities in the 1950s held that the *Doria* must have carried design flaws that led to her demise. This fight played itself out in the legal battle between the Italian and Swedish American Lines. At the beginning of January 1957, the Italian Line submitted the *Doria*'s stability booklet and ballasting charts.[38] But before these could be examined in court, both lines suddenly terminated the legal proceedings.[39] The assumption by many was that these materials proved the Swedish contention that the *Doria* had been lost because of instability, lack of ballasting, and inherent design flaws—a view popularized by author Alvin Moscow, who produced the first book on the disaster.[40]

This belief landed atop widespread tales of cowardice on the part of some of the *Doria*'s crew. In this respect, the Swedes had won the propaganda war: they had held frequent press conferences and were not shy in airing accusations against their Italian counterparts; the Italian Line chose not to respond in kind, and very quickly a narrative took hold among much of the public. In this, prejudiced opinion played its part. The Swedes, went this reasoning, were civilized, clean, and brisk, with a respectable heritage and a reputation for efficiency. The Italians, on the other hand, were just a decade from fighting alongside Hitler. Appreciation of Italian culture, films, and fascination had risen dramatically, but there were still doubts: Italy had the Mafia, questionable politics, and subservience to a somehow suspect Catholic Church. Imagination painted them as hotheaded, erratic, and corrupt. "There was still a lot of suspicion and even jealousy," recalls Joseph D'Andrea, former honorary Italian consul in Pittsburgh. "It was easy for many people to blame the Italian shipbuilders and the Italian crew, no matter the facts, because they were still seen as alien by many in America."[41]

Details of the decision to end litigation remain a mystery. Both the Italian and the Swedish American Lines agreed to settle the case out of court, without finding of fault or liability, a decision perhaps coerced by Lloyd's of London, which had an insurance stake in both ships. No one wanted to see a lengthy trial that would air potentially damning allegations. And so neither side received financial compensation from the other.[42] Perhaps the Italian Line, unaware of the extent of the damage caused by *Stockholm*, feared that the blame would fall on them, and so they agreed to accept terms they had fought against. In the end, Italian Line contributed 70 percent toward the claims, while the Swedish Line paid only 30 percent of the totals awarded.[43]

It is left to history to attempt to sort out precisely what went wrong that night and why two ships, both equipped with the latest technologies, should have met in a fatal collision. The first mistake was Nordenson's decision to take *Stockholm* east on a course some twenty miles north of the outbound sea lane recommended in the Safety of Life at Sea

Convention of 1948. Taking the recommended route would have added approximately two hours to his voyage.[44] Unfortunately, the northern eastbound route was only a recommended course: although this was widespread and accepted practice, neither the Swedish American or the Italian Line had signed the convention.[45] But this northern route *was* part of the 1953 North Atlantic Track Agreement, which Sweden *had* signed.[46] Nordenson was clearly in violation of this agreement.

When Nordenson retired to his cabin at ten, he reminded Carstens to summon him if they encountered any fog. The Swedish captain's decision to leave his young third officer in charge of the bridge is, in retrospect, puzzling. Nordenson had sailed these waters many times: he thus knew that fog frequently and suddenly appeared in the area, especially in summer and under similar conditions. "July and August," recalled Harry Grattidge, who captained both *Queen Mary* and *Queen Elizabeth*, "which bring smoky, blanketing fogs to the North Atlantic, were always my worst months. There is an old saying in the North Atlantic: 'For five hot weather months you blow on your foghorn, then for the other seven, you blow on your fingers to keep warm.'"[47] Four hours before the collision, when Nordenson was still on the bridge, Second Officer Lars Enestrom was puzzled when *Stockholm*'s radar picked up a signal from Block Island, which was ten miles beyond the equipment's range. Enestrom decided that this was a phantom signal, caused by warm air from the south flowing over waters from the Labrador Current—the very conditions that caused sudden banks of fog.[48] Yet this notation apparently passed without raising any sense of alarm that *Stockholm* was nearing an area of possible fog. Nordenson's warning that he should be summoned if *Stockholm* entered fog alone indicates that he recognized that this was a real possibility. Had he remained on the bridge as *Stockholm* approached an area infamous for summer fogs, the collision might have been avoided.

Carstens always maintained that the Swedish liner had not encountered any fog until the last minute before the collision. This has been among the most contentious claims concerning that evening. The *Nantucket Lightship* reported heavy fog in the area and issued its warning, and the United States Weather Bureau stated that the fog in the area was so dense that visibility was "probably less than a mile."[49] Lester Sinness, traveling aboard the *Ile de France*, noted, "A dense fog really settled in by nine o'clock, with visibility virtually zero."[50] Not only was *Ile de France* in a heavy fog that night, but so were *Cape Ann* and the *Private William H. Thomas* when they answered the *Doria*'s SOS message.[51]

Banks of fog came and went in patches in these waters: Carstens was under orders to summon Nordenson if *Stockholm* encountered any fog. It seems unlikely that he would have disobeyed such an order from his notoriously stern and fastidious captain, yet Carstens later admitted that a patch of fog had obscured his view of the *Doria*, and when Enestrom ran to *Stockholm*'s bridge after the collision he, too, noted that he could barely see the moon through the fog surrounding the ship.[52] And the fog was so thick within a minute of the collision that at first Nordenson believed the other ship was the Swedish liner *Kungsholm*.[53]

More to the point, though, the inexperienced Carstens never anticipated encountering fog, despite Nordenson's warning that this was a possibility. Although *Stockholm* picked up a fog warning from the *Nantucket Lightship*, Carstens was evidently unaware of its meaning.[54] Even when *Stockholm* neared its collision with the *Doria*, Carstens never questioned why he could not see her lights as the two ships approached each other. Captain Richard A. Cahill, who spent more than forty years at sea and served as visiting professor at the US Merchant Marine Academy at Kings Point on Long Island, analyzed the collision. He wrote of Carstens: "His inability to sight the other vessel when expected should have suggested the possibility of fog to him, but apparently it did not. To plunge ahead at full speed toward a high speed vessel he could not see and without making a substantial course change to the right or without calling the master or to reduce speed if he rejected the first two alternatives was a grave error."[55]

This last point underlines the third of the mistakes that night: Carstens was simply too inexperienced—and too overworked—to adequately assess the developing situation before him, anticipate problems, and respond to them in a timely manner. The Swedish American Line was one of the few shipping company carriers that required only one officer to stand watch.[56] Carstens was expected to monitor the radar, plot and maintain the ship's course, take radio direction readings, make navigational notes, and supervise the lookout; in addition, that night his attention was consumed by keeping track of the erratic steering of his helmsman Peder Larsen and ordering constant course corrections. It was an exhausting collection of responsibilities, and Carstens had been up since dawn, assisting as *Stockholm* left New York.[57]

Larsen's steering not only continually took *Stockholm* off course but also meant that Carstens had to spend some time watching and correcting the actions of his helmsman. Carstens had to rely on the readings Larsen called out: these were frequently in error, sometimes by as much as 4 degrees, and likely led the young Swedish officer to make mistakes in calculations.[58] These distractions are especially important in assessing the claim that Carstens first spotted the Doria off *Stockholm's* port side; he said he turned *Stockholm* 20 degrees to starboard to widen the distance between the ships, but insisted that the Italian liner had suddenly crossed to his starboard side and thus placed itself directly in the Swedish vessel's path.[59] Three recent expert, independent reviews of the data that night—by Richard Cahill, former president of the Royal Institute of Technology in Sweden Carl Nordling, and Samuel Halpern—all agree that Carstens was wrong in this assertion.[60] Cahill bluntly declared that "testimony from the *Stockholm* can in no way fit the established facts."[61]

Instead, Cahill believed that Carstens "expected to see a red light and, in retrospect, convinced himself and the helmsman that they did in fact see one, whereas he probably saw no distinct lights as *Andrea Doria* emerged from her murky shroud."[62] Using the known positions of the two ships, Cahill was convinced that "*Stockholm* could have seen only a green sidelight and never a red light. For both of the sidelights of the *Doria* to be showing, let alone the port by itself, *Stockholm* would have had to have been almost three-tenths of a mile further south. Had she been in that position, however, the collision could not have taken place."[63]

How much plotting Carstens actually did remains unknown. According to instructions aboard *Stockholm*, he was to record any plots and the times they were made in the ship's log. Carstens said that he plotted the oncoming ship three times that night, but only a single instance was entered in the log. More to the point, Second Officer Lars Enestrom ran to the bridge within a minute of the collision. He saw that the Bial maneuvering board next to the radar screen, where plotting was done, was blank. He asked Carstens why he hadn't plotted some of the positions. The third officer insisted that he had done so; despite the chaos surrounding the collision, Carstens insisted that the data had been erased in that tumultuous first minute.[64]

Stockholm's 20-degree turn to starboard, as Cahill noted, essentially caused the collision.[65] Carstens insisted that he ordered this change when the *Doria* was off his port side at a distance between 1.8 and 1.9 nautical miles. In fact, analysis of the data shows that the Italian liner was perhaps 1.3 miles ahead and about 3 degrees off *Stockholm*'s starboard bow.[66] "It does appear," says naval architect William Garzke, "that once that 20-degree turn was made, a collision was inevitable despite any corrective actions on the part of *Andrea Doria*."[67]

Captain Calamai was widely criticized for his decision to only slightly reduce his vessel's speed as he steamed west through the thick bank of fog. However, making port on time was important to avoid delays, overtime pay for longshoremen, and keeping to regular passenger schedules. Despite these three factors, it was recommended that vessels encountering such conditions should slow their speeds to enable a full emergency stop at no more than half the visibility distance.[68] In practical terms, this would have meant Captain Calamai slowing his liner down to 1–2 knots and crawling along at a snail's pace. Few mariners followed this suggestion, which would have resulted in significant delays and added expenses. On its 1952 maiden voyage, for example, *United States* ran at a record-setting pace through heavy fog.[69] As Captain Raoul de Beaudéan of the *Ile de France* later explained: "It would serve no purpose for a ship with a speed of 25 knots to sail at 20 or even 15 the moment the weather thickens, so long as the radar indicates no obstacles. In my opinion they should only slow down at the approach of another ship."[70] As Cahill summarized, the *Doria*'s "speed in fog was, therefore, in conformity with prevailing practice, and no realistic criticism of Captain Calamai can be leveled against him on that score."[71]

History has also asserted that Captain Calamai had not followed standard navigational practices when he ordered his ship to make a starboard-to-starboard passing rather than the regulation port-to-port maneuver. Had he done so, it is claimed, the collision would have been avoided. With the *Doria*'s radar showing the oncoming vessel to starboard, however, such a maneuver would have meant imperiling both ships as the Italian liner would have cut across the eastbound track of the Swedish ship. When, in the last minute before the collision Calamai turned sharply to port, he was acting according to the maritime principle of "in extremis," which authorized the master to take any measures necessary to avoid collision.

The accumulation of the various mistakes and errors in judgment made by Carstens all combined to make the collision inevitable. But there may have been another fatal factor at work that night. It was John Carrothers, a former chief engineer with the Matson Navigation Company, who in 1971 first theorized that Carstens had misread his radar on that fateful night.[72] The radar screen in use on *Stockholm* consisted of five concentric rings; a knob allowed the range to be adjusted from a fifteen- to a five-mile scale. Because the bridge was kept dark, a flashlight was needed to determine the correct adjustments.[73] A mistake was certainly possible: it was the first time that Carstens had been left to navigate *Stockholm* without supervision, using radar on which he had not been properly trained, and his attention was clearly divided that night.

Carstens testified that he first observed the *Andrea Doria* "about 11 P.M." as a blip in the fourth radar ring, and believed that she was then some twelve miles distant. During the inquest, when the impossibility of the two ships erasing such a distance between them in a mere ten minutes, Carstens altered his story, insisting that the 11:00 P.M. time had only been an estimate. But if his radar was actually set on the five- rather than the fifteen-mile scale, *Doria* would have been only four miles away—a scenario that accords with the collision ten minutes later.[74]

There is a possible hint that *Stockholm*'s officers were not as cautious in adjusting the radar range as they might have been. Four hours before the collision, Second Officer Lars Enestrom was surprised when the radar picked up signals from Block Island, which he then believed to be some forty-one miles away; this was particularly odd, as *Stockholm*'s radar generally could not pick up any signal more than thirty miles distant.[75]

Carstens certainly seems to have had difficulty accurately operating the radar. Having received no special training in its use, he had attempted to master the equipment by reading the manual in his spare time.[76] He admitted that he had trouble that night adjusting the light levels on the screen, which blurred the images he saw.[77] After the collision, when Nordenson asked Carstens to plot the location of the ship they had hit, the third officer actually miscalculated what he saw on the radar and placed the other vessel at a distance of some five miles.[78]

In the decades since Carrothers proposed this theory, it has been taken up and propounded by several maritime experts, chief among them Captain Robert J. Meurn, professor at the US Merchant Marine Academy. Working with the United States Maritime Administration, Meurn used the technology available at the academy to input all the known data and create a highly sophisticated simulation of events on *Stockholm*'s bridge that night. This only reinforced Meurn's conviction that Carstens had inadvertently been using the five-mile scale on his radar screen.[79] Meurn's conclusions have now become part of the academy's curriculum, used when training cadets. "I'm of Swedish descent," Meurn has said, "so instinctively I assumed that fault for the accident was the Italian captain's, not the Swedish. For many years afterwards, I scientifically analyzed elements of the collision and, with great contrition and absolute certainty, I can tell you that blame for the disaster belongs squarely on the shoulders of the *Stockholm*'s third officer, Carstens-Johannsen, who was in charge of the navigational watch."[80]

This conclusion has not gone without some criticism.[81] Not surprisingly, Carstens adamantly rejected the idea. "I did not make a mistake," he asserted in 2001.[82]

In the wake of *Andrea Doria*'s loss, the press widely described the disaster as "the first radar-assisted" collision, something that Captain Raoul de Beaudéan of the *Ile de France* warned against: "Mariners should not endow their gadgets with an infallibility that is not of this world. While making use of them they should always bear in mind that they are human fabrications, endowed with human imperfections."[83] Carstens's likely misreading of his radar may have played a considerable role in the collision, but it was merely one of many mistakes he made. Separately, they may have been minor in and of themselves: taken together, they coalesced into disaster that warm and foggy summer night in 1956.

Chapter Nineteen

At the end of World War I, survivors and relatives of those who perished in the sinking of the *Lusitania* brought suit against the German government. The lawsuit sought some $15.5 million in lost property, personal injury, and compensation. It took nearly a decade before the special Mixed Claims Commission rendered its judgments. In the end, just $2.5 million was awarded in damages. Survivors and those who had lost relatives felt ignored and cheated, their shattered lives and losses reduced to a few meager dollars in bureaucratic legal fights that seemed heartless.

As *Andrea Doria* survivors and the relatives of those lost in the disaster found, little had changed by 1956. Claims for lost possessions and lost lives totaled some $116 million.[1] The Dilworths sought $5,000 for lost property; Thure Peterson asked for $500,000 in compensation for his wife's life; the Di Sandros wanted $100,000 in consideration of Norma's death; and Ross Sergio sued for $500,000 for the loss of his wife and four young children.[2]

The Italian Line put up $4 million and the Swedish Line added $1.8 million to settle claims—a mere fraction of what was being sought.[3] Passengers or relatives of victims had two choices: accept a settlement on the terms offered, or hire lawyers and take their individual cases to court. Already scarred by their experiences, or often in no financial position to lodge new lawsuits, most of the claimants simply resigned themselves to this second tragedy. As had happened with the *Lusita-*

nia claims, cold calculation reduced the amounts awarded in the *Doria* disaster to just 5 percent of what was sought. Santino Porporino, his son recalls, felt that he was swindled in the settlement and received less than other survivors, perhaps because he did not speak English.[4] Thure Peterson received a mere $10,000 for Martha's death; the Di Sandros were given $9,000 for Norma's death, while Ross Sergio settled his claim for just $37,500.[5]

Some survivors quickly moved on with their lives. A year after the disaster, Philip and Arline Trachtenberg happily boarded *United States* for a voyage to Europe. "I wouldn't go any other way," Arline said. "I still prefer a ship. We might not be here this morning if we had been involved in a plane disaster."[6] Both lived on quietly before retiring to Florida. Arline, who died in 1997, outlived her husband by a decade.

The Daimler-Benz assembly plant project that Klaus Dorneich was to work with in Mexico City ended up snarled in government bureaucracy, and so he devoted himself to similar jobs in El Salvador and Guatemala, where he met his future wife, Hilly Wagner, whose father Herbert had been deported, along with hundreds of other Central American citizens of German descent, to a prison camp in America before he finally returned in 1947. When the Mexican government project was finally canceled, Klaus returned to Germany and began studying for a PhD in economics at Freiburg University; in 1958 he served as lecturer on the economic history of Europe before and after the war to a "Europa Seminar" for American students visiting from DePauw University held in Austria, and also became a Fulbright Scholar in the United States. He eventually took a job working for a communications company (ITT-SEL) in Stuttgart and married Hilly in Guatemala. In 1967 the family moved from Stuttgart to Mexico, where Klaus worked on microwave projects for the Olympic Games and the soccer World Cup; they remained in the country, where one of their three children (Regina) was born, until returning to Germany in 1972. Klaus was never scared of being on another liner: after retiring in 1995, he spent a decade as a "lecturer on board" for a number of cruise ships, mainly in the Mediterranean, the Red Sea, and the Caribbean. While he rarely discussed his experiences on the *Doria* with passengers, safety officers from the crew inevitably wanted to hear his memories of that night. Today, he and his wife, Hilly, continue to make regular visits to Guatemala each year, where they still have family of cousins.[7]

Robert Hudson, the last passenger off the *Doria*, was sent to Savannah for surgery on his injured back. In 1960 he finally returned to the sea.[8] Living in Texas, he married and had two daughters, the first named Andrea after the ship. He died in 2000.[9]

Having lost his wife in the tragedy, Walter Carlin survived her by less than two years, dying in 1958.

Less than six months after the disaster, American television broadcast a documentary on the disaster, which included a dramatic recreation of Martha Peterson's last hours trapped in the wreckage. The following year, Thure Peterson established a memorial chapel to Martha's memory in Gustavus Adolphus Lutheran Church in New York City, but the trauma was revived in 1960, when the film *The Last Voyage* debuted in theaters across the world. This was a fictionalized telling of the Petersons' story, starring Robert Stack and Dorothy Malone. The film managed an eerie sense of realism by using the *Ile de France*, the same vessel that had played such a pivotal role in safely rescuing hundreds of *Andrea Doria* passengers.

In 1959, just three years after the disaster, the French Line had sold the grand *Ile de France* for $1.29 million to a Japanese company for scrap.[10] The company, in turn, leased the liner to MGM Studios for use in filming *The Last Voyage* at the rate of $4,000 a day and with permission to destroy portions of the ship and partially sink it to lend an authentic touch to the film.[11] "We will do everything for real," producers Andrew and Virginia Stone announced. "When a boiler explodes—a boiler explodes. When a funnel collapses, bashing in the front deck, a funnel collapses and bashes into the front deck. Bulkheads really explode."[12] When the French Line learned of this desecration, they demanded that the liner's name not be visible in any scene under threat of legal action.[13] The liner thus became the SS *Claridon* in the film.

Names were changed, but there was no mistaking the fact the viewers of *The Last Voyage* were seeing the essentials of the Petersons' story, with fictional husband, Cliff Henderson, desperately attempting to rescue his wife, Laurie, from their cabin as she lay tangled in the wreckage. In place of heroic steward Giovanni Rovelli, the film offered up actor Woody Strode as a valiant member of the crew; instead of a hydraulic jack, the would-be rescuers awaited the arrival of an acetylene torch from a nearby ship. Hollywood being Hollywood, there was a happy ending, with the trapped woman rescued and spirited off the ship just as waves washed over the decks. No one, it seemed, wanted to embrace the reality. As for Thure Peterson, he did his best to move beyond the tragedy. He returned to his chiropractic practice in New Jersey and eventually remarried. He remained in contact with Jane Cianfarra and with Giovanni Rovelli, the waiter who had worked so desperately to save Martha Peterson's life.[14] Peterson died in 1970 at the age of seventy-one.[15]

Paul Sergio died in 1972, and his wife, Margaret, passed away six years later, never having recovered from losing her sister and nieces and nephews aboard the *Doria*. In 1960 Ross Sergio remarried: his new wife, Antoinette, was extremely sensitive about the situation, assuring young Anthony that she was not trying to take his mother's place but "just wanted to love his dad." She gave Ross three new children, including a daughter named after the lost Maria. Antoinette quickly established a close relationship with Anthony. Ross died in October 1997 at the age of eighty-eight. After a long career, Anthony retired to California. It took him many years to come to terms with losing his mother and his four siblings: a meeting with Mother Theresa proved pivotal in his personal journey. "Christ didn't do anything," he says, "but He was still crucified, and He still forgave. People die every day, killed in car accidents or other ways. My family is like that. I don't like it, but it's out of my hands. So I will forgive, but I won't forget."[16]

Shortly after the *Andrea Doria* disaster, Zsa Zsa, one of Richardson and Ann Dilworth's poodles, gave birth to twins: the pups were named Andrea and Doria.[17] The couple moved into their new colonial-style house in the Society Hill District of Philadelphia, and Dilworth continued his revitalization projects, winning national attention. He won a second term as mayor in 1959, but in 1962 he stepped down from the office to run for Pennsylvania governor, a race he lost to William

244 ~ Greg King and Penny Wilson

Scranton and which he called the biggest disappointment of his career.[18] In 1963 President John F. Kennedy asked him to head a board that would develop high-speed rail between Boston and Washington, DC, an assignment that ended when Kennedy was assassinated.[19] In 1965 Dilworth took over as president of the Philadelphia Board of Education and pushed through a controversial integration plan.[20] He had an uneasy alliance with Mayor Frank Rizzo, who joked, "Everything Dilworth has been with has gone down, even the *Andrea Doria*."[21] Dilworth died of a brain tumor on January 23, 1974, at the age of seventy-five; Ann outlived him by seven years, dying in 1981.

Most of the Gifford family suffered no lingering effects from the disaster. "The biggest thing for me," Dun said, "was how lucky we were. One second different, and the other five members of my family would have been killed. The people two through six doors ahead of us were all killed. That has always stuck with me." Only the youngest, Bambi, admitted to any sense of unease. When she was sixteen, a date took her to see *A Night to Remember* about the sinking of *Titanic*. "I freaked out and left," she recalls. "I was kind of upset because I kind of liked the guy. It's never happened since. I've never had nightmares."[22]

The Giffords tried to spend the anniversary of the collision together on Nantucket, reminiscing over drinks and dinner; they kept a buoy that had once marked the wreck site and that had washed up on the shore of the island as a planter in the garden.[23] "There are times you flash back," Jock says. "I can still see some of the artifacts in some of the staterooms on the ship. I still see the VW bus we traveled in, sitting in the bottom of the hold. Obviously it's an experience you don't want to have, but you feel so darn lucky to be alive."[24]

Clarence Gifford died at the age of ninety-one in 2004; his wife, Priscilla, died a year later, age ninety-three. "She didn't want us to be afraid of traveling," said her daughter, now Bambi Mleczko. "Going through something like that, you realize how lucky you are to survive. It's hard to articulate the bond it helps form."[25] Of all the Gifford children, it was Dun who unwittingly found himself at the center of ongoing tragedies. He went to Washington, DC, to work for the new Department of Housing and Urban Development but soon signed on as legislative aide to Senator Edward Kennedy. In 1968 he temporarily stepped away to work as national campaign coordinator for Robert Kennedy's presidential quest for the White House, taking charge of the famous "Boiler Room Girls" who did research for the candidate.[26] On the evening of June 5, he was just a few steps behind the candidate when Sirhan Sirhan opened fire in the pantry of the Ambassador Hotel in Los Angeles. Together with Rosey Grier, Dun flung himself at the assassin and managed to wrestle the gun away from him. Dun rode to the hospital in the ambulance with the wounded Bobby and his wife, Ethel, but his heroic action had been too late to save Kennedy's life.

A year later, Dun was back working on Edward Kennedy's behalf. In July he was at his house on Nantucket when an urgent telephone call summoned him to Martha's Vineyard to identify the body of Mary Jo Kopechne after Kennedy's accident at Chappaquiddick.[27] The senator then asked Dun to accompany the body and return it to Mary Jo's parents in Pennsylvania. Reporters ringed the small airplane as it left the island—the press dubbed Dun "the body snatcher" and accused him of participating in a cover-up of the accident.[28]

Dun soon left government service, though he remained close to Senator Kennedy and frequently joined him sailing off the Massachusetts coast. In 1976 he formed a cookie company with future senator John Kerry, and increasingly became drawn to the culinary world, befriending Julia Child before launching his own company, the Oldways Preservation Trust, in 1988 to promote healthy eating and a Mediterranean-style diet. He died of a heart attack in 2010 at the age of seventy-one.[29]

Almost exactly a year after the *Andrea Doria* sank, Andrew Stevens embarked on a summer voyage to France with a group of students.[30] His mother, Herminia, was nervous: "I wondered what time his ship would pass Nantucket Island," she said.[31] Andrew wasn't at all worried, at least not until his ship left the pier and passed another vessel entering the harbor. "No, it can't be," Andrew muttered to a friend.[32] It was *Stockholm*, newly repaired. "That night," he recalls, "I couldn't sleep, and spent the night on deck."[33]

Andrew lost his father in 1977 and his mother in 1982. In 1962, after two years of college, he enlisted in the US Army and was stationed at

Highlands Air Force Station in New Jersey and began taking classes at Monmouth College, graduating with honors in 1966. He married his wife, Linda, in 1963, and the couple raised three children, Nora, Richard, and Kimberly as Andrew taught math and history and acted as a coach at a private boys' school in Connecticut. After earning his master's degree at the University of Connecticut, Andrew went on to teach at several elite private schools before retiring to Florida in 2005. He is still active and enjoys bicycling, golf, pickleball, swimming, bridge, dominoes, and his five grandchildren.[34]

Cecilia and John Pick settled in Milwaukee as he returned to teaching at Marquette University. He died in 1981; Cecilia died in 1990.

Although Nora Kovach and her husband Istvan Rabovsky temporarily benefited from their fame as survivors of the *Doria*, the first appearances in the West of the Bolshoi Ballet soon eclipsed their artistic technique and they found less demand for their performances. The couple divorced, although both continued to be involved in the dance world. Nora died in 2009 at the age of seventy-seven.[35]

In the months after the disaster, Giovanni Vali went to Canada, where he got a job as an elevator operator in Winnipeg. He began writing to Melania Ansuini, unable to forget her. After six months of correspondence, he finally asked to marry her. On March 10, 1957, they were wed. It took some time for Giovanni to get a permanent visa; the paperwork finally came when Melania announced that she was pregnant. "Long before," he said, "we agreed that if we ever had a girl we'd call her Doria." True to their decision, when a daughter was born in June 1958, the couple named her Doria; a second daughter, Dina, was born five years later.[36]

Eventually Melania and Giovanni opened an Italian restaurant in San Jose, which they named *Andrea Doria*. The walls were decorated with newspaper clippings about the disaster and photographs of the liner. "When somebody asks about them," Giovanni explained, "I tell them it was a terrible thing. But one thing I'm glad for: it brought us together."[37] The couple retired from the restaurant many years ago, but remain happily married today. Melania's dreams of being trapped in the water, she says, largely dissipated after her marriage and the birth of her first daughter, but even after a half century, she feels "that the tragedy is always in front of me," an ever-present reminder of a life-changing ordeal. She never learned to swim, but her experience has not stopped her from enjoying several cruises, the last one to various ports on the Black Sea.[38]

Alda Raimengia also managed to put the disaster behind her. Five months after the sinking, she gave birth to a daughter, Luciana (another daughter, Josephine, arrived a few years later). Alda and Franco lived in the Bronx until his death in 1991. Today Alda lives near her daughter Josephine in Massachusetts, to be close to her grandchildren, Andrew and Kenny, who are fascinated by the *Andrea Doria* story. In 2019, to mark her eightieth birthday, they gave her a *New York Times* custom birthday book. It began with the newspaper's front page from the day of her birth. Alda opened the cover of this clever present and read that the major news story on the day of her birth covered the funeral of Pope Pius XI. Glancing through the article, she saw that one of the byline names was Camille Cianfarra. She paused for a moment. Alda knew she recognized the name, but she couldn't quite place it. But every modern household is equipped with a computer hooked to the internet, and a brief search reminded Alda where her fate and that of Camille Cianfarra had intersected. They had both been on the *Doria*. Alda had lived; Cianfarra had not. It was a reminder to her of how precious life is. She enjoys going out sailing—"I have no problem being on the water," she says. "My son-in-law takes me out on his boat."[39]

A few months after the tragedy, Ruth Roman wrote an article for *Parade* magazine detailing her experiences. "I know that in a way I profited from it," she said. "For I learned something which gave me a new feeling about my fellow man."[40] Having divorced Mortimer Hall a few months before the tragedy, she wed again in November, this time to entertainment executive Budd Burton Moss; this lasted less than four years before Ruth obtained an annulment on the grounds that her divorce from Hall had not been legally finalized (she would marry a fourth time, in 1976). Ruth continued to work in film, but starting in the 1960s began focusing more on television: over the next two decades she appeared in dozens of programs, including *Bonanza; I Spy;*

The Outer Limits; The Mod Squad; Murder, She Wrote; and *Knots Landing.* She died of natural causes at her home in Laguna Beach in September 1999 at the age of seventy-five. Her son, Richard, had her ashes scattered at sea.[41]

Ruth's fellow actress Betsy Drake, too, returned to Hollywood and to an unsettled private life. When Cary Grant finally came back from filming in Spain, he stunned Betsy by announcing that he wanted Sophia Loren to star in her place opposite him in *Houseboat,* which Betsy had written for herself. Worse, Grant handed off the script to be rewritten, and Betsy received no credit.[42] She pulled herself through a winning comic turn in *Will Success Spoil Rock Hunter?* the following year, but by this time Betsy was worn out. "My marriage was breaking up," she said, "and that took all my energies. And I was tired of acting in Hollywood. The work itself I loved. But everything that surrounded the business of acting seemed to me sheer idiocy."[43] The couple announced their separation in October 1958, while Grant was filming *North by Northwest,* saying, "Our marriage has not brought us the happiness we fully expected and mutually desired."[44]

After the separation, Betsy began seeing a therapist in Hollywood, who recommended that she try LSD, which was then still legal; she did and soon convinced Grant to do so as well; he became an avid devotee.[45] But nothing could save the marriage, and Betsy and Cary were finally divorced in 1962. She made only a few more films before retiring from acting in 1965. With her new freedom, Betsy began a serious study of therapy at UCLA's neuropsychiatric institute and wrote a novel, *Children, You Are Very Little,* that drew on her own unhappy childhood experiences. She eventually moved to London, where she lived quietly until her death in 2015 at the age of ninety-two.[46]

In October 1956 Robert Young took his family back to Europe aboard the SS *America.* "I especially remember the lifeboat drill," Madge says. "I'd been on a lot of ships but I'd never been through a drill like that before. There was an officer in charge, who lined us all up in military fashion on deck, inspected us, told us, 'No talking,' and checked that we all had our lifebelts on correctly. I was a bit of a brat, so when he came to me, I said, 'I know why you're doing this!'" She sailed again in 1959, this time alone on the *United States* with a friend whose father was in the diplomatic corps—"I was never afraid to get back on a ship," she recalls.[47]

Madge went to Tufts University, programmed computers in the 1960s, and later went into systems engineering. She found her job developing and operating a tracking system for F-14 fighter jets particularly fun. She married and raised four children in Massachusetts before retiring to New Hampshire. Her father, Robert, died from leukemia in 1996; her mother, Virginia, died in 2011 at the age of ninety-nine. "Her whole life had revolved around travel," Madge says. "When we buried her, I remembered what she had said about traveling with flannel when we were standing on the deck of the *Andrea Doria*, waiting to be rescued. So we buried her ashes in a little ladies' overnight suitcase, into which we put her last passport, and a flannel nightie for her final journey." Today, Madge devotes her time to keeping alive the memory of the Liberty Ships her father had helped create, volunteering and serving on boards of living-history museums and local historic sites. She is also involved in the efforts to preserve and save the liner *United States*, on which she had traveled. "In most of the interviews I do," she says, "all anyone seems interested in asking me about is what kind of trauma I suffered during the *Doria*'s sinking. But I was just a kid, and had no sense of danger as it was happening. Unlike others, I did not suffer any injury or loss."[48]

Mike Stoller returned to America to learn that Elvis Presley had made "Hound Dog" a hit. With partner Jerry Leiber (who died in 2011), Stoller now embarked on the most productive period of his prolific career, their work comprising a virtual hit parade of popular music. They followed "Hound Dog" with other Presley hits, including "Jailhouse Rock" and "King Creole"; "Charlie Brown" and "Yakety Yak" for the Coasters; "There Goes My Baby" for the Drifters; "Love Potion Number 9" for the Clovers; "Is That All There Is?" for Peggy Lee; and "Stuck in the Middle with You" for Stealers Wheel. They also collaborated with Ben E. King for his hit "Stand by Me," and with Barry

Mann and Cynthia Weil for "On Broadway." In 1987 the pair were inducted into the Rock and Roll Hall of Fame.

Mike and Meryl had three children, but by the mid-1960s the marriage faltered and they divorced a few years later. Mike remarried, to jazz pianist Corky Hale, had three more children, and, after many years of avoiding everything but small sailboats, he finally boarded a liner again for a Caribbean cruise. "I had no trouble with the experience," he says. He still occasionally sees Meryl, who lives in Manhattan, most recently at a birthday party for their daughter.[49]

Thomas Kelly left the priesthood in 1971 and married a former nun. For many years he taught sociology at Lake Superior State University in Sault Sainte Marie. Today he divides his time between Michigan and Arizona. Father Joseph Oppitz served in an Annapolis parish until his retirement. He died in 2011. The trio of priests from Chicago all enjoyed lengthy careers in the church. John Dolciamore took up a position on the Metropolitan Tribunal of the Archdiocese of Chicago, becoming chief judge in 1972 and reviewing questions of canon law and marriage while also presiding over several parishes. In an interview in the 1970s, he said that he no longer played Scrabble—it reminded him of the last night on the *Doria*.[50] He was never able to forget his experiences in 1956. He made the mistake of watching James Cameron's film *Titanic* and was "very sorry" he had done so: the beautiful ship, passengers sliding down the decks, and the struggle for survival, he said, were all too reminiscent of *Andrea Doria,* and he felt unwell for several days.[51] Dolciamore died at the age of eighty-six in November 2012, having served in the priesthood for sixty years.[52]

Father Richard Wojcik kept a large photograph of the *Andrea Doria* on his bedroom wall—"it tells me that everything that happens is providential," he said.[53] He, too, had a difficult time watching *Titanic,* "particularly the scenes in the water," which brought back all too vivid memories of July 1956.[54] For many years he taught liturgical communication at the University of Saint Mary of the Lake Seminary in Mundelein, Illinois, allowing him to share his love for music. In later years he developed an affinity for African, Hispanic, and Polish music.[55] He died in 2013 at the age of eighty-nine.

A color photo of the *Andrea Doria*, off the coast of Italy. *Authors' collection.*

An Italian Line advertisement for the *Andrea Doria*. *Authors' collection.*

Beauty sails the Sunny Southern Route

IN the sweeping modern décor of the handsome *Conte Biancamano* . . . in the rich
appointments and Old World artistry of the graceful *Saturnia* and *Vulcania*,
beauty sails this nature-favored route to Europe. The lovely *Andrea Doria*
is so lavishly decorated that she's been called "a floating guide to art."

Whichever ship you choose, the flawless service of Italian Line
is yours, the superb cuisine of Continental chefs . . .
and you'll dance, play, eat, swim, live in beauty
on the *Sunny Southern Route* to all Europe.

Coming this year:
s.s. *Cristoforo Colombo*, sister ship
of the lovely *Andrea Doria*.

Italian Line
"ITALIA" Società di Navigazione — Genova

See your Travel Agent or
AMERICAN EXPORT LINES (General Agents)
39 Broadway, New York 6, N. Y.

ANDREA DORIA EXPRESS SERVICE ON THE SUNNY SOUTHERN ROUTE • 6 DAYS TO GIBRALTAR • 8 DAYS TO NAPLES • 9 DAYS TO CANNES AND GENOA
SATURNIA • VULCANIA • CONTE BIANCAMANO TO AZORES • PORTUGAL • NORTH AFRICA • GIBRALTAR • SPAIN • MAJORCA • FRANCE • ITALY • SICILY

An Italian Line advertisement for the *Andrea Doria* from 1954. *Authors' collection.*

Adalgisa Di Fabio. *Courtesy of Adalgisa Di Fabio.*

The Porporino family, rescued and on board the *Stockholm*. From left: Santino with Giuseppe (Joe), and Antonietta holding Bruna. Santino is still wearing the curtain from the *Andrea Doria* that he had taken to wrap around himself as he escaped.
Courtesy of Joe Porporino.

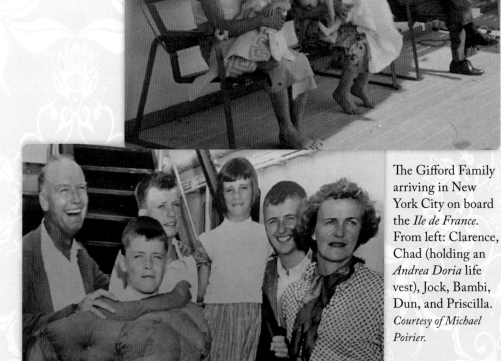

The Gifford Family arriving in New York City on board the *Ile de France*. From left: Clarence, Chad (holding an *Andrea Doria* life vest), Jock, Bambi, Dun, and Priscilla.
Courtesy of Michael Poirier.

Salvaged by The Doria Project from Italian Line flagship s.s. Andrea Doria, sunk July 26, 1956 in the Atlantic.

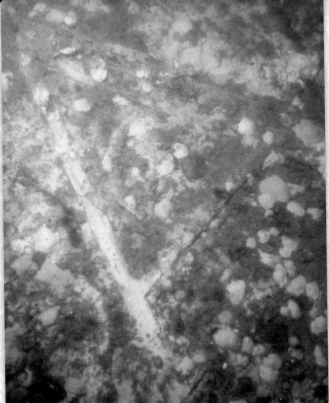

A mangled dollar bill taken by diver Peter Gimbel from the *Andrea Doria*'s safe. *Courtesy of Michael Poirier.*

An underwater photograph of the "A" on the *Andrea Doria*'s hull. *Courtesy of William Campbell.*

Diver John Moyer, on the right, and fellow diver Bill Nagle, with the bronze bell from the *Andrea Doria*'s stern auxiliary helm, 1985. *Courtesy of John Moyer.*

John Moyer with one of the recovered Gambone panels. *Courtesy of John Moyer.*

Diver Sherwood Probeck in the bow area of the *Andrea Doria* in July 2011, close to the ruins of a staircase. *Courtesy of Dan Wright.*

A photo from July 2011 of a diver, the late Ken Winter, 195 feet inside the wreck of the bow of the *Andrea Doria*, under the top deck. *Courtesy of Dan Wright.*

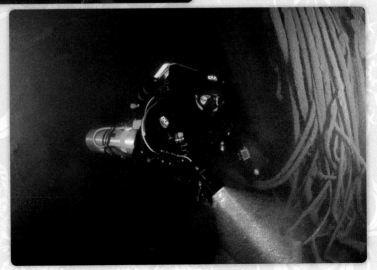

A 2011 photo of diver Sherwood Probeck, 230 feet inside the wreck of the *Andrea Doria*'s bow. *Courtesy of Dan Wright.*

A collection of wine bottles discovered by the divers Sherwood Probeck and Ken Winter in July 2011. They were located inside a closet approximately 220 feet deep in the bow section. *Courtesy of Dan Wright.*

A side-scan sonar image of the wreck of the *Andrea Doria*. *Courtesy of Dana Hall/OceanGate.*

Raymond Goedert, the last of the three Chicago priests, is today a retired auxiliary bishop for the archdiocese. For many years he served as the vicar of priests, offering pastoral services to his fellow religious leaders.[56] He had few bad experiences in the aftermath of the *Doria* tragedy: if anything, he says, it strengthened his resolve to be the best priest he could be. He had an unpleasant reminder of the disaster a few years ago, when he was on holiday in Maine. A friend had taken him out on a boat when a storm suddenly erupted; the situation looked desperate until another boat came to their assistance. When they finally got back to the shore, someone reminded Goedert that it was July 25, the anniversary of the collision.[57] Looking back on his experiences today, he has no regrets and remains grateful for the heroic work undertaken by the *Ile de France* that summer night.[58]

Nicola DiFiore settled in Scotch Plains, New Jersey, near his daughter and granddaughter and established his own successful business, Nick's Iron Works, which he operated until his death in 1992.[59]

Maria Coscia never quite recovered from her experience on the *Doria*. "She had always been a healthy person, very happy-go-lucky," says her daughter Sadie. "But after the sinking she became more nervous and more cautious, and her health went down." She never again went on any holiday except to visit relatives in Connecticut by train.[60] She died in July 1977. There was a coda to her story: In 1992 her son, Fred, visited Maria's native Carlantino and asked if anyone knew Giancinto, the prisoner of war his parents had welcomed into their house in the Bronx for Sunday dinners during World War II. Incredibly, he found him in the town square. "I am the son of Raffaele from New York," he announced. Giancinto was stunned: "That cannot be!" he insisted. "He is only a little boy!" The two embraced before the elderly man asked if Sadie had ever married. "Yes," Fred told him laughing, "two times."[61]

The *Doria* tragedy altered young Pat Mastrincola's ideas about one day joining the navy—"I decided I didn't want to be back out on the water," he says. "And I've never been on a ship since. I suppose I would go on a nice seven-day cruise now with my wife." The one lingering effect was that "the sinking gave me a kind of false sense of security.

I was cocky, and I felt like I could dodge almost anything thrown at me." Fortunately for Pat, he indeed seems to have an uncanny ability to emerge relatively unscathed from perilous situations. He joined the army and was sent to Vietnam and survived a jump when his parachute failed to open; back in America, a sniper shot out the windshield of the truck he was driving, and later still, a bus accident left him with a broken neck. "I figure I've lived this long," he says, "so why worry about it anymore?"[62] His sister, Arlene, had better luck, although the story of the *Andrea Doria* is still with her. "It's just part of my life," she says. "It's a reminder of how blessed I am to be here. If people are interested in hearing my story, I am always happy to share it and answer any questions." When the president of the company where she worked learned that she had survived the tragedy, he wanted to hear about her experiences. He had a collection of historical artifacts and, when Arlene retired, she presented him with a dinner plate that had been retrieved from the wreck by diver David Bright.[63] Today Pat lives on the East Coast and Arlene lives in the Midwest; their mother, Rosa, died in October 2018.

Adalgisa Di Fabio found her experiences on *Andrea Doria* difficult to forget. Her uncle Francesco liked to take her to the movies every Sunday: "the first thing I did when I entered the theater," she says, "is to look for the exit signs. I still do that today, so I know where I can run to if I need to suddenly escape." She found herself suffering from "a terrible phobia about being trapped, where everything seemed to close in on me and I had trouble breathing. My uncle and aunt took me to doctors to make sure that I was okay, but in those days no one thought that I needed to talk about what had happened, and so I kept it all in. It has taken me a lifetime to deal with all of the emotions. You learn that it gets easier, but it never goes away. The tragedy is always there, and I never know when it will suddenly wake up."[64]

A few years after the sinking Adalgisa's parents were finally able to join her in America. After attending a Catholic school, Adalgisa went to work as a seamstress, making clothing for Saks Fifth Avenue. In 1961 she married a young man she had actually known from her village in Italy and who had come to America to work as a carpenter and raised three children. It took twenty-three years for her to work up her courage to return to Italy on a visit—"I was afraid of flying, but I wouldn't get on a boat again; I never have," she says.

A few years ago, she had spinal surgery and, to recover, doctors had Adalgisa do physical therapy in a pool. She refused to go toward the deep end—"water and I don't get along." One day, a young lady who was a fellow patient suggested that Adalgisa go into the deeper part of the pool. "Oh, no," Adalgisa told her, "something happened to me in the water once. I had a terrible experience."

"Oh," the young lady replied. "My *nonna* Anita had a terrible experience in a shipwreck, but I never met her."

"My breath stopped," Adalgisa recalls. "I saw that the name on her tag was Joy."

"Don't say another word," she told Joy. "I'm going to tell you a story." And she did—of being on *Andrea Doria*, and of the beautiful young woman, Anita Leone, whom she had admired and who had been on her way to America for the birth of her grandchild. Adalgisa was stunned to learn that, after fifty-six years, she had come face-to-face with Anita's future granddaughter. "And so I met the mother and the granddaughter in the water. I have always said that Anita's soul had been following me around, waiting for me to give that message to her granddaughter." Today Adalgisa remains active in her church and tries to enjoy every day. "*Andrea Doria* taught me that life is very special," she says. "I have looked on my life since then as a gift. During those awful hours on the *Andrea Doria*, I knew I was there to die. I was really at peace with it. But the hand of God kept me and looked after me. I decided to remember that every day. I like to see colors, smiles, and enjoy my life: there are always tragedies and so much suffering, but when something like this happens to you it makes you appreciate everything that comes after it as a real gift."[65]

When, six months after the *Doria*'s sinking, Antonietta Porporino gave birth to a son, she and Santino named him Peter, in honor of Captain Calamai; three more children followed as the couple settled in Paterson, New Jersey. The disaster left Antonietta with a fear of water—"she was scared of being in it, or even being over it, like on a bridge," her son Joe says. Once the family went on a boat but as soon as she saw that it had a glass bottom, Antonietta became so distraught that the captain had to turn around so that she could disembark. Before Santino and Antonietta died, Joe found the card that Swedish professor Gösta Ekspong had given them on board *Stockholm* and managed to trace him to an address in Uppsala. "I am sure this letter will be a long and overdue surprise from a family who has not forgotten you," Joe wrote. He was stunned to receive an answer: "Your letter came as a surprise, a very pleasant one," Ekspong wrote. "We, my wife, Inga, and myself, have not forgotten your family from the dramatic event when *Andrea Doria* and *Stockholm* collided near Nantucket in 1956. In fact, we have wondered if your parents were able to settle properly in the USA." To-day, Joe still prizes the water-stained nightgown his mother had on at the time of the collision as well as the drapes from one of the *Doria*'s First Class cabins that his father had been given to wear over his boxer shorts.[66]

For Barbara Boggs, the collision only accelerated what had been a barely contained crisis of marital unhappiness and depression. Her brother, Marshall Field IV, was hospitalized with manic depression in October 1956 and a month later, her father, Marshall Field III, died of a brain tumor.[67] Sharing what seemed to be a tendency in the Field family for depression, Barbara soon suffered a complete breakdown—a "total psychotic break," as her daughter Barbara Bliss recalled, "that included delusions and hallucinations." Boggs had her committed to a rest home, the euphemistically named Four Winds Katonah, where she stayed for two months. There followed periods at facilities in Connecticut and Massachusetts before Barbara entered a ward at New York City's Pres-byterian Hospital.[68] Diagnosed as suffering from pathological depres-sion, with delusions and suicidal tendencies, she endured several years of therapy and even shock treatments.[69]

Barbara finally recovered and attempted to reclaim some semblance of normalcy in her life. She divorced Boggs and in March 1961 she married for the third time. Ironically her new husband, Peter Benziger, was the grandson of the famous "Unsinkable" Molly Brown of *Titanic* fame. Barbara died on February 7, 1984, at the age of sixty-six.

Barbara's son, Bobby, who had been just twelve at the time of the collision, recalls how, before his mother died, some men who had dived to the wreck of the *Doria* came to visit her to show some of the china they had recovered. Barbara had hoped they might present her with a plate or cup as a small souvenir, but they left with all of their treasures. As for Bobby, he says, "I went on ships again after the *Andrea Doria*. I never even thought about it." In 1981, he met fellow survivor Mike Stoller for lunch at the Beverly Hills Hotel, and the two men spent time reenacting the collision using models of the ships. Midway through the meal, the head waiter came over and said he'd recognized the *Doria* model; his father, he explained, had been a fireman aboard the liner.[70]

As for Bobby's sister Barbara Bliss, she never managed to completely escape from the turmoil that ringed her life as a descendant of Marshall Field. Despite "the enormous life of privilege I experienced as a young person," she wrote, "life held only despair and mental illness for many members of my family."[71] She likened the sense to being "expelled from the Garden of Eden," with all of the "incredible beauty" and wealth forming its own Paradise Lost.[72] She was, her daughter, Adelaide, remembers, "tortured by the past. She was raised to be a socialite but her own heart was Bohemian. The kind of WASP society in which she was brought up was in direct opposition to her own temperament. Everything that she had been taught was important—society, expectation, wealth—had been whittled down and eroded to a great sense of loss, always harking back to a past full of what might have been."[73]

Barbara's brief romance on the *Doria* with Dun Gifford came to nothing—he "lost some of his allure without a crisis to contend with," she admitted.[74] After graduating from Sarah Lawrence, Barbara enjoyed an operatic career, appearing in numerous international productions but, as her daughter says, "was not aggressive in pursuing it or in promoting herself." Still, she never abandoned music and became a respected voice coach in both New York and Los Angeles.[75] Both of her marriages—the first to diplomat Ambler Moss, Jr., in 1960, and the second to exiled Cuban pianist Luis Mestre in 1967—ended in divorce. "In the process of learning about myself and understanding the dynamics of the illness that haunted my family," Barbara wrote, "I drew closer to my own heart; indeed my own center or inner core.

The peace and serenity that surround my life today make all the luxury and opulence of the past pale in comparison. But it was a long struggle to arrive at this point."[76] Barbara died on December 27, 2014.[77] Her daughter, actress Adelaide Mestre, has successfully woven together her family's tangled history and conflicting inheritance in a one-woman show, *Top Drawer: Stories of Dysfunction and Redemption from Park Avenue to Havana,* which premiered in 2011.

Although she remains the best known of all *Andrea Doria* survivors, Linda Morgan has done her best to put the "miracle girl" appellation in the past. "I hope," her mother, Jane, said a year after the disaster, "that people will not keep reminding Linda of her terrifying experience and will let her grow up and forget."[78] Linda thought it was absurd when her Campfire Girls troop presented her with a lifesaving badge. When she graduated from boarding school, her father convinced her to take a voyage on RMS *Queen Elizabeth;* she found the experience so unnerving that for the next forty years she refused to board another ship.[79]

Jane never entirely recovered from the ordeal. Physically, she was left with a limp and pain in her hand; emotionally, Linda remembers, she "was never the same. Each year, around the anniversary, she suffered from depression when thinking about Cian and Joan." In September 1957 she wed reporter George Kirstein: "I think she just didn't want to be alone," Linda says. On July 25, 1968—the twelfth anniversary of the disaster—Jane died of a heart attack at the age of fifty-two.[80]

Just two months earlier, Linda had married lawyer Phil Hardberger. They had met while working on an anti-poverty campaign at the Office of Economic Opportunity in Washington, DC. The couple moved to Texas, where Linda raised their daughter and worked for many years as curator of the McNay Art Museum in San Antonio and then for the Tobin Theatre Arts Fund. Although she had little taste for publicity, she was thrust back into the spotlight when her husband successfully ran for mayor of San Antonio and she used her position to push for expansion of civic spaces and gardens.

Today, Linda spends much of her time alongside her husband on their boat; it took some time for her to overcome a hesitancy about being on the water—"my only stipulation," she recalls, "was that we could see land at all times."[81] She is philosophical about her inexorable link to the *Doria*. "People don't remember plane crashes or other tragedies like they do a ship sinking. I'm just one survivor, and I survived not because of anything I did. There was nothing heroic about it. But I know that when I go, my obituary will read, 'Miracle Girl Dies.' It's absurd."[82]

"I had no ill effects of which I am aware from the disaster," says Peter Thieriot. "I never had any nightmares, panic attacks, or psychological problems, unless the experience contributed to my less than stellar comportment as a teenager." He returned to California, where an aunt and uncle raised Peter and his three brothers in Hillsborough with their own two sons. Following a rough term at Bellarmine College Preparatory in San Jose, he attended a Benedictine school Portsmouth Abbey in Rhode Island which, he says, "did me a lot of good." After a stint in the army, he married and raised three children. Peter spent a few years working in the family newspaper business before taking a break, during which he built patio furniture in Redwood City.[83] He briefly returned to the newspaper business only to take up ranching in Wyoming, where he raised bison and promoted their meat as a healthier alternative to beef.[84] His nephew Max Thieriot has become an actor, currently starring in the CBS Television drama *SEAL Team*. Now retired to a small ranch in the Midwest, Peter enjoys spending time with his children and grandchildren.[85] "An experience like the *Andrea Doria*," Peter has said, "makes some of the less tasty things in life easier to deal with. An awful lot can happen, and it doesn't seem like any big deal."[86]

Tullio and Filomena Di Sandro moved to Providence, Rhode Island, near where their daughter Norma's grave is in Pawtucket. They had three more children: son, Ermanno, and two daughters, the first named Norma in honor of their lost girl, and Brigida Marilena. Ermanno recalls that while his living sister Norma assumed a central place in the family's life, "the little Norma lost in the shipwreck was never known, and never included as part of my childhood or adolescence, because she was not spoken about at home at all. The pain and embarrassment of my parents did not spill out, or if it did, only sporadically. My parents had always kept us in the dark about everything, because it was not their intention to relive those moments of pure bewilderment, of breathlessness, of depression at having lost everything, and above all the loss of their most dear jewel, their beautiful daughter." When one of the children asked about the photographs of Norma displayed in their house, Tullio and Filomena, Ermanno recalls, "would simply say that she was a little angel, a distant little sister who was in paradise."[87]

After eleven years in America, the Di Sandros returned to Italy; they exhumed Norma's remains for reburial in Marzano Appio, although her tombstone still remains at the St. Francis Cemetery in Pawtucket. Tullio taught electronics until he retired in 1986—"he was a great, respected, friendly, and honest worker," his son, Ermanno, says. Tullio died on Christmas Day 2007. Filomena today lives in a house her architect son, Ermanno, renovated for her, adding a beautiful redbrick portico with white arches. "She knows that she will be reunited with Norma just after her death," he says.[88]

Of the three children, it is Ermanno who most keenly felt the constant presence of the sister he had never known. "I feel that she protects me from danger," he says. "I always hear her next to me, and she dictates my life because she is my powerful guardian angel." In 2007 he published his first book about his family's experiences on *Andrea Doria* and dedicated it to Norma's memory; two others have followed. The central square of Marzano Appio, Filomena's birthplace, has also been dedicated to Norma. With the contribution of three artists and sculptors, Ermanno has designed a monument to his sister, which is to be erected in Tullio's native Colli a Volturno. The town's mayor is developing a public park named in her memory and dedicated to the area's emigrants, where the monument—along with a carousel, also designed by Ermanno and donated by his living sister Norma—will soon be placed. "I want her to remain eternal," Ermanno says of his lost sister, "so that her memory and her short life on earth have not been useless in an unjust world like this."[89]

Chapter Twenty

———◆◆◆———

A day after the sinking, a spokesman from the United States Navy
cautioned that it would be "next to impossible" to raise the *Andrea Doria*. "A ship the size of that Italian liner is nothing but a pile of
junk when she hits the bottom."[1] This didn't stop many from offering
a variety of proposals. In 1965, marine salvage expert Captain Don
Henry announced that he planned to fill the hull with liquid plastic
foam, which he hoped would then miraculously float it to the surface.[2]
Nothing came of this, nor did suggestions that she could somehow be
winched up, or given buoyancy by cramming her full of Ping-Pong balls
ever get beyond idle chatter.[3]

Even as the US Navy shot down fanciful ideas of raising the sunken
liner, an expedition to the *Doria* was under way, led by twenty-nine-
year-old department store heir Peter Gimbel. Joined by fellow diver
Joseph Fox, Gimbel hired a commercial fishing vessel to take them out
to the site on July 27, 1956.[4] Before leaving the scene on the morning of
July 26, *Hornbeam* had anchored a yellow drum over the wreck; now,
there was no sign of the marker. Clues gradually revealed themselves: a
steady stream of bubbles breaking the surface as air continued to escape
from the sunken liner; a jumble of floating flotsam that had broken
free; and long, filmy stretches of machine oil seeping up from the hull.
Aware that the *Doria* must be somewhere below, Gimbel and Fox prepared to make the dive.

They donned bulky rubber wet suits, pulled on tightly over powdered limbs, strapped on weighted belts holding knives and compasses, slipped their feet into fins, and adjusted masks over their faces. Finally came two air tanks, slung heavily on their backs and linked by thin tubing to mouthpieces before the pair tumbled over the side and began their plunge downward, into the unknown. The dangers were real: they had to be alert for nitrogen narcosis—"the rapture of the deep," as Jacques Cousteau termed it—which occurred with increased pressure of dissolved inert gasses. As the gas levels accumulated, they started to affect perception and judgment: the effect was similar to being drunk—disorienting and, because it induced a feeling of careless euphoria, often dangerously lethal.[5]

In 1956 the danger of nitrogen narcosis seriously limited the time Gimbel and Fox could safely stay at a depth of more than 150 feet: beyond fifteen or twenty minutes and the accumulation of nitrogen in the body could lead to blackouts. Returning to the surface was just as dangerous: the divers had to carefully regulate their ascent, stopping at prescribed points along the dive line to decompress and allow the nitrogen in their blood to dissipate. This was how a diver spent the bulk of their time: a dive of twenty minutes meant almost eighty minutes decompressing during the ascent. Failure to do so caused decompression sickness—"the bends"—which could lead to fatal embolisms in the bloodstream, heart, and brain.[6]

The July sunlight faded as Gimbel and Fox descended: the water changed from blue to a murky, barely perceptible green: visibility lessened the deeper they went. Finally, out of the shadows the men spotted a shimmering white—the side of *Doria*'s superstructure. "She is lying on her starboard side," Gimbel said after the dive, "and her port side seems in excellent condition. Her paint isn't even blemished. The portholes are unbroken. Even the lights along the promenade deck are unbroken."[7]

Gimbel and Fox captured small vignettes of the liner in a few hazy black-and-white photographs: the dim light and limited visibility made it impossible to see more than twenty or thirty feet of the ship at any one time. *Life* published the photographs and a few weeks later decided to finance another expedition. Along with three other divers, Gimbel and Fox returned to the site armed with color film. Six weeks beneath the surface had changed the ship: she was covered in a thin layer of slime; small bubbles of air and machine oil trapped within the hull still continued to float toward the surface. Peering through windows, Gimbel and Fox could see curtains, furniture, and mattresses floating in the murk: heavier objects rested in disordered jumbles on walls that had now become floors. They found piles of luggage still awaiting a disembarkation in New York that would never come; hundreds of shoes, abandoned by passengers as they attempted to keep their footing on the tilted, slippery decks; and documents—postcards, letters, menus, charts—that waved back and forth in the gentle current that swept through the ship. In the wheelhouse, the telegraphs and instruments gleamed brightly; the teak decks showed no sign of decay. Now and then, there was an eerie rumble or distant crash, as fittings and furniture continued to break loose and tumble from deep within the hull.[8]

The world once again saw the *Doria,* abandoned yet still intact, dignified in her isolation and evocatively whispering her siren song to other adventurers. They would come in waves, lured by the pull of a fabled sunken liner still full of potential treasures and, with her port side some 150 feet below the surface, within reach of experienced divers. Divers in the 1960s had labeled the *Doria* "the Mount Everest" of shipwrecks, an appellation that somehow made it seem even more alluring. As one man put it, "I can think of no more fitting tribute than beholding the magnificent lady up close and touching her now silent remains, and maybe if lucky and bold enough even bringing back some artifact from her to preserve and display."[9]

Over the years, hundreds have visited the wreckage, drawn by the allure of treasure in the form of artifacts—china, crystal, silver, and other souvenirs, as well as more substantial remnants of the vessel, including its fittings. The development of Trimix gas, in which helium replaced a portion of oxygen and nitrogen used in breathing tanks, allowed many more divers to visit the wreck as it lessened the chance of nitrogen narcosis, but danger still remains.[10] "You have to contemplate the very real possibility that you may not get out alive," was how one man summed up the situation.[11]

The first salvage efforts came in 1964, when two businessmen, Glenn Garvin and Robert Solomon, purchased a surplus US Coast Guard cutter that they renamed *Top Cat*, hired a crew of experienced divers, and visited the site to retrieve the statue of Admiral Andrea Doria that stood in the First Class Lounge. It took the team several attempts and involved considerable effort. To create an opening large enough to bring out the life-size statue, the men broke the windows along the Promenade Deck free from their frames; they hauled the frames to the surface, then used explosives to create an opening into the lounge beyond. The divers didn't know what to expect: with the *Doria* on her starboard side they anticipated that the heavy bronze statue would have toppled from its pedestal and was now probably half-buried in silt and debris at the bottom of the room. But amazingly the ship's namesake still stood atop his base, jutting out horizontally from a floor that had now become a wall. The divers decided not to use torches to cut the statue free: instead, with cables secured around the heavy figure, they spent several days manually sawing through its ankles until it was free and could be raised to the surface.[12]

Rescued but lacking its feet, the amputated statue had a kind of curious half-life, displayed at various venues before Garvin installed it in the banquet hall of his Sea Garden Hotel in Pompano Beach, Florida. When the hotel closed, the statue next surfaced back aboard *Top Cat* as a kind of good-luck charm before it ended up in Florida again, first at a beach bar and then as a lawn ornament in the yard of *Top Cat* captain Dan Turner.[13] In 1996 divers dove the wreck and recovered the statue's feet. A Florida artisan used these as models to re-create the original base and the restored statue briefly went on display in Genoa before returning to its Florida home.

It was not until 1981 that the most famous of the *Doria*'s items was salvaged. That year Peter Gimbel returned to the site in quest of one of the liner's safes. Before making his expedition he met with Barbara Boggs's son, Robert, who wondered whether the purser's safe might still hold his mother's jewelry as well as other items that passengers had been unable to retrieve after the collision.[14] But a meeting with Peter Thieriot changed Gimbel's plan. "I told Gimbel that he wouldn't find the purser's safe," Thieriot says, "because the hole in *Andrea Doria*'s side that I saw when I left encompassed the Purser's Office."[15] The Purser's Office had been just off the fore side of the First Class Foyer, the area that had been crushed in the collision. Gimbel then decided to try to find the Bank of Rome safe, which had been in an office just aft of the First Class Foyer, which was undamaged by *Stockholm*'s bow. He burned through the hinges of the double doors on the port side of the Foyer Deck, which had given First Class passengers access to the foyer beyond when they boarded, leaving a hole some eight by twenty feet.[16] After removing the doors, Gimbel was able to swim down, locate the Bank of Rome safe, and haul it out of the ship and to the surface.[17]

Recovery of the *Doria*'s safe made headlines around the world. Gimbel was certain that it contained a fortune in bank notes and valuable coins. Curiosity had to wait three years to be satisfied, as the safe sat in a shark tank at Coney Island to keep it in a familiar environment while Gimbel touted its discovery and arranged for an attendant television special to provide maximum publicity. Not until August 16, 1984, was the safe finally opened, on a live television broadcast hosted by George Plimpton and aired throughout the world.[18] Revelation of the safe's contents proved to be a disappointment: instead of the anticipated fantastic riches and rare coins, the safe held only a collection of disintegrating and waterlogged American, Italian, and Canadian currency, along with some unclaimed travelers' checks.[19] Gimbel had spent some $2 million to retrieve a safe whose contents were worth only an estimated $20,000. Hoping to recoup some of his expenditure, Gimbel dried the bills, had them encased in plastic, and sold them off to the public for up to $300 each.[20]

It was a sad coda to Gimbel's adventures with the *Doria*. He had been the first to see her after her sinking; had discovered that her keel was broken and that the damage inflicted by *Stockholm* was far more devastating than anyone had suspected; and had produced two fascinating documentary chronicles of his experiences, *The Mystery of the Andrea Doria*, and *Andrea Doria: The Final Chapter*. He died in 1987 at the age of fifty-nine; his third wife, former actress Elga Andersen, made arrangements before her own death that, after her passing, Peter's ashes, as well as those of his brother and of herself, would be placed inside the *Andrea Doria*. When she died, divers took the three sets of cremated remains down to the ship and settled them through a portside porthole on A Deck into the wreckage.[21]

John Moyer was trapped in the wreckage of *Andrea Doria*. It was the summer of 1984, and the thirty-two-year-old native of Vineland, New Jersey, had joined a team of divers making an annual expedition to the sunken liner. Growing up near the Jersey shore, Moyer had spent weekends diving on the multitude of wrecks—from Revolutionary War–era ships to vessels sunk in World War II—that lay littered along the coast. After obtaining a biology degree from Stockton University in Pomona, New Jersey, Moyer went into business but continued recreational diving in his spare time.

"When I first got involved," he says, "I was more interested in diving than in any specific wreck. I only knew about *Andrea Doria* because other divers kept telling me about it. I knew right away that it was something that I wanted to see for myself."[22]

One of those who had told Moyer to visit the *Doria* was Gary Gentile. Born in 1946, Gentile is one of the pioneers of technical diving, publishing classic books on the subject and on his extensive underwater expeditions. Moyer first met Gentile in 1975, and the two became immediate friends; together they have dived on hundreds of wrecks. And so, in 1982, Moyer first joined Gentile in an expedition to the *Doria*.

"All we really had for reference were a few books," Moyer recalls. "We had to figure out how to negotiate our way in and out of the wreck without a lot of clear reference points. The first year I went down, I looked for the bridge. But as I swam around, I saw that it was gone—it had broken away and fallen off the wreck. I was floating in the dim light, looking down to where the bridge should have been, and there was nothing there, just a big, black gaping hole."[23]

In 1983 Moyer had swum into the Promenade Deck toward the Winter Garden. Entering the ship meant safely avoiding the jagged edges of windows and doors, the jumble of collapsed walls, and the tangle of hanging electrical cables that swath the dark corridors and warren of rooms in deadly tendrils.[24] Every movement stirred up silt that swirled in obstructing clouds; broken furniture, rotting panels, and shattered glass only added to the dangers in an environment where everything was disorienting and askew. Barnacles, sea anemones, mussels, starfish, and other marine organisms gradually cloaked and concealed recognizable features. "The wooden partitions of the rooms," Moyer recalls, "were all gone, but structural walls were still in place. It was very confusing: you had to remember that what used to be ceilings and floors were now walls, and that staircases were now sideways."[25]

On his first dive, Moyer had found two silver boxes in the silt of the Promenade Deck—"they had probably belonged to a passenger," he says. But a year later there was a new goal. On a previous dive, Gary Gentile had swum aft, into the First Class Dining Room, and become the first to discover a treasure trove of china, porcelain, and crystal still lodged in the remnants of storage cabinets.[26]

The allure of this cache was irresistible. Now, in 1984, Moyer and two fellow divers swam through "Gimbel's Hole" and into the ruined First Class Foyer. Passage to the First Class Dining Room and its china closets was restricted: "as soon as you enter the corridor," Moyer says, "you were hit by dozens of electrical cables, hanging down like a curtain. You had to swim around them carefully to reach the china."[27]

By agreement, Moyer was the first of the trio to swim down the corridor to the china closets, and he began retrieving plates, cups and saucers from the muck. "At first visibility was good," he recalls, "but as soon as I started picking up the china the silt got stirred up into thick clouds, making it almost impossible to see." When Moyer turned and began to swim through this murk, he felt himself suddenly stopped short. At first he couldn't see what was preventing him from returning to the Foyer, but as the silt began to clear, he realized that the hanging electrical cables had wrapped themselves around the valves of his air tanks and trapped him in place. "I was maybe thirty feet down the corridor from the other two divers, and they had no idea that I was caught up. I grabbed my light and flashed it on and off down the ruined corridor to signal that I needed help. Luckily they saw it and swam over and got me untangled. If they hadn't, I don't know what would have happened."[28] The following summer, fellow diver John Ormsby died in almost exactly the same spot after his feet got caught in the tangled cables, becoming one of eighteen men to lose their lives exploring the the legendary *Doria*.[29]

Subsequent expeditions to the wreck continued to retrieve artifacts. In the summer of 1985, Moyer was slated to join Gentile and five other divers on an expedition to the wreck, hoping to retrieve one of the ship's bells. While testing a new underwater torch a week prior to the dive, though, Moyer suffered severe decompression sickness and had to be airlifted by a Coast Guard helicopter; he spent six hours decompressing in a chamber only to be told by his doctor that he was not allowed to dive for two weeks. Still, Moyer went out with his fellow divers and was present when they surfaced, bringing with them the bronze bell from *Andrea Doria*'s stern auxiliary helm.[30] Diver Steve Gatto later retrieved the auxiliary helm, and Gentile raised several of the Richard Riu ceramic panels from the ruins of the First Class Cocktail Lounge.[31]

One great prize remained: the *Doria*'s main bell, which had normally hung in a mounting on the bow. No one had reported ever seeing it on a dive, and it had never been recovered. Thinking that there must be an explanation, Moyer began a lengthy correspondence with officials at Ansaldo about the ship. Before the internet age, this was a long, drawn-out process by regular mail; impatient, Moyer finally traveled to Genoa, where he was able to meet a number of the *Doria*'s former officers and crew and studied the shipyard's archives. "Ansaldo," he remembers, "couldn't have been more helpful. I had been worried about their reaction—I was pillaging their ship, and wasn't Italian—but they assigned an assistant to me and were as interested in me diving the wreck as I was in their having built the ship." Moyer's efforts were rewarded. He learned that during the *Doria*'s voyages, the bell was usually taken down from its mountings and stored in the bow's paint locker, to prevent it from becoming weathered in the transatlantic sprays. It was remounted only just before the liner arrived in port.[32]

This information gave Moyer a road map to follow when he returned to the wreck with his friend and fellow diver Billy Deans, whom he had befriended while working in Key West. They swam into the liner's bow through a missing hatch cover and managed to reach the paint locker only to find that the door was locked. They ended up prying the door open, but their lights revealed only a layer of silt and debris some three feet thick. That winter, Moyer worked on developing a new airlift system to suction out and remove the silt. When he and a team of divers returned the following summer, armed with the new airlift hose, they broke out the paint locker's porthole and eased the hose down into the room. Five teams of two men spent hours slowly excavating the room. "It was a pretty grueling process," Moyer recalls. "Every day a team of divers had to take the airlift down and set it up in the porthole. Sometimes, when the current was especially strong, it took two or three dives to get it in place, and at the end of the day we had to break it all down again and bring it up, only to repeat the process again the next morning. We vacuumed out as much as we could. There was debris, mud, and silt, but no bell."[33]

Moyer wanted that bell, but he also had become aware of the large, futuristic ceramic panels by Guido Gambone that had decorated the Winter Garden: officials at Ansaldo had shown him photographs depicting how they had not only adorned the walls but also stood as partitions along the port and starboard sides. On a previous dive into the Winter Garden Moyer and Deans had spotted two large panels in the silt, and believed that they might be two of the Gambones. Having spent considerable time and resources in his quest, Moyer decided that he should protect his interests by filing an Admiralty Court claim on the wreck. His suit sought only to protect rights to any items he might discover from the specified areas in the bow or Winter Garden. Other divers would still be permitted to visit the wreck and retrieve souvenirs that could be carried to the surface by hand. Before the case could advance, Moyer had to meet first with the judge and show him china he had recovered from the site to prove that he had visited the wreck and was capable of diving it.[34]

Legal clarification of ownership was a necessity: the Italian insurance company Societa D'Assicurazione had acquired title to the wreck when it reimbursed the Italian Line for the *Doria*'s loss. The Societa

D'Assicurazione had never before objected to salvage of the wreck or asserted rights over recovered relics like the statue of Admiral Andrea Doria or the safe, but Moyer had no guarantee that they would not sue for ownership. The United States District Court for the District of New Jersey eventually agreed that the Italian company had abandoned the vessel and duly named Moyer as "salvor in possession" of the wreck.[35]

Armed with the court's "arrest warrant," Moyer went out to the wreck, dove down, and placed the legal notice in a watertight canister on the *Doria*. His lawyer also sent letters to the vessels that regularly took divers out to the *Doria* each summer, warning that while they were free to visit the liner they were not allowed to investigate the forward section and the bow when Moyer was at work.[36]

On July 4, 1993, the RV *Wahoo*, which Moyer had chartered for the expedition, brought him and a specially selected team to the wreck site. "They were twelve of my best friends," Moyer recalls, "and the best wreck divers around, three from Canada and the rest from the East Coast, including Evelyn Dudas, who had been the first woman to dive the *Doria*." The divers returned to the paint locker, hoping to find the ship's bell, but it again proved elusive. Moyer then turned his attention to the ship's Winter Garden. Swimming in through the port side, he again found the two large objects that had aroused his interest on earlier dives. They *were* two of the Gambone panels that had served as partitions. During the sinking they had broken free and landed against the Winter Garden's inner port wall, one faceup and the other facedown, and both buried in layers of silt. At roughly five by six feet and each weighing some seven hundred pounds, safely recovering these panels proved a considerable challenge. "We worked in teams," Moyer recalls. "We tied big nylon straps around them to hold them in place, and then used airlift bags to raise them. The really tricky part was trying to get them out: we had to carefully guide them out through an open doorway on the port side, which was now the ceiling, and get them into a position where the airlift bags could be fully filled to raise them to the surface."[37] It was a nerve-racking proposition, but after much effort the two panels finally emerged and saw sunlight for the first time in nearly forty years.[38]

The last significant recovery of an artifact from the wreck came in 2010, when New Jersey divers Ernest Rookey and Carl Bayer discovered the *Doria*'s small bronze bridge bell, emblazoned with the vessel's name, lying half-concealed in a layer of silt on the ocean floor. "All we hoped for was to get a little trinket to take home to remember our dive," an astonished Rookey told reporters.[39]

Moyer has continued to explore the wreck and renewed his rights as "salvor in possession." When he returned to the *Doria* in 1995, he found that the entire Winter Garden was gone: the deck had simply collapsed and slid off into the seabed. Had he not rescued the Gambone panels, they would have been lost to the world. He hopes that one day his extensive collection of *Doria* artifacts will find a home with a museum willing to preserve them and share them with the public.[40]

Recovery of artifacts from shipwrecks is not without controversy. Some, who suffered personal losses on the ship, quite naturally regard the wreck as a sacred space. "I feel very strongly about the divers who have visited the ship and brought things back," says Linda Morgan Hardberger. "There is nothing I can do to stop it. But for me the wreck is a burial ground for people I loved, not a tourist attraction."[41]

It is unlikely that future expeditions to the *Doria* will succeed in locating further prized treasures unless, like the bridge bell, they fell clear of the ship and wait to be found embedded in the seabed. Time has taken a cruel toll on the once-proud liner. She has been on the ocean floor for only a little over sixty years and one might imagine that she would be relatively well-preserved. The bow section of *Titanic*, after all, is still quite recognizable after more than a century beneath the waves. But ironically the *Doria*'s modern construction materials and the relatively shallow depth of her grave have each contributed to her premature demise. The aluminum of her superstructure could not long resist the underwater pressure and the decay of corrosion. And whereas *Titanic* rests some 2.5 miles down in a natural deep freeze unaffected by the surface environment, the *Doria* is, at 240 feet, too shallow to have escaped the destructive growth of sea life and the constant battering by Atlantic currents that have whipped through the wreck every year.

Andrea Doria existed in pristine form on the Atlantic seabed for less than twenty years. She was not engineered to withstand the constant water pressure nor the downward pull of gravity. Her funnel went first, collapsing into oblivion; by 1973 massive parts of her aluminum upper superstructure, including the wheelhouse, had fallen off the wreck and crashed into the seabed. The ensuing decline was rapid as the ship continued to disintegrate. The Belvedere Deck and the Sun Deck disappeared, sliding from the top of the ship to rest in a jumble of twisted wreckage along her side; by 1995, the Boat and Promenade Decks had also begun to slough off the ship as the inexorable pull of gravity took its toll. Within the hull, what remained of the *Doria*'s fittings—walls, ceilings, and floors—began their inevitable collapse; doorways caved in, staircases disappeared, and partitions pulled away, further weakening the interior. This also had the effect of reducing the beam of the *Doria* herself: she'd once been nearly ninety feet across but as decks slid off, they also took with them internal support and the port side of the hull began to flatten, pancaking in on itself until the wreck was bowed in the middle. Similar pressures widened fissures and cracks along the length of the vessel. By 2000, everything down to the Foyer Deck was gone, fallen to the ocean floor. The stern began to collapse, and by 2004 the bow had begun to separate itself from the hull.[42]

In 2016, Argus Expeditions contracted with OceanGate, a company based in Everett, Washington, to undertake an expedition to the wreck. Founded by Stockton Rush, OceanGate has been utilizing manned submersibles for maritime expeditions since 2009 and has undertaken a number of investigations in Alaska, off the Pacific Coast, and in the shipwreck-rich waters of Puget Sound in Washington State. On June 2, the support vessel *Warren Jr.* took the team and its submersible, called *Cyclops I* and designed using technology from the Applied Physics Lab at the University of Washington, out to the wreck site. During two dives, the small crew was able to maneuver the submersible around the wreck, taking seventeen sonar scans of the liner in time to record its pitiful state just before the sixtieth anniversary of its sinking to provide a scientific database against which future deterioration could be assessed. Unlike divers, the submersible was able to remain at the wreck for some four hours. Cracks noticed in prior years had widened to yawning chasms; chaos now reigned on the formerly elegant liner. The superstructure was gone: the broken-off bow sagged forlornly away from the ship, and the stern had separated. But the weather, as so often happens at the site in summer, soon turned and remained ugly, with high winds, heavy seas, and even a bank of fog that offered an eerie echo of July 25, 1956; this prevented plans to more fully explore the wreck. "It was simply too dangerous to continue the operation," says Joel Perry of OceanGate.[43]

Diving the *Doria* had always been perilous, but it is no longer safe to enter the majority of the remaining hull. From time to time, ominous, eerie crashes can still be heard coming from deep within the hull as the disintegration continues. "It must be clearly understood that the *Andrea Doria* is no longer a ship," Gary Gentile wrote in 2005. "It is very much a wreck—a sadly distorted caricature of her former self."[44] No one knows how long she has left before the final collapse, but the *Doria*'s fate is certain. Remaining steel will tumble to the sea, tearing the hull downward until it is flattened against the ocean floor. Everything will totter and fall in an incredible pile of rubbish: steel and ravaged teak, bits of broken china and gleaming silver, pieces of tile and twisted electrical cables, barnacle-encrusted portholes and rusted beams from watertight bulkheads. The ocean will reclaim the wreck, reducing the once great *Andrea Doria* to a jumble of oxide at the bottom of the Atlantic.

Epilogue

———◆◆◆———

On Saturday, July 28, 1956, tugs towed *Stockholm* from Pier 97 to the Bethlehem Steel Company Dry Dock in Brooklyn, where, at a cost of $1 million, she was fitted with a new bow.[1] By December 1956 she was back at sea, sailing her usual route for the Swedish American Line. But in 1959, Sweden sold her to an East German firm, which renamed her *Völkerfreundschaft* (People's Friendship) and used her as a holiday transport on the North and Black Seas. In 1983 she had a second brush with destiny, when she rammed and seriously damaged a West German submarine.[2]

Time has not been kind to the former Swedish liner. After extensive renovations, she went through six changes of ownership and name in a mere fifteen years.[3] In December 2008, while she was sailing as MV *Athena* for the Lisbon-based Classic International Cruises, pirates attacked the ship in the Gulf of Aden; thankfully no one was injured, and the vessel was soon cruising under yet another name, *Azores*. Like the fabled *Flying Dutchman*, the former *Stockholm* seems doomed to unhappily roam the oceans, forever shadowed by her tumultuous past.

Gunnar Nordenson, *Stockholm*'s former captain, was given command of the new Swedish liner *Gripsholm* in May 1957, with Carstens following as his third officer. There was an uncomfortable diplomatic incident at the time. The new *Gripsholm* was built in the same Ansaldo Shipyard that had given birth to *Andrea Doria*. When word came that the captain of *Stockholm* and the man who had been at her helm during the collision were to arrive in Genoa and take possession of the new liner, the workers at Ansaldo revolted. Still mourning the loss of their beloved *Andrea Doria,* they refused to complete the transfer if Nordenson and Carstens were involved. In the end, the Swedish American Line sent another captain.[4]

Nordenson retired from the Swedish American Line and died in 1981. Carstens remained at sea until 1965, when he took a management position with Bostroms, which operated the Swedish American Line.[5] He refused to accept any responsibility for the collision: "I did what I did," he once said, "and I know it is right, so I have no problem with it, but it is something you never forget because I have to live with it all my life."[6] After participating in an Italian program on the disaster, Carstens objected to its defense of the *Doria*'s captain—"I really thought it was wrong to honor the memory of Captain Calamai in that way," he complained. He even added his own unique spin on the tragedy, claiming that it was *Andrea Doria* that had collided with *Stockholm.* Now deceased, Carstens seemed unaffected by events that July of 1956. "I can claim with a clear conscience that I have never lain awake at night agonizing over what happened," he said.[7]

Perhaps this could be put down to Swedish reticence; the contrast in attitudes between Carstens and Captain Calamai, however, was stark. Calamai returned to Genoa a broken man. The hearings in New York had ended without resolution. The Swedish American Line's determined efforts to win over the press had been largely successful, leaving a widespread perception among much of the public that Calamai had somehow been culpable in the disaster. Unfortunately the Italian Line's agreement to secretly settle the case only fueled such beliefs. The Italian Maritime Marine commissioned their own inquiry into the collision; this is said to have absolved Calamai of blame, but the results were never made public.[8]

Captain Calamai was left to shoulder the public blame. In the aftermath of the tragedy, the Italian Line wanted nothing to do with their previously celebrated captain and treated him shabbily: he was no longer welcome to take over the helm of the *Doria*'s sister ship, *Cristoforo Colombo,* which had been promised to him, and never went to sea again. Guido Badano, his former junior second officer, recalled that he felt himself "alone, unsupported, and wronged by the media and his people . . . He became depressed and unwilling to confront unreasonable questioning."[9]

Calamai formally retired from the Italian Line in 1957. "When I was a boy," he said sadly, "and all my life, I loved the sea. Now I hate it."[10] People in Genoa would see him occasionally, strolling on the streets "like a zombie."[11] The emotional burden crushed him: not only had he lost his ship, but he also was haunted by the forty-six passengers who had perished that night. His daughter Silvia recalled that he was "like a father who has lost his son." Calamai died on April 9, 1972, at the age of seventy-five. His last words were, "Is it all right? Are the passengers saved?"[12]

The passage of time has scattered *Doria*'s surviving passengers. A few in the New York area began holding informal reunions in the early 1990s. In 1996, to mark the fortieth anniversary of the disaster, the US Merchant Marine Academy played host to the reunion. "A lot of them are coming for closure," said Captain Robert Meurn. "They want to reconcile it once and for all." Twenty-eight survivors attended, including Guido Badano, and enjoyed a dinner modeled after the last meal served on the *Doria*.[13]

Those attending the forty-fifth reunion, in July 2001, were able to share not only memories but also to relive the moment of disaster through the immersive computer simulation developed by Captain Robert Meurn at the US Merchant Marine Academy. They entered the thirty-foot-high Computer Assisted Operational Research Facility simulator, which, for this exercise, replicated the bridge of the *Stockholm:* windows gave a nearly 300-degree view of the virtual environment unfolding beyond on arced, twenty-foot-high screens and the floor vibrated with the simulated rumble of engines. Using the course recorders of *Andrea Doria* and *Stockholm*, Meurn programmed the minutes leading up to the crash to play out in realistic animated form through the windows. At first survivors saw only the *Stockholm*'s bow as it plunged forward, surrounded by fog then, suddenly, the lights of the *Doria* loomed out of the darkness as the Swedish ship abruptly turned into the Italian liner's side amid the sounds of metal crunching.[14] The experience was all too vivid for some survivors. "I never screamed when it happened," said one after watching the re-creation, "but I sure did at the simulation."[15]

For many years, survivor Anthony Grillo helped organize reunions. He was just three at the time of the collision, and had few memories of that night in July 1956, but he was determined to keep the memory of the *Doria* alive. He established a website, www.andreadoria.org, which presented information on the ship along with previously unpublished memoirs contributed by his fellow survivors, making it an invaluable resource. Grillo died in 2004, but his sister Vivian maintains the site as a tribute to her brother and to the lost liner.

It is another survivor, Pierette Domenica Burzio Simpson, who has, in a way, both taken on Grillo's mantle as a sort of gatekeeper to her remaining fellow passengers while also expanding her efforts into print and film. As a nine-year-old Italian girl coming to America to join her mother, Pierette lived through the disaster and rescue, retaining vivid memories of the experience. "The impact of that collision," she has said, "hurled me out of childhood innocence."[16] It was in her career as a teacher that the story first began resurfacing. The director of the private school where she taught French asked her to do a last-minute presentation to the elementary-aged pupils; though reluctant to highlight herself, she decided to use her experiences on the *Doria* as an opportunity to speak about immigration and the American dream. "I was so worried that I'd scare these poor kids to death, talking about a shipwreck," she says, "they knew about *Titanic* and so I went ahead. Most of them had never experienced sacrifice, so I talked about coming to America as a nine-year-old, leaving my friends and country behind to find a better life, and how I ended up on the ship and was rescued. The kids were so quiet as they listened, and I saw some fellow teachers wiping tears as I spoke about the importance of having a dream, working hard to achieve it, and never giving up even when faced with a tragedy. At the end, kids were begging me to tell my story again and my colleagues said that I should publish it."[17]

After discussing the idea with another *Andrea Doria* survivor,

Germaine Strobel-Donofrio, Pierette decided to write about her experiences. But the book took on a life of its own as she met others who had traveled aboard the *Doria;* spoke to maritime authorities; and felt a growing sense of injustice about the way Captain Calamai and his crew had been treated. Her 2006 book, *Alive on the* Andrea Doria*! The Greatest Sea Rescue in History* (published in Italy by Sperling & Kupfer as *L'ultima notte dell'*Andrea Doria) related not merely Pierette's own story but also included memoirs from a wide swath of fellow survivors. The real strength of the book, though, lay in Pierette's dedicated efforts to thoroughly address the cause of the collision and the technical aspects of the sinking. She learned naval architecture in English and in Italian so that she could fully explain the details, and worked closely with naval architects and maritime forensic experts and engineers in both countries. "It was a fascinating process," she recalls, "and I had to really beef up my Italian language skills, but the rewards were substantial." Publication made Pierette unique: she went beyond personal chronicle and became the first survivor of any shipwreck to challenge and disprove the accepted historical record through scientific explanation. "This book," she says, "was a way of giving back to the country of my birth and bring forth the truth that had been buried in the coffers of injustice. Captain Calamai and the *Doria*'s crew became scapegoats after the disaster, and it angered me that the Italian Line did nothing to defend their own. Their public relations people didn't want to speak to the media or correct the record but instead thought it best to maintain a dignified silence. It became my mission to set the historical record straight."[18]

Pierette followed *Alive on the* Andrea Doria*!* with a semifictionalized book for young readers, *I Was Shipwrecked on the* Andrea Doria*! The Titanic of the 1950s* in 2012. Along with members of the Society of Naval Architects and Marine Engineers, she planned the First International Marine Forensics Symposium as well as coauthoring, with naval architect and maritime forensics expert William H. Gazke, Jr., a scholarly, technical study of the disaster, *The Loss of* Andrea Doria: *A Marine Forensic Analysis,* published in the *Journal of Ship Production* in 2010.

Pierette ventured into film by accident. As a member of the Dante

Alighieri Society in Detroit, she helped organize speaking events and occasionally ushered guests around the city. One such visitor was Luca Guardabascio of Rome, a young but ambitious Italian director with several television movies and series as well as documentaries to his credit. After forming a friendship, the subject of making a film about the *Doria* came up. Multiple documentaries had already appeared: eventually Pierette and director decided that the best approach would be one that melded her personal story to a larger narrative encompassing the entirety of the *Doria* story.

This proved to be an immense learning curve, especially when Guardabascio urged Pierette to write an original script herself. There were many sleepless nights and additionally Pierette took on the role of producer, hiring actors and crew both in America and in Italy. "Being shot in two different countries, in two different languages, and under difficult circumstances including funding the project to a large extent," she recalls, "the film was a huge challenge." In the process, she again made history: the first survivor to write and produce a documentary feature about their own shipwreck; it was also unique in that fellow survivor, songwriter, and composer Mike Stoller contributed the main parts of the score.[19] The result, Andrea Doria: *Are the Passengers Saved?* is a beautifully shot, lyrical meditation, not merely on the collision but also a chronicle of Pierette's journey to rediscover her childhood roots in Italy. "Without roots," her mother told her, "there is no strength."[20] Combining dramatic re-creations with the memories of fellow survivors and interviews with naval architects, Italian art historians, maritime experts and engineers, and divers to the wreck, this is a tribute to the meaning of identity and honor and stands as an impressive work of art.

Andrea Doria: *Are the Passengers Saved?* has appeared on PBS, at international film festivals, and won numerous awards. Her work has brought deserved recognition, including Honorary Citizenship from her native town in the Piemonte region in Italy; a Piemonte region Leadership Award; and honorary membership in the Marine Forensics Committee of the Society of Naval Architects and Marine Engineers. Pierette has also received two proclamations from the State of Michigan and the Collegian Award from her alma mater, Wayne State University in Detroit. The success of Andrea Doria: *Are the Passengers Saved?* has spurred both Pierette and Guardabascio to explore the possibility of a feature film. The Italian Ministry of Culture expressed interest in such an idea, but funding for such a production is elusive. Despite setbacks, Pierette's belief in the *Doria* legacy remains undaunted. "I continue to work full-time on confronting the historical record that was surrounded by prejudice toward my people," she says. "It is through the *Andrea Doria* tragedy that I leave my statement to the world: to teach future generations that safety at sea must continue to be improved; about pride in one's origins; that after adversity there is transcendence; and that through art one can convey a social mission."[21]

Despite the loss of *Andrea Doria*, the Italian Line actually saw an increase in bookings for the 1957 season. They still ran the *Doria*'s near-twin, *Cristoforo Colombo*, between Genoa and New York: the experiences of her passengers must have been similar to those who traveled on *Titanic*'s sister ship, *Olympic*, after 1912. But the following year saw an unexpected development when British Overseas Airways Corporation (BOAC) and Pan Am began offering regular commercial flights across the Atlantic. As de Havilland Comets, Boeing 707s, and Douglas DC-7s roared across the skies, travelers began choosing temporary discomfort in order to spend more time on their business trips and holidays. Over the next few years, transatlantic bookings steadily declined as the number of those traveling by air increased dramatically: by 1966 some four million people annually traveled across the Atlantic by plane, while just 650,000 did so by ocean liner.[22]

Increasingly crowded skies slowly but surely erased the demand for travel by sea as, one by one, most of the remaining liners fell victim in the name of progress. None of *Andrea Doria*'s contemporary rivals remain afloat. Withdrawn from service in 1967, Cunard's *Queen Mary* has become a floating hotel in Long Beach, California; *Queen Elizabeth* was sold the following year, and, in 1972, caught fire in Hong Kong harbor before being scrapped. And the great *United States* sits forlornly in a Philadelphia shipyard. Stripped of her interior fittings, left to the elements, and now clad in discoloring bursts of rust, she awaits an uncertain fate, the last of the grande dames, whispering evocatively of an era long since past.

The Italian Line took delivery of new liner *Leonardo da Vinci* in 1960, but by 1965, when their twin ships, *Michelangelo* and *Raffaello*, were finished, the industry was already racking up considerable losses. In 1975, the Italian Line sold both *Michelangelo* and *Raffaello;* a year later, they abandoned transatlantic service altogether. Efforts to operate *Leonardo da Vinci* as a cruise ship proved futile and, one by one, the Italian Line's remaining ships were scrapped: *Andrea Doria's* twin, *Cristoforo Colombo,* and *Leonardo da Vinci* in 1982, *Raffaello* in 1983, and *Michelangelo* in 1991. Privatized in 1998, the Italian Line formally ceased to exist in 2005, ending more than a century of seafaring tradition.

Ironically, as Gary Gentile has pointed out, fate was in many ways kinder to *Andrea Doria* than to her rivals. "She would not," he wrote, "become as other ships: a forgotten, rusting hulk, lost in the dim memories of seafarers and insurance files. . . . By her celebrated if untimely demise the *Andrea Doria* avoided the humiliating fate of many of her contemporaries: the long ocean tow to a third world scrap yard, to be torched apart and recast in everlasting obscurity. Instead, she still resides serenely in her last port of call."[23]

It is easy to look back and see in the *Doria's* unfortunate end the last gasp of an era. She burst forth from a resurgent Italy, a floating repository of art and tradition, and wove a glamorous spell over her passengers. Yet she existed uneasily between two worlds: the already doomed golden age of ocean liners and the encroaching modern era of jet travel. Her noble lines, sleek black hull, and gleaming white superstructure hinted at tradition, while her dramatically bold interiors represented all of the modernity of the coming space age. The reconciliation of past and future depended on a kind of resigned stasis: as tastes and trends changed, most travelers no longer wanted to dress for dinner or expend their limited holiday time sitting idly on deck chairs. The new cruise ships, when they came, seem monstrous by comparison: massive, multidecked behemoths with six-story atria, water slides, and throngs of flip-flop–wearing revelers gambling at slot machines and noisily slurping drinks during endless cabaret performances.

Andrea Doria's final voyage had its own clash of cultures. There were, to be sure, those accustomed to tradition, like Cecilia Pick and Barbara Boggs, who appreciated the white-jacketed stewards and air of formality that still existed. And emigrants had always accounted for a large number of transatlantic travels. But the modern age was also represented by celebrity movie stars like Ruth Roman and Betsy Drake, and rock-and-roll pioneer musician Mike Stoller. Yet whatever their backgrounds, these passengers all found themselves thrown together in a shattering maritime drama. Their struggle to survive reveals itself as an uplifting tale of physical and moral courage, a testament to the power of humanity to face seemingly overwhelming adversity and, for the most part, emerge even more resilient.

Unfortunately the *Doria*'s legacy remains overshadowed by questions of responsibility for the collision. In the first half century following the disaster, public opinion largely blamed the Italians. Captain Calamai was thought to have acted recklessly; some members of his crew were portrayed as cowards, and experts opined that the ship's poor design led to her unfortunate demise. In refusing to engage in an ongoing public-relations battle with their Swedish counterparts, officials at the Italian Line unfortunately ceded the propaganda war. Only in the last decade has a new narrative finally begun to emerge. It now seems obvious that it is Carstens who must shoulder blame for the collision. Shipping lines usually protected their captains: after the sinking of *Titanic* in 1912, the White Star Line went to great lengths to mythologize its captain, Edward Smith, as a hero to the last, ignoring his undoubted negligence in racing his liner at top speed into an area where ice was known to lurk. The Italian Line's shameful treatment of Captain Calamai went against this tradition: it proved easier to let him linger in the public imagination as a scapegoat than to bear the long and costly expenses of extended maritime trials.

It is undoubtedly true that some of the *Doria*'s service personnel abandoned the ship and left its passengers to their fates. But the captain and his officers, along with ordinary crew members, able-bodied seamen, and engineers, remained aboard the liner. That only forty-six lives were lost on the *Doria* that night is surely the most compelling argument in favor of her crew's competence and professionalism in the face of unexpected disaster. And the loss of the liner itself was inevitable: no matter how well built or how many watertight doors, no ship meant to stay afloat if only two compartments flooded could survive the devastation caused when a third is opened to the sea.

In 1956 the collision and loss of *Andrea Doria* seemed so startling because, in its collective arrogance, mankind once again believed that technology had conquered the unpredictable oceans. *Titanic* should have taught that no amount of modern equipment or misplaced belief could compensate for human error. Unfortunately on that foggy July night in 1956, fatal miscalculation and inexperience on the part of one ship doomed the other, the pride of Italy's Renaissance Fleet, to an eternal Atlantic grave.

Acknowledgments

In the beginning, this book was inspired by a conversation Greg had with our editor at St. Martin's Press, Charles Spicer. From there, the project took root. We thank our agent, Dorie Simmonds, for helping spearhead the process, and working diligently on our behalves to bring it to fruition. We also thank Sarah Grill, editorial assistant at St. Martin's Press, for her help with the manuscript and the illustrations.

The book grew thanks to the enthusiasm and assistance of Mike Poirier, a liner and shipping expert whom we met during the time we wrote our *Lusitania* book. Mike's devotion to his subject is evident through his willingness to advise us, to read all the versions of our manuscript, and to answer so, so many questions. By now Mike is a firm personal friend of both of us, and to him we owe many thanks for bringing us to the history of this ship, an experience that has both deepened and enriched our lives.

It is not an overstatement to say that this book would not exist without the generosity and support of the extraordinary Pierette Domenica Burzio Simpson. At the age of nine, she survived the sinking of *Andrea Doria* and has since become one of the world authorities on the subject, helping keep the story alive through her books, her film, and her websites. Even when faced with a personal crisis, Pierette remained steadfast in her efforts on our behalf, coordinating introductions to her fellow survivors, assisting with corrections to the manuscript, and helping us locate images to use in illustrating the book. She has our inexpressible gratitude and friendship.

Normally, a King and Wilson book develops steadily and in a controlled fashion, as research takes us hither and yon in revealing the deeper aspects of the subject at hand. This book, however, was slowed by events beyond our control when, on June 6, 2018, Penny's mother died at the age of ninety-three, and then—perhaps predictably after seventy-two years of marriage—her father followed on June 29. They were apart for only twenty-three days.

The passing of Penny's parents followed closely after the unexpected death of her nephew in 2017. For Penny, this book was very much a labor of love in immortal memory of three people who had given her support, encouragement, and love all her life and theirs: Edward O'Hanlon, Mary O'Hanlon, and Jon Phillips.

An author relies on relationships with family and friends—not only to buoy him or her up through the process of writing a book but also to willingly forgo movie nights, get-togethers, and parties. For their patience and forbearance, Penny thanks: James and Tricia Manara; Jamie and Lindsey Phillips and their daughters, Georgia and Charlotte; Barbara Wilson; Beth Kelsey; Peggy, Eric, and Ryan Cartwright; John Phillips; Bill and Anne O'Hanlon; Margaret McPherson; Stephanie Douglas; Ann Howes; Richard Osborne and the whole extended family in Rutherglen, Scotland.

For their continued support and friendship, many, many thanks go to Dominic Albanese; Mark Andersen; Janet Ashton; Arturo Beeche; Simon Donoghue; Annette Fletcher; Jake Gariepy; Coryne Hall; Emma Hampton and Sally Criddle; Christopher Kinsman; Chuck and Eileen Knaus; Angela and Mark Manning, who reconnected with Greg just as this book demanded all of his attention; Barton Maxwell; Eugene Mejia; Ilana Miller; Michael Revis; Jennifer Rider; Larry Russell; Charles Stewart; Katrina Warne; Sue Woolmans; and Kelly Wright. Special thanks to the wonderful Antonio Perez Caballero, who gives us so much support and encouragement always. To the good people of Planetsocks, whom Penny has now known online for something approaching twenty years—thanks for the wit, wisdom, humor, friendship, and puns.

Penny's husband, Tom, has been the go-to guy for all our computer and printing needs for almost twenty years. Even on this, the last day of work on this book, he is helping with glitches and questions. We literally could not do this without him. So much love from Penny and gratitude from Greg.

Should anyone wish to follow our future projects and talk about history, please join us on our Facebook Group: King and Wilson History: The Romanovs and Beyond.

Many people helped in the research and writing of this book, offering advice, information, and guidance. We received assistance from the following archives and individuals for articles, newspapers, photographs, and other documents: James Huntoon and Randy Thompson of the US National Archives and Records Administration (NARA) at Riverside (California); Lisa Williams of the Mariners' Museum, Newport News, Virginia; and Meg Romero Hall, director of Archives and Records, the Archdiocese of Chicago. For sharing materials and their memories, we thank Rose Calvelli, who acted as a translator for survivors arriving in New York; Joseph D'Andrea, former honorary Italian counsel in Pittsburgh; former *Doria* passenger Iole Dole; Christina Crawford, who shared memories of her 1956 voyage aboard the *Doria* with her mother, Joan Crawford, and allowed us to quote from her unpublished diaries; William H. Garzke, Jr., former chairman of the Marine Forensic Panel of the Society of Naval Architects and Marine Engineers, for correcting and advising on technical portions of the book; Marlene Eilers Koenig; Cathy Crawford LaLonde and her son, Casey LaLonde, Joan Crawford's daughter and grandson, for sharing memories of Cathy's time on both the *Andrea Doria* and her experience on the *Ile de France* when it rescued passengers from the Italian liner; and Larry Russell, for recalling the day he saw the *Ile de France* arrive in New York City with survivors. And once again Susanne Meslans opened her extensive library to us, which helped us better tell this story and that of the lives of a few of the *Doria*'s more privileged passengers. Susanne remains a treasured friend, and one day Greg will convince her to finally write a book.

Once again Joan Blacker of the Everett Public Library worked miracles on our behalf, scouring databases and obtaining obscure titles that helped us portray the scope of this story. Joan has been an integral part in the research process for our last few books, and her friendly assistance will be greatly missed as she retires from her position.

In helping us understand the wreckage of *Andrea Doria* and the various expeditions to her, we must thank John Moyer. John is "salvor in possession" of the wreck—essentially the owner—and has made more than 120 dives on the site. His knowledge is extraordinary, and his generosity in sharing his experiences helped shape this book. His fantastic photographs documenting his efforts and recovery of artifacts from the ship are amazing. In the summer of 2016, OceanGate, an underwater exploration company based in Everett, Washington, undertook a survey of the wreck site. Joel Perry of OceanGate freely shared information and allowed Greg to tour their submersible, *Cyclops I,* which had visited the site, and Dana Hall and Amber Bay shared the company's images from their work. Dan Wright and William Campbell also generously shared with us important images of their dives to the wreck.

In the writing of this book, we were most fortunate to get to meet and talk to survivors of the *Andrea Doria* tragedy. Without exception, they are wonderful people—welcoming, friendly, open, and deeply committed to the accurate recording of their memories of the beautiful liner and the summer of 1956. This book would not have been possible without the participation of the following survivors, who submitted themselves to interviews, email follow-ups and reading and rereading the completed manuscript: Robert F. Boggs; Adalgisa Di Fabio; Klaus Dorneich; Melania Ansuini Vali; Auxiliary Bishop Raymond Goedert; Linda Morgan Hardberger; Pat Mastrincola; Arlene Mastrincola Meisner; Madge Young Nickerson; Joe Porporino; Alda Raimengia; Tony Sergio; Andrea Stevens; Mike Stoller; and Peter Thieriot.

We were also fortunate to have survivors' family members lend a helping hand. We extend our thanks to: Maria Coscia's daughter Sadie Onorato and her granddaughter Renee Coscia, who went to extraordinary lengths to help us tell their family's story; Adelaide Mestre, who shared memories of her mother, Barbara Bliss, as well as Barbara's unpublished memoirs; Nicholas, the Marquis de Piro, for composing a short biography of his aunt Cecelia Pick and allowing us to tell her story; Alda Raimengia's daughter Lucy Raimengia for providing additional details; Nicola DiFiore's granddaughter Daniela Sellinger, who helped us re-create his time on the ship; Antonio Sergio's daughter Maria Sergio, for helping coordinate interviews and information; Ermanno Di Sandro; Linda Stevens; Maria Tusa; and Doria Weeks.

In winding down this project, we are thinking of all the wonderful people and unique challenges that we encountered in the course of the last two and a half years. The survivors have been brilliant and are the stars of this production. We have been awed by their courage, grace, wit, and humanity. But as we end this tale, our thoughts inevitably drift to the fifty-one people who did not come back from the sea. In particular, we lament the loss of the children of the *Andrea Doria*, some of whose stories are told in this book: Joan Cianfarra; Guiseppe, Anna Maria, Margaret Dominica, and Rocco Sergio; and always, *la principessina*, Norma di Sandro.

Notes

Chapter One

1 Levy, 25–26, 51; Buckley.
2 Levy, 75; Buckley.
3 Levy, 200.
4 Ibid., 523.
5 Maxtone-Graham, 401–02, 406; Wealleans, 137.
6 Steele, 202.
7 Maxtone-Graham, 409.
8 Grattidge, 250.
9 Brinnin, *Sway of the Grand Saloon*, 532–33.
10 Goldstein, 11.
11 Kohler, 321.
12 Ibid., 176.
13 Eliseo, 18.
14 *New York Times*, May 22, 1951.
15 Eliseo, 44–46.
16 Moscow, 20; Goldstein, 14; Kohler, 188.
17 Moscow, 110.
18 Hoffer, 11.
19 Ibid.
20 Kohler, 189.
21 Goldstein, 14; Hoffer, 11; Moscow, 158.
22 Moscow, 16, 88, 90; Garzke and Simpson, 100; Kohler, 188–89.
23 Goldstein, 14; Simpson, 248–49; Moscow, 88–89.
24 Moscow, 22.
25 Maxtone-Graham, 169.
26 Ibid., 260; Kohler, 66–67, 73.

27 Kohler, 322.

28 Ibid., 190.

29 Kohler, 328; Roccella, 41.

30 Tinterri, 91–92; Eliseo, 92.

31 Kohler, 1.

32 Moscow, 19.

33 Eliseo, 2.

34 Kohler, 184.

35 Ibid., 184–85.

36 Hoffer, xiii.

37 Mattsson, 5.

38 Information from Cathy Crawford LaLonde and her son Casey LaLonde.

39 Excerpt from Christina Crawford's diary, courtesy of Christina Crawford.

40 Ibid.

41 Ibid.

42 Information from Cathy Crawford LaLonde and her son Casey LaLonde.

43 Crawford, 83.

Chapter Two

1 Moscow, 22–23; Goldstein, 9; Tinterri, 75–76, 82, 86–87; Eliseo, 36.

2 Hoffer, 8.

3 Kohler, 194.

4 Moscow, 14.

5 Eliseo, 87.

6 Eugenio Giannini, in *The Sinking of the Andrea Doria*, DVD.

7 Brinnin, *Beau Voyage*, 60–61.

8 Moscow, 14.

9 Brinnin, *Beau Voyage*, 53–54.

10 Eliseo, 91; Kohler, 188.

11 Eliseo, 148. Adjusted for inflation, the value of $100 in 1956 is approximately $925 in 2020. For the sake of comparison with the *Doria* rates, the average annual income for an American household in 1956 was $4,500; the median price for a new house was some $11,000; new Fords began at $1,748; a Kodak Brownie movie camera cost $59; a six-pack of beer could be had for $1.20; and a gallon of gas cost roughly .22 cents. See https://fiftiesweb.com/pop/prices-1956/.

12 Gentile, *Deep, Dark, and Dangerous*, 60, 73, 100–1.

13 Simpson, 30.

14 Interview with Andrew Stevens.

15 *Sarasota Herald-Tribune*, July 25, 2006.

16 Kohler, 189–90.

17 Moscow, 102; Goldstein, 20; Hoffer, 32.

18 *New York Times,* January 24, 2009; details drawn from Miles, *Leap Through.*
19 *New York Times,* November 13, 1953.
20 Miles, 194–97.
21 *New York Times,* January 24, 2009.
22 "Recruits for Freedom," in *Time,* September 7, 1953.
23 *New York Times,* August 26, 1953.
24 *The Spectator,* September 11, 1953.
25 Goldstein, 20.
26 Becker, 61, 65–66; Madsen, 155–57, 173; Bessell, 37.
27 Caumsett Foundation, 8.
28 Bessell, 14–15, 20; Randall, 145–46.
29 Benziger, 86–87.
30 Caumsett Foundation, 11.
31 Kiernan, 81.
32 Becker, 119; Bliss, *Barbara's Tarnished Bliss,* 50; Madsen, 278.
33 Marling, 87; Caumsett Foundation, 18, 26; *Life,* October 18, 1943, 108.
34 Marling, 87.
35 Benziger, 122.
36 Bliss, *Barbara's Tarnished Bliss,* 42, 50, 86.
37 Interview with Adelaide Mestre.
38 Bliss, *A Grandchild Remembers.*
39 Interview with Adelaide Mestre.
40 Bliss, *Barbara's Tarnished Bliss,* 26.
41 Benziger, 121.
42 "Amazing Tale."
43 Information from Nicholas, the Marquis de Piro.
44 Ibid.
45 Ibid.
46 *Milwaukee Journal,* July 28, 1956.
47 Information from Klaus Dorneich.
48 NWZonline.de Stuttgart, July 20, 2006, "Atlantic Does Not Let Shipwrecked People Go."
49 Fagone.
50 Morris, 13, 15, 17–18; Binzen, 16, 32–34; *New York Times,* January 24, 1974.
51 Fagone.
52 Morris, 38–39; Binzen, 88.
53 Morris, 35.
54 Ibid., 94.
55 Ibid., 142.
56 Fagone.

57 Fagone; *Philadelphia Daily News,* October 2, 1956; *Philadelphia Inquirer,* October 18, 1970.
58 Fagone.
59 Binzen, 161.
60 Ibid., 141.
61 *Philadelphia Inquirer,* July 27, 1956; Hoffer, 36.
62 Hoffer, 37.
63 Roman, 6.
64 *The Guardian,* September 16, 1999.
65 "The Rapid Rise of Ruth Roman," *Life,* May 1, 1950, 55.
66 *New York Times,* September 11, 1999.
67 Ryan, 25.
68 *New York Times,* September 19, 1970.
69 Ryan, 26.
70 Ibid.
71 *Brooklyn Daily Eagle,* January 20, 1933; Hoffer, 28.
72 *Brooklyn Daily Eagle,* October 26 1956.

Chapter Three

1 "Amazing Tale."
2 Archdiocese of Chicago, "Archdiocesan Priest, Rev. Msgr. John V. Dolciamore, Dies," November 27, 2012, http://legacy.archchicago.org/news_releases/obituaries_12/obit_112712.html; www.FranzosenbuschHeritageProject.org.
3 Goldstein, 43.
4 *Daily Herald,* Chicago, June 3, 1999.
5 Ibid.
6 Hoffer, 101.
7 Interview with Auxiliary Bishop Raymond Goedert.
8 Hoffer, 33.
9 Lucy Gordan, "An Interview with Dun Gifford," November 6, 2007, http://epicurean-traveler.com/an-interview-with-dun-gifford/.
10 *Nantucket Inquirer and Mirror,* June 10, 2010; *Providence Sunday Journal,* December 9, 1956.
11 *Nantucket Inquirer and Mirror,* June 10, 2010.
12 *Providence Sunday Journal,* December 9, 1956.
13 *Nantucket Inquirer and Mirror,* June 10, 2010.
14 Interview with Madge Young Nickerson.
15 Ibid.
16 Young, 2.
17 Interview with Madge Young Nickerson.
18 Ibid.

19 *USA Today*, July 25, 1981.
20 Leiber and Stoller, 34.
21 Fricke.
22 Leiber and Stoller, 78.
23 Ibid., 86.
24 Interview with Mike Stoller.
25 Leiber and Stoller, 87.
26 Tinterri, 105; Gentile, *Deep, Dark, and Dangerous*, 74; interview with Mike Stoller.
27 Interview with Mike Stoller.
28 Interviews with Pat Mastrincola and Arlene Mastrincola Meisner.
29 Ibid.
30 Interview with Arlene Mastrincola Meisner.
31 Interview with Pat Mastrincola.
32 Interview with Sadie Onarato.
33 Interview with Renee Coscia.
34 Interview with Alda Raimengia.
35 Interview with Antonio Sergio.
36 Hoffer, 38; Moscow, 110, 119; Goldstein, 44, 73.
37 Hoffer, 38.
38 Interview with Antonio Sergio.
39 Hoffer, 65; *Detroit Free Press*, April 24, 1960; *The Journal News*, March 20, 1973.
40 Interview with Melania Vali.
41 Interview with Ermanno Di Sandro; Di Sandro, *In ricordo di Norma*, 99–101, 106–8.
42 Interview with Melania Vali.
43 Interview with Daniela Sellinger.
44 Interview with Joe Porporino.
45 Simpson, 32.
46 Interview with Joe Porporino.
47 Interview with Pierette Domenica Simpson.
48 Interview with Adalgisa Di Fabio.
49 Ibid.

Chapter Four

 1 *The Pantagraph*, July 26, 1981.
 2 Amory, 420.
 3 Moffat, 81.
 4 Brechin, 174–75; Bruce, 171–75.
 5 Brechin, 175–77; Birmingham, 76.
 6 Moffat, 179.

7 Brechin, 195; Birmingham, 77, 236.

8 Interview with Peter Thieriot.

9 Ibid.

10 Ibid.

11 *The Pantagraph*, July 26, 1981; Goldstein, 22; Hoffer, 35; Moscow, 105.

12 Tinterri, 137; Moscow, 20; Goldstein, 13; Eliseo, 95; Kohler, 190.

13 *The Pantagraph*, July 26, 1981; Goldstein, 22; Hoffer, 35; Moscow, 105.

14 Interview with Peter Thieriot.

15 Interview with Linda Morgan Hardberger.

16 Ibid.

17 Ibid.

18 Ibid.

19 Ibid.

20 Ibid.

21 *Time*, August 6, 1956; Goldstein, 23; *New York Times*, April 1, 1951.

22 Morgan, 238.

23 Interview with Linda Morgan Hardberger.

24 Goldstein, 62.

25 Eliot, 259–60.

26 Nelson, 165.

27 Eliot, 260–61.

28 Ibid., 261–62.

29 Nelson, 167.

30 *Photoplay*, January 1959, 72–73; Eliot, 272.

31 *Los Angeles Times*, November 12, 2015.

32 Ibid.

33 Ibid.

34 Eliot, 292–93.

35 Ibid., 299.

36 Hotchner 110–12.

37 Loren, 122.

38 Eliot, 300.

39 Goldstein, 62.

40 Nelson, 196; Eliot, 301; *The Washington Post*, November 11, 2015; *Los Angeles Times*, November 12, 2015.

41 Di Sandro, *In ricordo di Norma*, 135.

Chapter Five

1 Eugenio Giannini, in *The Sinking of the* Andrea Doria.

2 Moscow, 23; Gentile, Andrea Doria: *Dive to an Era*, 19–20; Kohler, 195.

3 Hoffer, 23; Goldstein, 71.

4 Moscow, 107.

5 Ibid.; Hoffer, 40.

6 Bliss, *Barbara's Tarnished Bliss*, 30.

7 http://www.forwardlook.net/features/chrysler_norseman_en.htm.

8 Hoffer, 5.

9 Interview with Madge Young Nickerson.

10 Hoffer, 5–6; Goldstein, 17.

11 *Daily Times*, August 15, 1956.

12 Bliss, *Barbara's Tarnished Bliss*, 22.

13 Interview with Madge Young Nickerson.

14 Lee, John Dolciamore interview.

15 Interview with Adalgisa Di Fabio.

16 de Beaudéan, 170.

17 Eliseo, 266–68.

18 Brinnin, *Beau Voyage*, 138–39.

19 Eliseo, 143.

20 *Nantucket Inquirer and Mirror*, June 10, 2010.

21 Eliseo, 153.

22 Hoffer, 22; Goldstein, 13; Eliseo, 138.

23 Simpson, 97.

24 Eliseo, 152.

25 de Beaudéan, 163.

26 Tinterri, 127; Haberstroh, 22; Eliseo, 150.

27 Eliseo, 158–61.

28 Brinnin, *Beau Voyage*, 57.

29 Gentile, Andrea Doria: *Dive to an Era*, 117; Gentile, *Deep, Dark, and Dangerous*, 125.

30 Hoffer, 22, 59.

31 Eliseo, 94.

32 Interview with Pat Mastrincola.

33 Ibid.

34 Ryan, 27.

35 "Amazing Tale."

36 Eliseo, 153.

37 Ibid., 160.

38 de Beaudéan, 167.

39 Interview with Madge Young Nickerson.

40 Interview with Linda Morgan Hardberger.

41 Simpson, 179.

42 Eliseo, 94; Maxtone-Graham, 258.

43 Moscow, 20.

44 Simpson, 32.

45 Interview with Madge Young Nickerson.

46 Interview with Linda Morgan Hardberger.
47 Interview with Melania Vali.
48 Interview with Arlene Mastrincola Meisner.
49 Interview with Andrew Stevens; *Sarasota Herald-Tribune,* July 25, 2006.
50 Simpson, 157.
51 *The Pantagraph,* July 26, 1981.
52 Eliseo, 159.
53 Ibid., 153.
54 Goldstein, 12–13; Hoffer, 24; Moscow, 21; Gentile, Andrea Doria: *Dive to an Era,* 19; Haberstroh, 33; Kohler, 191; Eliseo 93.
55 Maxtone-Graham, 239.
56 Gentile, *Deep, Dark, and Dangerous,* 53–54.
57 Hoffer, 35.
58 Brinnon, *Beau Voyage,* 56.
59 Eliseo, 145.
60 Ibid.; Moscow, 24.
61 Eliseo, 143–45; Goldstein, 13; Haberstroh, 12; Gentile, *Deep, Dark, and Dangerous,* 66; Gentile, Andrea Doria: *Dive to an Era,* 103.
62 Maxtone-Graham, 248.
63 www.pierettesimpson.com.
64 Simpson, 212–13.
65 Interview with Iole Dole.
66 Interview with Pierette Simpson.
67 Interview with Adalgisa Di Fabio.
68 Hoffer, 27; Simpson, 170.
69 Hoffer, 35; www.pierettesimpson.com.
70 Eliseo, 155.
71 Tinterri, 134–35; Gentile, Andrea Doria: *Dive to an Era,* 30; Kohler, 191; Eliseo, 92–93.
72 Gentile, *Deep, Dark, and Dangerous,* 127.
73 Bliss, *Barbara's Tarnished Bliss,* 23.
74 Eliseo, 159.
75 de Beaudéan, 178.
76 Interview with Adalgisa Di Fabio.
77 Gentile, *Deep, Dark, and Dangerous,* 70, 84; Tinterri, 132–33.
78 Maxtone-Graham, 191–92.
79 Brinnin, *Beau Voyage,* 56.
80 Bliss, *Barbara's Tarnished Bliss,* 22.
81 Interview with Adalgisa Di Fabio.
82 Interview with Pat Mastrincola.
83 Hoffer, 24.
84 David Hollyer, at www.andreadoria.org; *USA Today,* July 25, 1981.

85 *Brooklyn Daily Eagle,* October 26, 1956.
86 Interview with Alda Raimengia.
87 Interview with Mike Stoller.

Chapter Six

1 Mattsson, 41.
2 Ryan, 27.
3 Goldstein, 31; Moscow, 25.
4 Bliss, *Barbara's Tarnished Bliss,* 23.
5 *USA Today,* July 25, 1981.
6 Hoffer, 30.
7 Binzen, 136.
8 Mattsson, 41.
9 Moscow, 27.
10 Benziger, 118.
11 Lee, interview with Richard Wojcik.
12 "Amazing Tale."
13 Hoffer, 30.
14 Simpson, 179.
15 *San Bernardino County Sun,* July 24, 1981.
16 Hoffer, 30.
17 Interview with Linda Morgan Hardberger.
18 Binzen, 136.
19 Ryan, 27.
20 In *The Sinking of the* Andrea Doria.
21 *Brooklyn Daily Eagle,* October 26, 1956.
22 *Providence Sunday Journal,* December 9, 1956.
23 Hoffer, 30.
24 *Providence Sunday Journal,* December 9, 1956.
25 *Sarasota Herald-Tribune,* July 25, 2006.
26 Interview with Madge Young Nickerson.
27 Hoffer, 30.
28 Simpson, 180.
29 *Redlands Daily Facts,* Redlands, California, July 22, 1957.
30 Simpson, 180.
31 Ryan, 27.
32 Hoffer, 36.
33 *The Times Record,* Troy, New York, August 27, 1956.
34 Hoffer, 37.
35 Bliss, *Barbara's Tarnished Bliss,* 23.
36 *Asheville Citizen-Times,* July 26, 1981.
37 *Providence Sunday Journal,* December 9, 1956.

38 Bliss, *Barbara's Tarnished Bliss*, 23–24.

39 Eliseo, 94, 128; interview with Andrew Stevens.

40 Hoffer, 33; *Bulletin of the Catholic Laymen's Association of Georgia*, August 3, 1956; *Daily Herald*, Chicago, June 3, 1999.

41 Benziger, 118.

42 Eliseo, 94.

43 Simpson, 157.

44 *Milwaukee Journal*, July 28, 1956.

45 Cecilia Pick, undated letter, courtesy of Nicholas, Marquis de Piro.

46 Hoffler, 37.

47 Interview with Antonio Sergio.

48 Hoffer, 38.

49 Interview with Adalgisa Di Fabio.

50 Interview with Renee Coscia.

51 Interview with Alda Raimengia.

52 Interview with Joe Porporino.

53 Interview with Melania Vali.

54 *Detroit Free Press*, April 24, 1960; Morgan Hill Life; *The Journal News*, March 20, 1973.

55 Interview with Daniela Sellinger.

56 Interview with Pat Mastrincola.

57 Roman, 6; Goldstein, 57.

Chapter Seven

1 Goldstein, 31; Moscow, 25.

2 Moscow, 26.

3 Halpern.

4 Moscow, 62.

5 Goldstein, 31.

6 Moscow, 17, 74; Goldstein, 26; Brinnin, *Sway of the Grand Saloon*, 528.

7 Moscow, 17.

8 Goldstein, 27–28; Moscow, 34; Mattsson, 24.

9 de Beaudéan, 190.

10 Halpern; Goldstein, 36; Garzke and Simpson, 2.

11 Garzke and Simpson, 1.

12 Moscow, 27.

13 Goldstein, 32.

14 Moscow, 28.

15 Ibid., 57.

16 Moscow, 57–60; Hoffer, 1–2

17 de Beaudéan, 186.

18 Hoffer, 11; Goldstein, 32.

19 Moscow, 61; Hoffer, 13; Goldstein, 32.

20 Moscow, 61.

21 Hoffer, 14.

22 Goldstein, 40; Moscow, 66.

23 Hoffer, 15.

24 Moscow, 67.

25 Hoffer, 15; Goldstein, 41.

26 Goldstein, 36; Moscow, 38–39.

27 Moscow, 41.

28 Moscow, 36; Goldstein, 35.

29 Moscow, 29, 31.

30 Halpern; Hoffer, 44; Goldstein, 36.

31 Hoffer, 47; Goldstein, 37; Garzke and Simpson, 2–3.

32 Hoffer, 48; Moscow, 38–39, 44.

33 Halpern.

34 Mattsson, 36.

35 Goldstein, 37.

36 Moscow, 45.

37 Hoffer, 199; Goldstein, 38; Halpern.

38 Halpern; Goldstein, 38, 228.

39 Goldstein, 39; Halpern.

40 Moscow, 68; Goldstein, 49.

41 Kohler, 196.

42 Goldstein, 49; Moscow, 70; Kohler, 196.

43 Moscow, 70–71.

44 Simpson, 220.

45 *New York World-Telegram*, October 5, 1956.

46 Simpson, 220.

47 Ibid.

48 Moscow, 72.

49 Goldstein, 55.

50 Garzke and Simpson, 2; Moscow, 75.

51 Moscow, 87.

Chapter Eight

1 Moscow, 100; Hoffer, 57; *Daily Independent Journal*, July 27, 1956.

2 Ryan, 28.

3 Hoffer, 57.

4 *San Bernardino County Sun*, July 24, 1981.

5 Moscow, 111; Hoffer, 56.

6 *Providence Sunday Journal*, December 9, 1956.

7 *Longview News-Journal*, July 25, 1986.

8 *Providence Sunday Journal,* December 9, 1956.

9 Bliss, *Barbara's Tarnished Bliss,* 24.

10 *Nantucket Inquirer and Mirror,* June 10, 2010.

11 Bliss, *Barbara's Tarnished Bliss,* 24.

12 *The Daily Herald,* July 27, 1956.

13 Roman, 6.

14 *San Francisco Chronicle,* July 27, 1956.

15 Roman, 6.

16 Interview with Andrew Stevens.

17 *Sarasota Herald-Tribune,* July 25, 2006.

18 Benziger, 115.

19 *Bulletin of the Catholic Laymen's Association of Georgia,* August 3, 1956.

20 Lee, interview with John Dolciamore.

21 *Daily Herald,* Chicago, June 3, 1999.

22 *Bulletin of the Catholic Laymen's Association of Georgia,* August 3, 1956.

23 *Brooklyn Daily Eagle,* October 26, 1956.

24 Interview with Madge Young Nickerson.

25 Young, *Transfer in the Atlantic,* 2. Madge wrote *Transfer in the Atlantic* just after the disaster, when a friend suggested she submit her experiences to *Seventeen.* Unfortunately the magazine opted not to publish the article.

26 Interview with Madge Young Nickerson.

27 *Providence Sunday Journal,* December 9, 1956.

28 *Nantucket Inquirer and Mirror,* June 10, 2010.

29 *Providence Sunday Journal,* December 9, 1956.

30 Ibid.; *Nantucket Inquirer and Mirror,* June 10, 2010.

31 *Providence Sunday Journal,* December 9, 1956.

32 *Marion Star,* July 27, 1956.

33 *Los Angeles Times,* July 27, 1956.

34 Hoffer, 63–64.

35 *Cincinnati Enquirer,* July 27, 1956; *Los Angeles Times,* July 27, 1956.

36 *Daily Herald,* Provo, Utah, July 27, 1956.

37 *Niagara Falls Gazette,* February 16, 1957.

38 Goldstein, 62; it is usually said that Drake left without her jewels, but in an interview printed in *Niagara Falls Gazette,* February 16, 1957, she explicitly said that she took them with her but lost them during the ensuing chaos.

39 *Niagara Falls Gazette,* February 16, 1957.

40 Goldstein, 66.

41 Interview with Mike Stoller.

42 *Milwaukee Journal,* July 28, 1956.

43 Interview with Auxiliary Bishop Raymond Goedert.

44 Interview with Daniela Sellinger.

45 Interview with Pat Mastrincola.

46 Dorneich, *Sinking.*
47 *Detroit Free Press,* April 24, 1960; *The Journal News,* March 20, 1973; Hoffer, 65.
48 Interview with Melania Vali.
49 Morgan Hill Life.
50 Interview with Renee Coscia.
51 Interview with Alda Raimengia.
52 Interview with Adalgisa Di Fabio.
53 Interview with and information from Joe Porporino.
54 Di Sandro, *In ricordo di Norma,* 174–84.

Chapter Nine

1 Moscow, 87.
2 Information from William H. Garzke, Jr.
3 Moscow, 91; Garzke and Simpson, 4.
4 Gentile, Andrea Doria: *Dive to an Era,* 75; Kohler, 198; Garzke and Simpson, 6.
5 Garzke and Simpson, 6.
6 Information from William H. Garzke, Jr.
7 Garzke and Simpson, 5; Simpson, 149; Kohler, 198; Moscow, 90.
8 Garzke and Simpson, 5.
9 Moscow, 89.
10 Ibid., 97–98.
11 Moscow, 88–96; *New York World-Telegram,* October 5, 1956.
12 Moscow, 94; Hoffer, 81.
13 King and Wilson, 194.
14 Moscow, 94–95.
15 Ibid., 95.
16 *New York World-Telegram,* October 5, 1956.
17 Simpson, 56.
18 Kohler, 199.
19 Hoffer, 78; Simpson, 56.
20 *Cincinnati Enquirer,* July 27, 1956.
21 Interview with Alda Raimengia.
22 *Philadelphia Inquirer,* July 27, 1956.
23 Di Sandro, *In ricordo di Norma,* 184–85.
24 *Daily Herald,* Chicago, June 3, 1999.
25 Lee, interview with John Dolciamore.
26 Interview with Auxiliary Bishop Raymond Goedert.
27 Gladstone, 7.
28 Cecilia Pick, undated letter, courtesy of Nicholas, Marquis de Piro.
29 *Providence Sunday Journal,* December 9, 1956.

30 www.pierettesimpson.com.

31 Benziger, 115.

32 Bliss, *Barbara's Tarnished Bliss*, 25.

33 Dorneich, *Sinking*.

34 Interview with Adalgisa Di Fabio.

35 Simpson, 208.

36 *USA Today*, July 25, 1981.

37 Simpson, 57.

38 Moscow, 122.

39 Ibid., 123; Goldstein, 87.

40 Simpson, 189; Goldstein, 89; Moscow, 124.

41 Moscow, 125; Goldstein, 94.

42 Moscow, 126.

43 *Pilot*, August 2, 1956. In 1963 *Cape Ann* was sold to American Union Transport and operated as *Transunion* until it was scrapped in 1968.

44 Goldstein, 85.

45 Moscow, 126; *Daily Herald*, Provo, Utah, July 27, 1956. In 1957 *Thomas* was transferred to the Maritime Administration and in 1971 was sold for scrap.

46 Moscow, 126.

47 Ibid., 128; *Daily Independent Journal*, July 26, 1956.

48 de Beaudéan, 193.

49 *New York Times*, July 26, 1956.

50 de Beaudéan, 195.

51 Ibid.

52 Moscow, 130.

53 de Beaudéan, 196.

54 Moscow, 130.

55 *Daily Independent Journal*, July 26, 1956.

56 Moscow, 131; Stanford, 203.

57 Goldstein, 53; Moscow, 76–77.

58 Goldstein, 54.

59 Moscow, 140.

60 Hoffer, 59; Goldstein, 77–78.

61 Goldstein, 81; Moscow, 133.

62 Goldstein, 104; Moscow 132–33.

63 Moscow, 134–36; Hoffer, 59.

64 Moscow, 136.

65 *Redlands Daily Facts*, July 22, 1957.

66 Simpson, 180.

67 Ibid.

68 Moscow, 137.

69 Ibid.
70 Simpson, 180; Moscow, 158.
71 *San Bernardino County Sun,* July 24, 1981.
72 Simpson, 180.
73 Hoffer, 84.
74 Simpson, 180.
75 Goldstein, 103.
76 Mattsson, 63.
77 Moscow, 139.
78 Moscow, 82, 139; Hoffer, 59–60.
79 Moscow, 140.
80 Simpson, 190–91.
81 Moscow, 140–41.
82 Goldstein, 105.
83 Moscow, 141.
84 Ibid.
85 Hoffer, 110.

Chapter Ten

1 *Niagara Falls Gazette,* February 16, 1957.
2 *San Francisco Chronicle,* July 27, 1956; *Times Record,* August 27, 1956.
3 Roman, 6.
4 *Los Angeles Times,* July 27, 1956.
5 *Philadelphia Inquirer,* July 27, 1956.
6 *Daily Herald,* Provo, Utah, July 27, 1956.
7 *Philadelphia Inquirer,* July 27, 1956.
8 Interview with Andrew Stevens.
9 *Sarasota Herald-Tribune,* July 25, 2006.
10 Hoffer, 94.
11 *Brooklyn Daily Eagle,* October 26, 1956.
12 Young, *Transfer,* 2.
13 Interview with Madge Young Nickerson.
14 Interview with Robert F. Boggs.
15 Meisner.
16 Benziger, 115.
17 Interview with Robert F. Boggs.
18 Benziger, 115.
19 Bliss, *Barbara's Tarnished Bliss,* 24.
20 Benziger, 115.
21 *Providence Sunday Journal,* December 9, 1956.
22 *Nantucket Inquirer and Mirror,* June 10, 2010.
23 *Providence Sunday Journal,* December 9, 1956.

24 Ibid.

25 *Daily Herald,* Chicago, June 3, 1999.

26 Lee, interview with John Dolciamore; *Bulletin of the Catholic Laymen's Association of Georgia.*

27 Lee, interview with Richard Wojcik.

28 Interview with Auxiliary Bishop Raymond Goedert.

29 Goldstein, 116.

30 Hoffer, 101–2.

31 *The Pantagraph,* July 26, 1981.

32 *Providence Sunday Journal,* December 9, 1956.

33 Interview with Peter Thieriot.

34 *The Pantagraph,* July 26, 1981.

35 Hoffer, 71.

36 Ibid., 95.

37 Ibid., 103.

38 Interview with Mike Stoller.

39 Simpson, 158.

40 Interview with Mike Stoller.

41 Leiber and Stoller, 89.

42 Interview with Mike Stoller.

43 Hoffer, 103–4.

44 Ibid., 104.

45 Simpson, 158.

46 Hoffer, 105.

47 Simpson, 158.

48 Leiber and Stoller, 89.

49 Cecilia Pick, undated letter, courtesy Nicholas, Marquis de Piro.

50 *Nantucket Inquirer and Mirror,* June 10, 2010.

51 *Brooklyn Daily Eagle,* October 26, 1956.

52 Young, *Transfer,* 3.

53 Interview with Joe Porporino.

54 *Morning Call,* July 28, 1956.

55 Interview with Joe Porporino.

56 Ibid.

57 Interview with Melania Vali.

58 Di Sandro, *In ricordo di Norma,* 184–85.

59 Interview with Daniela Sellinger.

60 Interview with Alda Raimengia.

61 Dorneich, *Sinking.*

62 Interview with Adalgisa Di Fabio.

63 Interview with Pat Mastrincola.

64 Interview with Arlene Mastrincola Meisner.

65 Interview with Pat Mastrincola.
66 Interview with Arlene Mastrincola Meisner.
67 Interview with Pat Mastrincola.
68 Interview with Arlene Mastrincola Meisner.
69 Interview with Pat Mastrincola.
70 Moscow, 106–9; Hoffer, 71; Goldstein, 71.
71 Hoffer, 62.
72 Moscow, 120.
73 Hoffer, 91–92.

Chapter Eleven

1 *Brooklyn Daily Eagle,* October 26, 1956.
2 Interview with Madge Young Nickerson.
3 Young, *Transfer,* 3.
4 *Philadelphia Inquirer,* July 27, 1956.
5 *Nantucket Inquirer and Mirror,* June 10, 2010.
6 www.pierettesimpson.com.
7 *Providence Sunday Journal,* December 9, 1956.
8 Benziger, 59.
9 Ibid., 116–18.
10 Bliss, *Barbara's Tarnished Bliss,* 24–25.
11 *Providence Sunday Journal,* December 9, 1956.
12 Young, *Transfer,* 3.
13 *Brooklyn Daily Eagle,* October 26, 1956; Hoffer, 143.
14 Interview with Pat Mastrincola.
15 Simpson, 38.
16 *Nantucket Inquirer and Mirror,* June 10, 2010.
17 *Providence Sunday Journal,* December 9, 1956.
18 *Longview News-Journal,* July 25, 1986.
19 *Niagara Falls Gazette,* February 16, 1957.
20 *Brooklyn Daily Eagle,* October 26, 1956.
21 Interview with Adalgisa Di Fabio.
22 Hoffer, 143.
23 Simpson, 159.
24 Bliss, *Barbara's Tarnished Bliss,* 26.
25 Moscow, 180.
26 Ibid.
27 Hoffer, 103.
28 Lee, interview with Richard Wojcik.
29 *Bulletin of the Catholic Laymen's Association of Georgia,* August 3, 1956.
30 *Daily Herald,* Chicago, June 3, 1999.
31 *Providence Sunday Journal,* December 9, 1956.

32 Hoffer, 96.

33 Hoffer, 94–95; interview with Auxiliary Bishop Raymond Goedert.

34 *Chicago Tribune,* November 21, 1996.

35 Goldstein, 94.

36 de Beaudéan, 197; Goldstein, 125; *New York Times,* July 26, 1956; Moscow, 171.

37 Moscow, 175.

38 Goldstein, 104.

39 Simpson, 204.

40 Moscow, 143–44.

41 Simpson, 202.

42 Mattsson, 58–59.

43 Moscow, 169.

44 Hoffer, 115.

45 Ibid., 118.

46 Moscow, 223.

47 Simpson, 203.

48 *Brooklyn Daily Eagle,* October 26, 1956.

49 *Daily Herald,* Provo, Utah, July 27, 1956.

50 *Providence Sunday Journal,* December 9, 1956.

51 Hoffer, 123.

52 Simpson, 203.

53 Hoffer, 137.

54 Ibid.; Moscow, 146; Simpson, 203.

55 www.pierettesimpson.com.

56 *Nantucket Inquirer and Mirror,* June 10, 2010.

57 *Providence Sunday Journal,* December 9, 1956.

58 Benziger, 116.

59 Meisner.

60 Bliss, *Barbara's Tarnished Bliss,* 27.

61 Meisner.

62 *Brooklyn Daily Eagle,* October 26, 1956.

63 *Philadelphia Inquirer,* July 27, 1956; *Post-Standard,* July 27, 1956; *Los Angeles Times,* July 27, 1956; Hoffer, 128.

64 Interview with Pat Mastrincola.

65 Interview with Arlene Mastrincola Meisner.

66 Moscow, 192.

67 Dorneich, *Sinking.*

68 Moscow, 141–42.

69 Moscow, 168, 171; Goldstein, 105, 107.

70 Mattsson, 59.

71 Goldstein, 107.

72 Mattsson, 59.
73 Moscow, 172.
74 At http://www.oceanliner.org/johnson.htm.
75 Hoffer, 119–20.
76 Goldstein, 107.
77 Moscow, 172.
78 Hoffer, 120–21.
79 Mattsson, 59–60.
80 Interview with Joe Porporino.
81 *San Francisco Chronicle,* July 27, 1956.
82 Interview with Daniela Sellinger.
83 Moscow, 186; *San Francisco Chronicle,* July 27, 1956; Roman, 6.
84 Interview with Melania Vali.
85 Information from Ermanno Di Sandro to authors.
86 Moscow, 174.
87 *Plainfield Courier-News,* July 27, 1956.
88 Di Sandro, *In ricordo di Norma,* 202; Hoffer, 121; Moscow, 173.
89 Information from Ermanno Di Sandro to authors.

Chapter Twelve

1 Ernest Melby, at www.andreadoria.org.
2 Simpson, 205–6; Moscow, 193–95; Goldstein, 162; Garzke and Simpson, 5–6.
3 Moscow, 182.
4 de Beaudéan, 199.
5 Ibid.
6 Goldstein, 139; Moscow, 183.
7 Ernest Melby, at www.andreadoria.org.
8 Benziger, 116.
9 Interview with Robert F. Boggs.
10 Hoffer, 129.
11 www.pierettesimpson.com.
12 Interview with Auxiliary Bishop Raymond Goedert.
13 Interview with Pat Mastrincola.
14 *Brooklyn Daily Eagle,* October 26, 1956.
15 *Daily Independent Journal,* July 26, 1956; de Beaudéan, 197; Stanford, 201.
16 de Beaudéan, 199–200.
17 *Detroit Free Press,* April 24, 1960.
18 Hoffer, 133.
19 Interview with Melania Vali.
20 Information from Ermanno Di Sandro to authors.
21 *Detroit Free Press,* April 24, 1960.
22 *Brooklyn Daily Eagle,* October 26, 1956.

23 *Providence Sunday Journal,* December 9, 1956.

24 *Nantucket Inquirer and Mirror,* June 10, 2010.

25 Dorneich, *Sinking.*

26 *Brooklyn Daily Eagle,* October 26, 1956.

27 Goldstein, 142.

28 *Niagara Falls Gazette,* February 16, 1957.

29 Roman, 6; *San Francisco Chronicle,* July 27, 1956; *Ogden Standard-Examiner,* July 27, 1956.

30 *Nantucket Inquirer and Mirror,* June 10, 2010.

31 Ibid.

32 www.pierettesimpson.com.

33 *Providence Sunday Journal,* December 9, 1956.

34 *Sarasota Herald Tribune,* July 25, 2006; interview with Andrew Stevens.

35 Benziger, 116–19.

36 Bliss, *Barbara's Tarnished Bliss,* 27.

37 Meisner.

38 Benziger, 116.

39 *Philadelphia Inquirer,* July 27, 1956.

40 Young, *Transfer,* 3–4.

41 Interview with Madge Young Nickerson.

42 Young, *Transfer,* 4–5.

43 Interview with Arlene Mastrincola Meisner.

44 Interview with Pat Mastrincola.

45 Interview with Arlene Mastrincola Meisner.

46 Interview with Pat Mastrincola.

47 Interview with Arlene Mastrincola Meisner.

48 Interview with Pat Mastrincola.

49 Interview with Arlene Mastrincola Meisner.

50 Interview with Pat Mastrincola.

51 *Plainfield Courier-News,* July 25, 1957; information from Daniela Sellinger.

52 Hoffer, 135.

53 Interview with Alda Raimengia.

54 Interviews with Sadie Onorato and Renee Coscia.

55 Interview with Adalgisa Di Fabio.

56 Hoffer, 96.

57 *The Pantagraph,* July 26, 1981.

58 Hoffer, 146.

59 *The Pantagraph,* July 26, 1981.

60 Hoffer, 143.

61 Interview with Mike Stoller.

62 Simpson, 159.

63 Hoffer, 144.

64 Simpson, 159.

65 Interview with Mike Stoller.

66 Simpson, 159–60.

67 Cecilia Pick, undated letter, courtesy Nicholas, Marquis de Piro.

68 Interview with Andrew Stevens.

69 *Sarasota Herald-Tribune*, July 25, 2006.

70 Binzen, 137.

71 *Times Record*, August 27, 1956.

72 *Philadelphia Inquirer*, July 27, 1956.

73 *Brooklyn Daily Eagle*, October 26, 1956.

74 Dorneich, *Lost Liners*.

75 *USA Today*, July 25, 1981.

76 *Daily Herald*, Chicago, June 3, 1999.

77 *USA Today*, July 25, 1981.

78 *Daily Herald*, Chicago, June 3, 1999.

79 Lee, interview with Reverend John Dolciamore.

80 Lee, interview with Reverend Richard Wojcik.

81 Lee, interview with Auxiliary Bishop Raymond Goedert; Hoffer, 141.

82 Hoffer, 142.

83 Meisner.

84 Ryan, 28.

85 Ibid.

86 Ibid., 28–29.

87 Ibid., 29.

88 Ibid.

89 Ibid.

90 Ibid., 27–28.

91 Ibid., 29.

92 Ibid.

93 Ibid., 29; Moscow, 146.

94 Ryan, 30.

95 Ibid.

96 Ibid.

97 Ryan, 30.

98 *New York Times*, September 19, 1970.

99 *Sacramento Bee*, August 14, 1956.

100 Ryan, 30.

101 Ibid., 30–31.

102 Ryan, 31; Hoffer, 140.

103 Ryan, 31.

104 Ibid.

105 Ibid.

Chapter Thirteen

1 Moscow, 197.

2 Dorneich, *Sinking.*

3 Cecilia Pick, undated letter, courtesy of Nicholas, Marquis de Piro.

4 *Milwaukee Journal,* July 28, 1956.

5 Moscow, 165.

6 Mattsson, 65.

7 Dorneich, *Sinking.*

8 *Milwaukee Journal,* July 28, 1956.

9 Brinnin, *Sway of the Grand Saloon,* 528.

10 Ibid., 202.

11 Hoffer, 163.

12 Cecelia Pick, undated letter, courtesy of Nicholas, Marquis de Piro.

13 Interview with Joe Porporino.

14 *New York Daily News,* July 27, 1956.

15 Young, *Transfer,* 5.

16 Interview with Pat Mastrincola.

17 *Marion Star,* July 27, 1956.

18 Goldstein, 153.

19 Ibid., 149–50.

20 Benziger, 116–17.

21 Interview with Robert F. Boggs.

22 Hoffer, 163.

23 Stanford, 203.

24 Interview with Arlene Mastrincola Meisner.

25 de Beaudéan, 201.

26 Dr. Lester S. Sinness, at www.andreadoria.org.

27 Interview with Pat Mastrincola.

28 Bliss, *Barbara's Tarnished Bliss,* 28.

29 Benziger, 119.

30 *Asheville Citizen-Times,* July 26, 1981.

31 Young, *Transfer,* 7.

32 Interview with Andrew Stevens.

33 Interview with Melania Vali.

34 *Plainfield Courier-News,* July 27, 1956.

35 de Beaudéan, 210–11.

36 Hoffer, 162.

37 *Delaware County Daily Times,* July 27, 1956.

38 *Long Beach Independent,* July 28, 1956.

39 de Beaudéan, 209.

40 *Detroit Free Press,* April 24, 1960.

41 *The Pantagraph,* July 26, 1981.

42 *Sacramento Bee,* August 14, 1956.

43 Young, *Transfer,* 6.

44 *Providence Sunday Journal,* December 9, 1956.

45 Interview with Robert F. Boggs.

46 de Beaudéan, 209–10.

47 Stanford, 202.

48 Ibid., 206.

49 Interview with Arlene Mastrincola Meisner.

50 Information from Cathy Crawford LaLonde.

51 Crawford, 83.

52 Moscow, 207.

53 *Bulletin of the Catholic Laymen's Association of Georgia,* August 3, 1956.

54 Young, *Transfer,* 6.

55 Interview with Madge Young Nickerson.

56 Interview with Mike Stoller.

57 Simpson, 160.

58 Moscow, 198.

59 de Beaudéan, 202.

60 Moscow, 198.

61 de Beaudéan, 203.

62 Ibid., 204.

63 Ibid.

64 *New York Times,* July 26, 1956.

65 de Beaudéan, 205.

66 Moscow, 208.

Chapter Fourteen

1 Simpson, 63; Moscow, 251; Hoffer, 149.

2 Simpson, 63.

3 Ibid.

4 Hoffer, 149.

5 Moscow, 251.

6 Ibid., 192–93.

7 Ibid., 100.

8 Goldstein, 163.

9 Hoffer, 148.

10 Goldstein, 231.

11 Hoffer, 58, 89; Goldstein, 67–68, 232.

12 https://www.encyclopedia-titanica.org/community/threads/trapped-alive
  -aboard-the-andrea-doria.25953/.

13 Moscow, 109.

14 Hoffer, 58, 89; Goldstein, 67–68, 232.

15 Hoffer, 40.
16 Hoffer, 151–53; Moscow, 103.
17 Hoffer, 151–53.
18 Ibid., 154–55.
19 Ibid.
20 Moscow, 104.
21 Ibid., 195.
22 Hoffer, 147.
23 Moscow, 202.
24 Ibid., 204–5.
25 Ibid., 205.
26 Hoffer, 149.
27 Moscow, 205.
28 Ibid., 206.
29 Ibid., 210.
30 Dorneich, *Sinking*.
31 *Los Angeles Times,* July 27, 1956; *Cincinnati Enquirer,* July 27, 1956.
32 Moscow, 211; Goldstein, 170.
33 Moscow, 124.
34 Ibid., 217.
35 Simpson, 72.
36 Dorneich, *Sinking*.
37 Guido Badano, in *The Sinking of the* Andrea Doria.
38 Goldstein, 178.

Chapter Fifteen

1 *New York Times,* July 26, 1956.
2 *Cincinnati Enquirer,* July 27, 1956.
3 Simpson, 74; Moscow, 215.
4 Moscow, 215.
5 Ibid.
6 *Marion Star,* July 27, 1956.
7 *Corriere della Sera,* July 27, 1956.
8 Hoffer, 162.
9 Goldstein, 180.
10 Interviews with Sadie Onorato and Renee Coscia.
11 Morgan, 238–39.
12 Ibid., 239.
13 Moscow, 221–22.
14 Goldstein, 181–82.
15 Ibid., 180.
16 Ibid., 221.

17 *Bulletin of the Catholic Laymen's Association of Georgia,* August 3, 1956.
18 Eliseo, 209.
19 *Cincinnati Enquirer,* July 27, 1956; Hoffer, 161.
20 Lester Siness, at www.andreadoria.org.
21 *Daily Herald,* Chicago, June 3, 1999.
22 Interviews with Sadie Onorato and Renee Coscia.
23 Young, *Transfer,* 7.
24 Interview with Madge Young Nickerson; Young, *Transfer,* 7.
25 Bliss, *Barbara's Tarnished Bliss,* 29.
26 Young, *Transfer,* 8.
27 Interview with Adalgisa Di Fabio.
28 Benziger, 117.
29 Young, *Transfer,* 8.
30 Interview with Madge Young Nickerson.
31 de Beaudéan, 212.
32 Ibid., 208.
33 Interview with Rose Calvelli.
34 Morgan, 239–40.
35 *Philadelphia Inquirer,* July 27, 1956.
36 *Cincinnati Enquirer,* July 27, 1956.
37 Binzen, 137.
38 *Cincinnati Enquirer,* July 27, 1956.
39 Nelson, 195.
40 Interview with Larry Russell.
41 *The Pantagraph,* July 26, 1981.
42 Bliss, *Barbara's Tarnished Bliss,* 30.
43 Interview with Madge Young Nickerson.
44 Young, *Transfer,* 8.
45 Lee, interview with Reverend Richard Wojcik.
46 Interviews with Sadie Onorato and Renee Coscia.
47 Interview with Daniela Sellinger; *Plainfield Courier-News,* July 27, 1956.
48 Interview with Arlene Mastrincola Meisner.
49 Interview with Pat Mastrincola.
50 Interview with Adalgisa Di Fabio.
51 Interview with Antonio Sergio.
52 *L'Espresso,* August 2, 1956.
53 *Cincinnati Enquirer,* July 27, 1956; *Los Angeles Times,* July 27, 1956.
54 *L'Espresso,* August 2, 1956.
55 Hoffer, 170.
56 Moscow, 223.
57 *Cincinnati Enquirer,* July 27, 1956; Moscow, 223.
58 *Brooklyn Daily Eagle,* October 26, 1956.

59 Moscow, 223.

60 Leiber and Stoller, 90.

61 Interview with Alda Raimengia.

62 Simpson, 74.

63 Angela Galassi, in Andrea Doria: *Are the Passengers Saved?*.

64 Morgan, 240.

65 Ibid.

66 Ibid., 241–45.

67 Ibid., 245.

68 Ibid., 245–46.

Chapter Sixteen

1 Moscow, 212.

2 Ibid., 220.

3 Interview with Auxiliary Bishop Raymond Goedert.

4 Moscow, 220.

5 *Asbury Park Press,* July 28, 1956.

6 Hoffer, 164.

7 *Des Moines Register,* July 28, 1956.

8 Goldstein, 201.

9 Dorneich, *What Happened After.*

10 Interview with Auxiliary Bishop Raymond Goedert.

11 Interview with Joe Porporino.

12 Hoffer, 171.

13 *The Times,* July 27, 1956; *Daily Reporter,* July 27, 1956.

14 Hoffer, 171.

15 *Long Beach Independent,* July 28, 1956.

16 *Milwaukee Journal,* July 28, 1956.

17 Interview with Auxiliary Bishop Raymond Goedert.

18 Interview with Joe Porporino.

19 Dorneich, *What Happened After.*

20 Letter from John C. Wilson, Vice President of the American Red Cross, August 1, 1956, courtesy of Joseph D'Andrea.

21 Morgan, 246.

22 Ibid.

23 Simpson, 181.

24 *The Times,* July 27, 1956.

25 Simpson, 181.

26 Morgan, 246–47.

27 Simpson, 181.

28 Morgan, 247.

29 Ibid., 247–49.

30 Hoffer, 170.

31 Eliseo, 209.

32 Information from Ermanno Di Sandro.

Chapter Seventeen

1 Goldstein, 220.

2 Ibid., 221.

3 Dorneich, *What Happened After.*

4 *New York Post,* July 29, 1956.

5 Hoffer, 167–68.

6 *New York Times,* July 27, 1956.

7 Interview with Alda Raimengia.

8 Simpson, 160.

9 Goldstein, 222.

10 Ibid., 108.

11 *Des Moines Register,* July 28, 1956.

12 Benziger, 119.

13 *Nantucket Inquirer and Mirror,* June 10, 2010.

14 Dorneich, *Sinking.*

15 Leiber and Stoller, 89.

16 Cecelia Pick, undated letter, courtesy of Nicholas, Marquis de Piro.

17 Richardson Dilworth, undated letter, in Italian Line Press release of August 6, 1956, courtesy of Joseph D'Andrea.

18 Hoffer, 179.

19 *Cincinnati Enquirer,* July 27, 1956.

20 *Long Beach Independent,* July 27, 1956.

21 Interview with Pat Mastrincola.

22 Hoffer, 178.

23 *Long Beach Independent,* July 27, 1956.

24 *Niagara Falls Gazette,* July 28, 1956.

25 *Des Moines Register,* July 28, 1956.

26 *The Pilot,* August 2, 1956.

27 *New York Times,* August 3, 1956.

28 Italian Line press release, August 6, 1956, courtesy of Joseph D'Andrea.

29 King and Wilson, 194.

30 Ibid., 260.

31 Moscow, 222.

32 *USA Today,* July 25, 1981.

33 Hoffer, 178.

34 Simpson, 204.

35 Interview with Madge Young Nickerson.

36 Ibid.

37 Simpson, 182.

38 Goldstein, 222.

39 Hoffer, 205–6.

40 Simpson, 182.

41 Ibid., 183–84.

42 Morris, 110.

43 Goldstein, 251.

44 Bliss, *Barbara's Tarnished Bliss,* 30–31.

45 Benziger, 118–20; Bessell, 29.

46 Dorneich, *What Happened After.*

47 *Daily Herald,* Chicago, June 3, 1999.

48 Interview with Arlene Mastrincola Meisner.

49 Interview with Pat Mastrincola.

50 Interview with Adalgisa Di Fabio.

51 Interview with Melania Vali.

52 Cecelia Pick, undated letter, courtesy of Nicholas, Marquis de Piro.

53 *The Pantagraph,* July 26, 1981.

54 Interview with Antonio Sergio.

55 *Herald Statesman,* July 26, 1957.

Chapter Eighteen

1 Hoffer, 178.

2 Goldstein, 224.

3 Hoffler, 180.

4 Mattsson, 94; *Corsicana Daily Sun,* August 7, 1956.

5 Eliseo, 217.

6 Goldstein, 225.

7 Moscow, 227–28.

8 Moscow, 230; Goldstein, 225.

9 Moscow, 232.

10 *New York World-Telegram,* September 22, 1956.

11 Ibid.

12 Goldstein, 226.

13 Moscow, 234, 236; Kohler, 201.

14 *New York World-Telegram,* September 21, 1956.

15 Moscow, 234–37.

16 *New York World-Telegram,* September 21, 1956.

17 Ibid.

18 Moscow, 239.

19 Goldstein, 228–29.

20 Moscow, 240–41.

21 Ibid., 245; Goldstein, 235.

22 Moscow, 247.

23 Ibid., 259.

24 Report of US House of Representatives, 2, December 21, 1956.

25 Ibid., 7, 11.

26 Ibid., 7–8.

27 Information from William H. Garzke, Jr.

28 Report of US House of Representatives, 8.

29 Information from William H. Garzke, Jr.; Gentile, Andrea Doria: *Dive to an Era*, 69, 75; Kohler, 198.

30 Kohler, 198.

31 Kohler, 198; Simpson, 149.

32 Mattsson, 158–59.

33 Ibid., 126.

34 Ibid., 127–29.

35 Kohler, 197–98.

36 Moscow, 81.

37 Garzke and Simpson, 2.

38 Moscow, 270.

39 Mattsson, 105.

40 Moscow, 273.

41 Interview with Joseph D'Andrea.

42 Moscow, 273; Kohler, 202.

43 Goldstein, 238.

44 Garzke and Simpson, 2; Halpern.

45 Moscow, 18.

46 Garzke and Simpson, 2–3.

47 Grattidge, 145–46.

48 Halpern.

49 *New York Times*, July 26, 1956.

50 Lester Sinness, at www.andreadoria.org.

51 *New York Times*, July 26, 1956; *Daily Herald*, Provo, Utah, July 27 1956.

52 Moscow, 169; Goldstein, 77.

53 Goldstein, 53; Moscow, 76–77.

54 Garzke and Simpson, 3; Halpern.

55 Cahill, 4.

56 McMurray, 45.

57 Halpern.

58 Hoffer, 199; Nordling.

59 Kohler, 196–97.

60 Cahill, 2–4; Nordling; Halpern.

61 Cahill, 153.

62 Ibid., 2.

63 Ibid., 153.
64 Goldstein, 39, 54.
65 Cahill, 2.
66 Halpern; Nordling.
67 Information from William H. Garzke, Jr.
68 Hoffer, 196.
69 McMurray, 58.
70 de Beaudéan, 216.
71 Cahill, 4.
72 Meurn, 173.
73 McMurray, 57–58; Haberstroh, 49.
74 Goldstein, 243; Haberstoh, 49; Halpern; Simpson, 232.
75 Halpern.
76 Goldstein, 37.
77 Moscow, 45.
78 Ibid., 140.
79 Meurn, 174.
80 *New York Times*, August 1, 1999.
81 See, for example, Halpern.
82 *New York Times*, September 13, 2001.
83 de Beaudéan, 220.

Chapter Nineteen

1 Averbach and Price, 145.
2 Goldstein, 238–39; Hoffer, 181.
3 Moscow, 229.
4 Interview with Joe Porporino.
5 Goldstein, 238–39.
6 *Long Beach Independent,* July 26, 1957.
7 Interview with Klaus Dorneich.
8 Hoffer, 206.
9 Andrea Doria *Newsletter.*
10 Stanford, 5.
11 Brinnin, *Sway of the Grand Saloon,* 533–34.
12 *New York Herald,* April 19, 1959.
13 Brinnin, *Sway of the Grand Saloon,* 534; Stanford, 243–44.
14 Hoffer, 207.
15 *New York Times,* September 19, 1970.
16 Interview with Antonio Sergio.
17 Morris, 100–1.
18 *New York Times,* January 24, 1974.
19 Binzen, 155.

20 *New York Times,* January 24, 1974.

21 Fagone.

22 *Nantucket Inquirer and Mirror,* June, 10 2010.

23 *Asheville Citizen-Times,* July 26, 1981.

24 *Nantucket Inquirer and Mirror,* June 10, 2010.

25 *Boston Globe,* July 21, 2005.

26 Canellos, 149.

27 Hersh, 372

28 Hersh, 374; Taraborrelli, 97.

29 *Boston Globe,* May 12, 2010; http://epicurean-traveler.com/an-interview
    -with-dun-gifford/; *New York Times,* May 15, 2010.

30 Interview with Andrew Stevens.

31 *Herald Statesman,* July 26, 1957.

32 *Sarasota Herald-Tribune,* July 25, 2006.

33 Interview with Andrew Stevens.

34 Ibid.

35 *New York Times,* January 24, 2009.

36 *Detroit Free Press,* April 24, 1960.

37 Ibid.

38 Interview with Melania Vali.

39 Interview with Alda Raimengia.

40 Roman, 6.

41 *New York Times,* September 11, 1999; *Los Angeles Times,* September 11,
    1999.

42 *Washington Post,* November 11, 2015.

43 Associated Press, November 12, 2015.

44 *Los Angeles Times,* October 17, 1958.

45 Nelson, 234–35.

46 Associated Press, November 12, 2015; *Los Angeles Times,* November 12,
    2015; *Washington Post,* November 11, 2015.

47 Interview with Madge Young Nickerson.

48 Ibid.

49 Interview with Mike Stoller.

50 Hoffer, 206.

51 Lee, interview with Reverend John Dolciamore.

52 *Chicago Tribune,* November 27, 2012.

53 Lee, interview with Reverend Richard Wojcik.

54 *Daily Herald,* Chicago, June 3, 1999.

55 Ibid., January 30, 2013.

56 *Chicago Tribune,* November 21, 1996.

57 Lee, interview with Auxiliary Bishop Raymond Goedert.

58 Interview with Auxiliary Bishop Raymond Goedert.

59 Interview with Daniela Sellinger.

60 Interviews with Sadie Onorato and Renee Coscia.

61 Interview with Renee Coscia.

62 Interview with Pat Mastrincola.

63 Interview with Arlene Mastrincola Meisner.

64 Interview with Adalgisa Di Fabio.

65 Ibid.

66 Interview with Joe Porporino.

67 Bliss, *Barbara's Tarnished Bliss*, 42.

68 Ibid., 34–37.

69 Benziger, 126.

70 Interview with Robert F. Boggs.

71 Bliss, *Barbara's Tarnished Bliss*, 8.

72 Ibid., 12.

73 Interview with Adelaide Mestre.

74 Bliss, *Barbara's Tarnished Bliss*, 31.

75 Interview with Adelaide Mestre.

76 Bliss, *Barbara's Tarnished Bliss*, 13.

77 *New York Times*, January 7, 2015.

78 *Redlands Daily Facts*, July 22, 1957.

79 Goldstein, 253–54.

80 Interview with Linda Morgan Hardberger.

81 Simpson, 186.

82 Interview with Linda Morgan Hardberger.

83 Interview with Peter Thieriot.

84 *San Francisco Examiner*, January 17, 2010.

85 Interview with Peter Thieriot.

86 Hoffer, 208.

87 Interview with Ermanno Di Sandro.

88 Ibid.

89 Ibid.

Chapter Twenty

1 *Long Beach Independent*, July 27, 1956.

2 *Delaware County Daily Times*, September 15, 1965.

3 See Gentile, *Andrea Doria: Dive to an Era*, 20–29 on discussion of these various proposals.

4 McMurray, 111.

5 Haberstroh, 18; McMurray, 9.

6 McMurray, 10; Haberstroh, 20.

7 *New York Times*, July 29, 1956.

8 *Life*, September 17, 1956, 46–51.

9 McMurray, xii.

10 Ibid., 102; Haberstroh, 18.

11 McMurray, 8.

12 McMurray, 113; Gentile, Andrea Doria: *Dive to an Era*, 39–41.

13 Gentile, *Deep, Dark, and Dangerous*, 9.

14 Interview with Robert F. Boggs.

15 Interview with Peter Thieriot.

16 Sims, Moyer, and Gatto, 191; McMurray, 19; Gentile, Andrea Doria: *Dive to an Era*, 71; Gentile, *Deep, Dark, and Dangerous*, 50.

17 Sims, Moyer, and Gatto, 191; McMurray, 19; Gentile, Andrea Doria: *Dive to an Era*, 71; Gentile, *Deep, Dark, and Dangerous*, 50.

18 Goldstein, 277.

19 Gentile, Andrea Doria: *Dive to an Era*, 79.

20 Goldstein, 278; Mattsson, 135–36.

21 McMurray, 260–61.

22 Interview with John Moyer.

23 Interview with John Moyer.

24 Gentile, *Deep, Dark, and Dangerous*, 196; McMurray, 19; Sims, Moyer, and Gatto, 195.

25 Interview with John Moyer.

26 Gentile, Andrea Doria: *Dive to an Era*, 103.

27 Interview with John Moyer.

28 Ibid.

29 Gentile, *Deep, Dark, and Dangerous*, 144–65, 195; Sims, Moyer, and Gatto, 190; *Nantucket Inquirer and Mirror,* July 25, 2015.

30 Interview with John Moyer; Gentile, Andrea Doria: *Dive to an Era,* 137–38.

31 District of New Jersey 1993 *Moyer v. Wrecked & Abandoned Vessel,* 836 F. Supp. 1099 (DNJ 1993) US District Court for the District of New Jersey. *John F. Moyer, Plaintiff, v. the Wrecked and Abandoned Vessel Known as the* Andrea Doria, Defendant. Civ. A. No. 93–2377. United States District Court, D. New Jersey. November 18, 1993, Peter E. Hess, Wilmington, DE, for plaintiff; Gentile, *Deep, Dark, and Dangerous,* 70.

32 Interview with John Moyer.

33 Ibid.

34 Ibid.

35 District of New Jersey 1993 *Moyer v. Wrecked & Abandoned Vessel,* 836 F. Supp. 1099 (DNJ 1993) US District Court for the District of New Jersey. *John F. Moyer, Plaintiff, v. the Wrecked and Abandoned Vessel Known as the* Andrea Doria, Defendant. Civ. A. No. 93–2377. United States District Court, D. New Jersey. November 18, 1993, Peter E. Hess, Wilmington, DE, for plaintiff; Sims, Moyer, and Gatto, 191–92;

Washington Post, November 28, 1993; Gentile, *Deep, Dark, and Dangerous,* 82–83.

36 District of New Jersey 1993 *Moyer v. Wrecked & Abandoned Vessel,* 836 F. Supp. 1099 (DNJ 1993) US District Court for the District of New Jersey. *John F. Moyer, Plaintiff, v. the Wrecked and Abandoned Vessel Known as the* Andrea Doria, Defendant. Civ. A. No. 93–2377. United States District Court, D. New Jersey. November 18, 1993, Peter E. Hess, Wilmington, DE, for plaintiff.

37 Interview with John Moyer.

38 District of New Jersey 1993 *Moyer v. Wrecked & Abandoned Vessel,* 836 F. Supp. 1099 (DNJ 1993) US District Court for the District of New Jersey. *John F. Moyer, Plaintiff, v. the Wrecked and Abandoned Vessel Known as the* Andrea Doria, Defendant. Civ. A. No. 93–2377. United States District Court, D. New Jersey. November 18, 1993, Peter E. Hess, Wilmington, DE, for plaintiff; Sims, Moyer, and Gatto, 192.

39 *New Jersey Star-Ledger,* June 29, 2010.

40 Interview with John Moyer.

41 Interview with Linda Morgan Hardberger.

42 Sims, Moyer, and Gatto, 193; Gentile, *Deep, Dark, and Dangerous,* 199–200, 202, 206, 210.

43 Interview with Joel Perry; http://www.oceangate.com; *Christian Science Monitor,* June 14, 2016.

44 Gentile, *Deep, Dark, and Dangerous,* 197.

Epilogue

1 Goldstein, 209; *Baltimore Sun,* August 19, 2006.

2 Goldstein, 266.

3 *Baltimore Sun,* August 19, 2006; Goldstein, 267.

4 Goldstein, 266.

5 Hoffer, 109.

6 Carstens, in *The Sinking of the* Andrea Doria.

7 Mattsson, 137.

8 See Andrea Doria: *Are the Passengers Saved?*

9 Simpson, 267.

10 Moscow, 276.

11 Hoffer, 107.

12 Hoffer, 210.

13 *New York Daily News,* July 25, 1996.

14 *New York Times,* September 13, 2001.

15 *Orlando Sentinel,* July 25, 2006.

16 Andrea Doria: *Are the Passengers Saved?*

17 Interview with Pierette Simpson.

18 Ibid.
19 Ibid.
20 Andrea Doria: *Are the Passengers Saved?*
21 Interview with Pierette Simpson.
22 Steele, 218; Maxtone-Graham, ix.
23 Gentile, Andrea Doria: *Dive to an Era*, 13.

Bibliography

Books

Amory, Cleveland. *Who Killed Society?* New York: Harper & Brothers, 1960.

Aslet, Clive. *The American Country House.* New Haven, CT: Yale University Press, 1990.

———. *The Last Country Houses.* New Haven, CT: Yale University Press, 1982.

Averbach, Albert, and Charles Price, eds. *The Verdicts Were Just: Eight Famous Lawyers Present Their Most Memorable Cases.* New York: David McKay, 1966.

Bayley, Stephen. *La Dolce Vita: The Golden Age of Italian Style and Celebrity.* London: Fiell, 2011.

Becker, Stephen. *Marshall Field III: A Biography.* New York: Simon & Schuster, 1964.

Benziger, Barbara Field. *Prison of My Mind.* New York: Walker, 1969.

Bessel, Matthew. *Caumsett: The Home of Marshall Field III in Lloyd Harbor, New York.* Huntington, NY: Huntington Town Board, 1991.

Binzen, Peter, with Jonathan Binzen. *Richardson Dilworth: Last of the Bare-Knuckled Aristocrats.* Philadelphia: Camino Books, 2004.

Birmingham, Stephen. *California Rich.* New York: Simon & Schuster, 1980.

Bisset, Sir James. *Commodore.* New York: Criterion, 1961.

Bonnett, Wayne, ed. *Gabriel Moulin's San Francisco Peninsula: Town & Country Homes 1910–1930.* San Francisco: Windgate Press, 1990.

Brechin, Gray. *Imperial San Francisco: Urban Power, Earthly Ruin.* Berkeley: University of California Press, 1999.

Brinnin, John Malcolm. *Beau Voyage: Life Aboard the Last Great Ships.* New York: Dorset Press, 1987.

———. *The Sway of the Grand Saloon.* London: Arlington Books, 1971.

Bruce, John. *Gaudy Century: The Story of San Francisco's Hundred Years of Robust Journalism.* New York: Random House, 1948.

Cahill, Captain Richard A. *Collisions and Their Causes.* London: The Nautical Institute, 2002.

Cannon, Dyan. *Dear Cary: My Life with Cary Grant.* New York: It Books/HarperCollins, 2011.

Caumsett Foundation. *Caumsett: The Marshall Field III Gold Coast Estate.* New York: Caumsett Foundation/Arcadia Publishing, 2016.

Celant, Germano. *The Italian Metamorphosis, 1943–1968.* New York: Guggenheim Museum, 1994.

Crawford, Joan. *My Way of Life.* Los Angeles: Greymalkin Media, 2017.

de Beaudéan, Raoul. *Captain of the Ile.* New York: McGraw-Hill, 1960.

Decurtis, Anthony, and Holly George-Warren, eds. *The Rolling Stone Illustrated History of Rock & Roll.* New York: Random House, 1976.

Della Casa, Stefano, and Dario E. Viganò. *Hollywood sul Tevere: Anatomia di un Fenomeno.* Milan: Mondadori Electa, 2010.

Diufreigne, Jean-Pierre. *Dolce Vita Style.* Paris: Assouline, 2005.

Di Sandro, Ermanno. *Bella Addormentata (Andrea Doria 1956).* Rome: Bel-Ami Edizioni, 2013.

———. *In ricordo di Norma: Storie di due sopravvissuti e di Norma, la "Principessina Addormentata."* Amazon: Kindle, 2017.

———. *Le insorgenze del cuore. Naufragio sull'Andrea Doria.* Genoa: Lupo, 2007.

Donzel, Catherine. *Luxury Liners: Life on Board.* New York: Harry N. Abrams, 2006.

Eliot, Marc. *Cary Grant.* New York: Harmony, 2004.

Eliseo, Maurizio. Andrea Doria: *Cento Uno Viaggi.* Milan: Hoepli, 2006.

Canellos, Peter S., ed. *Last Lion: The Rise and Fall of Ted Kennedy.* New York: Simon & Schuster, 2009.

Flayhart, William H. *Disaster at Sea: Shipwrecks, Storms, and Collisions on the Atlantic.* New York: W. W. Norton, 2005.

Garfield, David. *A Player's Place: The Story of the Actors Studio.* New York: Macmillan, 1980.

Garrison, James B. *Mastering Tradition: The Residential Architecture of John Russell Pope.* New York: Acanthus Press, 2004.

Gentile, Gary. Andrea Doria: *Dive to an Era.* Philadelphia: Gary Gentile Productions, 1989.

———. *Deep, Dark, and Dangerous: Adventures and Reflections on the* Andrea Doria. Philadelphia: Gary Gentile Productions, 2005.

Gladstone, Eugene W. *In the Wake of the* Andrea Doria. Toronto: McClelland & Steward, 1966.

Goldstein, Richard. *Desperate Hours: The Epic Rescue of the* Andrea Doria. New York: John Wiley & Sons, Inc., 2001.

Grattidge, Captain Harry. *Captain of the Queens.* New York: E. P. Dutton, 1956.

Gundle, Stephen. *Death and the Dolce Vita: The Dark Side of Rome in the 1950s.* Edinburgh: Canongate, 2012.

Haberstroh, Joe. *Fatal Depth: Deep Sea Diving, China Fever, and the Wreck of the Andrea Doria.* Guilford, CT: Lyons Press, 2004.

Harris, Warren. *Cary Grant: A Touch of Elegance.* New York: Doubleday, 1987.

Hersh, Burton. *Edward Kennedy: An Intimate Biography.* Berkeley, CA: Counterpoint, 2010.

Hewitt, Mark Alan. *The Architect and the American Country House.* New Haven, CT: Yale University Press, 1990.

Hoffer, William. *Saved! The Story of the* Andrea Doria—*The Greatest Sea Rescue in History.* New York: Simon & Schuster, 1979.

Hotchner, A. E. *Sophia: Living and Loving, Her Own Story.* London: Michael Joseph, 1979.

Kathrens, Michael C. *Great Houses of New York 1880–1940, Volume 2.* New York: Acanthus Press, 2013.

Kavaler, Lucy. *The Private World of High Society: Its Rules and Rituals.* New York: David McKay, 1960.

Kiernan, Frances. *The Last Mrs. Astor: A New York Story.* New York: W. W. Norton, 2007.

King, Greg, and Penny Wilson. Lusitania: *Triumph, Tragedy, and the End of the Edwardian Age.* New York: St. Martin's Press, 2015.

Kohler, Peter C. *The Lido Fleet: Italian Line Passenger Ships & Services.* Alexandria, VA: Seadragon Press, 1998.

Leiber, Jerry, and Mike Stoller, with David Ritz. *Hound Dog: The Leiber and Stoller Autobiography.* New York: Simon & Schuster, 2009.

Levy, Shawn. *Dolce Vita Confidential: Fellini, Loren, Pucci, Paparazzi, and the Swinging High Life of 1950s Rome.* New York: W. W. Norton, 2016.

Licitra-Ponti, Lisa. *Gio Ponti: The Complete Work 1928–1978.* Cambridge, MA: MIT Press, 1990.

Loren, Sophia. *Yesterday, Today, Tomorrow: My Life.* New York: Atria Books, 2014.

MacKay, Robert B., Anthony Baker, and Carol A Traynor. *Long Island Country Houses and Their Architects 1860–1940.* New York: New York Society for the Preservation of Long Island Antiquities and W. W. Norton, 1997.

Madsen, Axel. *The Marshall Fields: The Evolution of an American Business Dynasty.* Hoboken, NJ: John Wiley & Sons, 2002.

Marling, Karal Ann. *Debutante.* Lawrence: University Press of Kansas, 2004.

Mattsson, Algot. *Out of the Fog: The Sinking of the* Andrea Doria. Centreville, MD: Cornell Maritime Press, 2003.

Maxtone-Graham, John. *The Only Way to Cross.* New York: Macmillan, 1972.

McMurray, Kevin F. *Deep Descent: Adventure and Death Diving the* Andrea Doria. New York: Pocket Books, 2001.

Meurn, Robert J. *Watchstanding Guide for the Merchant Officer.* Centreville, MD: Cornell Maritime Press, 1990.

Miles, George. *Leap Through the Iron Curtain, The Story of Nora Kovach & Istvan Rabovsky.* London: Weidenfeld and Nicolson, 1955.

Miller. William H., Jr. *The Great Luxury Liners, 1927–1954: A Photographic Record.* New York: Dover, 1981.

Moffat, Frances. *Dancing on the Brink of the World: The Rise and Fall of San Francisco Society.* New York: G. P. Putnam's Sons, 1977.

Morgan, Edward P. *Clearing the Air.* Washington, DC: Robert B. Luce, 1963.

Morris, Joe Alex. *The Richardson Dilworth Story.* Philadelphia: Mercury, 1962.

Moscow, Alvin. *Collision Course.* New York: G. P. Putnam's Sons, 1959.

Nelson, Nancy. *Evenings with Cary Grant.* New York: William Morrow, 1991.

Randall, Monica. *The Mansions of Long Island's Gold Coast.* New York: Rizzoli, 2003.

Roccella, Graziella. *Gio Ponti 1891–1979, Master of Lightness.* Cologne: Taschen, 2017.

Simpson, Pierette Domenica. *Alive on the* Andrea Doria! *The Greatest Sea Rescue in History.* Garden City, NY: Morgan James, 2006.

Stanford, Don. *The* Ile de France. New York: Appleton-Century-Crofts, 1960.

Steele, James. *Queen Mary.* London: Phaidon, 1995.

Taraborrelli, J. Randy. *After Camelot: A Personal History of the Kennedy Family 1968 to the Present.* New York: Grand Central, 2012.

Tinterri, Alessandro, ed. Andrea Doria *L'Elegante Signora Del Mare.* Genoa: Fondazione Ansaldo, 2016.

Wall, Robert. *Ocean Liners.* New York: E. P. Dutton, 1977.

Wealleans, Anne. *Designing Liners: A History of Interior Design Afloat.* London: Routledge, 2006.

Young, Robert T. *The Lessons of the Liberties.* New Hampshire: privately printed, 2016.

Journals and Magazines

Andrea Doria *Newsletter* 1, no. 11 (February 16, 2003).

Garzke, William H., Jr., and Pierette Domenica Simpson. "The Loss of the Andrea Doria—A Marine Forensic Analysis." *The Journal of Ship Production and Design* 26, no. 2 (May 2010): 1–9.

Life (dates referenced within the citations)

Photoplay

The Pilot

Roman, Ruth. "What I Learned from the *Andrea Doria.*" In *Parade,* September 9, 1965.

Ryan, Cornelius. "Five Desperate Hours in Cabin 56." *Collier's,* September 28, 1956.

Sims, Philip, John Moyer, and Steven Gatto. "The Decay of the *Andrea Doria*." *The Journal of Ship Production and Design* 26, no. 3 (August 2010): 187–98.

Time (dates referenced within the citations)

Newspapers

Individual newspapers are referenced by date in the citations

Canada

    Ottawa Journal

Italy

    Corriere della Sera

    L'Espresso

United Kingdom

    The Guardian

    The Spectator

United States

    Abilene Reporter-News, Abilene, Texas

    Asbury Park Press, Asbury Park, New Jersey

    Asheville Citizen-Times, Asheville, North Carolina

    Associated Press

    Boston Globe

    Brooklyn Daily Eagle

    Bulletin of the Catholic Laymen's Association of Georgia, Savannah, Georgia

    Chester Times, Chester, Pennsylvania

    Christian Science Monitor

    Cincinnati Enquirer, Cincinnati, Ohio

    Corsicana Daily Sun, Corsicana, Texas

    Council Bluffs Nonpareil, Council Bluffs, Iowa

    Daily Herald, Chicago

    Daily Herald, Provo, Utah

    Daily Independent Journal, San Rafael, California

    Daily Reporter, Greenfield, Indiana

    Daily Times, Burlington, North Carolina

    Delaware County Daily & Sunday Times, Chester, Pennsylvania

    Des Moines Register

    Detroit Free Press

    Herald Statesman, Yonkers, New York

    The Journal News, Hamilton, Ohio

    Long Beach Independent, Long Beach, California

    Longview News-Journal, Longview, Texas

    Los Angeles Times

    Marion Star, Marion, Ohio

    Milwaukee Journal

Morning Call, Allentown, Pennsylvania
Nantucket Inquirer and Mirror
New Jersey Star-Ledger
New York Daily News
New York Times
New York World-Telegram
Niagara Falls Gazette, Niagara Falls, New York
Ogden Standard-Examiner, Ogden, Utah
Orlando Sentinel
Palm Beach Daily News, Palm Beach, Florida
The Pantagraph, Bloomington, Illinois
Philadelphia Daily News
Philadelphia Inquirer
Pittsburgh Post-Gazette
Plainfield Courier-News, Plainfield, New Jersey
Post Standard, Syracuse, New York
Providence Sunday Journal
Redlands Daily Facts, Redlands, California
San Bernardino County Sun, San Bernardino, California
San Francisco Chronicle
San Francisco Examiner
Sarasota Herald-Tribune
The Telegram, Worcester, Massachusetts
The Times, Hammond, Indiana
The Times, San Mateo, California
The Times Record, Troy, New York
USA Today
The Washington Post
Wichita Eagle, Wichita, Kansas

Websites

Airoldi, Robert. "Local Survives Sinking of Andrea Doria." *Morgan Hill Life*,
 Morgan Hill, California. August 6–19, 2014, http://morganhilllife.com
 /2014/08/01/local-survives-sinking-of-andrea-doria.
"The Amazing Tale of Father Oppitz and the Sinking Ship," *Catholic Review*,
 October 14, 2011, https://www.archbalt.org/the-amazing-tale-of-father
 -oppitz-and-the-sinking-ship.
www.andreadoria.org.
www.AndreaDoriaMovie.com.
Archdiocese of Chicago, at http://legacy.archchicago.org/news_releases
 /obituaries_13/obit_130129.html; http://legacy.archchicago.org/news
 _releases/obituaries_12/obit_112712.html.

Balaban, Judy, and Cari Beauchamp. "Cary in the Sky with Diamonds." *Vanity Fair,* August 2010, https://www.vanityfair.com/culture/2010/08/drugs-in-hollywood-201008.

Bliss, Barbara. *A Grandchild Remembers Caumsett,* http://caumsett1.tripod.com/index_files/Page665.htm.

Buckley, Réka. "Glamour and the Italian Female Stars of the 1950s." *The Historical Journal of Film, Radio and Television* 28, no. 3 (2008), https://doi.org/10.1080/01439680802230688.

http://conglimbo.blogspot.com/2012/01/that-sinking-feeling-loss-of-ss-andrea.html.

https://www.encyclopedia-titanica.org/community/threads/trapped-alive-aboard-the-andrea-doria.25953.

Fagone, Jason. "Searching for Richardson Dilworth." *Best of Philly Magazine,* http://www.phillymag.com/articles/2008/11/24/searching-for-richardson-dilworth/.

Gordan, Lucy. "An Interview with Dun Gifford," http://epicurean-traveler.com/an-interview-with-dun-gifford/.

https://fiftiesweb.com/pop/prices-1956/.

http://www.forwardlook.net/features/chrysler_norseman_en.htm.

www.FranzosenbuschHeritageProject.org.

Fricke, David. "Rolling Stone's Leiber and Stoller 1990 Interview with the Songwriting Legends," *Rolling Stone,* August 22, 2011, http://www.rollingstone.com/music/news/leiber-stoller-rolling-stones-1990-interview-with-the-songwriting-legends-20110822.

https://www.growingbolder.com/david-and-louise-hollyer-2002/telegram.com.

Halpern, Samuel. *An Objective Forensic Analysis of the Collision Between* Stockholm *and* Andrea Doria, http://www.titanicology.com/AndreaDoria/Stockholm-Andrea_Doria_Collision_Analysis.pdf.

Lee, Kyle. "Voices from the Andrea Doria." 2011. Vimeo. https://vimeo.com/33910689.

Meisner, Cynthia. "Saving Grace," https://vineyardgazette.com/news/2011/07/28/gazette-chronicle-saving-grace.

Nordling, Carl O., *A Reconstruction of the* Andrea Doria/Stockholm *Collision.* Carl Nordling apparently died in 2007, and in the few months since we accessed the link below, his on-line presences have been collected and archived. His *A Reconstruction* can now be found at: https://web.archive.org/web/20070211184947/http://www.carlonordling.se/doria/doria.html.

https://www.nwzonline.de/atlantik-laesst-schiffbruechigen-nicht-los_a_6,1,2068860687.html.

http://www.oceangate.com.

http://www.oceanliner.org/johnson.htm.

www.pierettesimpson.com.

www.ShipwreckedontheAndreaDoria.com.

http://thisamericanhouse.com/betsy-drake-the-last-lioness.

DVDs

Andrea Doria: *Are the Passengers Saved?* Produced by Pierette Domenica Simpson. Andrea Doria Project, 2016.

The Sinking of the Andrea Doria: *Secrets of the Dead.* Produced by Margi Kerns, executive producers Roberto Dall'Angelo and Jared Lipworth. New York: PBS/Thirteen/WNET, 2005.

Other Media

Bliss, Barbara. *Barbara's Tarnished Bliss.* Unpublished memoirs, courtesy of Adelaide Mestre.

District of New Jersey 1993 *Moyer v. Wrecked & Abandoned Vessel,* 836 F. Supp. 1099 (DNJ 1993) US District Court for the District of New Jersey. *John F. Moyer, Plaintiff, v. the Wrecked and Abandoned Vessel, Known as the* Andrea Doria, Defendant. Civ. A. No. 93–2377. United States District Court, D. New Jersey. November 18, 1993, Peter E. Hess, Wilmington, DE, for plaintiff.

Dorneich, Klaus. *Sinking of the* Andrea Doria. Manuscript, courtesy of Klaus Dorneich.

———. *Lost Liners.* Manuscript, courtesy of Klaus Dorneich.

———. *What Happened After.* Manuscript, courtesy of Klaus Dorneich.

Report of the US House of Representatives, Committee on Merchant Marine and Fisheries, December 21, 1956, by Vice Admiral USN Retired EL Cochrane, HL Seward Emeritus Professor of Mechanical and Marine Engineering Yale University, HC Shepheard Rear Admiral USCH Retired, EM Webster Commodore USCG Retired.

Troppauer, Chelsea Elizabeth. *Go with the Faux: Re-Evaluating the Design of the Richardson Dilworth House.* Unpublished PhD thesis, University of Pennsylvania, 2013, http://repository.upenn.edu/hb_theses/213.

Young, Madge. *Transfer in the Atlantic.* Manuscript, courtesy of Madge Young Nickerson.

Index

DATE DUE